POWER FAILURE

New York City
Politics and
Policy since 1960

POWER FAILURE

Charles Brecher

Raymond D. Horton

with

Robert A. Cropf

Dean Michael Mead

New York   Oxford
OXFORD UNIVERSITY PRESS
1993

Oxford University Press

Oxford   New York   Toronto
Delhi   Bombay   Calcutta   Madras   Karachi
Kuala Lumpur   Singapore   Hong Kong   Tokyo
Nairobi   Dar es Salaam   Cape Town
Melbourne   Auckland   Madrid

and associated companies in
Berlin   Ibadan

Copyright © 1993 by Oxford University Press, Inc.

Published by Oxford University Press, Inc.,
200 Madison Avenue, New York, New York 10016

Oxford is a registered trademark of Oxford University Press

Library of Congress Cataloging-in-Publication Data
Brecher, Charles.
Power failure : New York City politics and policy since 1960 /
Charles Brecher, Raymond D. Horton with Robert A. Cropf, Dean
Michael Mead.
p. cm.   Includes index.
ISBN 0-19-504427-4
1. New York (N.Y.)—Politics and government—1951-
2. Elections—New York (N.Y.)—History—20th century.
3. Budget—New York (N.Y.)—History—20th century.
I. Horton, Raymond D. II. Title.
F128.52.B725 1993
324.9747'1043—dc20   92-427

9 8 7 6 5 4 3 2 1

Printed in the United States of America
on acid-free paper

PREFACE

The origins of this book can be traced to the mid-1960s when the two senior authors arrived separately in New York to begin graduate study in political science—one at Columbia University and one at the Graduate Division of the City University. Each of us quickly developed an interest in local politics, and both were stimulated by Wallace Sayre and Herbert Kaufman's *Governing New York City*. By the time of his sudden death, Wallace Sayre had personally aided one author's pursuit of a specialization in urban politics as teacher and dissertation supervisor. Herb Kaufman's changed research interests led him in other directions, but he never failed to reply to our inquiries and consistently encouraged us to update his classic. Like all students of New York City, we owe a great intellectual debt to Sayre and Kaufman.

Our separate interests in New York City were brought together through another of Columbia's outstanding professors, Eli Ginzberg. He hired us early in our academic careers. Eli and his colleagues at the Conservation of Human Resources (CHR) project provided an incredibly stimulating social science environment that shaped our minds and our notions of what research should seek to accomplish. Eli has been a friend and mentor for more than 20 years. This book—indeed many of the things professional we have enjoyed in our careers—would not have occurred without Eli's interventions. In addition to Eli, three CHR staffers played important roles. Miriam Cukier and Penny Peace provided research assistance and administrative support during the years when the idea of a book on New York City government began to shape our research interests; Charles Frederick has kept our books for almost as long as we have been lucky enough to receive grants to support this work.

Our collaboration in studying the city's politics intensified when the city of

New York experienced its 1975 fiscal crisis. Events in the mid-1970s strengthened our emerging view that the politics of the city were not as self-regulating as Sayre and Kaufman theorized. That fiscal crisis also led to the appointment by Mayor Abraham Beame of a Temporary Commission on City Finances (TCCF). Between 1975 and 1977, we worked together for the TCCF on a series of studies which added immeasurably to our understanding of the city's policies and politics. Several members and staff of the TCCF made important contributions to this book in subsequent years. Former Mayor Robert F. Wagner, Jr., was a member of the commission, and from that relationship came a series of illuminating interviews with "our" first mayor. Mary McCormick, from whom we learned much, was a colleague at the TCCF, as well as before and after. The TCCF introduced us to Barbara Thornton Valentine, who provided support services at the commission and subsequently typed, and more recently word-processed, innumerable pages of material related to this manuscript in her position at the Columbia University Graduate School of Business.

The experience with the TCCF led us to embark on a new project intended to provide an independent base from which to analyze municipal prospects, problems, and policies. With the support of several foundations, we initiated the Setting Municipal Priorities (SMP) project in 1978. The annual (1980 through 1986) SMP volumes became biennial (1988 and 1990) and were suspended to complete this book, but the opportunity as co-editors to pick the brains of those who wrote SMP chapters contributed mightily to the development of this book. The following list of chapter authors includes some special friends and colleagues whose contributions extend well beyond their writing one or more chapters: Roy Bahl, Thomas Bailey, Margaret Bald, Robert Berne, Tom Boast, Howard Chernick, Robert Cropf, Maarten de Kadt, Fred Doolittle, Matthew Drennan, Elizabeth Durbin, Mary Bryna Sanger, Jack Freidgut, Ester Fuchs, Marilyn Gittel, Cynthia Green, David Grossman, James Hartman, John Kaiser, Kurt Katzmar, Eugene Keilin, James Knickman, Peter Kolesar, James Krauskopf, Reynold Levy, David Listokin, Dale Mann, Mary McCormick, Brenda McGowan, Julia Vitullo-Martin, John Mollenkopf, Richard Nathan, Dick Netzer, Kenneth Rider, Elizabeth Roistacher, Diana Roswick, Ross Sandler, Edward Seeley, Jr., Dennis Smith, John Palmer Smith, Walter Stafford, Michael Stegman, Georgia Nanopoulous-Stergiou, George Sternlieb, Kenneth Thorpe, Emanuel Tobier, David Tobis, Roger Vaughn, Bruce Vladeck, Roger Waldinger, Elaine Walsh, and Mark Willis.

Shortly after initiating the SMP project we began an association with an old (by New York standards) civic group, the Citizens Budget Commission (CBC). We had some reservations about the compatibility of two academics and a high-powered group of trustees drawn predominantly from the city's businesses, but we hoped a shared concern for responsive and efficient municipal government would provide the basis for serious policy research applied to those ends. We were not disappointed.

In one way the contributions of the CBC experiences to this book mirrors those of our other associations. We have been able to draw upon the intellectual capital of others, notably CBC trustees and staff. But we also gained something unique, something we could not have gained had we kept our feet planted firmly in academia—the opportunity to witness close up, indeed participate in, the process by which the city raises, allocates, and manages its scarce resources. Being participant-observers complicates the understanding of events but it helps too. Working for the CBC has vividly and repeatedly underscored a point we might have understood only intellectually—that the concept of a business community is a figment of imagination, or ideology. Our interactions with CBC's trustees confirms that the political values of the city's business leaders are anything but monolithic.

Our most immediate bosses at the CBC have been those who chaired the organization's board and its five standing research committees. The chairmen of the board whom we have been privileged to serve are Lawrence S. Huntington, Frank P. Smeal, Richard A. Levine, and Richard Ravitch; the research committee chairs are Gordon Binns, Bud Gibbs, David Greenbaum, William Hayden, Eugene Keilin, and Jack Miller.

In addition, we have had the opportunity to work with a dedicated group of CBC staffers: Mary De La Fuente typed the manuscript in its various iterations with assistance from Fondia Thompson. Jim Hartman and John Palmer Smith were CBC colleagues as well as SMP contributors; Cindy Green continues to be an informative colleague at CBC as well as an SMP contributor, doctoral student, and valued friend. During Patricia Fry's tenure at CBC she taught us a great deal about the city's finances, some of which is reflected in Chapter 6, which draws heavily on work she undertook. James Lo, CBC's newest staffer, helped as fact-finder and fact-checker in the preparation of the final manuscript.

Robert Cropf and Dean Mead also made their contributions to the book while serving as CBC staff. Bob started as a research assistant while pursuing a masters degree at New York University; he left to work at the New York City Office of Management and Budget but returned to collaborate with us at CBC and to complete a doctoral degree. His dissertation provided a basis for his important contribution to Chapter 5, and his work at CBC is reflected in several other chapters. Dean joined us at CBC directly after completing undergraduate work at Cornell University; for more than four years he eagerly and successfully took on ever more demanding assignments including research reflected in several chapters. Both deserve the recognition and credit symbolized by their names on the title page.

Another group of individuals who made continuous contributions to this book are the employees of New York City government who shared their data and their insights with an openness that is all the more noteworthy because much of our professional life has been devoted to critical examination of their behavior. These employees range from mayors and commissioners to clerks; it is impossible to acknowledge them all individually, but to "officialdom" we give special thanks.

Financial support for this book came in many forms. The most direct is grants from the Charles H. Revson Foundation and the Commonwealth Fund for preparation of the book. We are sincerely grateful to the boards of these organizations for their funding, and we are especially thankful for the encouragement and patience of Margaret Mahoney and Thomas Moloney of the Commonwealth Fund and Eli Evans of the Revson Foundation in seeing this project to its completion.

The drafting of several chapters was facilitated by support from the Rockefeller Foundation in the form of a one-month period as scholars in residence at the Villa Serbelloni. Perhaps only those who enjoy this special status can appreciate its contribution to the development of a book; it is a memorable and productive period for which we are deeply appreciative.

Indirect financial support for this book was derived from the foundations that supported our related work in the form of grants to Conservation of Human Resources, the SMP project, or the Citizens Budget Commission. These are the Ford Foundation, Rockefeller Brothers Fund, New York Community Trust, Robert Sterling Clark Foundation, Josiah Macy, Jr. Foundation, NYNEX Foundation, Robert Wood Johnson Foundation, Foundation for Child Development, and Russell Sage Foundation. In addition in its initial years the SMP project benefited from federal support from the Economic Development Administration of the Department of Commerce, the Employment and Training Administration of the Department of Labor, the National Institute of Education of the Department of Education, and the Office of Policy Development and Research of the Department of Housing and Urban Development.

Finally, no one can emerge sane (or nearly so) from 20 years of involvement in local politics, from the rigors of co-editing nine volumes, and from the pains of authorship of hundreds of manuscript pages without a good deal of tender, loving care. Fortunately we have devoted families who supply an abundance of this scarce resource, so our ultimate thanks go to Radley Horton and Madeline, Sari, and Beth Brecher.

New York   C. B.
April 1992   R. D. H.

CONTENTS

Service Delivery

LIST OF TABLES

I

INTRODUCTION AND OVERVIEW

1

INTRODUCTION

This book is intended to serve as a guide for those seeking to explore the subject of New York City's government. Like most good guidebooks, it aims to be useful for those visiting for the first time, those on return sojourns, and even for natives willing to view their city from a new vantage.

There are two essential elements for a successful guidebook. The first is abundant information. But for the politically oriented, the key facts and figures are not hotel addresses and rates, restaurant menus, or museum fees and hours. Instead the key descriptors of governmental arrangements include the number, terms, and authority of various elected officials, the size of agency budgets and payrolls, and the procedures for reaching authoritative decisions. This information is presented in the following chapters, but it would be far less interesting and far less useful without the second ingredient of this guidebook.

Information about a city's political life, like its cultural or culinary attractions, should be presented with a point of view that reflects the guide's judgment. This book has a point of view about municipal politics, and readers are apt to like or dislike it depending on whether they share the authors' views. The chapters that follow are rooted in the belief that New York City's government, like all such public entities, should be judged on two standards—efficiency and responsiveness. Municipal government should respond to the preferences of its citizens in a democratic fashion, and it should perform its selected tasks in a manner that delivers the greatest results while extracting the smallest tax burden.

Imposing this dual standard on city politics means that politics and policy cannot be separated. Simply knowing if the political process works in accord with democratic norms and yields policies responsive to citizens' expectations is not enough. The resulting policies should also be measured to determine if they are establishing governmental practices that are efficient and effective. Hence, this book is about the policies of the city of New York as well as about its politics.

The authors' point of view has a third element: Money is important to both politics and policy. The character "Deep Throat" of Watergate fame repeatedly told the investigators to "follow the money." It was good advice then, and it is generally good advice for those seeking to examine political processes. Consequently, this book emphasizes budgetary decisions as key to understanding the priorities of government and to revealing the influence of diverse community groups. It also uses cost data to assess how efficiently local government is doing its jobs.

The 14 chapters that follow this Introduction elaborate on these themes while also providing abundant information about the structure and activities of New York City's government. The remainder of this Introduction serves three other purposes. First, the need for a new guidebook to municipal government is expounded, and the differences between this book and those that preceded it are emphasized. Next the organization of the book is explained and its contents are highlighted. Finally, a summary judgment on the status of the city of New York is presented in terms of its responsiveness and efficiency.

The Case for a New Guidebook

More than 30 years ago Professors Wallace Sayre of Columbia University and Herbert Kaufman of Yale University collaborated to write *Governing New York City: Politics in the Metropolis*.[1] It served long and well as a guidebook because it contained the two ingredients identified earlier—abundant information and a clear point of view. In more than 775 pages and 19 chapters the book described virtually every aspect of all organizations within municipal government. As a portrait of a city's political life at the close of the 1950s it was unrivaled in the richness of its detail. And the effort remains unduplicated; it remains to be seen if the ambitious *Encyclopedia of New York City* initiated by the New York Historical Society will replace *Governing New York City* as a comprehensive reference.

Sayre and Kaufman also had a point of view. They wrote in the midst of an intellectual debate contested largely between sociologists and political scientists over the answer to the question, "Who governs?" Many sociologists saw a dominant "power elite" of wealthy businessmen who used local politicians as instruments for governing American municipalities in ways that served the wealthy at the expense of workers. In contrast, many political scientists interpreted local politics as a healthy contest among numerous diverse competing interests with none excluded and none consistently dominant. Their "pluralist" interpretation suggested a certain satisfaction with the nature of urban politics, while those who favored the power elite perspective typically were dissatisfied with the local political manifestations of capital's power over the working class.

Sayre and Kaufman were clearly in the pluralist camp. They concluded, "No single ruling elite dominates the political and governmental system of New York City." Instead they found a system that is "vigorously and incessantly competitive."[2] They also hailed the openness of the city's politics: "No part of the city's large and varied population is alienated from participation in the system. . . . All the diverse elements in the city, in competition with each other, can and do partake of the stakes of politics; if none gets all it wants, neither is any excluded."[3]

Given their findings, it is not surprising that Sayre and Kaufman shared their political science colleagues' prevailing sense of satisfaction with American urban politics. In fact, they viewed New York City as a model for other urban centers. Their book's conclusion was nearly a paean for its subject:

> The most lasting impression created by a systematic analysis of New York City's political and governmental system as a whole are of its democratic virtues: its qualities of openness, its commitments to bargaining and accommodation among participants, its receptivity to new participants, its opportunities for the exercise of leadership by an unmatched variety and number of the city's residents new and old. Defects accompany these virtues, and in some situations overshadow them, but the City of New York can confidently ask: What other large American city is as democratically and as well governed?[4]

The case for seeking a replacement for Sayre and Kaufman's 31-year-old analysis is twofold. First, its descriptive information is no longer accurate. Guidebooks must be updated. Just as hotel prices, restaurant menus, and museum hours change, so too do the specifics of a city's governmental apparatus from the composition of its legislature to the powers of its mayor. Second, the pluralist interpretation is no longer valid. Some scholars argue Sayre and Kaufman's views were wrong in 1960; less debatable is that time has eroded the openness and competitiveness they praised. Each of these arguments warrants further elaboration.

The Changing City

Cities seem to be in a constant process of change. Hence descriptions at one point in time are quickly outdated. Dramatic changes in the population, economy, and political structure of New York City have occurred in the past three decades.

In 1960 New York was not only the nation's largest city; it was a place whose population seemed relatively stable. The city's earlier rapid growth was rooted in foreign migration, and the national government had virtually halted that immigration in the 1920s. Postwar economic growth and the "baby boom" increased the number of New Yorkers in the late 1940s, but in the 1950s the population size remained nearly steady. Sayre and Kaufman commented, "As the city looked forward to the census of 1960, a stabilization of population was expected."[5]

The overall size of the city's population did remain almost constant in the 1960s, but there were few signs of true stabilization in New York's demography in the past three decades. Three powerful demographic forces have yielded dramatic changes—suburbanization, interregional migration, and international migration.[6] Suburbanization, a national force driven by cultural values and selected federal housing and transportation policies, led to migration of city residents to nearby counties. Interregional migration is more sensitive to economic trends with net inmigration—largely of blacks and Puerto Ricans from rural areas—during growth periods, and net outmigration—including all groups, but disproportionately among better educated whites—during periods of economic decline. International migration increased significantly in the mid-1960s following changes in federal laws regulating migration, remained at a steady pace of about 75,000 annually during much of the 1970s, and was reported at between 85,000 and 90,000 annually in more recent years.[7]

The coming and going of large numbers of New Yorkers have led to dramatic changes in the composition of the population. (See Table 1.1.) In racial and ethnic terms, the city shifted from 77 percent non-Hispanic whites in 1960 to 43 percent in 1990. Blacks increased from 13 to 25 percent, and

Table 1.1 Selected Characteristics of New York City Population, 1960–1990

Characteristic	1960	1970	1980	1986	1990
Total population (000s)	7,782	7,807	7,071	7,263	7,323
Population under age 18	2,164	2,263	1,777	1,780	1,687
Ethnic composition (%)	100.0	100.0	100.0	100.0	100.0
White (non-Hispanic)	76.5	63.2	52.0	44.1	43.2
Black	13.1	19.2	24.0	25.9	25.2
Hispanic	9.2	15.2	20.1	24.6	24.4
Other	1.3	2.3	3.8	5.4	7.2
Percent foreign born	20.4	18.2	23.5	NA	28.4
Percent below poverty level	16.0	14.9	20.0	23.9	19.3
Percent of families headed by female	11.2	19.4	25.8	NA	29.0
Percent of households that are single individuals	19.4	25.2	32.7	33.7	37.7
Components of change					
Births	—	1,504	1,118	654	NA
Deaths	—	987	805	436	NA
Net migration	—	(494)	(1,192)	(26)	NA

Sources: Figures for 1960, 1970, and 1980 are from the decennial census. Ethnic composition for 1960 partially estimated by Professor Emanuel Tobier. Figures for 1986 from *Current Population Survey* with estimates for population under 18 by Emanuel Tobier; ethnic composition in 1986 estimated by Tobier from the Census Bureau's 1987 Housing and Vacancy Survey for New York City; and female head and single-person households in 1986 estimated by Tobier from 1987 Housing and Vacancy Survey. The 1990 data are from Census Bureau public use tapes analyzed by the New York City Planning Commission and published in *The New York Times*, March 22, 1991.

Note: NA, not available.

Table 1.2   Employment in New York City, 1960–1990

	1960	1969	1977	1987	1990
Total					
Number (000s)	3,538.1	3,797.7	3,187.3	3,590.0	3,569.9
Percent	100.0	100.0	100.0	100.0	100.0
Government					
Number (000s)	408.2	547.0	508.0	580.0	608.3
Percent	11.5	14.4	15.9	16.2	17.0
Total private					
Number (000s)	3,129.9	3,250.7	2,680.0	3,010.0	2,961.6
Percent	88.5	85.6	84.1	83.8	83.0
Private by industry (percent)					
Manufacturing	30.3	21.7	16.9	10.6	11.4
Construction	4.1	2.8	2.0	3.3	3.8
Transportation and utilities	10.2	8.5	8.1	6.0	7.6
Wholesale and retail trade	23.8	19.7	19.4	17.8	20.4
Finance, insurance, and real estate	12.3	12.3	13.0	15.3	17.5
Services and miscellaneous[a]	19.4	20.6	24.6	30.9	39.3

Source: New York State Department of Labor.

Note: Totals may not add due to rounding.

[a]Includes mining.

Hispanics from 9 to 24 percent in the same period. Persons of foreign birth increased from 18 percent in 1970 to 28 percent in 1990.

The new population also has a different age and family structure. The share of the population who are children has fallen, the share of families headed by females has grown from 11 to 29 percent, and the share of households consisting of single individuals has grown from under one-fifth to over one-third.

The new population also has a significantly altered income distribution. The share of the population living below the federal poverty level fell from 16 percent in 1960 to 15 percent in 1970, but it then grew to 20 percent in 1980 and almost 24 percent in 1986. In this sense, New York is a much poorer city now than when Sayre and Kaufman studied it.

The population changes are related to profound economic changes. (See Table 1.2.) The post-1960 economic record can be divided into three periods: from 1960 through 1969 there was modest growth with total employment increasing about 260,000, or over 7 percent; from 1969 to 1977 there was a sharp decline with job losses totaling over 610,000, or 16 percent; from 1977 to 1987 the economy again grew with employment up 403,000, or 13 percent. After the October 1987 stock market crash the economy began to reverse, and the 1990 data point to private sector job losses of about 48,000.

However, throughout each period of growth or decline there has been a nearly steady shift in the industrial composition of the local economy. Manufacturing has steadily declined from 30 to 11 percent of the total. At the same time, services employment has been on a steady rise from 19 to 39 percent. The finance sector also has grown in significance from 12 to 18 percent. Thus, in both size and character, the local economy is different from the 1950s.

Like its people and jobs, the city's governmental institutions also have changed. Specifically, the City Charter—the municipal equivalent of a constitution—was revised significantly by referendum in 1961, 1975, 1983, and 1989. (These changes are described in detail in Chapter 3.) In addition to charter changes, other aspects of local government have been changed through local legislation or executive orders creating new agencies (such as the Human Resources Administration) and abolishing others, and through state legislative action creating new entities such as the Health and Hospitals Corporation and the Metropolitan Transportation Authority. For these reasons, the constitutional design of the government now in place differs in important ways from that described by Sayre and Kaufman.

The Validity of the Interpretation

Time has not only made the descriptive details of *Governing New York City* inaccurate; it also has invalidated its pluralist interpretation of local political processes. Since 1960, numerous studies have pointed out that the openness and competitiveness which Sayre and Kaufman praised were either exaggerated at the time or have diminished notably since then.

Most critics agree no single elite dominates New York City, but they describe a system of "multiple elites." That is, there are multiple subdivisions of city politics and each is dominated by a single group. This group may be challenged occasionally by those with conflicting interests, but it possesses sufficient skill and resources to consistently maintain its self-interest.

Often the dominant group in a specific policy area is the organized civil servants whose jobs and working conditions are at stake. Early studies of the city's public schools by David Rogers and Marilyn Gittell stressed that educational politics consisted largely of matters over which the system's employees, particularly through the United Federation of Teachers, were able to pursue their interests even when in conflict with parent groups or civil rights organizations.[8] Others presented evidence that the organized municipal employees were able to retain control over the operations of their pieces of local government. For example, the Patrolman's Benevolent Association was able to defeat proposals for a civilian review board despite strong support for the board from civil rights groups and leading politicians; this led political scientists reviewing the experience to conclude: "The rules of the game have prescribed that any alteration in enforcement policy must be a product of decision-making wholly within the Department, and few mayors (or commissioners) have had the temerity to challenge the power of the entrenched bureaucracy."[9]

But it is not always organized civil servants who dominate particular policy areas. Land use policy is often the domain of real estate owners and developers, assisted by specialized real estate lawyers. The ability of these interests to use local government to promote downtown or central business district development has been noted in various cities.[10] In New York City the pattern has been documented by Jack Newfield and Paul DuBrul as well as by Norman and Susan Fainstein.[11]

The connections between this pattern of multiple elite influence over policy decisions and the coalition politics of mayoral elections were insightfully drawn by Martin Shefter. He viewed mayoral candidates as obliged to put together a coalition that would provide the funds and votes necessary for electoral success. Generally this involves forming alliances with and supporting the preferences of the groups of organized civil servants and others who seek greater public expenditures for their own members. The result of this type of political coalition is a fiscal crisis in which the city commits to more expenditures than it can raise in taxes or borrowing; the fiscal crisis, in turn, leads to a new regime that temporarily curbs spending pressures. But the political strength of the unions and other pro-expenditure groups eventually is revived, leading to a new electoral success for their candidate and, eventually, to a new fiscal crisis. Shefter concluded, "Fiscal crises should be regarded not as aberrations but as an integral part of urban politics."[12]

In sum, the pluralist lenses through which Sayre and Kaufman examined New York City are no longer recognized as the most appropriate. New models recognize the disproportionate influence of some groups, notably the organized civil servants, and the potential for fiscal crises which their influence on electoral politics can cause.

Organization of the Book

This book is organized into four parts—Introduction and Overview, Electoral Politics, Budgetary Politics and Policy, and Service Delivery. The first part consists of this introduction and an "Overview of Political Change." The overview chapter has two purposes: it highlights the significance of local politics in shaping municipal policy, and it presents an interest group model for explaining policy changes over the 1960–1990 period.[13]

By focusing on budget decisions it is possible to identify four periods, each distinguished by different policies. From 1961 to 1969 total spending increased and so did the share for redistributive purposes; from 1969 to 1975 total spending continued to rise, but there was less redistribution and more borrowing; from 1975 to 1983 there was reduced spending and reduced borrowing; from 1983 to 1989 spending again rose but it was allocated primarily to nonredistributive purposes.

The model for explaining fiscal policy changes includes three broad factors—the performance of the local economy, intergovernmental interventions, and power relations among local interest groups, who are comprised of the business community, municipal financiers, the dependent poor, civil servants, and middle-class residents. Applying this model to expenditure decisions over the four periods reveals that the role of intergovernmental aid was the dominant force shaping expenditure policy during the 1960s, but for the two decades after 1969 local political decisions have been far more significant than either intergovernmental interventions or local economic forces. This was true during both the retrenchment of the late 1970s and the expansion of the 1980s. It is shifting alliances and power balances among local interest groups that account for most policy changes; the city's budgetary actions are not simply at the mercy of national economic trends or officials of higher levels of government.

The approach and findings of Chapter 2 relate only to budgetary decisions. While taxing and spending are critical to municipal politics, they do not exhaust its scope. Another important dimension is regulation of a wider range of activities including building codes and taxi medallions; perhaps the most significant of these regulatory powers is the ability to control land use. Local regulatory politics, particularly land use politics, are not given special attention in this book. Such analysis would be important, but it was beyond the resources of the authors. The exclusion of regulatory decisions is an important limitation to the scope of this book.

Electoral Politics

Part II is devoted to electoral politics. Its initial chapter, "Local Elections and Local Democracy," identifies three prerequisites for a healthy democracy and asks if New York City meets these conditions. The first criterion is a local constitution that creates public offices that have sufficient authority to determine policy and that are filled by popular election. A review of the charter changes indicates these conditions are met; currently the mayor, comptroller, city council president, and members of the city council comprise such officials. The second criterion is that these offices be filled through competitive elections. With the exception of the mayoralty, this condition is rarely met. Not only does the Democratic party dominate local politics; it also is characterized by little intraparty competition in the form of primary election contests. From 1961 to the present, Democrats have continuously filled the borough presidencies in Brooklyn, Queens, and Manhattan and lost the Bronx only from 1961 to 1965; Democrats have filled the comptroller's post throughout the period and the council presidency in seven of the eight terms. The mayoralty was occupied by a Republican for just two of the eight terms. Democrats also have comprised an overwhelming majority of the city council throughout the period.

Limited intraparty competition is particularly evident in the council races. Of the 283 contests for council seats between 1961 and 1989 less than half involved a primary election, and most of those contests were not even close— in only 41 cases was the margin of victory less than 10 percentage points. In comptroller contests there also was limited competitiveness; a primary was not even required in 1977 and in only one of the seven other contests was the margin of victory less than 10 percentage points. With regard to council president, three of the last eight primary contests can be viewed as competitive, but there has not been a close election since 1977. The mayoralty is the only office seriously contested in the primary and general elections.

The third condition for a healthy democracy is widespread citizen participation. On this score, New York City also is found wanting. Although a long-term trend toward declining voter turnout was reversed in 1989, most eligible New Yorkers still do not participate in picking their leaders. Only slightly more than one-third of those eligible voted for mayor in 1989, and that was up from about one-fifth in 1985.

Because it is mayoral contests that are closest to providing democratic choices for New Yorkers, the second chapter in Part II focuses on them. "Mayoral Elections" addresses the question, "What do mayoral elections decide?" Four basic issues are identified, and each of the eight contests since 1961 is analyzed to determine the significance of these issues. The finding is that mayoral elections have never posed viable choices between "service-demanders" and "money-providers"; with few exceptions, all candidates have presented themselves as supporters of enhanced services, and those who did not received relatively few votes. Instead elections provide a mixture of choices between "reform" and "regular" styles of politics and between different attitudes over race relations, and they provide opportunities for ethnic groups to assert their identity and pride. However, the roles of ethnic politics and of splits between reformers and party "bosses" have become less prominent, and electoral politics in the 1980s became increasingly a matter of positions on race relations.

The third chapter in Part II focuses on the role of money in electoral campaigns. "Public Financing of Campaigns" describes the scandalous state of affairs in 1985 when incumbent Mayor Edward I. Koch spent over $7 million to defeat a challenger with less than $1 million, with much of Koch's money coming from large contributors who did business with the city.[14] The state legislature refused to either better regulate contributions or establish a public financing program, but local scandals spurred city officials to create a public financing program for municipal elections. The results are mixed: Spending in the 1989 mayoral contest was curbed, and the candidates had a more even fiscal base. But through "bundling" and other devices large contributions were apparently still influential in citywide contests, and the program had little impact on the council races.

Budgetary Politics and Policy

The five chapters in Part III are devoted to budgetary politics and policy. The first is concerned with improving the process through which the city formulates its now $29 billion annual operating budget. "Improving the Operating Budget Process" begins by reviewing the changes in procedures mandated during the fiscal crisis period and the benefits realized from these reforms.[15] Next it indicates how the "sunset" of the Financial Control Board in 1986 eased these requirements and identifies some of the issues related to current practices. The agenda for reform flowing from this analysis includes new procedural safeguards, more rigorous updating of the Financial Plan, new methods for projecting "gaps," an internalized monitoring function, and reduced reliance on fiscal gimmickry.

"Bargaining and Budgeting" examines the relationship between the budgetary process and the collective bargaining process.[16] Because the bulk of the city's operating expenses are for compensation of its employees, the budget is determined in large part by collective bargaining decisions. But because the wages the city pays should be determined partly in light of its budgetary situation and the "affordability" of a settlement, bargaining cannot be independent of budgeting. To better relate the processes, two measures are recommended. First, the city and its unions should agree to a system of "final-offer arbitration" that would be relied upon when collective bargaining does not yield a timely settlement. Second, collective bargaining agreements should be required, either through bargaining or arbitration, before the start of a fiscal year.

The city of New York has a capital budget as well as an operating budget, and the third chapter in this section is devoted to this now $4 billion annual activity. "The Capital Budget and Capital Projects" examines both the formulation and implementation of the capital budget.[17] It traces the growth of the capital budget from its dormancy during the late 1970s to its nearly $4.7 billion in planned contract commitments in fiscal year 1990. However, analysis of the construction activity actually taking place reveals that the city is better at spending money than at completing projects, let alone on time and within budget. Specifically, among a group of important projects analyzed, less than one in ten was finished in accord with a reasonable timetable. The chapter uses case studies to identify the sources of delay and makes recommendations for improved performance.

Budgeting has a revenue as well as an expenditure side, and the last two chapters in this section consider the sources of municipal funds. "Tax Policy" identifies criteria for distinguishing "good" from "bad" taxes with greatest emphasis on the concepts of economic efficiency and equity.[18] It applies these standards to each of the city's major taxes. The results highlight the shortcomings of two taxes, the unincorporated business tax (yielding $356 million in fiscal year 1990) and the commercial rent tax ($685 million). Both are forms of double taxation that do harm to local economic development and create inequities among different forms of businesses. The recommendation is to eliminate each, a move that would be possible if the state assumed more responsibility for financing redistributive activities now relying on a local tax base.

The single largest revenue source for the city is the property tax, and it is the subject of the final chapter in this section.[19] The chapter has a single theme: political decisions have made New York City's property tax an economic nightmare. Legislation effective in 1983 legitimized different tax rates for four different classes of property, thereby permitting the mayor and city council to tax small residential property at much lower rates than other classes. This initial inequity has been amplified since then. By fiscal year 1991 the effective tax rate for home owners was $0.84 per $100 of market value; in contrast, commercial property owners paid over five times as much, or $4.31 per $100 of market value. This subsidy of home owners by owners of other types of property is politically motivated, as well as economically harmful and grossly unfair to renters and businesses.

Service Delivery

City government does more than raise and spend money; it delivers services to citizens. Part IV, "Service Delivery," considers how well municipal leaders perform their task. The first chapter, "Expenditures and Services," presents a conceptual model for examining the relationship between spending and service delivery.[20] The key concepts are resources, or inputs, and outputs in the form of services to citizens. Productivity is a relationship between inputs and outputs; it is determined by the skill with which management utilizes the available resources. Application of the model to municipal services is difficult because inputs and especially outputs are difficult to measure, but an illustration from the task of refuse collection shows it can be done. The results provide useful information for mayors seeking to improve productivity as well as for citizens seeking to judge how well elected officials are doing their service delivery job.

Using an input–output approach highlights the fact that the major input to municipal services is labor. Hence a major determinant of productivity is the unit cost of labor, and the price of labor is in large part a function of municipal wage policy as set in collective bargaining. Chapter 12, "Municipal Wage Policy," seeks to identify guidelines for setting municipal wages.[21] After describing the structure of municipal labor relations and the outcomes of bargaining from the mid-1970s through fiscal year 1991, it presents guidelines for contracts covering the next few years. These include keeping pay increases below the rate of inflation (since they have exceeded inflation in most recent years), permitting substantial variation in rates of pay increase among different occupations to reflect external labor market conditions (tens of thousands of people apply for posts as sanitation workers; nursing positions go vacant); and using "gainsharing" to provide additional compensation to groups of workers who agree to changes in work rules that yield recurring productivity gains.

The last three chapters examine the performance of specific municipal agencies. "The Uniformed Services" is broadest in scope, covering the Police, Fire, Correction, and Sanitation departments.[22] In each case the services performed by the agency are identified and the input–output model is used to assess performance during the late 1980s. The findings vary among the services, but a general conclusion is that the "uniformed" bureaucracies successfully resist changes that might improve productivity. The chapter ends with 20 specific steps that could be taken promptly to improve the performance of the uniformed services.

The Department of Parks and Recreation is among the smallest of municipal agencies in terms of budget and employees, but the chapter reviewing its history and performance is instructive.[23] It relates how the department's inventory of facilities was expanded through Robert Moses's entrepreneurship and with the help of substantial federal funding in the form of Depression-era public works projects. As a result, since Moses left office in 1960, parks commissioners have consistently faced the task of maintaining a large system with limited local resources. There is a mismatch between the size of the city's park system and the size of the department's budget that causes much of the system to be in a state of neglect. Given the reality of limited resources, the ways suggested for avoiding the need to abandon some parks are (1) to obtain more earmarked revenues for parks from private philanthropy and from increased user fees; and (2) to reduce the number of personnel required to maintain parks by introducing competitive arrangements involving private contractors to replace the insulated, quasi-military civil service system that now prevails.

"The Health and Hospitals Corporation" examines the agency responsible for operating the nation's largest municipal hospital system.[24] It traces the system's origins from the infirmaries of poorhouses, to a separate Hospitals Department, to the creation of the public benefit corporation in 1970, to the impact of the 1975 fiscal crisis on the corporation's autonomy. The analysis then shifts to the performance of the agency in delivering its services during the late 1980s. As with other agencies the trends are mixed, but the evidence includes examples of services whose unit costs have risen sharply with little or no sign of improved quality. The analysis points to the affiliation system—under which contracts with private teaching institutions are the principal means for obtaining physician staff—as a source of high costs and weak management. Exploration of alternatives for staffing the municipal hospitals would require changing the political balance between the private and public sectors in the local health care sector, but such initiatives could lower costs and yield higher-quality services.

The agencies assessed in Part IV do not comprise a comprehensive or even representative set of municipal services. Large and important functions, including education, social services, and transportation, are omitted. Consequently, general conclusions should be drawn cautiously. But the cumulative evidence points in a consistent direction: There is much inertia within the system, which makes change difficult. This is true whether current practices rely heavily on civil servants (as in the uniformed services) or on private contractors (as with the HHC). The major difficulty is in putting forward changes, regardless of the direction of the change. There may be no single solution for improving productivity, but because innovation is essential the common obstacle is a reluctance to change.

An Assessment

If we are successful, the remainder of this book will supply readers with abundant information about the government of New York City. But more than offering information, we want to convey a point of view and permit an educated judgment about the political status of the nation's largest municipality.

As noted earlier, the values guiding the inquiry are responsiveness and efficiency. Good government should reflect the preferences of its citizens in its policy choices and should provide its residents with services that are delivered efficiently. Unfortunately, New York City falls short in both respects.

Municipal political institutions do not meet high standards for the relevant criteria. Elections for key offices are rarely competitive; not surprisingly, they attract, at best, only one-third of the eligible electorate. Equally important, the few mayoral contests that meet the competitiveness standard are decided on the basis of voters' views on race relations rather than the candidates' capacity to formulate policies bearing more directly on the operation of municipal government. In sum, for most municipal offices the electoral mechanisms for promoting responsiveness are rusty and performing poorly; for the mayoralty, the somewhat healthier competition is distorted by issues of race.

These political weaknesses are matched by managerial faults. Reviews of several city agencies indicate that innovation is rarely promoted and difficult to implement. As a result, services are costly, and new resources are as likely to be allocated to enriching those who provide the services as to expanding or improving the benefits received by citizens.

Just as municipal officials often do not spend wisely, they also do not tax wisely. The current mix of revenues includes taxes that give unjustified subsidies to some home owners while imposing harmful burdens on renters and businesses who remain. The highest local taxes in the nation are neither raised sensibly nor spent effectively.

As these final paragraphs indicate, we completed this analysis of New York City government in a far less congratulatory frame of mind than did Sayre and Kaufman over 30 years ago. It would be depressing to think that the standards of responsiveness and efficiency set by New York City are the best an American city can achieve. The lasting impressions which New York City politics provides its contemporary students are not uplifting. We hope the potential rewards in the form of a vibrant local democracy serving over 7 million of the world's most diverse citizens will be sufficient to draw those bold enough to explore the subject into the fray of promoting reform.

2

OVERVIEW OF POLITICAL CHANGE

The field of urban politics has changed dramatically since the early 1960s, which many regard as its heyday. Then, some of political science's major figures mounted a counterattack against a loose assemblage of neo-Marxists, mostly sociologists, who had concluded that American cities, like the larger society, were governed by a "power elite." The issue seemed important at the time. The efforts of the political scientists involved served as evidence that their discipline was capable of providing intellectual leadership in a period when national political leaders were showing increased concern for urban problems.

Unfortunately, the field's prominence was short lived. Critics from within and outside the discipline identified methodological weaknesses in evidence supporting the new interpretations. As quantitative methods became more fashionable in the social sciences, the perceived lack of rigor in the research techniques of the field of urban politics led many promising young scholars to view it as a career dead end. Perhaps equally important, changes in the national political mood lessened concern for the political and social ills prevalent in urban areas.

The fiscal problems experienced by many American cities in the 1970s rekindled interest in urban politics. The neo-Marxists returned. Since it was hard to square the fiscal disorder of cities with the notion that local elites had everything under control, they broadened their argument to include the workings of capitalism nationally and internationally. However, few political scientists were interested in recreating the community power debate by either attacking the new models or seeking to deal with deficiencies in the earlier counterarguments. Instead, some used well-developed quantitative techniques to study the determinants of urban fiscal problems; others turned toward more normative policy research with a goal of developing a "national urban policy."

These varied research strands continued through the 1980s. Racial tensions and obstacles to political incorporation of minorities in urban areas also matured as a subfield in this decade. But a common legacy of this diverse set of inquiries is the view that local politics plays a relatively unimportant role in shaping the development of American cities. Some scholars emphasize the economic constraints imposed by competition within a capitalist system; others emphasize the dominance of intergovernmental constraints and stimuli with an emphasis initially on the federal government and, more recently, state governments. Few now emphasize local politics as the principal mechanism shaping the fate of urban America.

This chapter pursues this theme by examining political change in New York City. The first section identifies a set of fiscal policy choices whose varying resolution distinguishes four periods in the political history of New York City since 1960. The second section proposes a model of political change that relies on three causal factors: intergovernmental influences, the performance of the local economy, and changes in power relationships among local political groups. The third section applies the model to explain political change in New York City. The concluding section discusses the implications of the findings.

Identifying Political Change

A meaningful definition of local political change requires some explicit assumptions about what local government does. Political scientists generally point to three activities over which local government officials exercise discretion. These "stakes and prizes" of local politics involve the expenditure of public funds, the raising of revenues, and regulation.[1]

Elements of Political Change

Public expenditure policies have two fundamental dimensions, how much to spend and what to spend it on. The scale of spending indicates the size of local government; over time, municipal spending may shrink or expand. The distribution or mix of spending among types of services and groups of beneficiaries indicates the priorities of local government; over time municipal priorities also may change.

Government officials also decide who pays for municipal activities. These decisions involve choices between "exporting" taxes and burdening local resident; in addition, the local burden must be distributed among groups of residents. Changes in the incidence of taxation typically are described in terms of progressivity or regressivity.

Cities also regulate individual and business behavior, ranging from the establishment and enforcement of building and health codes to land use. While regulation is an important local function, it is not addressed in this chapter. This is a significant limitation, but fiscal behavior remains an important element of local political change.

The focus on spending and finance requires some elaboration of the data appropriate for describing these policies. Each dimension of local fiscal policy can be measured quantitatively.

Spending

Inflation and economic growth make current-dollar spending a misleading indicator. Constant-dollar (that is, inflation-adjusted) expenditures and expenditures as a share of local economic output are more appropriate yardsticks. Table 2.1 presents spending by the city of New York in current dollars, constant (1982) dollars, and as a share of value added by the local economy. (Unless noted, textual references to spending are in constant dollars and are to fiscal years.)

With respect to the functional distribution of spending, local government expenditures can be divided into three broad categories—developmental, redistributive, and allocative.[2] Developmental spending is intended primarily to enhance business activity. It includes infrastructure investments, subsidies for industrial parks, and the maintenance and improvement of transportation facilities, including mass transit, which is particularly significant in New York City.

Redistributive expenditures are aimed at improving the living conditions of residents at the low end of the income distribution. The major redistributive items in the New York City budget are public assistance or "welfare" payments, medical care, social services for the poor, and housing subsidies.

The remaining city services are considered allocative. These expenditures are not viewed as having differential impacts among income groups or classes but as serving residents generally. Examples include refuse collection and fire protection. For the most part, political disputes over this type of spending are based on geographic areas or neighborhoods.

However, in New York and other large cities allocative functions include activities that have significant developmental and redistributive impacts, particularly education and criminal justice. Education has an important developmental purpose as an investment in future labor supply. In addition, education expenditures have a redistributive quality because the student population is disproportionately poor.[3]

Criminal justice also has strong developmental and redistributive implications. To the extent that police, prosecutorial, judicial, and correctional services promote public safety, they contribute to a city's economic competi-

Table 2.1 Spending by the City of New York, Fiscal Years
1961–1990 (dollars in millions)

Fiscal Year	Current Dollars	Constant (1982) Dollars	Percentage of Local Value Added
1961	$2,734.4	$8,572.0	9.7%
1962	2,958.9	9,185.1	10.2
1963	3,237.3	9,856.7	10.7
1964	3,540.9	10,545.2	11.2
1965	3,844.2	11,342.2	11.8
1966	4,240.5	12,209.1	12.5
1967	4,977.6	13,870.3	14.0
1968	5,517.5	14,938.0	14.8
1969	6,329.9	16,216.1	15.7
1970	6,893.0	16,546.7	15.9
1971	7,938.6	17,843.1	17.5
1972	8,820.0	18,846.3	18.5
1973	9,525.6	19,480.5	19.1
1974	10,721.9	20,114.1	20.2
1975	12,377.3	21,139.0	22.2
1976	12,261.3	19,638.7	21.0
1977	12,989.7	19,775.1	21.2
1978	13,090.1	18,958.8	20.1
1979	13,216.4	17,891.0	18.8
1980	14,290.2	17,482.1	18.4
1981	15,108.5	16,742.3	17.4
1982	16,370.8	16,793.7	17.4
1983	16,992.2	16,524.0	17.0
1984	18,537.1	17,251.8	17.2
1985	20,484.2	18,278.5	17.8
1986	21,745.2	18,737.0	17.9
1987	23,289.2	19,350.1	18.0
1988	24,647.0	19,428.1	17.8
1989	27,624.9	20,713.2	19.1
1990	29,682.9	21,063.1	NA

Average annual percentage change		
FYs 1961–69	11.1%	8.3%
FYs 1969–75	11.8	4.5
FYs 1975–83	4.0	(2.7)
FYs 1983–89	8.3	3.5

Sources: Expenditure data are from City of New York, *Comprehensive Annual Financial Report of the Comptroller,* fiscal years 1961–1990 editions. The expenditure totals include operating and capital expenses. The totals for fiscal years 1968–80 have been adjusted by the authors to take into account changed practices in the reporting of the state and federal portions of expenditures under the Medicaid program. Specifically, estimates of state and federal reimbursement for Medicaid expenditures have been subtracted from these years' spending totals; this makes the 1968–80 fiscal-year spending totals consistent with later years. Constant-dollar conversions for expenditures are based on U.S. Department of Labor, Bureau of Labor Statistics, Middle-Atlantic Regional Office, "Consumer Price Index for All Urban Consumers (CPI-U) for the New York–Northeastern New Jersey Area." Value added estimates were provided by Matthew Drennan based on the econometric model described in his *Modeling Metropolitan Economies for Forecasting and Policy Analysis* (New York: New York University Press, 1985). Figures are fiscal year estimates based on averages of calendar year figures. Value added figures are in constant-dollar values based on the national GNP price deflator.

Note: NA, not available.

Table 2.2 City of New York Expenditures by Function, Selected Fiscal Years (percentage distribution)

Function	1961	1969	1975	1983	1989
Primarily redistributive functions	25.8%	35.8%	32.6%	33.2%	30.8%
Public assistance	8.7	15.9	11.5	9.2	6.5
Health	11.0	11.7	9.6	9.9	9.9
Social services	5.3	7.5	9.8	11.8	11.0
Housing	0.8	0.7	1.6	2.3	3.4
Primarily developmental functions	11.0	5.6	11.2	8.4	9.5
Infrastructure	5.2	4.9	8.6	4.4	4.8
Transportation	5.8	0.7	2.6	4.0	4.7
Education	27.4	29.0	28.6	26.9	25.6
Elementary and secondary	24.9	25.6	24.0	25.7	24.3
Higher	2.5	3.3	4.5	1.2	1.3
Criminal justice	13.7	11.3	12.7	12.3	14.7
Police	10.6	9.1	9.9	9.7	10.3
Other	3.1	2.2	2.8	2.7	4.5
Other allocative functions	22.2	18.4	15.0	19.1	19.4
Total	100.0%	100.0%	100.0%	100.0%	100.0%
Total expenditure ($ millions)	$2,290.6	$5,800.7	$10,444.8	$15,353.3	$25,656.1

Source: See Table 2.1. Total includes capital and operating expenses. Total adjusted by authors to account for change in Medicaid reporting. Total excludes debt service; see Note 4. Details on the allocation of items to each function are available from the authors; the method follows closely that presented in Charles Brecher and Raymond D. Horton, "Expenditures," in Charles Brecher and Raymond D. Horton, eds., *Setting Municipal Priorities, 1984* (New York: New York University Press, 1983), pp. 68–96.

tiveness. In addition, they are redistributive in that the poor are disproportionately represented among the victims of crime. Thus, it is appropriate to examine the mix of city spending in terms of five categories: primarily developmental, primarily redistributive, educational, criminal justice, and other allocative services. Table 2.2 presents a distribution of the city of New York's expenditures in selected years using these categories.[4]

Finance

Public expenditures must be financed. Determining "who pays" is as important as determining "who gets." Three basic sources of public funds can be tapped: lenders, other governments, and local taxpayers.

Borrowing, which mostly takes the form of issuing long-term bonds, transfers the burden of financing local government from current to future city residents. It is regarded as an appropriate financing mechanism when the benefits of expenditure are received primarily by future residents, as is the case for most capital improvements. However, capital improvements also may be financed from current revenue sources on a "pay as you go" basis. Moreover, borrowing sometimes is used to finance current operations.

Intergovernmental aid shifts the financial burden from city residents to taxpayers in the "outside" world. Although city residents pay taxes to state and federal governments, these payments need not be returned in the form of aid. Thus, most federal and state aid is viewed as "free" money.

Local revenues consist primarily of taxes, but they also include user charges such as license fees, water bills, and a variety of other items. The burden of taxes varies with the type of tax. Some, such as the local personal income tax, residential property taxes, and sales taxes on items consumed by residents, are paid by residents. Others are exported, such as the hotel occupancy tax, the commuter income tax, and taxes on business income earned by selling goods or services to nonresidents. The ultimate burden of other taxes, such as the commercial occupancy tax, is a source of controversy among economists. Nevertheless, the mix of taxes determined by local government choices strongly influences the extent of which residents provide funds for municipal expenditure.

Local taxes also have distributive consequences. A progressive local income tax requires higher-income residents to finance a greater share of local expenditures than does a sales tax. And the residential property tax, which has been characterized as a "rent tax," places a disproportionate burden on low-income households because so much of their income is devoted to housing costs.

Although comprehensive data on the incidence of the city of New York's taxes over the past three decades are not available, Tables 2.3 and 2.4 present some instructive information. Table 2.3 categorizes municipal income among borrowing, intergovernmental aid, and local sources; Table 2.4 divides local revenues among the real estate tax, sales tax, personal income tax, business income taxes, commercial rent tax, and others.

Table 2.3 City of New York Revenue Sources, Fiscal Years 1961–1990 (percentage distribution)

Fiscal Year	Borrowing[a]			Intergovernmental Aid			Local Taxes	Total		
	Capital	Operating[b]	Total	Capital[c]	Operating	Total	Operating	Capital	Operating	Total
1961	10.6%	—	10.6%	0.5%	17.7%	18.2%	71.2%	11.2%	88.8%	100.0%
1962	10.9	—	10.9	0.5	18.4	18.9	70.2	11.4	88.6	100.0
1963	13.0	0.8%	13.8	0.9	19.8	20.7	65.5	13.9	86.1	100.0
1964	12.5	2.4	14.9	0.8	19.2	20.1	65.0	13.3	86.7	100.0
1965	12.4	1.6	14.0	0.4	19.8	20.2	65.8	12.8	87.2	100.0
1966	10.9	1.1	12.0	0.3	23.4	23.7	64.3	11.2	88.8	100.0
1967	8.3	1.9	10.2	0.7	27.4	28.1	61.7	9.0	91.0	100.0
1968	7.9	3.4	11.3	0.7	28.6	29.4	59.4	8.6	91.4	100.0
1969	7.5	1.5	9.0	0.5	32.1	32.6	58.5	8.0	92.0	100.0
1970	9.6	2.6	12.2	0.4	29.3	29.7	58.1	10.0	90.0	100.0
1971	12.1	1.7	13.8	1.3	30.0	31.3	54.9	13.5	86.5	100.0
1972	12.7	3.2	15.8	1.0	28.6	29.6	54.6	13.7	86.3	100.0
1973	12.4	2.3	14.6	1.6	28.2	29.7	55.6	14.0	86.0	100.0
1974	10.7	8.6	19.3	2.8	26.7	29.5	51.2	13.5	86.5	100.0
1975	8.8	7.2	16.0	3.0	26.8	29.8	54.1	11.8	88.2	100.0
1976	5.9	9.4	15.3	3.0	31.2	34.2	50.4	8.9	91.1	100.0
1977	8.2	7.6	15.8	1.8	30.3	32.2	52.0	10.0	90.0	100.0
1978	2.2	5.4	7.6	2.6	35.3	37.9	54.5	4.8	95.2	100.0
1979	3.7	3.1	6.8	2.9	36.5	39.4	53.8	6.5	93.5	100.0
1980	2.5	2.5	5.0	2.0	36.9	38.9	56.1	4.5	95.5	100.0
1981[d]	3.9	—	3.9	2.4	35.8	38.1	58.0	6.2	93.8	100.0

(continued)

Table 2.3 (Continued)

Fiscal Year	Borrowing[a]			Intergovernmental Aid			Local Taxes	Total		
	Capital	Operating[b]	Total	Capital[c]	Operating	Total	Operating	Capital	Operating	Total
1982	6.5	—	6.5	2.9	34.5	37.4	56.1	9.4	90.6	100.0
1983	5.3	—	5.3	2.1	34.1	36.2	58.5	7.4	92.6	100.0
1984	5.7	—	5.7	1.7	34.0	35.8	58.6	7.4	92.6	100.0
1985	5.1	—	5.1	2.1	33.7	35.8	59.1	7.2	92.8	100.0
1986	7.9	—	7.9	0.9	32.9	33.8	58.2	8.9	91.1	100.0
1987	6.4	—	6.4	1.3	30.3	31.6	62.1	7.6	92.4	100.0
1988	8.3	—	8.3	0.7	30.0	30.7	61.0	9.0	91.0	100.0
1989	8.9	—	8.9	0.9	29.6	30.4	60.7	9.7	90.3	100.0
1990	10.3	—	10.3	1.2	29.5	30.7	59.0	11.5	88.5	100.0

Sources: City of New York, *Comprehensive Annual Financial Report of the Comptroller*, fiscal years 1961–1990 editions. The figures for fiscal years 1968–80 have been adjusted by the authors to take into account changed practices in the reporting of the state and federal portions of expenditures under the Medicaid program.

[a]Capital borrowing includes Other Revenues category, as well as small items such as Interest, Miscellaneous, Transfers to/from Other Funds, and Reimbursements.

[b]Assumes excess of expenditures over revenues as amount borrowed for fiscal years 1976–80. Fiscal years 1961–75 include New York City Stabilization Reserve Corporation, Borrowed from Other City Funds, Borrowed from Other City Funds, Revenue Anticipation Notes in Lieu of Revenue Anticipation Notes, Transfers to/from Other City-Owned funds, Stabilization Reserve Fund Revenue Anticipation Notes Issued, and Budget Notes Issued for State Guaranteed Federal Revenue Sharing.

[c]Also includes aid revenue from sources other than state and federal government.

[d]Capital figures do not include $147 million transfer from the General Fund.

Fiscal Year	Real Estate	Sales	Personal Income	Business Income	Commercial Rent	Other	Total
1961	63.6%	19.1%	—	11.3%	0.1%	5.9%	100.0%
1962	63.3	19.3	—	11.6	0.1	5.7	100.0
1963	62.7	18.5	—	13.3	0.1	5.4	100.0
1964	59.9	21.1	—	9.9	3.3	5.8	100.0
1965	59.0	20.4	—	11.4	3.2	6.0	100.0
1966	60.7	17.0	—	9.5	3.2	9.6	100.0
1967	57.9	14.6	5.0%	9.7	2.8	15.0	100.0
1968	54.8	14.1	5.8	10.8	2.7	11.8	100.0
1969	54.1	14.3	6.5	11.2	2.6	11.3	100.0
1970	56.8	14.5	6.4	11.5	2.9	7.9	100.0
1971	57.6	14.3	5.8	8.7	4.0	9.6	100.0
1972	51.6	12.8	10.9	10.6	3.8	10.3	100.0
1973	54.4	12.8	10.2	10.0	3.9	8.7	100.0
1974	55.4	12.8	10.1	9.7	3.9	8.1	100.0
1975	53.6	16.0	9.4	10.8	3.9	6.3	100.0
1976	51.5	14.3	9.2	13.6	3.4	8.0	100.0
1977	51.4	13.8	9.9	13.1	3.2	8.6	100.0
1978	50.3	14.5	10.9	12.5	3.0	8.8	100.0
1979	48.8	15.7	11.2	12.4	3.2	8.7	100.0
1980	45.9	16.4	12.6	13.6	3.1	8.4	100.0
1981	42.8	17.0	13.2	15.0	3.1	8.9	100.0
1982	43.6	17.1	14.1	14.5	3.4	7.3	100.0
1983	43.3	17.3	15.2	14.0	3.8	6.4	100.0
1984	41.3	17.6	16.2	14.5	4.1	6.3	100.0
1985	39.9	17.3	16.5	15.3	4.1	6.9	100.0
1986	40.9	17.0	16.2	14.5	4.2	7.2	100.0
1987	39.1	16.1	17.1	15.3	4.1	8.3	100.0
1988	40.4	16.7	15.8	15.4	4.4	7.3	100.0
1989	41.3	16.2	17.1	14.4	4.5	6.5	100.0
1990	43.6	16.2	17.0	12.4	4.6	6.2	100.0

Sources: City of New York, *Comprehensive Annual Financial Report of the Comptroller,* fiscal years 1961–1990 editions. Individual items shown as a percentage of total taxes, rather than total local revenue. Total local revenue, as shown in Table 2.2, includes non-tax revenues.

Four Periods with Different Fiscal Policies

The categories and data presented thus far can be used to identify four periods during which different fiscal policies were followed. The distinguishing factors of each period are summarized next.

1961–1969: Rapid Growth and Increased Redistribution

This period was marked by rapid growth in municipal spending, increased priority for redistributive expenditures, and further enhancement of income redistribution through greater reliance on progressive taxes. Between 1961 and 1969, municipal spending rose 89 percent, or an average of 8.3 percent annually; this near-doubling caused municipal spending to rise from 10 to 16 percent of local value added. In the same period, the share of total spending allocated to redistributive services increased from 26 to 36 percent. The introduction of the local personal income tax in 1967 also made revenue raising a more progressive activity. The personal income tax accounted for 7 percent of all tax revenue by 1969, while the regressive sales tax fell from 19 to 14 percent.

1969–1975: Continued Growth with Less Redistribution and More Borrowing

In this period local spending continued to grow. The rate of increase slowed to 4.5 percent annually, but spending as a share of local value added rose from 16 to 22 percent. Expenditures were allocated somewhat differently, with redistributive spending falling from 36 to 33 percent and developmental expenditures rising from 6 to 11 percent.

The most noteworthy change is evident in the sources of municipal funds. Borrowings grew from 9 to 16 percent of the total, while local tax revenues fell from 59 to 54 percent. Among local revenue sources the personal income tax continued to become more prominent, rising from 7 to 9 percent of the total, but the sales tax share also rose—from 14 to 16 percent.

1975–1983: Retrenchment and Reduced Borrowing

The most noteworthy change in fiscal policy during this period was the abrupt shift from growth to decline in municipal spending. Expenditures fell 22 percent, or 2.7 percent annually, and declined as a share of local value added from 22 to 17 percent. This period was one of relative stability in the functional distribution of spending. In 1975 and 1983, redistributive services accounted for 33 percent of total spending, and education and criminal justice also retained nearly identical shares.

However, the sources of funds changed markedly. Borrowings dropped from 16 percent of total income in 1975 to 5 percent in 1983, and local taxes increased from 54 to 59 percent. Among local revenues the real estate tax declined in importance, falling from 54 to 43 percent of the total. Personal income tax and sales tax shares increased, the former from 9 to 15 percent and the latter from 14 to 17 percent.

1983–1989: Growth with Less Redistribution

From 1983 to 1989, municipal spending again increased significantly. Expenditures rose 25 percent, or an annual average of 3.8 percent. As a share of local value added, spending rose from 17 to 19 percent.

The distribution of municipal expenditure also shifted. The proportion for redistributive activities declined from 33 to 31 percent with a simultaneous rise from 12 to 15 percent in the share for criminal justice. Other functions retained relatively stable shares.

With respect to finance, policy changes also are evident. Intergovernmental aid fell from 36 to 30 percent of total income. To offset this decline both borrowed funds and local taxes increased. Borrowings grew from 5 to 9 percent of the total, and local taxes increased from 59 to 61 percent.

In sum, political change in New York City during the past three decades can be described in terms of four periods based on differences in spending and finance policies. These four periods differ in two ways from time spans used in other contexts to analyze political change in New York City. First, the categorization is not simply between pre- and post–fiscal crisis eras. Two distinct periods are evident both before and after the 1975 fiscal crisis.

Second, the periods do not correspond neatly to periods of individual mayoral rule. The first period transcends two different mayors (Robert F. Wagner, Jr., and John V. Lindsay); the second period also spans two mayors (Lindsay and Abraham D. Beame); the third also spans two mayors (Beame and Edward I. Koch). Although the last period includes only one mayor, Koch, it is not clear that Koch's defeat and the election of David N. Dinkins in 1989 will change local fiscal policies.

Factors Causing Change in Fiscal Policies

Three variables are hypothesized to account for change in fiscal policy: the performance of the local economy, intergovernmental interventions, and power relationships among local interest groups. Changes in each of these factors can be linked to changes in one or more of the elements of local fiscal policy defined earlier.

Local Economic Activity

Changes in the size of the local economic base can be expected to influence at least two elements of local fiscal policy. First, local economic growth (decline) affects the amount of local government spending. All things being equal, public expenditure will grow along with private income during periods of local economic growth (and decline along with private income during economic decline).

Second, economic growth (decline) exerts an independent influence on the sources of local revenue since some local taxes are more economically sensitive than others. For example, personal income tax and sales tax revenues rise and fall more closely in line with private income than real estate tax revenues (because of assessment practices). Thus, the independent effect of economic growth (decline) is to increase (decrease) reliance on sales and personal income taxes. Since this effect, at least in New York City, is most evident in the personal income tax, the net effect of economic growth (decline) is to make the local tax system more (less) progressive.

Intergovernmental Relations

The state of New York and the federal government influence local fiscal policy through legislation providing financial aid and through judicial and administrative interventions. Each has an independent effect on local fiscal policy.

Financial Aid

The impact of intergovernmental aid depends on the form it takes. Three types of programs can be distinguished—unrestricted aid, categorical aid, and mandated matching aid.

Unrestricted aid is "free" money since localities can use it as they see fit (so long as they meet minimal accounting standards and do not use the funds in violation of constitutional standards). Such aid has an "income effect" in that the grant funds will be used like any other additional revenue source.[5]

Categorical aid is provided for a specific purpose. Its impact depends on what the locality would have done without the funds. If the locality would *not* have spent funds for the purpose, then categorical aid generates new local spending. However, if the locality would have spent local money for a particular purpose, then categorical aid merely substitutes intergovernmental funds for local funds. In the latter case, categorical aid has an income effect similar to unrestricted aid. Since New York City has a history of local spending at relatively high levels for a wide range of services, much categorical aid presumably is substitutive and carries an income effect.

Mandated matching programs are designed to achieve a stimulative effect, that is, to ensure that more will be spent than would have been spent without the program. These state and federal government initiatives provide categorical aid but with the added string attached that a locality must spend some of its own funds to receive the aid. The most significant mandated matching programs in New York City are public assistance and Medicaid. The public assistance programs require the city to pay state-determined benefits to all who are eligible under the laws of New York State; the city then receives state and federal aid (the latter passed through the state) which *partly* reimburses it for program costs. Under Medicaid, the state pays the costs of medical care for indigent residents meeting its eligibility requirements; the city and the federal government then are obliged to reimburse the state for a share of the costs.

Other Interventions

Higher governments also influence local fiscal policy through judicial and administrative regulations. The precise fiscal impacts of court decisions vary from case to case, but judicial interventions typically increase local spending for specific services or population groups.[6] Thus, judicial intervention has a direct fiscal effect by altering the distribution of spending in favor of the affected service or group. Notable illustrations in New York City include court orders requiring spending to upgrade jails, special education for disadvantaged students, and shelters for homeless individuals. Administrative regulations, sometimes enforced by judicial action, also shape the distribution of local funds. For example, the city is required by state administrators to develop new solid waste management policies.

Local Interest Group Competition

A third factor hypothesized to exert an independent effect on local policy decisions is the balance of power among local interest groups. Virtually all models of local politics assume that such groups exist, that such groups have competing interests, and that local government decisions reflect their relative power. However, the specification of these groups and the methodologies for identifying their relative power differ.

These differences were evident in the community power debate. The elite models viewed the community as divided between a "business community" (the capitalists) and residents who were either unemployed or worked for private firms and local government in the area (labor). This paradigm posited enduring conflicts between these two broad groups or classes in most policy areas; the "reputational" and other methodologies employed by its adherents confirmed their hypothesis.

In contrast, pluralists saw local political competition as involving numerous interest groups with specialized interests and few, if any, enduring conflicts. Important government decisions were hypothesized to be the product of bargaining among multiple groups; the pluralist methodology relied on detailed case studies of the decision-making process that confirmed the hypothesis that community power was not dominated by local elites.

Subsequent studies of local fiscal policy dispute the elitist view of recurring conflict between two classes but at the same time suggest that a relatively small number of groups compete with one another over recurring interests. In four case studies of communities experiencing fiscal stress, Levine, Rubin, and Wolohojian relied on a theoretical model that identified both interest groups and formal authority structures as independent variables influencing policy responses to reductions in spending.[7] They interpreted the evidence as supporting the hypothesis that retrenchment policies were affected by informal relationships among local interest groups.

Clark and Ferguson's more comprehensive analysis comparing fiscal policy decisions in 62 American cities employed a theoretical model predicting that spending outcomes were determined by community wealth, the preferences of elected leaders, local political culture, and competition among four groups: the business community, the poor, municipal employees, and middle-class residents.[8] Regression analysis generally confirmed the hypothesized relationship between the size and influence of the four groups and fiscal decisions.

These studies are consistent with the hypothesis that the balance of power among local interest groups exerts a direct influence on New York City government's fiscal policies. The analysis that follows adopts the Clark-Ferguson categories except that it distinguishes municipal financiers from the remainder of the business community. The municipal financiers, investment bankers who underwrite bond sales, are no less interested in increased profits than the business community, but their profits are served by different local government fiscal policies. In this section, the identity and the interests of the business community and the municipal financiers are specified, along with those of the dependent poor, civil servants, and privately employed residents (in more common parlance, the "middle class").

The Business Community

The concept of "business community" has been questioned by critics of elite theories of community power, including Sayre and Kaufman.[9] The city's businesses are numerous and differ in several ways: size (big versus small); control (managers versus entrepreneur-owners); products (services versus goods); markets (local versus national and international); and location (one area of the city versus another). The pluralists celebrated these differences and concluded that business firms comprise multiple competing communities.

This view overlooks the growing interdependence of a core group of New York City firms which has been called the "corporate headquarters complex" or the "advanced business service sector."[10] These businesses include headquarters of manufacturing enterprises, financial institutions, law firms, advertising and public relations firms, management consultants, and others. They are big businesses which are run by managers, sell the bulk of their services to organizations located outside the city, and are concentrated in a dense central business district. Closely allied are the realtors, who develop and/or own the buildings that house the advanced business service firms. Although the realtors' interests are not identical to those who buy or rent commercial buildings, they are similar enough to be defined here as within the business community.

So defined, the business community's major interest in local fiscal policy is to reduce, or at least contain the growth of, public expenditure. The managers of the city's businesses associate increased local spending with higher taxes and lower profits.

With respect to the mix of local spending, they are particularly adverse to redistributive expenditures since the dependent poor are not purchasers of advanced business services. However, the business community selectively supports increased developmental and allocative spending. Capital improvements that provide general economic benefits (mass transit, for example) are supported, but projects that convey specific real benefits (for example, the central business district's west side) are opposed by those businesses that would suffer competitively. The business community generally supports increased expenditures for police (to improve public safety) and street cleaning (particularly in areas where their businesses are located). Since they associate improvements in allocative services with staffing additions and do not want public sector compensation levels to drive up the cost of labor generally, the business community prefers that increases in spending be devoted to expanding the number of civil servants rather than to enhancing their compensation.

As noted earlier, the business community prefers low taxes. They share a particular aversion to higher personal income taxes. The managers of the advanced business service firms are highly paid; those who escape the full brunt of the city's personal income tax by living in the suburbs still view it as anathema because it complicates recruitment of their managerial subordinates.

Municipal Financiers

Lenders are an important source of municipal income. However, municipalities do not sell bonds and notes directly to creditors. Instead, they are sold to firms that "underwrite" the securities and then resell them in the "public" credit market. When underwriters are able to resell the securities at a higher price, they pocket the difference. Ordinarily, underwriting is a profitable activity.

Investment bankers are a second intermediary in the pipeline of municipal credit. They typically are associated with one of the firms that underwrite municipal debt, but the investment bankers are hired by cities to help structure the sale of municipal debt to the underwriters and, indirectly, to creditors in the capital markets. The fees of the investment bankers are based on the volume of loans they facilitate. Generally, the interests of the investment bankers and the underwriters coincide, but not always. If the investment bankers facilitate loans that the underwriters cannot resell for a profit, then the underwriters will be forced to sell for a loss or, alternatively, to hold the bonds "on the shelf."

The nature of their business means municipal financiers are served by local fiscal policies that conflict with those of the larger business community. Whereas the business community prefers reduced municipal expenditure, the municipal financiers prefer more spending since some of that spending is likely to be supported by increased borrowings—particularly spending for capital investments.

The municipal financiers also have different local tax preferences. Although they tend to earn as much as (if not more than) the business managers, the financiers favor high local (and state) personal income taxes because these taxes exempt the interest on municipal bonds and notes. Thus, the higher the marginal tax rate on personal income, the more attractive municipal debt is to the larger investment community.

The Dependent Poor

A major segment of the local population has little or no private income and depends on government to support their food, shelter, medical care, and other social services needs. The poor occasionally organize for collective action, but their interests typically are represented in local politics by organizations that are "in the business" of providing social services and, therefore, are themselves dependent on public expenditures. These organizations are predominantly nonprofit but include firms and government agencies as well. Although their respective interests sometimes diverge, the dependent poor and the organizations designed to serve them usually share a common interest in enhanced benefits and broader eligibility for social welfare programs.

The poor and their organizational providers favor greater local spending since it is likely to provide improved benefits to them; among the functional categories they favor spending for redistribution over other purposes. (It is worth noting, however, that the dependent poor are most likely to favor greater cash assistance, whereas the providers tend to favor spending for in-kind services.) With respect to tax policy, this group, like the municipal financiers, favors a progressive personal income tax.

Civil Servants

Since most municipal services require relatively large labor inputs, a large share of municipal expenditure goes to compensate civil servants. To advance their substantial interests in municipal fiscal policy, the city's municipal employees have organized into civil service unions. The "organized bureaucracy" seeks to influence municipal fiscal policy both through collective bargaining, which has expanded in scope to include many issues in addition to the determination of compensation, and through lobbying, endorsements, campaign contributions, and other common political strategies.

Civil servants generally favor more public expenditure since a large percentage of additional funds is likely to find its way into their pocketbooks. As a group, civil servants are indifferent to the functional distribution of expenditures. However, they seek to increase "labor's share" of total expenditure, and like most salaried workers, including professors, they tend to prefer increased compensation to higher staffing. With respect to revenue sources, civil servants favor progressive taxes. They perceive themselves as lower wage earners, but beyond that progressive taxes like the personal income tax yield more revenue to support government spending in times of growth.

Privately Employed Residents

This group is more heterogeneous than the others, which complicates the specification of its interests. Its members work for private organizations located in New York City, though some residents are reverse commuters. As noted earlier, this group corresponds broadly to the "middle class" in that the earned incomes of its members usually exceed the poverty level; at the same time, relatively few reach the high-income bracket. While large in number, this group is not well organized. Its interests usually are articulated by small groups organized on a neighborhood basis or on the basis of common concern over a particular service, such as public education or police protection.

The expenditure preferences of this group are similar to those of the business community. Its members prefer reduced expenditure because they consider themselves heavily taxed. They also favor shifting expenditures from redistributive purposes. In general, their support for allocative spending is broader than that of the business community because middle-class New Yorkers consume a wider range of such services than business managers. However, the middle class shares with the business community an interest in obtaining better services as cheaply as possible; this leads them also to prefer additions to the municipal work force over higher compensation per worker.

This group's tax preferences vary with the living arrangements of its members. Those who own their own homes (nearly one-quarter of the city's households) assign a high priority to keeping the residential property tax low. The large majority who rent are less concerned with property taxes because many are protected by various forms of rent regulation. In general, however, the city's privately employed residents oppose the more visible taxes, including the personal income tax and the sales tax.

To summarize, the model posits that the fiscal policies of New York City government change because of changes in intergovernmental interventions, the local economy, and the balance of power among five key local interest groups. Three of the groups—the dependent poor, civil servants, and municipal financiers—generally prefer to see municipal expenditure increase. The same groups also favor greater progressivity in local taxation, particularly in the form of higher personal income taxes. The business community and privately employed residents prefer reduced levels of local public expenditure and less progressive taxes.

The groups that prefer increased expenditure also compete for spending increments. The clearest competition is between the dependent poor and civil servants. However, the financiers are also competitors for municipal funds since debt service (the payment of principal and interest to creditors) must be paid in order for loans to continue.

The division of labor's share of expenditure between compensation and employment is another basic cleavage. Civil servants prefer that the compensation–employment tradeoff be drawn in favor of compensation. The others, particularly the poor, the middle class, and the business community, favor increased employment over higher compensation.

Causal Factors During the Four Periods

To test the model elaborated in the previous section, changes in municipal expenditures are disaggregated in three ways. Table 2.5 shows the contribution of each independent variable to the spending change in the four periods identified earlier. Intergovernmental interventions are divided into two components: change resulting from mandated spending (which includes aid for

Table 2.5 Components of Change in City of New York Spending During Four Periods (amounts in millions of constant 1982 dollars)

Fiscal Period	Total Change in Spending	Intergovernmental Impact			Local Economy Impact	Local Political Impact		
		Mandate Effects	Other Aid	Subtotal		Change in Borrowing	Remainder	Subtotal
1961–69	$7,644.1	$1,967.9	$2,623.3	$4,591.2	$1,036.4	$531.3	$1,485.2	$2,016.5
	100.0%	25.7%	34.3%	60.1%	13.6%	7.0%	19.4%	26.4%
1969–75	$4,992.9	$98.5	$1,127.1	$1,225.6	($664.4)	$1,893.0	$2,468.7	$4,361.7
	100.0%	2.0%	22.9%	24.9%	(13.5%)	38.5%	50.1%	88.6%
1975–83	($4,615.0)	($404.4)	$119.0	($285.4)	$214.5	($2,460.4)	($2,083.7)	($4,544.1)
	100.0%	8.8%	(2.6%)	6.2%	(4.6%)	53.3%	45.2%	98.5%
1983–89	$4,189.2	$22.3	$217.5	$239.8	$968.1	$934.0	$2,047.3	$2,981.3
	100.0%	0.5%	5.2%	5.7%	23.1%	22.3%	48.9%	71.2%

Sources: The change in total spending is derived from Table 2.1. The mandate effect is the change in expenditures accounted for by spending in public assistance from all sources and locally funded spending on Medicaid. Data for these expenditures are estimated from *Annual Report of the New York State Department of Social Services, Statistical Supplement.* Other aid is calculated by subtracting the estimated state and federal share of public assistance spending from total intergovernmental aid as shown in Table 2.3. The local economy impact is calculated by applying the percentage change in value added during the period to nonmandated local spending in the base year. Nonmandated local spending is calculated as total spending from Table 2.1 minus the mandate effect and other aid.

Table 2.6 Change in Spending by Selected Objects of Expenditure During Four Periods (percentage distribution)

	Fiscal Period			
	1961–69	1969–75	1975–83	1983–89
Total change (in millions of 1982 dollars)	$7,644.1	$4,992.9	($4,615.0)	$4,189.2
Labor costs	42.9%	43.0%	36.3%	56.3%
Redistributive spending	48.7	9.7	18.3	23.1
Public assistance transfer	26.1	(6.2)	14.8	(2.9)
Indirect redistributive spending	22.6	16.0	3.5	26.1
Debt service	6.1	28.0	31.4	(8.2)

Sources: Change in total spending from Table 2.1. Change in redistributive spending from sources noted in Table 2.2. Change in debt service from sources noted in Table 2.1. Change in labor spending from Table 2.7; figure for 1969–75 period includes Health and Hospitals Corporation expenditures. Percentages do not add to 100 because indirect redistributive spending includes some municipal labor costs.

public assistance as well as mandated local spending for public assistance and Medicaid) and change attributable to other forms of intergovernmental aid. The "local economy impact" in Table 2.5 represents the spending change that would have resulted if locally funded, nonmandated spending had increased (decreased) at the same rate as local value added. The remainder, attributable neither to intergovernmental interventions nor to local economic change, is attributed to local political change. The amount within this remainder reflecting changes in borrowing also is identified in Table 2.5, since it relates to the role of the municipal financiers.

Table 2.6 disaggregates the spending change during each period into three categories that are closely related to key local interest groups: labor costs or payments to civil servants, redistributive services, and debt service. The redistributive category is subdivided into direct transfers to the poor (public assistance payments) and indirect transfers (to organizations providing services to the poor, including municipal agencies). The debt service category reflects payments of principal and interest on outstanding debt.

Finally, Table 2.7 disaggregates the change in spending for labor costs into shares attributable to changes in the number of civil servants and their average compensation. These figures help gauge the relative political influence of civil servants, who favor higher compensation, and the poor, the middle class, and the business managers, who favor increased numbers of employees.

The 1961–1969 Period

The rapid expansion in municipal expenditure during this period resulted largely from intergovernmental interventions, which explain 60 percent of the total increase. (See Table 2.5.) Increases in categorical and unrestricted aid account for 34 percent of the overall spending change; the expansion of public assistance eligibility and the enactment of Medicaid underlay the jump in the city's mandated expenses, which caused 26 percent of the overall increase.

Table 2.7 Components of Change in City of New York Labor Costs During Four Periods

	Fiscal Year					Percentage Change			
	1961	1969	1975	1983	1989	1961–69	1969–75	1975–83	1983–89
Labor costs (millions of 1982 constant dollars)									
Salaries and wages	$3,706.4	$6,329.8	$6,803.5	$5,261.7	$7,240.7	70.8%	7.5%	(22.7%)	37.6%
Pensions and fringes	852.7	1,511.5	2,402.5	2,270.6	2,649.9	77.3	58.9	(5.5)	16.7
Total	4,559.0	7,841.2	9,206.0 [10,198.1]a	7,532.3	9,890.6	72.0	17.4 [29.9]a	18.2	31.3
Number of employees	200,706	278,161	247,871 [294,522]a	194,623	238,383	38.5	(10.9) [5.9]a	(21.5)	22.5
Compensation per employee (1982 constant dollars)									
Salaries and wages	$18,467	$22,756	$27,448	$27,035	$30,374	23.2%	20.6%	(1.5%)	12.4%
Pensions and fringes	4,248	5,434	9,693	11,667	11,116	27.9	78.4	20.4	(4.7)
Total	22,715	28,189	37,140	38,702	41,490	24.1	31.8	4.2	7.2
Components of change									
Employment change	—	—	—	—	—	53.6%	19.6%	118.2%	71.8%
Compensation change	—	—	—	—	—	46.4	80.4	(18.2)	28.2
Total change	—	—	—	—	—	100.0%	100.0%	100.0%	100.0%

Sources: Expenditure figures are from City of New York, Comprehensive Annual Financial Report of the Comptroller, fiscal years 1961, 1969, 1975, 1983, and 1989 editions. Constant-dollar conversions based on U.S. Department of Labor, Bureau of Labor Statistics, Middle Atlantic Regional Office, "Consumer Price Index for All Urban Consumers (CPI-U) in the New York–Northeastern New Jersey Area" (fiscal-year average). Employment data for 1975 (without HHC), 1983, and 1989 are also from the respective Comptroller's Reports. Employment data for 1961, 1969, and 1975 (with HHC) are from The City in Transition: Prospects and Policies for New York, Final Report of the Temporary Commission on City Finances, June 1977.

aThe creation of the Health and Hospitals Corporation in 1970 removed employees of the former Department of Hospitals from the city's payroll. Bracketed figures include HHC employment and labor costs to ensure consistency with fiscal year 1969 data. These figures use personal service expenditures for HHC as reported in the Corporation's Financial Report for Fiscal Years 1975 and 1976 prepared by Arthur Andersen and Company. The figures including HHC employment and expenditures are used to calculate the composition of change in the 1969–1975 period.

During this period the local economy (measured by local value added) grew at an average annual rate of 2 percent. Assuming local revenue growth at this rate, the local economy's growth caused 14 percent of total spending growth. Thus, 74 percent of the total spending increase between 1961 and 1969 can be attributed to intergovernmental interventions and local economic growth.

The remaining portion, 26 percent, can be attributed to increased influence in the local political system of one or more of the groups favoring higher spending. Their relative influence in shaping the expenditure increment during this period is shown in Table 2.6, most clearly for the poor and civil servants.[11]

As noted earlier, spending for redistributive purposes rose from 26 to 36 percent of the total between 1961 and 1969. (See Table 2.2.) Restated as a share of the increment, redistributive spending accounted for 49 percent of the growth. (See Table 2.6.) Direct transfers via public assistance payments accounted for 26 percent of the increment; indirect spending or organizations that serve the poor consumed 23 percent.

Civil servants captured 43 percent of the total spending increase. (See Table 2.6.) As Table 2.7 shows, the additional dollars supported a 39 percent increase in employment and a 24 percent gain in average compensation. Although their numbers and living standards rose, the resolution of the compensation–employment tradeoff did not heavily favor the preference of civil servants. Employment growth accounted for 54 percent of the increase in labor spending; increased compensation 46 percent.

The evidence pertaining to the influence of the financiers is more ambiguous. As Table 2.5 shows, borrowed funds contributed only 7 percent of the increase in local expenditure, a result that reduced the proportion of borrowings to total income from 11 to 8 percent. (See Table 2.3.) However, the introduction of the personal income tax in 1967 served the current (and future) interests of the investment bankers.

The evidence suggests that the policies of the 1961–1969 period were not implemented at the behest of the business community and the middle class. They were unsuccessful in holding the line on public expenditure and shifting spending from redistribution, as Tables 2.1 and 2.2 show, respectively. In addition, the period saw introduction of the local personal income tax. The compensation–employment tradeoff, however, was resolved in a manner that gave substantial recognition to their interests.

The 1969–1975 Period

In this period the local economy declined at an average annual rate of 1.4 percent. If local public spending had followed this pattern, municipal expenditures would have declined by 14 percent. Since spending actually rose 28 percent between 1969 and 1975, the other variables more than offset the negative local economic effect.

Unlike the previous period, intergovernmental interventions were not the dominant factor pushing up spending. Only 25 percent of the total spending increase was caused by intergovernmental policies. The mandate effect was reduced to 2 percent in this period by curbs on eligibility for public assistance and passage of the federal Supplemental Security Income (SSI) program (which removed from the city's budget substantial sums previously required to aid the aged and disabled). However, the other forms of intergovernmental aid continued to grow at a substantial rate as federal revenue sharing, worker training, and other programs were enacted. These nonmandated programs accounted for 23 percent of the spending growth during the 1969–1975 period.

Since only 11 percent of the spending change between 1969 and 1975 is explained by the combination of intergovernmental and local economic variables, local politics was the dominant force. However, there was a notable shift in the explanation of the spending increase. In the prior period, increased spending for public assistance payments to the poor and payments to civil servants accounted for 69 percent of the increment. Between 1969 and 1975 payment to civil servants and borrowings explain as much as 82 percent of the increase.[12]

Civil servants captured the same share of the spending increment, 43 percent, in both periods. (See Table 2.6.) During the 1969–1975 period, however, the increase in average compensation (32 percent) accounted for 80 percent of the total increase in spending for labor; employment gains (6 percent) accounted for only 20 percent of the increment. (See Table 2.7.)

The increasing influence of municipal financiers is evident in Tables 2.3, 2.5, and 2.6. Borrowings rose from 9 to 16 percent of total income, accounting for 39 percent of the increment. Debt service payments, which accounted for only 6 percent of the spending increase between 1961 and 1969, accounted for 28 percent of the increase in the 1969–1975 period.

In contrast to civil servants and municipal financiers, the influence of the poor declined in this period. Redistributive spending accounted for only 10 percent of the 1969–1975 increment, compared to 49 percent in the prior period. (See Table 2.6.) Moreover, all of the incremental spending for the poor went to organizations designed to provide services to the poor (though some of the absolute decline in direct payments reflected the aforementioned passage of the SSI program).

For the most part, the fiscal policies of the 1969–1975 period were not consistent with the interests of the business community or the middle class. The annual rate of expenditure growth slowed somewhat, from 8.3 to 4.5 percent, but in the face of economic decline this raised local spending from 16 to 22 percent of local value added. (See Table 2.1.) While the relative importance of redistributive spending declined, the resolution of the compensation–employment tradeoff was not drawn in favor of the business community and the middle class. The average compensation of civil servants increased nearly a third, but their numbers declined. In addition, the personal income tax continued to grow more important in financing municipal government, notwithstanding the sharp increase in borrowed funds.

The 1975–1983 Period

The fiscal policies of the 1975–1983 period are attributable almost entirely to local political forces. The local economic impact in these years was expansionary, since local value added began to increase after 1975. As Table 2.5 shows, municipal expenditure would have increased $215 million had locally funded spending paralleled local economic trends. Instead, spending declined $4.6 billion.

Intergovernmental actions explain only a small portion of the spending change. Tight curbs on public assistance and Medicaid spending led to reductions in mandated programs, which were offset by slight increases in other forms of intergovernmental aid. (See Table 2.5.) Overall, the intergovernmental effect accounts for only 6 percent of the total reduction. Together, the intergovernmental and local economy variables explain only 1.5 percent of the expenditure reduction between 1975 and 1983.

The strong role of local politics in both the 1969–1975 and 1975–1983 periods combined with the strikingly different fiscal policies in these periods suggests that the balance of influence among groups shifted radically. However, observation of decision making in the period reveals that the two groups found to be most influential in the 1969–1975 period—civil servants and municipal financiers—were also the parties in the key decision-making position during the post–fiscal crisis period. Why did the same groups pursue different policies?

The answer to this question derives from the fact that the lenders who supplied capital to underwriters refused to continue to make additional funds available. This refusal stemmed from changes in the financial markets that made tax-exempt loans less desirable for many institutional investors and a loss of confidence among traditional investors in the city's ability to manage its finances and repay its loans.

When the traditional source of borrowed capital withdrew, the prospending coalition of the 1969–1975 period changed course. The goal of each group was to reduce its potential losses. An agreement was reached between the civil servants and municipal financiers to pursue their goals through private negotiations that would exclude other groups (notably the poor and the middle class) and would prevent the outcome from being determined by a bankruptcy master—a potential new outside party whose independence was threatening to both civil servants and financiers. The uncertain outcome of bankruptcy proceedings was the cement that held together negotiations between civil servants and municipal financiers over the pattern of retrenchment.

As the largest recipient of municipal expenditures, civil servants had much to lose. Whereas their pensions were protected by the state constitution, their jobs and their salaries and fringe benefits were at risk. A bankruptcy master seeking to protect residents and businesses from reductions in services might have cut salaries and fringe benefits rather than jobs. Although their exposure was great, civil servants also possessed the period's scarcest resource—capital.

The gains in municipal employment and salaries, plus the liberalization of pension benefits realized in the post-1960 era, resulted in a large increase in pension fund assets which could be reinvested. This ensured that civil servants—more accurately, civil service union leaders—had a seat in the negotiating room.

The municipal financiers also were exposed. The investment banks still holding unsold bonds suffered an immediate loss when the credit markets closed. But they held a longer-term interest in restoring the city's access to public credit, which would allow them to resume their traditional function, and their expertise was required to help devise new financing methods.

The business community was exposed because large tax increases were one option for mitigating losses to the direct beneficiaries of municipal spending. Business leaders were able to gain a seat at the negotiating table (principally in the form of appointment to membership on the Emergency Financial Control Board) because the deterioration of the previously dominant coalition weakened the civil servants and because in such uncertain times American ideology favors reliance on "businesslike" approaches to restoring fiscal order.

The poor also had much to lose, but they were not represented among the negotiators. To some extent their interests were protected by federal entitlement programs (though this did not prevent the state from reducing benefits or the city from reducing the welfare rolls administratively). In addition, the lack of organization among this group made it difficult to identify widely accepted representatives who might participate in negotiations.

The middle class had a lot to lose, too. The services they consumed were at risk, and like businesses they were a potential target for increased taxes. But, like the poor, the middle class had no direct representation in the negotiations.

How did the competing groups fare in the retrenchment period? Payments to civil servants fell 18 percent, accounting for 36 percent of the total decrement. (See Tables 2.7 and 2.6, respectively.) However, the entire reduction was made by cutting the work force 22 percent; the average compensation of civil servants actually increased 4 percent.

This outcome served the interests of union leaders. Since they are elected by union members, they preferred to have fewer—but better compensated—voters than more members with reduced compensation. In addition, this outcome served the interest of most municipal employees. Most of the work force reduction was accomplished by attrition rather than layoffs, and seniority rules reduced uncertainty over which workers would be fired. In addition, the collective bargaining system was retained, continuing the right of municipal workers to union representation. Civil servants were among retrenchment's losers, but they retained a strong voice in the allocation of the losses.

The municipal financiers fared better than municipal workers, although neither the investment bankers nor the underwriters emerged unscathed. The investment bankers earned fees for their services in restructuring municipal loans during the period between 1975 and the reopening of the public credit market in 1981. As Table 2.6 suggests, there was a substantial restructuring business during this period; cuts in debt service accounted for 31 percent of the total spending decrement during the period. This is explained largely by the conversion of outstanding debt from "short to long," a stretching exercise that delayed repayment of principal and interest. Whereas the underwriters were spared capital losses by avoidance of bankruptcy, the funds they invested in bonds remaining in their inventories were effectively frozen. (The same can be said of the larger investment community, though some investors feared the worst and sold their holdings at a loss. Of course, for each unwise seller, there was a wise buyer.)

The poor suffered absolute cuts, but not of a magnitude to reduce their share of municipal expenditure. Cuts in redistributive spending contributed 18 percent of the decrement in expenditures, near enough the overall average to preserve their 33 percent share of total spending. (See Tables 2.6 and 2.2, respectively.) However, the mix of redistributive spending changed. Direct payments contributed 15 percent of the overall spending decline; indirect payments contributed only 4 percent. In this sense the dependent poor suffered greater losses than did their service-providing benefactors. The poor were ill-served in another sense. Like the business community and privately employed workers, who were interested in the maintenance of municipal services, the poor suffered because the resolution of the compensation–employment tradeoff favored the living standards of civil servants over maintenance of service standards.

The interests of the business community generally were well-served. Its primary interest is in seeing local expenditure and taxation held down. Retrenchment clearly satisfied the first goal. The second was satisfied too, though this is not evident fully from the tabular material. Taxes were cut during the 1975–1983 period. The rationale for this policy, later popularized at the federal level, was that tax cuts would stimulate economic growth.

To the extent that privately employed New Yorkers pursue lower spending and reduced taxes, the fiscal policies of the retrenchment period also served them. However, the terms of the compensation–employment tradeoff ensured service cuts in most areas.

The 1983–1989 Period

The role of local politics diminished somewhat in the most recent period, but it remained the most important of the explanatory variables. As Table 2.5 shows, local economic growth accounted for 23 percent of the total increase in spending in the postretrenchment period. Intergovernmental interventions continued to play a relatively small role, accounting for less than 6 percent of the total growth in spending.

Whereas the average annual growth rate in the 1983–1989 period was less than in the two previous expansionary periods (1961–1969 and 1969–1975), it exceeded the rate of decline in the 1975–1983 period. As a result, by 1989 spending had returned nearly to the 1975 high-water mark.

The fiscal policies of this period suggest the prospending coalition of civil servants and municipal financiers remained influential, while the business community was no longer in a position to exercise its will strongly. Civil servants received 56 percent of the expenditure increment during this period. (See Table 2.6.) This exceeded their capture rate in the two earlier growth periods (43 percent) and their loss rate during retrenchment (36 percent). However, the division of labor spending favored employment over compensation gains. Average compensation rose 7 percent, but the number of employees rose 23 percent. (See Table 2.7.) Nearly three-quarters (72 percent) of the increase in labor spending is attributable to the employment variable.

Municipal financiers also played an increasingly important role. While borrowed funds were more difficult to use for operations because of restrictions set in place after the fiscal crisis, the diversion of capital funds for operations prior to 1975 and the near cessation of capital improvement after 1975 meant that huge sums were needed for infrastructure. Borrowings rose from 5 to 9 percent of total income, and new borrowing accounted for 22 percent of the spending increment in this period. (See Tables 2.3 and 2.5, respectively.)

As noted earlier, the redistributive share of total spending fell from 33 to 31 percent in the latest period. Spending for redistributive services accounted for 23 percent of the total increment, but public assistance expenditures declined. (See Table 2.6.) In the last three periods, redistributive spending favored payments to organizations designed to serve the poor over direct cash assistance to the poor.

The influence of the business community declined in the most recent period. Spending returned to an upward trend, although at a slower rate than during any pre-1975 period. However, the continued influence of the business community is evident in the shifting mix of expenditures, which deemphasized redistribution. Also, the mix of taxes was altered little during this period, although local taxes account for an increased share of total revenues. (See Tables 2.3 and 2.4.)

With respect to the middle class, its interests overlap significantly with those of the business community. Moreover, the relatively large share of labor costs attributable to employment growth rather than compensation enhancement suggests that the middle class and the business community benefited from service enhancement during this period.

Conclusion

This chapter began with the suggestion that the field of urban politics suffered from intellectual neglect after the 1960s. The perception of the community power debate as a disciplinary "dead end" had a chilling effect. The fiscal problems of American cities in the next decade resurrected some scholarly interest in the field, but the consensus that emerged—that urban fiscal problems were caused by forces over which municipal officials have little control—further dampened interest in urban politics.

This chapter suggests that reports of the death of local politics have been greatly exaggerated. In New York City, at least, local politics was the dominant factor in three of the four periods considered—and overwhelmingly so. Changes in intergovernmental policies and in the city's economic base—two variables frequently cited as reducing the realm of local politics—were not unimportant determinants of New York City fiscal policies. Indeed, their combined effects were dominant in the 1960s and are not trivial now. But local politics, at least as defined and measured here, has been far more important for the last 20 years.

If local politics is important, then what does this chapter suggest about its study? Given the strong correlation between findings and methodology which characterized the earlier study of community power, it is appropriate to consider briefly the assumptions underlying the methodology employed here. They are (1) money is the most important of the "stakes and prizes" of local politics; (2) the outcomes of the competition over money are measurable; and (3) the outcomes represent the best evidence available for developing a positive theory of political change. The method employed in this chapter relies on budget decisions. These decisions provide scholars a neutral and quantifiable data base for developing inferences about community power.

The chapter also points to two conceptual errors in earlier models of urban politics. First, they presented change as consistently incremental; in fact, New York City fiscal policies shifted abruptly and rapidly. Second, they mistakenly viewed the "business community" as homogeneous and failed to identify the distinct interests and influence of the municipal financiers within this community.

The leading pluralist students of New York, Sayre and Kaufman, saw a competition for power among numerous interest groups, which they aggregated into two broad coalitions: those who wanted public expenditure to grow because of the benefits this would bestow on them (the "service-demanders") and those who wanted public expenditure to shrink because of the costs it entailed (the "money-providers").[13] Had the two groups' power been equal, the local political system would have been static. However, one or the other of these broad coalitions occasionally mobilized enough resources to extract a more favorable compromise. Yet Sayre and Kaufman viewed the overriding "balance" as such that incremental change was the rule.

In this sense, the political economy of the pluralists was not unlike that of the elitists. The main difference is that the elitists assumed that the money providers would dominate the relationship. But both paradigms predicted slow change, pluralist because of its theory of bargaining and the elitist because it stipulated that those who have community power hold onto it.

But change in New York City's fiscal policies cannot be aptly characterized as incremental. The immediate post–fiscal crisis period, when spending shifted from a 4.5 percent average annual increase to a 3.0 percent average annual decline, is widely viewed as an example of dramatic change. However, the rapid rate of expansion and the shifts in spending priorities in the other three periods also are inconsistent with an incremental interpretation of political change.

The misperception of the interests of municipal financiers has also misled earlier inquiries into the nature of political change. There is more common ground between municipal financiers and civil servants than has been appreciated. Civil servants seek added municipal expenditure because the chances are strong that some of it will accrue to their self-interest, either in terms of having more employees with whom to share the work or—an even stronger inducement—in terms of improved living standards for them and their families. The financiers also prefer added expenditures because, again, the chances are strong that some of it will accrue to their self-interest. More debt means higher fees for investment bankers and normally, though not always, more opportunities to profit from underwriting.

This reconceptualization makes the political changes in New York City in the post-1960 era easier to explain. In the period leading to 1975, municipal financiers were active in facilitating greater spending with greater reliance on borrowing. In this political context it is not surprising that the municipal financiers were reluctant to be whistle-blowers in the years preceding the 1975 fiscal crisis.

The proximate cause of the 1975 fiscal crisis, the event that ushered in the retrenchment period, was the decision of the underwriters and their retail customers to stop loans. The financiers redefined their interest in local politics, and in so doing occupied the place in the local political system traditionally assigned them. With the aid of the state of New York, the business community—now including municipal financiers—sought to preserve its capital by ensuring that outstanding obligations would be repaid and, eventually, by restoring access to public credit. This required new sources of funds, the largest available source being the pension funds of municipal workers. Thus, the symbiosis between civil servants and financiers continued, though their goals were to minimize loss instead of maximizing gain.

During the most recent period, investment bankers were able to resume their traditional function of facilitating increased sales of municipal debt. The symbiosis between the civil servants and the investment bankers was reduced somewhat because of restrictions on the use of bond proceeds to pay civil servants that were adopted during the fiscal crisis. However, the events preceding the fiscal crisis make it clear that "where there's a will, there's a way." And recent (fiscal year 1990) New York City refinancings intended to provide budget relief (that is, to support the jobs or compensation of civil servants) while increasing future debt service costs suggest a revitalized alliance of municipal financiers and civil servants.

This chapter also sheds some light on how and why the poor gain or lose in local politics. It suggests that whatever benefits the urban poor gain are derived primarily from the interventions of higher governments rather than their own local power. The poor were allocated an increasing share of municipal expenditure during the 1961–1969 period largely because this was commanded by decisions reached in Washington and Albany. The relationship between intergovernmental interventions and the poor's ability to capture a growing share of local spending, directly or indirectly, is complex but it is noteworthy that their influence declined with the contribution of the intergovernmental variable to the determination of municipal expenditure. Stated differently, the poor did less well when local politics became more important. This is evident in the contrast between their experience in the 1961–1969 and 1983–1989 growth periods. In the first period, they captured 49 percent of the expenditure increment; in the second period, the share fell to 23 percent.

Finally, this chapter raises an important, but unanswered, question: What is the role of electoral politics, and particularly of elected mayors, in achieving political change? By relying primarily on a model of local politics that emphasizes group bargaining, the chapter's approach implicitly places mayors in the role of legitimizing decisions reached by group leaders. But the chapter also suggests that the interests of groups often not well organized and lacking recognized spokesmen—notably the privately employed, or the "middle class"—are not completely sacrificed in local political contests. At times spending is curbed, the share of spending for allocative services increases, and a substantial share of expenditures for labor are used to increase municipal employment rather than enhance real wages. The next two chapters shift in focus from interest group politics to electoral politics. They explore, respectively, the role of elections in the city's political structure and the nature of mayoral campaigns and elections in linking public opinion to government policies and priorities.

II

ELECTORAL POLITICS

3

LOCAL ELECTIONS AND LOCAL DEMOCRACY

In democratic theory the most meaningful link between the preferences of a government's constituents and its policy decisions is the election of those with political authority. The citizenry translates its policy preferences into municipal action by electing leaders who promise to pursue policies that reflect their objectives.

But to make this theory work, certain conditions must be met. First, a local constitution must define public offices that have sufficient authority to change policy and are filled by election. Second, the elections for these offices must be competitive, that is, candidates with opposing views must have a realistic chance of victory. Third, the citizens themselves must support their preferences by voting in an informed manner.

The thesis of this chapter is that New York City's local political system often fails to meet these conditions. Its constitution, the Charter of the City of New York, does create a few elected offices with sufficient power to change policy. But the contests for filling the available elected positions, both powerful and not, are often noncompetitive. Finally, the citizens fail to vote in relatively large numbers, and their scarcer votes increasingly are based on values and policy preferences unrelated to the decisions municipal officials are empowered to make.

The Powers of Municipal Officials

The basic structure of the government of the city of New York is set forth in a charter. The charter must conform to general conditions established by state law, and its basic provisions can be amended only by the state legislature or by local referendum. Since 1960 the state legislature has not altered the charter, but four charter revision commissions have offered reforms to the voters, who approved them in elections in November 1961, 1975, 1983, and 1989.[1]

The three initial rounds of charter reform did not alter the basic design of city government. Three offices or bodies remained at the heart of municipal affairs: the mayor, the Board of Estimate, and the city council. However, the 1989 reforms abolished the Board of Estimate while retaining the offices of the board's members. The way in which the reforms affected the authority of each body is considered next.

The Mayor

The city's chief executive, the mayor, is elected to a four-year term in years following national presidential elections with no limit on the number of terms. Mayoral powers—some of which are shared with the council—include the preparation and administration of the city's operating and capital budgets, the conduct of collective bargaining with municipal employee unions, and the appointment of most commissioners to head municipal agencies. For performing these duties, the mayor's salary is $130,000 annually, a sum which has been raised five times from its 1960 level of $40,000. (See Table 3.1.) In

Table 3.1 Salaries of Municipal Officials, 1960–1990

	Mayor	Comptroller	Borough President	Council President	Council Member
1960 level	$40,000	$30,000	$25,000	$25,000	$10,000[a]
Year of increase					
1961	50,000	40,000	35,000	35,000	13,000[b]
1966	—[c]	—[c]	—[c]	—[c]	15,000[d]
1970	—[c]	—[c]	—[c]	40,000	25,000[e]
1974	60,000	50,000	45,000	50,000	—[c]
1979	80,000	66,000	61,000	66,000	35,000
1983	110,000	90,000	80,000	90,000	47,500
1987	130,000	105,000	95,000	105,000	55,000

[a]$7,000 salary plus $3,000 for contingent expenses.

[b]$10,000 salary plus $3,000 for contingent expenses.

[c]No increase.

[d]$10,000 salary plus $5,000 for contingent expenses.

[e]$20,000 salary plus $5,000 for contingent expenses.

addition, the mayor is provided a city-owned residence known as Gracie Mansion and many other perquisites, including a chef.

The charter reforms of 1961 significantly strengthened the Office of the Mayor. They increased the budgetary authority by requiring the mayor to prepare the capital budget, which formerly was done by the City Planning Commission; gave the mayor greater discretion over the administration of the operating budget, a role previously shared with the board; and increased the mayor's ability to reorganize the executive office as well as the divisions of departments headed by mayoral appointees, powers also previously shared with the board.

The 1975 reforms had less impact on the mayoralty. An effort was made to encourage decentralization within the executive branch by permitting commissioners to exercise greater discretion in personnel and budget decisions previously reserved to the central budget and personnel offices. However, these measures have not been implemented, partly because the mid-1970s fiscal crisis required strong central controls and partly because mayors prefer central control.

The 1975 reforms also weakened the mayor's appointment powers modestly by requiring city council approval for several positions previously appointed exclusively "at the pleasure of the mayor." These positions were members of the Municipal Arts Commission (which reviews designs for public structures and purchases of art for city buildings), the Board of Health, the Board of Standards and Appeals, the City Planning Commission, the Civil Service Commission, the Landmarks Preservation Commission, the Tax Commission, the Taxi and Limousine Commission, and public members of the Environmental Control Board. However, the commissioners who head the major executive agencies are appointed and reviewed at the discretion of the mayor without city council participation.

To plan, supervise, and coordinate the activities of the executive branch, the mayor has a staff working directly for him. The mayor designates one or more deputy mayors, and the mayor and the deputies each have assistants working for them. Mayors also typically appoint special commissions to investigate selected issues affecting more than one line agency, and these commissions are staffed and financed through the mayor's office. Also working directly for the mayor are a budget unit, headed by the director of the Office of Management and Budget, and a management-oriented unit which monitors agency operations and is headed by the director of the Office of Operations. Additional important units within the Office of the Mayor are the Office of Labor Relations, which conducts collective bargaining on the mayor's behalf, and the city's lobbying offices in Albany and Washington.

The scale of activity conducted directly within the mayor's office has grown significantly since the 1960s. Official data probably understate the trend, because mayors commonly borrow staff from agencies without transferring the budget line. Nevertheless, reported expenditures of the mayor's office have grown from $1.1 million to $135.3 million over the period, and the mayor's staff from 127 to 1,635. (See Table 3.2.)

Table 3.2 Budgeted Expenditures and Positions for the
Office of the Mayor, Fiscal Years 1960–1991

Fiscal Year	Expenditures	Positions
1960	$1,075,055	127
1961	1,123,525	129
1962	1,165,783	130
1963	1,672,870	179
1964[a]	3,631,826	346
1965	4,904,875	359
1966	5,944,748	389
1967	4,609,776	383
1968[b]	9,844,959	705
1969	10,850,790	746
1970	15,933,645	1,011
1971	13,231,150	777
1972	15,156,625	813
1973	17,338,619	939
1974	20,468,404	1,050
1975	27,178,593	1,084
1976	33,062,709	1,164
1977	28,663,975	908
1978	35,293,063	1,097
1979	35,640,109	1,231
1980	39,048,279	1,222
1981	46,285,989	1,252
1982	54,160,459	1,153
1983	68,406,648	1,242
1984	73,465,307	1,360
1985	92,132,828	1,503
1986	106,381,005	1,732
1987	118,350,622	1,717
1988	134,031,054	1,723
1989	145,237,690	1,855
1990	129,487,301	1,736
1991	135,296,523	1,635

Sources: The City of New York, *Adopted Budget*, fiscal year 1960–1991
editions.

[a]First year Bureau of the Budget (later Office of Management and Budget) included in Office of the Mayor.

[b]First year Office of Labor Relations and Model Cities Program included in Office of the Mayor. Model Cities not included after 1970.

The City Council

The city charter, following the general principle of separation of powers, creates a local legislature to share power with the mayor. The composition of this body has been altered in different ways and for different purposes over the last three decades.

Composition

From 1949, when a system of proportional representation was abandoned, to 1963 the city council consisted of 25 members, each elected to a single-member district on the basis of a majority vote. The 1961 charter reforms, effective in 1963, added 10 members to the council.[2] These new members were elected two from each borough with the stipulation that these "at-large" members be drawn from different parties. This way, at least five members of the council would not be Democrats.

In the early 1960s the U.S. Supreme Court began applying the "one-person, one-vote" principle to state legislatures, and the historical overlay of city council district boundaries on state legislative district boundaries led to council reapportionment for the 1965 elections. To protect the seats of incumbents while complying with the new principle, the council enlarged its membership from 25 to 27.

Subsequently, the federal courts extended the one-person, one-vote principle to local legislatures, and the federal Voting Rights Act required that changes in local legislative districts and rules not adversely affect minority groups. After the 1970 census the city council reapportioned itself and expanded the number of districts to 33. Elections were held for these districts in 1973, but a successful challenge to the new boundaries under the Voting Rights Act led to federally mandated elections using revised district lines in 1974.

The elections scheduled for 1981 also required redistricting based on the 1980 census, but the system devised by the council was challenged successfully on two fronts. First, the new district lines drawn by the council were found to violate the Voting Rights Act because they reduced the representation of racial minorities. This led to postponement of the election of district members until 1982 while new district boundaries were drawn. To accommodate the interests of minority groups and incumbents, the number of districts was expanded from 33 to 35 for the 1982 elections. Second, the 10 at-large seats were held unconstitutional because they violated the one-person, one-vote principle. This court ruling prevented the election of new at-large members in both 1981 and 1982.

The city sought to comply with the one-person, one-vote principle by appointing a charter revision commission. The commission placed a referendum before the citizens in November 1983 which abolished the at-large seats. Thus, the at-large members elected in 1977 served through 1983, but there have been no at-large members since 1983.

The next regularly scheduled elections were held in 1985. They involved contests for the 35 district seats which then comprised the full city council.

In 1989 elections again were held for the 35 district seats. However, the charter reforms passed that November increased the size of the council to 51 members. Election for the 51 new district seats were held in November 1991, based on district lines drawn using data from the 1990 census. The members elected in 1991 serve two-year terms, but beginning in 1993 council terms will be four years.

Council members are paid $55,000 per year, a sum that has been increased six times from its 1960 level of $10,000. (See Table 3.1.) About 40 percent of the members regard themselves as full-time legislators or public servants; the others report earned income from other occupations.[3] The council typically meets twice a month for ten months (excluding July and August) of the year. However, some members, especially the leadership, spend considerable additional time on committee work and other duties.

Powers

Historically, the city council has been characterized as a "weak" legislature. This appelation resulted from legal factors that limit the council's formal authority coupled with political recruitment practices that led members to exercise little initiative.

The council's legislative authority is limited in two respects. First, the scope for local legislative action is relatively narrow. State laws define most aspects of urban life, and state legislative authority overrides local action. Second, its limited local legislative authority is shared with the mayor, who has veto power over most local laws.

Because of its limited scope and shared authority, most of the city council's "legislative" activity has been ceremonial or administrative in character, involving changes in street names and similar matters. The activity has not been studied recently, but an analysis of the 1963–1972 period found that over 61 percent of the 1,015 council-enacted bills did not involve broad policy issues.[4]

The council's legislative authority was expanded significantly by the 1989 reforms. As discussed later, these reforms abolished the Board of Estimate. At the same time, zoning and land use powers—previously resting with the board—were transferred to the council. Since zoning and land use are the most significant legislative powers resting with local, rather than state, officials, this change has the potential to enhance the role of the council in local development and related decisions.

The council's budgetary role also has been strengthened by successive charter reforms. The 1961 reforms gave the council authority essentially equal to the board's to modify the mayor's budget proposals, and additional discretion was given these bodies in the 1975 reforms. The later reforms also established a staff unit, intended to parallel the functions of the mayor's Office of Management and Budget, to serve the council and board. However, this unit was abolished at the initiative of its dual masters in 1980 in favor of more staff for the council's standing committees, particularly its Finance Committee.

Despite this increased authority, the council did not become an aggressive actor in the budgetary process. Typically it did relatively little to alter the mayor's proposed operating budget, and it generally left review and modification of the capital budget to the board. A study of council actions in fiscal years 1980–1982 found that council actions changed the size of the expense budget less than 0.5 percent each year.[5]

The 1989 reforms abolishing the Board of Estimate left the council with sole legislative authority over the operating and capital budgets. The first budget adopted under these new procedures was for fiscal year 1991, and the speaker of the council (formerly the majority leader) played a prominent role in negotiating the budget with the mayor.

The council's appointive powers also have been strengthened over time. In 1969 the state law establishing the New York City Health and Hospitals Corporation, a public benefit corporation empowered to operate the municipal hospitals, required that 5 of the 16 members of the corporation's board be nominated by the council. As noted earlier, the 1975 charter reforms also designated several positions, primarily board memberships, which required approval of the council.

The council's oversight and investigative powers historically have been extensive. Its standing committees can investigate the operations of the executive branch related to their jurisdiction, and the council may appoint special committees with full investigative powers. Yet this power has not been used effectively by the council. Recurring waves of corruption and scandal and repeated charges of inefficiency have not led to prominent council investigations.

The historical incapacity of the council to use its powers effectively usually is explained in "chicken and egg" terms: The council's limited powers prevent it from drawing dynamic members, and its lackluster record deters charter reformers from granting it more powers. However, this explanation ignores the substantial influence of party leaders in selecting council candidates and the mayor's ability to use executive powers and patronage to obtain the acquiescence of the council. The dominance of the Democratic party in the council, discussed more fully later, and the willingness of this party's leadership to follow mayoral leadership for a small price better explain the historically weak status of the council. Whether the 1989 charter reforms will change this underlying problem remains to be seen.

The Board of Estimate

The board was a unique institution, combining both legislative and executive functions. Its major legislative powers were control over zoning laws and budgetary review and approval. Its executive powers included approval of noncompetitive contracts, changes in the use of city property, and the granting of franchises. These administrative powers involved the board closely in the operation of many city agencies and permitted it to delay or modify actions sought by the mayor and commissioners.

The composition of the board did not change from its creation in 1902 to its abolition in 1990. Its eight members served as a result of their election to separate positions. The mayor, council president, and comptroller represented citywide constituencies, whereas the five borough presidents were elected by voters in their respective counties. Each citywide official had twice the number of votes as each borough president, which ensured them a majority of votes if they held together on issues involving a conflict between the interest of the city as a whole and that of a particular borough.

Of the eight members, only the mayor and the comptroller had substantial powers outside their board activities. The mayor, as noted earlier, has important executive functions. The comptroller serves as the city's chief financial officer. He or she is responsible for maintaining the city's cash flow by accounting for revenues and expenditures, issuing and repaying city debt, and auditing agency activities. The fiscal duties place the comptroller at the center of many important budgetary decisions, and the audit functions involve the comptroller in reviewing, often critically, the performance of agencies under the executive jurisdiction of the mayor. The office's substantial powers and the incumbent's frequent stance in "looking over the shoulder" of the mayor cause the comptroller to be viewed as the city's second most important elected official and the mayor's leading political rival.

The comptroller is paid $105,000 annually, a sum that has been increased five times from its 1960 level of $30,000. (See Table 3.1.) The comptroller's office has not grown as rapidly as the mayor's, but its $69 million budget in fiscal year 1990 was five times larger than in 1960. (See Table 3.3.)

In contrast to the mayor and comptroller, the council president and the borough presidents had few significant powers outside their board activities. The council president presides over council meetings but votes only in the case of a tie (a rare occurrence). Typically the council president serves only a ceremonial role in the council; effective leadership is exercised by the council's majority leader, now speaker, who determines the legislative agenda and committee assignments. The borough presidents have had no significant executive powers since the charter reforms of 1961, which centralized municipal services under the mayor. When the board was abolished in 1989, the borough presidents became vestigial officials.

The council president is paid $105,000 annually, a salary that has been increased six times from its 1960 level of $25,000. (See Table 3.1.) In 1990 the council president's staff numbered 67 and the office's budget was under $3.3 million. (See Table 3.3.) This represented a substantial increase in staff and expenditures over 1960.

The borough presidents are each paid $95,000 annually, a sum that has been increased five times from its 1960 level of $25,000. The fiscal year 1990 budgets for the borough presidents' offices ranged from $5 million (Manhattan) to nearly $7.6 million (Bronx), with their staffs ranging in size from 98 to 140. Between 1960 and 1990 the number of staff positions for the five offices

Table 3.3 Budgeted Expenditures and Positions for Selected Municipal Officials, Fiscal Years 1960 and 1990

Official	Expenditures		Positions	
	1960	1990	1960	1990
Comptroller	$11,230,378	$68,976,065	1,848	998
Council president	102,396	3,269,138	11	67
Borough presidents				
Manhattan	6,318,013	5,011,482	1,132	116
Bronx	4,998,690	7,595,934	914	140
Brooklyn	7,391,177	5,785,027	1,311	112
Queens	9,693,557	6,036,422	1,732	125
Staten Island	2,986,816	5,135,173	535	98

Sources: The City of New York, Budget for the Fiscal Year 1959–60, and Adopted Budget, Fiscal Year 1990.

was reduced about 90 percent, and their budgets fell about 20 percent. The decline in resources for the borough presidents reflects the effect of charter reforms dating to 1961.

Deliberations preceding the 1961 reforms included consideration of abolishing the board, but less drastic measures eventually were put before the voters. The 1961 reforms obliged the board to act with the council in adopting the budget, gave the mayor sole control over most aspects of budget administration, and transferred administrative responsibility for selected construction activities from the borough presidents to a citywide agency under the control of the mayor.

The 1974 reforms had less impact on the board. Its powers were not altered significantly, and the borough presidents were authorized to appoint members to newly created community boards. The 59 boards were given an advisory role in land use decisions and serve as a forum for the expression of community interests relating to a range of issues. In addition, the community boards have small budgets with which to hire staff, including a district manager whose job is to facilitate cooperation among municipal agencies serving the local area.

The charter reform commission created in 1986 renewed interest in abolishing the board. The commission was established in response to a federal appeals court decision finding that the board's voting procedures violated the one-person, one-vote principle because borough presidents had equal votes despite their representing areas with widely varying populations. Research by the commission staff revealed that a system of weighted voting would likely violate the federal Voting Rights Act by diluting the strength of racial minorities, who were well represented among the borough presidents.[6]

After wrestling with these issues for more than two years, the commission recommended abolishing the board. Its zoning and budgetary powers were given to the council, and its contract and other administrative powers to the mayor. However, the positions of the council president and the borough presidents were retained as independent elected officers. The council president continues to preside over the council and is first in line to succeed should the mayor die or become disabled. The council president's other powers are limited, primarily to investigating citizen complaints as a "public ombudsman." The borough presidents' powers are restricted to largely advisory roles on budget and land use matters.

Other Municipal Officials

The cumulative effect of charter reforms since 1961 has been to make the mayor and council the key actors in municipal politics and to greatly diminish the authority of the council president and borough presidents. But New Yorkers also elect other local officials, including supreme court, civil court, and surrogate judges, district attorneys, and community school board members. These elected officials have relatively narrow powers in the city's policy-making process.

The judicial system created under New York State law is complex, including multiple types of courts and different appellate routes from the different lower-level courts. Many judicial appointments follow the reform model of appointment to long terms by the chief executive, the governor in the case of statewide courts and the mayor in the case of local courts. Thus the mayor appoints to ten-year terms judges to the New York City criminal and family courts.

However, a legacy of the unreformed era of party bosses is a state court system in which the lower court judges, known as State Supreme Court judges, are elected from local judicial districts. In New York City there are four judicial districts including 158 supreme court judges.[7] Nominations for these posts are not made through open primaries but are reserved to nominating conventions to which residents of each judicial district elect delegates. The result is a cadre of supreme court judges elected to 14-year terms after having been selected by party leaders. However, when vacancies occur the position is filled by gubernatorial appointment. Since many vacancies occur during terms as a result of retirements or deaths, this limits the number of serving judges who actually were elected to office. Supreme court judges handle significant criminal and civil matters arising under state law, but their decisions are subject to review by appellate courts, whose posts are filled by gubernatorial appointees. Typically, the appellate judges have more distinguished records than the supreme court judges they supervise.

Matters relating to estates are handled by county surrogates. In New York City one such official is elected from each borough for a 14-year term. Candidates are nominated by political parties through primaries. The election of a surrogate is often controversial and important to lawyers and others interested in the judges' discretionary powers to appoint executors. However, surrogates have no direct role in making broad policy decisions.

District attorneys, the top public prosecutors in the criminal justice system, are elected on a borough basis to four-year terms. District attorneys influence law enforcement practices and prison workloads by determining what types of crime will be enforced vigorously, but beyond this their policy role is relatively circumscribed. The offices also are important because they employ large numbers of lawyers as assistant district attorneys. In fiscal year 1990, the budgets of the five district attorneys' offices ranged from $3.6 million (Staten Island) to $42.6 million (Manhattan), and their staffs ranged in number from 70 to 1,200.[8]

The continued existence of a judicial system headed by elected judges and prosecutors is a legacy of the time when party organizations depended on patronage rather than a mechanism for promoting local democracy. The elections of district attorneys and supreme court judges help local party activists place associates in positions that control a significant number of jobs and, in the case of surrogates, lucrative legal assignments. In addition to serving the patronage function, judicial elections provide incentives for lawyers and others to become active in local politics.

The logic and significance of local school board elections is a different matter. Prior to 1969 there were no elected positions in the New York City

Board of Education. Public education was controlled by a board composed of mayoral appointees, with the candidates nominated by a "blue-ribbon" screening committee. The intention was to give professional educators a great deal of autonomy by "keeping politics out of education." This system led to deep dissatisfaction, particularly among members of racial minority groups, because the professional educators were not perceived as either sympathetic to minority needs or effective in educating minority youth. The result was a sweeping reform of local public school governance.

The 1969 school decentralization law changed the composition of the central governing board and decentralized authority by creating local, elected school boards. The central board was converted to a seven-member body, with one member appointed by each of the borough presidents and two appointed by the mayor. The new local school boards, which now number 32, were given authority over certain curriculum and staffing decisions for elementary and junior high schools in their districts. The local boards consist of nine members elected at-large on a nonpartisan basis. The elections are held in the spring, not in November with other elections, in an effort to keep school politics separate from party politics.

The election of community school boards has proved to be a disappointing exercise in representative democracy. An infinitesimal share of the potential electorate turns out to vote, and few significant issues are raised or decided in campaigns. The root of the problem is probably the limited authority of the local boards over educational matters, which remain largely under the authority of the central board or state law. Local boards hire district superintendents and control relatively small sums of "discretionary" funds provided by the board, but these powers are not enough to attract candidates concerned with broad issues of educational policy. The result is that local school board elections are dominated by the teachers' union, religious organizations, and local political clubs. The nearly 300 New Yorkers who are elected as school board members every three years are not important municipal policymakers.

This section began by asking whether municipal government provided opportunities for citizens to elect officials with significant authority. The answer is that there are multiple opportunities to elect public officials, though in most cases their authority is narrow in scope. Historically, only the mayor has exercised wide-ranging powers, but the 1989 charter reforms open up the opportunity for city council members, particularly the speaker, to exercise significant power. In addition, the comptroller enjoys substantial fiscal powers. However, the other citywide official—the council president—has no substantial formal authority, and the once-powerful borough presidents have been reduced to vestigial status. The remaining elected officials, ranging from district attorneys to school board members, exercise limited discretion in limited areas.

Limited Electoral Competition

The city charter provides voters the opportunity to elect officials who hold significant authority to shape policy, specifically the mayor, comptroller, and city council members. The failings of municipal democracy lie in the absence of meaningful competition for most of these offices whether in primary or general elections. Limited competition in turn is related to another failing of municipal democracy: Few of those eligible actually vote.

Democratic Party Dominance

The simple fact underlying the dominant position of the Democratic party in New York City is that seven of ten adult residents consistently identify with that party. (See Table 3.4.) And while allegiance to the Democratic party remained strong, it fell for the principal opposition, the Republican party. During the 1960–1989 period, Republican enrollment fell almost steadily from 24 to 14 percent of those registered. Some former Republicans became members of the Conservative party, which was established in 1964, but the strongest growth was among voters who registered as independent rather than with a party. The independents increased from 6 to 14 percent of total registrants.

The Democrats have translated their substantial enrollment majority into even larger majorities in the city council through the adroit drawing of boundary lines for single-member districts. From 1949, when proportional representation was abolished, to 1961 no more than two non-Democrats served on the 25-member council.[9] In subsequent elections the Democrats won 26 of 27 seats (1965), 25 of 27 (1969), 32 of 33 (1973 and 1977), all 35 (1982), and 34 of 35 (1985 and 1989). (See Table 3.5.) The Democratic majority on the council has never been less than 92 percent and has risen to 100 percent.

This Democratic dominance is achieved with little electoral competition. Between 1961 and 1989 there were 283 contests for council district seats. Using a 10 percent margin of victory as the standard for determining competitiveness, fully 247 contests were not competitive. This included 11 in which there was no opposition and another 150 in which the total exceeded 70 percent. (See Table 3.6.) And of the remaining 36 competitive elections, the

Table 3.4 Party Enrollment in New York City, 1961–1989 (percentage of distribution)

Year	Total	Democratic	Republican	Liberal	Conservative	Other and Independent
1961	100.0%	68.0%	23.7%	2.1%	NA	6.3%
1965	100.0	70.6	20.2	1.9	0.5%	6.8
1969	100.0	68.3	20.0	2.5	1.8	7.4
1973	100.0	68.2	18.1	2.7	1.8	9.2
1977	100.0	70.0	15.6	1.8	1.4	11.2
1981	100.0	70.1	13.9	1.2	1.1	13.6
1985	100.0	70.2	13.0	0.8	0.8	15.2
1989	100.0	69.8	14.2	0.8	0.8	14.4

Source: New York City Board of Elections.
Note: Totals may not add due to rounding. NA, not applicable.

Table 3.5 Number of New York City Council Members by Party, 1961–1989

Year	Total	Democratic	Republican	Liberal	Conservative
1961					
Total	25	23	2	—	—
1963					
Total	35	28	7	—	—
Districts (from 1961)	25	23	2	—	—
At-large (new)	10	5	5	—	—
1965					
Total	37	31	6	—	—
Districts	27	26	1	—	—
At-large	10	5	5	—	—
1969					
Total	37	30	3	4	—
Districts	27	25	1	1	—
At-large	10	5	2	3	—
1973					
Total	43	37[a]	5	1	—
Districts	33	32[a]	1	—	—
At-large	10	5	4	1	—
1974					
Total	43	37	5	1	—
Districts	33	32	1	—	—
At-large	10	5	4	1	—
1977					
Total	43	37	4	1	1
Districts	33	32	1	—	—
At-large	10	5	3	1	1
1982					
Total[b]	35	35	—	—	—
1985					
Total	35	34	1	—	—
1989					
Total	35	34	1	—	—

Sources: Final Report of the New York City Charter Revision Commission (1983), Research Memorandum C, pp. 387–402; City of New York, *Official Directory,* 1985 edition; and *The New York Times,* November 9, 1989, II, p. 6.

[a]Includes a member nominated by both the Republican and Democratic parties.

[b]Due to challenges to the drawing of districts under the Voting Rights Act, elections were postponed from 1981 to 1982. Due to challenges under the U.S. Constitution, the at-large seats were abolished in 1983; from 1977 to 1983 the same members served in the at-large seats.

victor received less than 55 percent of the total in 21 because more than two candidates were involved. Thus, by reasonable standards, only 15 of the 283 council district seat elections were competitive. Moreover, in the latest elections none were competitive.

The introduction in 1963 of at-large seats with restrictions on party representation was intended to reduce the Democratic majority, but it did so in only a limited fashion. As intended, five of the ten at-large seats were filled by non-Democrats. This reduced the Democratic majority to a still sizable 80 percent in 1963, but the figure rose to a steady 86 percent after the 1973 elections. (See Table 3.5.) Moreover, the opposition was divided, with Liber-

Table 3.6 New York City Council District Seat Elections by Degree of Competitiveness, 1961–1989 (number of seats)

Election Year	Winner's Vote Greater than 70%[a]	Winner's Vote 55–69%	Winner's Vote Under 55% but Margin Above 10%	Subtotal, Noncompetitive Elections	Competitive Elections	Total Elections
1961	2	15	2	19	6	25
1965	2	17	6	25	2	27
1969	4	10	10	24	3	27
1973	24	7	2	33	0	33
1974	16	17	0	33	0	33
1977	24	7	1	32	1	33
1982	27	6	0	33	2	35
1985	31	3	0	34	1	35
1989	31	4	0	35	0	35
Total	161	86	21	268	15	283

Sources: Data derived from election results printed in *The New York Times*, on the following dates: September 9, 1961, p. 10; November 9, 1961, p. 26; September 16, 1965, p. 50; November 4, 1965, pp. 52–54; June 19, 1969, p. 30; November 6, 1969, p. 41; June 6, 1973, p. 52; November 9, 1973, pp. 52–54; September 12, 1974, p. 34; November 7, 1974, p. 40; September 10, 1977, p. 16; November 10, 1977, IV, p. 13; September 25, 1982, p. 33; November 4, 1982, II, p. 9; September 11, 1985, II, p. 4; November 7, 1985, II, p. 6; September 14, 1989, II, p.2; and November 9, 1989, II, p. 6.

[a]Includes one unopposed candidate in 1973, four unopposed candidates in 1985, and six unopposed candidates in 1989.

als winning the second seat in some boroughs. Even this modest and divided opposition was virtually abolished with the elimination of the at-large seats in 1983. Since then the Democrats have had almost absolute control of the council.

Democratic control of the borough presidencies has been almost as firm. (See Table 3.7.) In the eight elections since 1960, a Democrat always won the contest in three boroughs—Manhattan, Brooklyn, and Queens—and none of these contests was competitive. In Manhattan the Democrat always won with at least 55 percent, and in two of these contests the majority exceeded 90 percent with the candidate receiving the endorsements of all three parties. In Brooklyn the Democratic majorities also always exceeded 55 percent. The Democratic majority in Queens exceeded 55 percent in seven of the eight contests; even the 1969 exception did not involve a close race. The Democrat won with 49 percent of the vote because of a four-person race. His closest competitor, the Liberal party candidate, received 23 percent.

In the Bronx the borough presidency has been in Democratic hands since 1965, but firm control was not established until 1969. In 1961 a candidate supported jointly by the Republican and Liberal parties defeated the Democrat in a very close race. In 1965 the Democrat won a very close election with 46.5 percent while the incumbent, again with joint Republican and Liberal endorsements, received 46.0 percent. The Democratic victory was related to the presence of a Conservative party candidate who apparently drew support

Table 3.7 Party and Percentage of Votes of Winning Candidates in Selected Municipal General Elections, 1961–1989

Office	1961	1965	1969	1973	1977	1981	1985	1989
Mayor	D-L/51%	R-L/45%	L/42%	D/56%	D/50%	D-R/75%	D/74%	D/50%
Comptroller	D-L/64	D/49	D/49	D/64	D-L/86	D-L/78	D-L/85	D-L/75
Council president	D-L/62	D/54	R-L/49	D/59	D-L/83	D-L/80	D-L/83	D-L/93
Borough president								
Brooklyn	D/56	D/60	D/57	D/67	D/66	D/79	D/77	D/76
Queens	D/58	D-R-L/89	D/49	D-R/82	D-L/73	D-L/88	D-L/84	D/84
Bronx	R-L/51	D/46	D/53	D-L/77	D-L/83	D-R/76	D-R-L-C/U	D-L/84
Manhattan	D-L/65	D-R-L/92	D-L/81	D-R-L/91	D/55	D/59	D/78	D-L/84
Staten Island	D-L/51	R-C/57	R-C/69	D-C/65	D-C/62	D-C/83	D-C/53	R-C-T/57

Sources: See Table 3.6.

Note: C, Conservative; D, Democratic; L, Liberal; R, Republican; T, Right to Life; U, unopposed.

from previous Republican voters. In 1969 the Republican–Liberal alliance in the Bronx dissolved, and the Democrat won with 53 percent of the vote. In subsequent Bronx contests the Democrat either won with a large majority or, as in 1985, ran unopposed.

Party competition is evident in Staten Island. In 1961 the Democrat won a close election with 51 percent of the vote. In both 1965 and 1969 the same candidate ran successfully with joint Republican and Conservative endorsements, increasing his margin from 57 to 69 percent. For the 1974 election the same incumbent changed party affiliations, running with joint Democratic and Conservative endorsements, and gained 65 percent of the vote. The Democratic–Conservative alliance then remained in place, providing one candidate 62 and 83 percent victories in the 1977 and 1981 elections, respectively. In 1985 the new joint Democratic–Conservative candidate won a narrower 53 percent victory as the Republican challenger gained over 45 percent of the vote. In 1989 a Republican gained the support of the Conservative and Right-to-Life parties and defeated the Democratic candidate with 57 percent of the vote.

Democrats have held the comptroller position throughout the post-1960 period. In all but two of the eight contests the victories were highly one-sided, with margins ranging from 59 to 83 percent. In 1965 and 1969 the margins were smaller, but this was due in large part to the presence of three candidates for the office. In 1965 the second-place Republican–Liberal candidate gained only 41 percent of the vote, while a Conservative received 11 percent. In 1969 the second-place Republican–Liberal won 42 percent and the Conservative 9 percent.

Seven of the eight elections for the council presidency were not competitive. In 1969 a Republican–Liberal candidate won with 49 percent of the vote as the Democrats and Conservatives split the remaining 43 percent and 8 percent, respectively. In six of the other contests the Democratic majority exceeded 59 percent (80 percent in the four most recent contests). Even the 1965 race—in which the Democrat gained just 54 percent—was not close because of the divided opposition. The Republican–Liberal candidate gained just 37 percent and the Conservative 8 percent.

The mayoralty is the only elected office where there is substantial evidence of party competition and even here four of the eight elections in the 1961–1989 period were not competitive. In 1981 the Democratic candidate, Edward I. Koch, enjoyed Republican endorsement and won 75 percent of the vote. The same incumbent received 74 percent of the vote in 1985. In 1973 the Democratic winner, Abraham Beame, won a 56 percent majority against separate Conservative, Republican, and Liberal candidates, with none getting more than 16 percent. The 1961 election saw Wagner win 51 percent of the vote in a three-way race in which the second-place Republican candidate received just 34 percent.

However, Democratic mayoral candidates either were defeated or won narrowly in four cases. The losses were to the same candidate, John V. Lindsay, who won as a Republican–Liberal candidate in 1965 and as a Liberal party candidate in 1969. In both instances Lindsay received less than half the votes. Another competitive election occurred in 1977, when the Democratic candidate, Koch, won with a bare 50 percent majority against the Liberal party candidate, Mario M. Cuomo, who received 41 percent of the total. The latest mayoral election also yielded a narrow Democratic victory. David Dinkins defeated his Republican–Liberal challenger, Rudolph Giuliani, with less than a 3 percent margin.

In sum, party competition is a rare phenomenon in New York City. Non-Democrats are a rare species in the city council; the borough presidencies also have been the province of Democrats spared close elections; the comptroller's office has not left Democratic hands in the entire period under consideration; and the council presidency has been won overwhelmingly by Democrats in six of the last seven races. Only mayoral elections evidence party competition, and even their record is mixed.

Intraparty Competition

Of course, limited party competition does not necessarily mean that elections cannot serve as instruments for changing policy. In a one-party city like New York, different policy preferences can be articulated in primary elections.

Since the early part of this century New York State election laws have recognized the importance of intraparty nominating decisions by establishing procedures to make the process democratic.[10] A system for conducting primary elections has been established to ensure that these contests are open to party members on an equal basis and decided in accord with democratic rules.

For municipal offices the nomination of a party, including the dominant Democratic party, is open to any candidate who files an appropriate nominating petition. The petition must contain the signatures of a designated number of enrolled party members. The requisite number of signatures varies with the office. Candidates for council seats must obtain 1,500 signatures, for borough president 5,000 signatures, and for the citywide offices 10,000 signatures.

If only one person files a nominating petition, he or she becomes the party's nominee. If more than one person files a qualified petition, then the state conducts a primary election in which enrolled party members are eligible to vote. The candidate receiving the most votes in the primary becomes the party's nominee for the general election, with the exception of citywide offices where, since 1973, a candidate must receive at least 40 percent of the primary vote to become the nominee. In a multicandidate race for mayor, comptroller, or council president a runoff primary is conducted between the two leading vote getters if the 40 percent requirement is not met.

Party activists are often characterized as seeking to avoid primary contests, which work against party unity and consume funds that could be employed to defeat the opposition party. According to this view, "strong parties" are ones whose leaders are able to agree upon candidates without resorting to primary elections. However, primary contests could be interpreted as signaling a healthy rather than weak party. Conflicts among factions within a party can

Table 3.8 New York City Council District Seat, Democratic Primary Elections, by Degree of Competitiveness, 1961–1989 (number of seats)

Election Year	Winner's Vote Greater than 70%	Winner's Vote 55–69%	Winner's Vote Under 55% but Margin Above 10%	Subtotal, Noncompetitive Elections	Competitive Elections	Total Elections
1961	2	9	0	11	0	11
1965	3	5	0	8	5	13
1969	3	8	2	13	6	19
1973	1	7	3	11	7	18
1974	0	7	0	7	4	11
1977	3	8	3	14	5	19
1982	5	5	0	10	8	18
1985	3	8	5	16	4	20
1989	2	4	2	8	2	10
Total	22	61	15	98	41	139

Sources: See Table 3.6.

be interpreted as responses to the need to change. From this perspective settling such conflicts through supervised electoral procedures is a democratic way to accomplish political change.

Do Democratic party primary elections satisfy the competitiveness criteria? With respect to city council positions, primaries are frequent but generally uncompetitive. (See Table 3.8.) Of the 283 contests for district seats in the 1961–1989 period, 139 involved a primary election. However, in only 41 of these cases was the margin of victory less than 10 percent. In other words, six of every seven nominations for council district seats were noncompetitive in the 1961–1989 period.

The competitiveness of nominations for borough president varies among the counties, reflecting in part the strength of each county's Democratic party organization. (See Table 3.9.) In Queens there was a primary battle in only one of the last eight elections, but even then the election was not close. The victor received 49 percent of the votes compared to 34 percent for the second-place candidate in a four-way race. Staten Island also has avoided competitive primaries. Such contests were required in only two of the eight elections, and in both cases the victor's margin was well in excess of 10 percent.

In Brooklyn borough president primaries have followed a somewhat different—but still uncompetitive—pattern. Nominees were selected by primary contests in five of the last eight elections, but in two of the five primaries the winner received more than 55 percent of the vote. And in the three exceptions the victor's margin exceeded 10 percentage points due to the presence of multiple candidates.

Nomination for the Manhattan borough presidency was competitive only in 1977 and 1981. There was no primary contest in 1973 and 1969, and in 1965 and 1961 the primary winners won lopsided victories. In 1977 and 1981 the same victorious candidate, Andrew Stein, spent large sums to defeat

Table 3.9 Winner's Share of Votes in Democratic Primary Elections, 1961–1989

Office	1961	1965	1969	1973	1977	1981	1985	1989
Mayor	61%	45%	33%[a]	I-35%/RO-61%	I-20%/RO-55%	60%	64%	51%
Comptroller	6	43	44	45	NP	66	78	47
Council president	61	49	24	41	I-31/RO-59	NP	49	75
Borough president								
Brooklyn	85	NP	56	46	43	NP	47	NP
Queens	NP	NP	49	NP	NP	NP	NP	NP
Bronx	NP	50	54	71	NP	NP	52	NP
Manhattan	60	86	NP	NP	36	53	65	84
Staten Island	59	NP	NP	68	NP	NP	NP	NP

Sources: See Table 3.6.

Note: I, initial primary; RO, runoff primary; NP, no primary.

[a]Democratic primary winner was not elected.

candidates backed by longer-term party activists. When he went on to run successfully for council president in 1985, a previously unsuccessful challenger, Dinkins, won the Manhattan borough president primary contest with a 65 percent majority. And when he ran successfully for mayor in 1989, Ruth Messinger won 84 percent of the votes.

Only the Bronx evidences substantial primary competition between candidates with different policy viewpoints. In 1961 the Democratic candidate was not contested for nomination, but his loss to a Republican–Liberal candidate in the general election intensified a reform–regular split within the Bronx Democratic party. The 1965 primary saw a reformer defeat a more traditional party activist with a narrow victory. When the Bronx borough president ran unsuccessfully for mayor in 1969, another hotly contested primary ensued between reformers and regulars. This time the reformer won with a 53 percent margin. He was renominated in a landslide primary in 1973, and in 1977 he was unopposed in the primary.

This three-term borough president, Robert Abrams, resigned after winning election as state attorney general in 1978, thereby permitting the Bronx city council delegation to name a successor to fill out the term. They selected a person identified with the regular faction of the party, who was challenged in the 1981 primary by a reformer. However, no primary resulted because the reformer's nominating petition was thrown out in state supreme court. In 1985 the incumbent faced a close primary challenge from another reformer and won with a bare 52 percent majority. In 1987 he was obliged to resign in the midst of corruption scandals, but this time the city council delegation named a reformer as successor. This person, Fernando Ferrer, won the 1989 nomination without a primary contest.

The record in the Bronx highlights two related factors that help explain the limited electoral competition for borough presidencies and city council seats. First, there are strong advantages to incumbency; second, one can become an incumbent without winning an election.

The advantages of incumbency are common to most elected offices, but they are especially pronounced for council members and borough presidents. These advantages include opportunities for public exposure and greater name recognition, control over budgets and staff appointments that may be used to reward supporters, and more general opportunities to use the powers of office to gain support. Since the powers and resources of borough presidents were greater than those of council members at least until 1989, the advantages of incumbency were greater for them.

The results of municipal election contests bear out the favored position of incumbents. In the 10 council elections since 1961 there were 323 contests for which incumbency was relevant (excluding ten seats for newly created at-large positions in 1963). (See Table 3.10.) In these contests incumbents sought reelection 269 times and succeeded in 236 instances. Of the 33 defeats, 25 were suffered in primary elections (only 118 of the 269 cases involved a primary challenge) and 8 in general elections.

For borough presidents the 8 elections since 1961 yielded a total of 40 possible contests. (See Table 3.11.) Of this total, incumbents sought reelection

Table 3.10 Challenges to Incumbency and Rate of Incumbent Reelection in City Council Races, 1961–1989

Year	Number of Positions Available	Number of Incumbent Races[a]	Number of General Election Victories by Incumbents	Number of Incumbents Facing Primary Contests	Number of Primary Victories by Incumbents
1961	25	18	14	7	4
1963	10	NA	NA	NA	NA
1965	37	28	25	10	7
1969	37	32	22	21	14
1973	43	26	22	9	7
1974[b]	33	33	33	12	12
1977	43	34	29	19	14
1982	35	31	27	14	11
1985	35	33	31	17	16
1989	35	34	33	9	8
Total	333	269	236	118	93

Sources: See Table 3.6.

Note: NA, not applicable.

[a]"Number of Incumbent Races" is defined as the number of elections in which an incumbent is running for reelection. For example, if an incumbent was running for reelection in every election year between 1961 and 1989, the number of incumbent races would be nine.

[b]All council members elected in 1973 were renominated by their respective parties, with the exception of Arthur J. Katzman. Katzman nevertheless won reelection.

in 34 races, winning 30 of the 34. Primary challenges occurred only 12 times, and none was successful. No incumbent borough president from Queens, Brooklyn, or Manhattan failed to be reelected.

Interestingly, many of the officials who enjoyed the advantages of incumbency were not initially elected to office. Until the 1988 charter reform a vacancy in a borough presidency was filled by the borough's council delegation. Between 1961 and 1987 fully 33 council members, more than one-fifth

Table 3.11 Challenges to Incumbency and Rate of Incumbent Reelection in Borough President Races, 1961–1989

Borough	Number of Incumbent Races[a]	Number of General Election Victories	Number of Primary Contests	Number of Primary Victories
Manhattan	5	5	3	3
Bronx	6	4	2	2
Brooklyn	7	7	4	4
Queens	8	8	1	1
Staten Island	8	6	2	2
Total	34	30	12	12

Sources: See Table 3.6.

[a]"Number of Incumbent Races" is defined as the number of elections in which an incumbent is running for reelection. For example, if an incumbent was running for reelection in every election year between 1961 and 1989, the number of incumbent races would be eight.

of all who served, were initially appointed rather than elected. In 1987, of the 35 council members, 8 were appointed initially. Among the 26 individuals who served as borough presidents between 1961 and 1987, fully 17 were initially appointed to fill vacancies. Of the 5 sitting borough presidents in 1987, 4 gained their positions through appointment.[11]

Among the citywide offices primary contests vary in their competitiveness. (See Table 3.9.) Nomination of the comptroller candidates has been least competitive. The 1961 race required a primary, but the candidate favored by the incumbent mayor won with 62 percent. Only the 1965 nomination was competitive. In that year the incumbent comptroller ran unsuccessfully for mayor, and four candidates were involved in a primary. The winner, a candidate supported by party regulars, defeated a reformer by a narrow 43–42 margin.

In 1969 the comptroller decided to run for mayor, which precipitated a primary contest for the comptroller's post. However, a former comptroller defeated his second-place rival by a 44–29 margin. The same pattern was repeated in 1973, when the incumbent comptroller again ran for mayor (this time successfully). The four-man primary battle that ensued once again was decided by a wide margin. A Bronx-based reformer defeated his closest rival with a margin of 45 to 24 percent. After winning election in 1973 he regained the Democratic nomination three times, once without a primary challenge and twice with majorities of two-thirds or more. When the four-term comptroller ran unsuccessfully for mayor in 1989, a three-way primary contest followed with the victor—formerly a member of Congress and Brooklyn district attorney—winning with 47 percent of the total vote compared to 24 percent for the second-place finisher.

The nomination for council president more frequently has involved competitive contests. The 1961 and 1965 nominations both involved primaries in which an incumbent was not competing, but neither was close. In the earlier year the winning candidate gained a 61 percent majority; in the later year the winner in a four-man contest defeated his second-place rival 49 versus 37 percent. However, each of the next three council president nominations was competitive. In 1969 five candidates entered a primary when the incumbent did not run again. The battle was exceptionally close, with a margin of a handful of votes. This nominee was unsuccessful in the general election, and in 1973 three aspirants (including the incumbent, who was initially elected as a Liberal–Republican candidate) competed in a primary. The winner received 41 percent of the vote with the second-place incumbent receiving 36 percent. In 1977 the incumbent Democrat faced a challenge from four candidates. The primary was again competitive, with the incumbent and his leading challenger receiving 31 and 25 percent, respectively. This required a runoff election, which the challenger won with 59 percent of the vote.

Since 1977, however, there have been no competitive contests for council president nomination. In 1981 nobody challenged the incumbent. When she ran for mayor in 1985, the former Manhattan borough president won in a six-person contest which saw him receive 49 percent of the vote—more than twice the number received by the runner-up. In 1989 he retained the nomination in a primary contest in which he gained 75 percent of the vote.

Mayoral nominations are the most competitive contests. Each of the last eight elections involved a primary, and only three were not competitive. In 1961, 1981, and 1985, incumbents were renominated with majorities ranging from 61 to 64 percent. But the other elections involved hotly contested primaries. Runoff elections were required twice (in 1973 and 1977) because no candidate received 40 percent of the vote, and a third (in 1969) would have been required if the runoff law had been in effect. In 1965 the primary winner received 45 percent of the vote, just 9 percentage points more than his leading rival. And the 1989 primary, a four-man contest, resulted in the victor receiving 51 percent of the vote and the second-place finisher 42 percent.

The foregoing analysis of competitiveness in general elections and in Democratic nominations leads to two general conclusions. First, interparty competition is virtually absent in New York City. The Democrats dominate the local legislature and most other elective offices. The leading exception to this rule is the occasional "fusion" candidate who succeeds as a Liberal–Republican candidate by gaining enough Democratic votes to win. Second, competition for Democratic party nomination also is relatively rare; incumbents and candidates designated by the established party leadership often do not face a primary challenge, and when they do they win easily. The principal exception to this general rule involves mayoral nominations.

Because the mayoralty is both the most important municipal office and the one most frequently involved in competitive electoral contests, it is important to explore more fully the nature of those contests. What is the basis for competition, and how does it relate to change in policy decisions? These issues are explored in the next chapter; but before beginning that task, another prerequisite for democratic responsiveness—voter participation—should be examined.

Limited Voter Participation

For the conditions of democratic theory to be realized, citizens must be offered electoral choices and participate in making the choices. One of the most striking trends in New York City during the post-1960 period is the sharp decline in voter participation in municipal elections.

The size of the potential electorate, the voting-age population, has remained relatively stable. (See Table 3.12.) An estimated 5.3 million people were over age 21 at the time of the 1961, 1965, and 1969 elections. For the 1973 election the potential electorate swelled to almost 5.6 million as the franchise was extended to those between the ages of 18 and 21. During the rest of the 1970s, population losses took their toll on the size of the electorate; by the 1981 election it again numbered about 5.3 million. Between 1981 and 1989 population growth increased the potential electorate to almost 5.5 million.

Table 3.12   Selected Measures of Voter Participation in New York City, 1961–1989

Year	Voting-Age Population	Registered Voters	Mayoral Vote	Percent of Eligible Voters Registered	Percent of Eligible Voters Voting	Percent of Registered Voters Voting
1961	5,341,080	3,239,879	2,424,990	60.7%	45.4%	74.8%
1965	5,320,903	3,281,689	2,554,210	61.7	48.0	77.8
1969	5,300,726	3,026,745	2,378,240	57.1	44.9	78.6
1973	5,599,343	3,565,147	1,705,660	63.7	30.5	47.8
1977	5,480,526	2,778,506	1,435,154	50.7	26.2	51.7
1981	5,302,472	2,585,464	1,222,648	48.8	23.1	47.3
1985	5,400,000	3,014,459	1,170,904	55.8	21.7	38.8
1989	5,475,000	3,183,741	1,899,845	58.2	34.7	59.7

Sources: Voting-age population figures are authors' estimates based on U.S. Census data. Other data from the New York City Board of Elections.

Despite the fact that the potential electorate was larger in 1985 than in 1961, fewer than half as many voted in the later year. The number of votes cast for mayor fell from more than 2.4 million in 1961 to less than 1.2 million in 1985, the lowest number in any municipal election in more than 50 years. As a proportion of the voting-age population, voters fell from 45 to 22 percent in the 1961–1985 period.

This decline in participation is partly explained by the changed characteristics of the voting-age population. More were recent immigrants not eligible to vote; more were younger adults, who have a tendency to be less active politically; more were poor, a condition that is also associated with nonparticipation. And national or cultural forces were also working to reduce voter participation. Turnout in presidential elections declined from 63 percent in 1969 to 53 percent in 1980 and 1984 to 50 percent in 1988.[12]

But the decline in municipal voter participation cannot be explained fully by national forces and local demographic change. To the extent demographic changes reduce participation, the decline should be evident in voter registration as well as turnout. Immigrants who cannot vote also cannot register; youth who ignore elections also fail to register; poor adults who are too pressed by life circumstances to vote are also unlikely to register. Yet the decline in registration was much less than the decline in votes. Registration in 1985 stood at 93 percent of the 1961 level, but voting was at 48 percent of the 1961 level.

Additional evidence that something unique to municipal politics was occurring is the divergence in trends between turnout among New Yorkers for local elections and for state and national elections. (See Table 3.13.) Although there was a general decline in turnout, the drop was greater for municipal elections. The halving of the mayoral vote from 1961 to 1985 compares unfavorably to the roughly one-fourth decline in presidential votes (from 1960 to 1984) and gubernatorial votes (from 1962 to 1986). In the 1960s there were likely to be slightly fewer New York City residents voting for governor than for mayor; by the early 1980s gubernatorial elections drew

Table 3.13   Votes in Presidential, Gubernatorial, and Mayoral Elections in New York City, 1960–1990

Election	Number of Votes	Votes as Percent of Closest Mayoral Votes	Votes as Share of Earliest Similar Votes Shown
1960—Presidential	3,143,782	127.4%	100.0%
1961—Mayoral	2,467,546	100.0	100.0
1962—Gubernatorial	2,481,849	100.6	100.0
1964—Presidential	3,076,230	116.0	97.9
1965—Mayoral	2,652,454	100.0	107.5
1966—Gubernatorial	2,532,237	95.5	102.0
1968—Presidential	2,719,869	111.2	86.5
1969—Mayoral	2,445,467	100.0	99.1
1970—Gubernatorial	2,359,228	96.5	95.1
1972—Presidential	2,697,278	150.7	85.8
1973—Mayoral	1,790,053	100.0	72.5
1974—Gubernatorial	1,846,305	103.1	74.4
1976—Presidential	2,231,220	150.1	71.0
1977—Mayoral	1,486,536	100.0	60.2
1978—Gubernatorial	1,526,574	102.7	61.5
1980—Presidential	2,013,164	154.2	64.0
1981—Mayoral	1,305,368	100.0	52.9
1982—Gubernatorial	1,685,931	129.2	67.9
1984—Presidential	2,340,181	199.9	74.4
1985—Mayoral	1,170,904	100.0	47.5
1986—Gubernatorial	1,288,842	110.1	51.9
1988—Presidential	2,126,418	111.9	67.6
1989—Mayoral	1,899,845	100.0	77.0
1990—Gubernatorial	1,159,127	61.0	46.7

Sources: New York City Board of Elections and New York State Board of Elections.

more than one-quarter more voters than mayoral contests. And while presidential elections always draw more voters than local elections, the disparity grew from 27 percent to 100 percent in the quarter century after 1960.

The unique character of the decline in municipal election turnout is also suggested by the absence of a similar decline in participation in primary elections. The decline in Democratic primary votes for mayor was neither as sharp nor as steady as the drop in general election turnout. (See Table 3.14.) While votes in the general election for mayor dropped 41 percent between 1961 and 1977, the number of primary votes increased almost 19 percent in the same period. Primary turnout dropped after 1977, but in 1985 the share of enrolled Democrats participating in the mayoral primary was still about the same as in the contests in the 1960s.

However, these disheartening trends in municipal electoral participation were reversed in the 1989 elections. For that contest the share of the population that was registered increased to more than 58 percent, and nearly 60 percent of registered voters actually voted, resulting in an overall turnout rate of 35 percent. The absolute number of voters rose nearly three-quarters of a million, or 62 percent. More people voted for mayor in the 1989 general

Table 3.14   Votes in New York City Democratic
Mayoral Primary Elections, 1961–1989

Election	Number of Votes	Votes as Percent of Eligible Democrats
1961—Primary	748,755	34.0%
1965—Primary	750,039	32.4
1969—Primary	777,796	37.6
1973—Primary	783,133	32.2
Runoff	901,496	37.1
1977—Primary	916,065	47.1
Runoff	787,897	40.5
1981—Primary	581,072	32.1
1985—Primary	682,014	32.2
1989—Primary	1,080,557	51.4

Source: New York City Board of Elections.

election than in any year since 1969, and in the primary nearly 1.1 million people voted. The results were related to the special character of that election, the subject to which we turn in the next chapter.

Conclusion

This analysis of elected offices and electoral behavior suggests that the conventional democratic mechanisms to link citizens' policy preferences with municipal policy decisions do not work very well in New York City. Locally elected officials possess the formal authority to shape local policy, but the process of selecting them does not provide voters with the opportunity to exercise effective political choice. The selection of members for the local legislature involves virtually no interparty competition and very limited intraparty competition. The selection of borough presidents, whose importance was primarily a function of their votes on the Board of Estimate, for all practical purposes was determined by a small group of party leaders. Most borough presidents were initially appointed rather than elected to the job, and very few incumbents failed to gain reelection when they sought it. Interparty competition for borough presidencies is rare, and only in one borough is there any evidence of substantial intraparty competition for these nominations.

Election of the three citywide officials offers a more meaningful opportunity for voters to exercise some policy influence. Although the Democratic party tends to dominate these positions, there is at least some party competition; in the last eight elections Republicans won the mayoralty twice and the council presidency once. In addition, there were three mayoral contests and one additional comptroller and council president race in which the Democrats won in a very competitive environment. Moreover, primary contests for the Democratic nomination for citywide office has provided another opportunity for policy change, particularly with respect to the mayoralty. Five of the eight most recent mayoral contests involved a competitive primary election among the city's Democrats, who comprise approximately 70 percent of the local electorate.

The nature of the connection between elections and municipal policy is most likely to be evident in elections for citywide office, and the office with the greatest opportunity for effecting change is the mayoralty. It is the most powerful of the citywide offices and the one that is most often obtained through competitive elections. Thus, a further exploration of mayoral contests is particularly important to understanding how municipal government responds to its citizens' preferences.

4

MAYORAL ELECTIONS

When a citizen pulls a lever in a mayoral election, the choice is more than among names. Candidates should, and generally do, stand for something; voters are giving a new or reelected chief executive a mandate to pursue a set of goals which have been emphasized in a campaign or a current administration. Unanticipated events and issues, often of great importance, inevitably arise; mayors cope with such events based on the broad values they hold. Other important aspects of municipal affairs are influenced, even determined, by people outside local government. Yet mayoral elections are the most meaningful opportunity for linking the desires of local residents and the decisions of local government.

What are the issues which mayoral elections decide, or at least provide policy guidance about? Students of American urban politics and observers of New York City politics have identified four basic issues which tend to divide a city's citizens.

One basic division is between what Sayre and Kaufman called the "service-demanding" and the "money-providing" groups.[1] Whereas they initially used these terms to describe patterns of interest group activity rather than electoral coalitions, this economic division was used to characterize mayoral coalitions by Shefter in his analysis of the successive fiscal crises in New York City's history.[2]

The initial formulation of Sayre and Kaufman had a highly redistributive emphasis, suggesting that municipal government was essentially a mechanism through which the poor obtained in-kind transfers from the wealthy. The following passage, intended to describe New York City politics in the decade before 1960, captures the issue well:

77

The insistence that service be rendered on an ever-increasing scale is unfailing, and the resistance of those who pay a large part of the bill is equally enduring. Lower income groups tend to make up the core of the service-demanders, who therefore count among their numbers the most depressed and deprived segments of the population, Negroes and Puerto Ricans especially. More advantaged groups, economically and socially, compose the money-providers. Observers unfamiliar with the New York City system of government might logically infer that the money-providers would have greater influence by far, since their access to the highest level of officialdom and their resources are presumably better. In fact, the quantity of services has steadily grown over the years; in the long run, despite temporary setback, the secular trend is unmistakable. The call for services has steadily won out.[3]

Shefter, who had the benefit of witnessing a period of contraction in local government, revised the formulation. He added municipal employees and their union leaders to the poor as prominent and powerful members of the prospending coalition. And he argued that the trends were cyclical, not secular. Rather than seeing a continued triumph of those favoring more government, he believed successful coalitions based on prospending policies would be driven from office by fiscal crises precipitated by the refusal of lending institutions to finance the ever-growing expenditures. Such crises discredit the ruling regime in the public's eye and lead to replacement coalitions who successfully, if only temporarily, reverse the policies of their predecessors.

A second enduring division within urban politics identified by scholars and practitioners is a battle between so-called regulars within the dominant (usually Democratic) party and reformers of both Democratic and Republican stripes.[4] The battle began in the late nineteenth century over the basic principles of local government. Regulars were characterized as "private-regarding," meaning they viewed government as a vocation with an emphasis on extracting private rewards from public service. The means of achieving this were patronage and closed party systems which permitted a small group of leaders chosen largely based on loyal service to the organization to control nominations and party finances. These leaders were typically known as "bosses."

Reformers were characterized as "public-regarding," meaning they wanted government to serve broader purposes, favored civil service as a staffing principle in order to make government operate more efficiently than under patronage, and sought to "open" local party organizations by having nominations made through primary elections and party finances a matter of public record. Reform policies oriented toward greater efficiency in government might reduce spending, but reformers also favor greater public spending for projects and activities that provide broad benefits such as infrastructure improvements and better educational services.[5]

The relative success of reform or regular policies in electoral contests has been linked, at least theoretically, to the social and economic composition of the population. Edward C. Banfield and James Q. Wilson argued that public-regarding approaches were more popular among middle-class and wealthier citizens, whereas recent immigrants and lower-income individuals were more likely to support private-regarding political leaders and organizations.[6] Thus older cities with large immigrant populations were likely to be dominated by regular party organizations and their policies while wealthier suburbs and newer Sunbelt cities with more homogeneous populations would install reform regimes.

A third interpretation of urban politics stresses the role of ethnic identity in dividing the electorate and in shaping electoral coalitions.[7] This view implies that elections are not determined primarily by individuals' policy preferences; rather they are one of several instruments through which people express their ethnic identity and pride. Having one of their members gain an elected position is seen as an opportunity for an ethnic group to promote its acceptance within a community and to express its feeling of importance.

According to this view electoral success will depend on the numerical strength of the ethnic group from which a candidate is drawn and the capacity to form "balanced" tickets in which candidates from different groups for different offices endorse each other. Successful party organizations will nominate candidates who represent the largest ethnic groups and will form coalitions by drawing candidates for different offices from different ethnic groups.

A fourth view of urban politics defines elections as a matter of race relations.[8] Blacks are seen as not "just another ethnic group" who are accommodated in the conventional ways of ethnic politics. Instead, citizens' attitudes toward the desire of blacks to become incorporated into political and other institutions become a dividing line. Elections are contests between candidates who favor greater accommodation to the desires of blacks and those who resist them. Symbolic terms and issues sometimes weakly disguise the conflicts. For example, those who are less sympathetic to minority concerns emphasize "law and order" and the priority of "merit" over "quotas" in hiring decisions; those more concerned with accommodation of minority interests emphasize the need to spend more public funds on social services and to take "affirmative action" to promote employment of blacks and Hispanics.

Those who oppose accommodation are themselves typically white, whereas a candidate urging more change may be a black or white supported by blacks. Position on the issue, rather than racial identity itself, is the decisive factor.

In this view the electoral success of problack candidates depends on several factors. If blacks comprise a substantial majority of the electorate, then their candidate will capture elected office. When blacks are a numerical minority, a problack candidate can be elected if either (1) there is a sufficient number of white supporters who ally with blacks or (2) the unsympathetic whites are divided and do not unite behind one candidate.[9]

These basic issues often overlap. For example, regular party organizations may employ ethnic politics in their battles with reformers; competition between service-demanders and money-providers may also be conflicts between those favoring and opposing more accommodation to blacks. But in some instances the explanations are competitive; that is, they comprise cross-pressures on individual voters. For example, positions in the battle between service-demanders and money-providers do not always overlap fully with those between citizens with different views of race relations; and party regulars and reformers do not comprise groups with inherently different views of spending and taxing policies.

This chapter examines New York City's mayoral elections in the post-1960 period to determine which, if any, of these issues are at stake in these contests. What are the policies and coalitions that each candidate represents? In essence, what do mayoral elections decide?

The next eight sections of this chapter examine each of the mayoral contests in the post-1960 period. The analysis relies primarily on narratives of the contests reconstructed from newspapers and other secondary sources, a few informal interviews with participants, and observations (and occasional participation) by the senior authors in all the contests except that in 1961. These qualitative analyses are supplemented by a more quantitative analysis of election results. In addition to presenting vote tallies by borough, the sections examine the role of race and ethnicity by assembling data for seven neighborhoods representing four groups. Specifically, the analysis focuses on two predominantly Jewish neighborhoods (Forest Hills and Williamsburg); two predominantly Hispanic neighborhoods (Bushwick and the Lower East Side); two predominantly black neighborhoods (Bedford-Stuyvesant and Harlem); and a predominantly Italian neighborhood (Bensonhurst). The method used is described more fully in an appendix to this chapter.

The 1961 Election

The incumbent mayor in 1961, Robert F. Wagner, Jr., had advanced largely by being a party regular. He had earlier served as Manhattan borough president and was elected mayor with the support of the county leaders, including the well-known Manhattan "boss" Carmine DeSapio. But reformers were gaining strength in New York. The 1956 presidential campaign of Adlai Stevenson had drawn many New York reformers into local politics, and after the 1960 election of President John F. Kennedy there was national party support for pursuing reform within the city. In addition, Wagner had close ties with organized labor in the city and likely could draw upon their support even without the endorsement of the party bosses.

In this context, Wagner made a decision to join the reformers and campaign against the bosses. He announced his candidacy for a third term on June 17, 1961, and he declared war on the bosses by naming his preferred running mates for the other citywide offices without consulting the county leaders. Wagner urged replacing the incumbent comptroller Lawrence Gerosa with the city budget director Abraham Beame and replacing the incumbent city council president Abraham Stark with his deputy mayor, Paul Screvane.

Wagner was endorsed by 39 reform Democratic clubs, the Liberal party, and labor unions. Abe Beame, who was a regular Brooklyn Democrat, agreed

Table 4.1 Votes in the 1961 Democratic Primary

County	Arthur Levitt	Robert Wagner	Total	Total Votes as a Percentage of Registered Democrats
New York	66,917	122,607	189,524	44.0%
Bronx	47,885	78,626	126,511	33.0
Kings	103,296	136,440	239,749[a]	32.0
Queens	64,157	102,845	167,002	30.9
Richmond	10,471	15,498	25,969	44.3
Total	292,726	456,016	748,755	34.0%

Source: New York City Board of Elections.
[a]Total includes 13 "scattered" votes.

to run with Wagner, indicating some shift in loyalties even among the regulars. Queens county leader Herbert Koeler also backed Wagner.

Wagner's new "reform" coalition proved successful in the Democratic primary. The Brooklyn, Bronx, and Manhattan county leaders had agreed to back State Comptroller Arthur Levitt as the "regular" candidate. But Levitt received only 39 percent of the 748,755 primary votes cast. Wagner gained a clear majority not only in Queens, where he was backed by the party regulars, but also in Manhattan, the Bronx, and Brooklyn. (See Table 4.1.) The bosses proved incapable of delivering the votes.

In the general election Wagner faced two significant opponents. The Republicans nominated the state attorney general Louis Lefkowitz. Gerosa, the city comptroller whom Wagner's running mate Beame had replaced on the Democratic ticket, decided to run against Wagner on a separate line, the newly formed Citizens party. His platform was to save New York City through "business leadership, financial reforms, and tax curbs."[10]

Wagner's ability to win the general election as a reformer was threatened by scandals in the public school system in the midst of the campaign. In response, Wagner proposed a joint city–state commission to investigate the matter, but Republican governor Nelson Rockefeller rejected this idea. Instead he called a special session of the legislature; a nine-month emergency was declared permitting the abolition of the old Board of Education and letting Wagner appoint a new one. This effectively defused the issue for the remainder of the campaign.

Wagner's reform image also was jeopardized by a fund-raising luncheon sponsored by Wagner's appointee to the City Planning Commission. The luncheon raised $25,000 for Wagner's campaign, largely from builders and realtors who had been invited by the planning commissioner. Lefkowitz charged the luncheon was "a corrupt political shakedown." The planning commissioner subsequently resigned, and Wagner rejected the funds offered. In part because of the scandal, The New York Times, which had recommended Wagner in the primary, endorsed Lefkowitz on its editorial page. The editors suggested voters split their tickets to elect a new Republican mayor and the Wagner-selected Democratic candidates for comptroller and city council president.

Table 4.2 Votes in the 1961 Mayoral Election

Candidate	Number	Percent
Wagner		
Total	1,237,421	51.0%
Democrat	970,383	40.0
Liberal	211,175	8.7
Brotherhood	55,863	2.3
Lefkowitz		
Total	835,691	34.5
Republican	779,088	32.1
Other[a]	56,603	2.3
Gerosa	321,604	13.3
Other candidates[b]	30,274	1.2
Total	2,424,990	100.0%

Source: New York City Board of Elections.

[a]Includes Civic Action Party and nonpartisan votes.

[b]Includes Vito Battista of United Taxpayers, Richard Garza of Socialist Workers, Eric Hass of Socialist Labor, and 5 "scattered" votes.

Partly because of these setbacks, Wagner's victory in the election was narrow for a Democrat in New York City. (See Table 4.2.) He received a bare majority (51 percent) of the 2.4 million votes cast, including 211,175 on the Liberal party line. Republican Lefkowitz received a third of all the votes, and Gerosa's Citizens party gained 321,604 votes, or about 13 percent. (Other minor party candidates accounted for the rest.)

From this account of the primary and general election campaigns, it is clear that the major issue dividing candidates was the classic reformers versus regulars battle. Wagner was able to position himself successfully as a reformer in the primary, and despite some setbacks in the general election campaign he maintained this image with enough strength to gain a bare majority.

However, other elements of urban politics were also present in the 1961 campaign. Ethnic political strategies were evident in the composition of Wagner's team, which included Beame, who was Jewish, and Screvane, originally named Scrivani, who was Italian-American, along with Wagner.[11] The

Table 4.3 Voting Distribution Index for General Election for Mayor in New York City, 1961

Neighborhood	Wagner	Lefkowitz	Gerosa
Williamsburg	1.38	0.74	0.28
Forest Hills	0.90	1.31	0.21
Bedford-Stuyvesant	1.37	0.71	0.18
Harlem	1.56	0.51	2.19
Bushwick	1.38	0.47	0.80
Lower East Side	1.25	0.89	0.10
Bensonhurst	0.48	1.07	0.31
Citywide percentage	50.10%	33.90%	13.00%

Source: New York City Board of Elections.

Note: See appendix for definition of Voting Distribution Index.

Republicans ran a Jewish candidate in part because he might attract Jewish voters, who traditionally voted Democratic. However, the strategy was only marginally successful based on the neighborhood voting data in Table 4.3. Although Lefkowitz ran well ahead of his citywide average in Forest Hills, this was not the case in Williamsburg.

The candidates' positions as champions of service-demanders or of money-providers also was relevant, if not most prominent, in the 1961 campaign. Wagner's closeness with labor and generally liberal stance implicitly placed him on the side of the spenders. In contrast, Gerosa positioned himself as a fiscal conservative and tried to make this his distinguishing feature (a characteristic the voters found either lacking credibility in a former regular Democratic or simply inconsistent with their values).

Racial politics was the most subdued division of the 1961 elections. There were no publicized efforts to raise the issue during the campaign, and the neighborhood voting data suggest blacks gave Wagner very strong support without his making any public promises on the issue. An account of the 1961 campaign by Harlem district leader J. Raymond Jones suggests he supported Wagner over Levitt out of dislike for his earlier treatment by the county bosses and his belief that better treatment in terms of patronage and career advancement might be forthcoming from Wagner, rather than out of differences on civil rights issues.[12]

The 1965 Election

Wagner's third term was a difficult one personally and professionally. The illness and death of his wife took an emotional toll, and management of municipal affairs posed increased challenges. A poll taken by Democrats in the spring of 1965 indicated only 44 percent of the citizens approved of the way the mayor was doing his job.[13] The budget prepared by the mayor in June showed the city to be in fiscal difficulties and relied on borrowing to bridge the budget gap, a practice denounced by several civic groups. Not surprisingly, on June 10, 1965, Wagner announced he would not seek a fourth term.

The Democratic primary to identify a successor to Wagner was a four-way battle. The regulars united behind Comptroller Beame, who received the early support of the Brooklyn and Bronx county leaders. Wagner promoted the candidacy of City Council President Screvane, who was closely identified with Wagner's administration. But two other aspirants also sought to run as reform candidates—Representative William Fitts Ryan and City Councilman Paul O'Dwyer. (Manhattan's district attorney, Frank O'Connor, was an announced candidate briefly but withdrew in favor of Beame.)

During the primary campaign, Beame took advantage of dissatisfaction with municipal government under Wagner to blemish Screvane's reputation because of his close association with Wagner. Beame repeatedly referred to the Wagner–Screvane administration. In contrast, Screvane could not effectively label Beame a boss, since Beame had been part of Wagner's reform ticket in 1961 and had been serving as an "independent" comptroller.

Table 4.4 Votes in the 1965 Democratic Primary

County	Paul Screvane	Abraham Beame	William Ryan	Paul O'Dwyer	Total	Total Votes as a Percentage of Registered Democrats
New York	66,444	53,386	48,744	6,775	175,349	37.7%
Bronx	54,260	66,064	16,632	5,876	142,832	33.3
Kings	79,485	128,146	24,588	8,332	240,551	31.3
Queens	63,680	82,601	22,570	6,895	175,746	29.7
Richmond	7,512	6,148	1,204	697	15,561	24.1
Total	271,381	336,345	113,738	28,575	750,039	32.4%

Source: New York City Board of Elections.

Predictably, the two reformers and Screvane divided their potential common support and Beame won the primary with a plurality of the votes. (See Table 4.4.) Of the 750,039 votes cast, Beame received 45 percent, Screvane 36 percent, Ryan 15 percent, and O'Dwyer 4 percent. Beame received a majority of the Brooklyn votes and outpolled Screvane in the Bronx, but he received less than a third of the votes in Manhattan, the reformers' base.

The Republican candidate in 1965, John V. Lindsay, was selected largely by the liberal, state-party wing of the Republicans, led most notably by Governor Nelson Rockefeller and Senator Jacob Javits. Local, and more conservative, Republican figures agreed to the candidate largely in deference to Rockefeller's influence in the party and with the hope that a well-publicized (even if unsuccessful) Republican mayoral race might help other Republicans in the campaign. In his campaign Lindsay generally distanced himself from the local Republican leaders and built an independent campaign organization. Lindsay also sought and received endorsement from the Liberal party. This nomination was linked to an agreement that Lindsay include Liberal party leader Timothy Costello as his running mate for city council president.

In reaction to the Republicans choosing a liberal candidate, the conservative Republican writer William Buckley announced he would run for mayor as a Conservative party candidate. Buckley acknowledged that he had little hope of winning but said that he wanted to prevent Lindsay's success and thus protect the "true" Republican philosophy.[14]

During the campaign three issues arose periodically: police misconduct, fiscal responsibility, and political extremism. Police brutality had arisen as an issue under Wagner, and civil rights organizations had proposed a civilian board to review such complaints. Wagner's police commissioner had resigned when a city council subcommittee recommended such a measure. In the campaign, Lindsay favored establishment of the civilian board; Beame and Buckley opposed it.

All three candidates criticized the "budget crisis" identified with Wagner's need to borrow to fund large expenditures in his last year. Buckley urged cutting services in order to deal with the problem, Lindsay urged more intergovernmental aid to help the situation, and Beame sought greater "home rule" as a way to deal with the revenue gaps.

The extremism issue was raised by both Beame and Lindsay as a criticism of Buckley. They linked Buckley to right-wing organizations such as the John Birch Society, the implication being that the antisemitic and racist views of that organization were acceptable to Buckley.

Beame obtained the endorsement of traditional Democratic supporters. He was supported not only by the regulars but also (albeit lukewarmly) by the incumbent mayor and President Lyndon Johnson, most labor unions and the Central Trades and Labor Council, and many Democratic reform leaders. However, Lindsay made significant inroads with the Democratic reformers, obtaining endorsements from several (including a Greenwich Village insurgent named Edward I. Koch).

John Lindsay won the election, but with less than a majority of the votes. (See Table 4.5.) Of more than 2.5 million votes cast, Lindsay received under 45 percent, including 11 percent on the Liberal party line. Beame drew 41 percent and Buckley 13 percent. Ironically, some observers believe Buckley drew more of his votes from conservative regular Democrats than from Republicans, thus helping rather than harming Lindsay's victory.

How relevant were each of the four broad issues to the 1965 elections? Reformism continued to play a dominant role. The key issue in the primary was whether the regulars, by supporting Beame, could regain control of the mayoralty from Wagner's "reform" administration. The division of the reformers among three candidates permitted Beame to win with a plurality. Similarly, in the general election the support of reform Democrats, who opposed Beame and his county leader coalition, was critical to Lindsay's plurality victory.

The service-demander versus the money-producer split was only a minor theme in the election. Lindsay was a liberal Republican (with Liberal party supporters); both he and Beame were clearly on the side of service-demanders. Only Buckley positioned himself as a friend of the money-providers, and he received the votes of only a small minority of New Yorkers.

Ethnic politics continued to play a role in 1965. The Democratic ticket was "balanced" with Abe Beame at the head; Mario Procaccino, an Italian-American, for comptroller; and Frank O'Connor, an Irish-American, for City

Table 4.5   Votes in the 1965 Mayoral Election

Candidate	Number	Percent
Lindsay		
Total	1,149,106	45.0%
Republican	867,310	34.0
Liberal	281,796	11.0
Beame		
Total	1,046,699	41.0
Democrat	983,109	38.5
Civil Service Fusion	63,590	2.5
William Buckley	341,226	13.4
Other candidates[a]	17,179	0.7
Total	2,554,210	100.0%

Source: New York City Board of Elections.

[a]Includes Vito Battista of United Taxpayers, Clifton DeBerry of Socialist Workers, and Eric Hass of Socialist Labor.

Table 4.6 Voting Distribution Index for General Election
for Mayor in New York City, 1965

Neighborhood	Lindsay	Beame	Buckley
Williamsburg	0.48	1.80	0.19
Forest Hills	1.14	0.97	0.33
Bedford-Stuyvesant	0.55	1.61	0.22
Harlem	0.69	1.48	0.11
Bushwick	0.62	1.58	0.32
Lower East Side	0.71	1.50	0.24
Bensonhurst	1.08	0.65	1.68
Citywide percentage	45.30%	39.50%	12.90%

Source: New York City Board of Elections.

Note: See appendix for definition of Voting Distribution Index.

Council president. However, the ethnic strategy did not work well for Beame; while his running mates won, Beame lost, in part because he was not strongly supported by Jewish voters. The data in Table 4.6 indicate Beame fared well in Williamsburg (part of his Brooklyn base), but Lindsay outdrew Beame in Forest Hills. For a significant number of Jews, the commitment to Lindsay's reform policies was more influential than Beame's heritage.

Racial politics emerged, though not significantly in the 1965 election. Lindsay distinguished himself from his opponents by favoring a civilian review board for police misconduct, an issue of symbolic importance in race relations. But this did not yield him much support among blacks. As Table 4.6 indicates, votes in black neighborhoods strongly favored Beame—a pattern consistent with their strong Democratic party allegiance. Lindsay won with a minority of the votes, but he was not the candidate backed most strongly by racial minorities.

The 1969 Election

Early in 1969 John Lindsay was widely perceived as having little chance for reelection. The mayor himself later wrote, "The last six months of 1968 had been the worst of my public life."[15] In that period the city suffered a bitter teachers' strike, which left deep rifts between Jews and blacks in the city. Other municipal unions also were battling with the mayor, and the police engaged in a work slowdown. To compound the troubles, the city was hit with a major snowstorm in February 1969, and the mayor bore the brunt of bitter citizen criticism over the inadequacy of clean-up efforts.

Despite these problems, in March 1969 Lindsay announced his intention to seek reelection and to do so as a joint Republican and Liberal candidate, as in 1965. He quickly received the Liberal party nomination at the party's convention in April.

Lindsay was less fortunate in seeking to duplicate his Republican nomination. He was not spared a primary battle. State Senator John Marchi announced his campaign for mayor under both the Republican and Conservative party banners. Marchi was nominated without a contest by the Conservatives, and he forced Lindsay into a Republican primary battle. About

Table 4.7 Votes in the 1969 Primary Elections

County	Democratic							Republican			
	Herman Badillo	Mario Procaccino	James Scheuer	Norman Mailer	Robert Wagner	Total	Total Votes as a Percentage of Registered Democrats	John Lindsay	John Marchi	Total	Total Votes as a Percentage of Registered Republicans
New York	74,809	26,804	7,117	17,372	40,978	167,080	41.1%	44,236	12,457	56,693	45.1%
Bronx	48,841	50,465	10,788	4,214	33,442	147,750	40.4	12,222	16,132	28,354	33.1
Kings	52,866	87,630	11,942	10,299	81,833	244,570	36.5	20,575	33,694	54,269	34.3
Queens	37,880	79,002	8,994	8,700	61,244	195,820	35.0	26,658	40,469	67,127	33.3
Richmond	2,769	11,628	509	703	6,967	22,576	33.9	3,675	10,946	14,621	44.5
Total	217,165	255,529	39,350	41,288	224,464	777,796	37.6%	107,366	113,698	221,064	36.6%

Source: New York City Board of Elections.

221,000 Republicans voted in that primary and they favored Marchi with 51 percent of the vote. (See Table 4.7.) Lindsay was left with only the Liberal nomination in what was a three-way mayoral race.

The Democrats also sensed Lindsay's vulnerability, and a contentious primary battle arose. The first announced candidate was James Scheuer, a liberal congressman. Next was Comptroller Mario Procaccino, described by *The New York Times* as "an almost unknown and somewhat inept clubhouse politician."[16] In the following weeks, six additional men announced candidacies, but three withdrew after brief campaigns. The remaining candidates to appear on the primary ballot were Bronx borough president Herman Badillo, former mayor Robert Wagner, and author Norman Mailer.

Among the candidates, Badillo and Scheuer competed for support among the reformers. Procaccino was the candidate of the regulars. Wagner was able to pull together only part of his winning 1961 coalition. The Liberal party was committed to Lindsay, but labor groups supported Wagner. Mailer campaigned on a platform of making the city the fifty-first state and drew support from unconventional quarters.

The main issue in the primary campaign was Procaccino's conservatism. He was attacked by the others as a racist appealing to a white backlash vote. He was portrayed as a "Yorty-type" (after the notorious Los Angeles mayor) who would polarize racial groups. Wagner was criticized by the reformers as lacking an ability to develop new policies.

The outcome of the primary was a victory for Procaccino, but without a clear majority. Of the 777,796 votes cast, the comptroller received just under one-third, barely enough to beat second-place Wagner with almost 29 percent. Badillo drew most of the remaining votes (28 percent), with Mailer and Scheuer getting only about 5 percent each. (See Table 4.7.)

After Procaccino's primary victory, many liberal Democrats gave thought to sponsoring a candidate on a new ballot line. But this strategy was rejected because no single candidate could be agreed upon, and because the result might be to dilute liberal voting and help Procaccino. Lindsay sought to encourage reform Democrats to support him by obtaining a second line on the ballot under the newly created Independent party. Lindsay was somewhat successful in gaining traditional liberal Democratic support. While the Central Trades and Labor Council remained in the Democratic camp, two public employee unions, District Council 37 and the Uniformed Sanitationmen's Association, eventually endorsed Lindsay. Lindsay also received endorsements from prominent liberal Democrats, including Howard Samuels, Herman Badillo, Shirley Chisholm, Arthur Goldberg, and Paul O'Dwyer. At the same time several prominent Republicans rejected Marchi and endorsed Lindsay, including Jacob Javitz and Louis Lefkowitz. Governor Rockefeller endorsed Marchi but declined to campaign for his party's candidate.

The most discussed issues in the 1969 general election were peace and safety. Lindsay raised the peace issue by taking an outspoken position on the Vietnam War. He argued the war was relevant to city politics, because financing it diverted federal tax dollars that otherwise could be used to deal with urban problems. Both Marchi and Procaccino opposed Lindsay's support for

Table 4.8 Votes in the 1969 Mayoral Election

Candidate	Number	Percent
Lindsay		
Total	999,933	42.0%
Liberal	859,960	36.2
Independent	139,973	5.9
Marchi		
Total	542,411	22.8
Republican	329,506	13.8
Conservative	212,905	9.0
Procaccino		
Total	831,727	35.0
Democrat	774,708	32.6
Civil Service	57,019	2.4
Other candidates[a]	4,169	0.2
Total	2,378,240	100.0%

Source: New York City Board of Elections.

[a]Includes Rasheed Storey of the Communist party and 151 "scattered" votes.

the peace movement. Public safety was made an issue by Procaccino and Marchi, who criticized the Lindsay administration's "lawlessness." They pointed to rapidly rising crime figures and held the mayor responsible.

The three-way contest resulted in a narrow victory for Lindsay. (See Table 4.8.) Of the nearly 2.4 million votes cast, Lindsay received 42 percent. This gave him a plurality over Procaccino's 35 percent and Marchi's 23 percent. For the second time Lindsay was elected by less than a majority of the voters.

With respect to the four issues in electoral contests, the 1969 campaigns evidenced both continuity and abrupt shifts. Continuity appeared in the continued significance of reform versus regular battles. In the Democratic primary, Procaccino won because he was the single regular against a divided reform opposition. In the general election many reform Democrats defected to Lindsay rather than support Procaccino.

Change was evident in the electoral significance of each of the other issues, making 1969 in many respects a watershed municipal election. In the battle between service-demanders and money-producers, public opinion seemed to shift. Lindsay was most clearly on the side of service-demanders and even, as a non-Democrat, gained some labor support. While Procaccino retained much labor support, he was more fiscally (and otherwise) conservative; Marchi also held conservative views. Thus, in contrast to previous elections, the majority of votes went to candidates who sided with the revenue-providers, although the champion of the service-demanders did win with a plurality.

Change was also evident in the declining role of ethnic politics. Multiple Democratic primary contests prevented mayoral candidates from following a strategy of presenting a traditionally "balanced" ticket. In addition, the Democratic candidate for council president lost to Lindsay's running mate, Sanford Garelick.

The most dramatic change in 1969 was the sharply increased role of race

Table 4.9 Voting Distribution Index for General Election
for Mayor in New York City, 1969

Neighborhood	Lindsay	Procaccino	Marchi
Williamsburg	0.54	1.96	0.32
Forest Hills	1.36	0.84	0.57
Bedford-Stuyvesant	2.02	0.26	0.20
Harlem	1.86	0.39	0.21
Bushwick	0.48	1.47	1.03
Lower East Side	1.47	0.79	0.31
Bensonhurst	0.24	1.60	1.50
Citywide percentage	41.00%	34.00%	22.20%

Source: New York City Board of Elections.

Note: See appendix for definition of Voting Distribution Index.

relations as a political issue. This had national as well as distinctly local origins. In the late 1960s the civil disorders in urban centers around the nation generated a white "backlash," and this movement was intensified by local events in New York City. The divisive campaign relating to a referendum over the creation of a civilian complaint review board for the Police Department in 1966 and the bitter struggle over school decentralization in 1968 divided New Yorkers over racial issues in enduring ways. In 1970 Nathan Glazer and Pat Moynihan, in a new introduction to their classic book, pronounced that "for the first time in New York City's history, as far as we know it, racial conflict became determinative for the city's politics."[17]

The neighborhood voting data for 1969 in Table 4.9, especially compared to the earlier years, reveals the growing significance of racial issues. The two black neighborhoods evidence an important shift in the 1969 election. In both 1961 and 1965, these areas gave strong support to the Democratic candidate; in 1965, Beame did far better than Lindsay in these areas as blacks seemed to support the regular Democrat over the reform or fusion candidate. In 1969, however, the black areas gave extremely strong support to Lindsay, the candidate seen as favoring their aspirations, and very weak support to the regular Democrat Procaccino, who was seen as a "law-and-order" candidate opposed to promoting civil rights causes. A similar, if less pronounced shift is evident in the Hispanic neighborhoods, especially the Lower East Side. Voters in both Bushwick and the Lower East Side favored the Democratic candidate in both 1961 and 1965; in 1969, voters on the Lower East Side dramatically shifted their support to Lindsay and gave relatively few votes to Procaccino. (However, the trend is not evident in Bushwick, perhaps because it was a more mixed than purely Hispanic area at that time.)

A shift in voting behavior also is evident in the Italian neighborhood of Bensonhurst. In 1961 these voters favored the Republican over the Democratic candidate, and they also favored Lindsay over Beame in 1965. In 1969, however, the Italians virtually abandoned Lindsay and gave strong support to Procaccino, the regular Democrat. Positions on issues of race relations appear to be the major factor in this shift.

The pattern in Jewish neighborhoods is less consistent, with a divergence between the wealthier area of Forest Hills and the poorer area of Williamsburg. In 1961, Williamsburg voters favored Wagner, and in 1965 they favored Beame; in 1969 they strongly favored Procaccino. In Forest Hills the voters gave disproportionately strong support to Lefkowitz in 1961 and favored Lindsay in 1965; in 1969, they still supported Lindsay. Thus, in 1969 upper-income Jews still appeared to be favoring reform values and/or greater concern for promoting the status of blacks.

The 1973 Election

After being denied the Republican nomination in 1969, Lindsay converted to the Democratic party, a move consistent with his ambitions for national office. But Lindsay's Democratic candidacy in the 1972 presidential primary contests was unsuccessful, and in 1973 he was still mayor.

Many Democrats felt Lindsay was vulnerable in a primary election, and five announced their candidacies before Lindsay withdrew from the race in early March 1973. The early entrants (in order of formal announcement) were Congressman Edward Koch, former Lindsay commissioner Jerome Kretchmer, Assemblyman Albert Blumenthal, Congressman Herman Badillo, and City Council President Sanford Garelick. The first four were regarded as liberal reformers, but Koch distinguished himself by asserting that crime was the overriding issue in the election. Garelick had been elected as part of Lindsay's ticket in 1969 with the joint nomination of the Republican and Liberal parties.

The day after Lindsay withdrew, Comptroller Beame announced his candidacy. Next, congressman and former police hero Mario Biaggi joined the race. Biaggi also was nominated by the Conservative party leadership without a contest at their March nominating convention.

The nomination of the Republican and Liberal parties remained open as their nominating conventions approached in mid-March. At this point Governor Rockefeller made a surprise proposal that both parties endorse former mayor Robert Wagner as a "fusion" candidate. The Liberals seemed ready to agree, but the local Republican party leaders balked and Wagner himself seemed uneasy with the idea. The plan was aborted, and the two parties made separate nominations. The Republicans again chose Marchi; the Liberals gave their nomination to Blumenthal, thus assuring him a line on the ballot even if he lost the Democratic primary. Within about one month of announcing their candidacies, two of the Democrats were obliged to withdraw because of an inability to raise sufficient campaign funds: Koch in March and Garelick in April.

The four-way Democratic primary was marked by few clashes over policy and frequent disagreement among the candidates over each others' personal qualifications. The controversy receiving the most attention was a revelation in May that Biaggi had invoked the Fifth Amendment in a federal grand jury investigation. Biaggi first denied this, then recanted the denial.

Biaggi received little press support and his labor strength was limited to a few construction trade unions. Badillo received endorsements from *The New*

Table 4.10   Votes in the 1973 Democratic Primary Elections

County	Herman Badillo	Abraham Beame	Mario Biaggi	Albert Blumenthal	Total	Total Votes as a Percentage of Registered Democrats
Initial Primary						
New York	74,496	46,519	18,218	41,794	181,027	35.1%
Bronx	57,258	42,537	39,893	18,713	158,401	34.4
Kings	58,546	98,121	48,952	32,412	238,031	30.8
Queens	34,742	74,223	45,949	29,173	184,087	30.4
Richmond	2,977	9,021	7,775	1,814	21,587	28.3
Total	228,019	270,421	160,787	123,906	783,133	32.2%
Runoff						
New York	113,642	78,849			192,491	37.3%
Bronx	85,827	96,590			182,417	39.3
Kings	91,776	201,862			293,638	38.0
Queens	56,933	153,377			210,310	34.8
Richmond	4,796	17,844			22,640	29.7
Total	352,974	548,522			901,496	37.1%

Source: New York City Board of Elections.

York Times and the *New York Post* and was backed by the hospital workers union and District Council 65, a large retail workers union. Both had large numbers of black and Hispanic members. Beame received support from most of the regular Democratic party organizations and from the Central Trades and Labor Council and the United Federation of Teachers.

With support divided in this way, no candidate was able to gain the 40 percent of the vote in the primary needed to secure the nomination.[18] Beame led in the race with 35 percent of the 783,133 votes, but Badillo ran a close second with 29 percent. Beame won large margins in Brooklyn and Queens, but Badillo received the largest number of votes in Manhattan and the Bronx. (See Table 4.10.)

To select the Democratic candidate, a runoff election was held three weeks after the initial primary. Beame and Badillo had a bitter contest, reflecting their different ethnic backgrounds and personalities. Beame won with a substantial margin (61 percent) in an election that saw turnout increase by about 120,000, or 15 percent over the contest three weeks earlier. After the difficult contest Badillo, in his concession speech, refused to either congratulate Beame or pledge to support him.

The general election campaign was a tepid race despite the presence of four candidates from four different parties. Beame, as a Democrat, was the clear favorite, and he ran a defensive campaign raising few issues. Marchi and Biaggi raised issues of law and order, stressing the rise of crime in recent years, but the appeal drew only limited support for their candidacies. In the end Beame won with about 56 percent of the vote. Marchi and Biaggi drew 16 and 11 percent, respectively. (See Table 4.11.) But the turnout in the election indicated a decline in voter interest; only about 1.7 million people voted, a drop of about 650,000, or more than one-quarter from the 1969 election.

Table 4.11 Votes in the 1973 Mayoral
Election

Candidate	Number	Percent
Beame		
Total	963,542	56.5%
Democrat	896,265	52.5
Civil Service	67,277	3.9
Marchi		
Total	274,052	16.1
Republican	259,781	15.2
Integrity	14,271	0.8
Biaggi		
Total	186,977	11.0
Conservative	178,967	10.5
Safe City	8,010	0.5
Blumenthal		
Total	262,600	15.4
Liberal	233,265	13.7
Good Government	29,335	1.7
Other candidates[a]	18,489	1.1
Total	1,705,660	100.1%

Source: New York City Board of Elections.

[a]Includes Francine Youngstein of Free Libertarian party,
Norman Oliver of Socialist Workers, Anton Chaitkin of
Labor party, John Emanuel of Socialist Labor, Rasheed
Storey of Communist party, and 26 other votes.

With respect to the underlying issues, the 1973 campaigns continued the trend toward a greater role for divisions over racial issues. Although Beame and Badillo could be differentiated as a regular and a reformer, respectively, their campaign strategies highlighted their differences over support for black and Hispanic citizens' concerns. As a consequence of this and some traditional patterns of ethnic politics, Hispanic neighborhoods gave strong support to Badillo in both the initial primary and the runoff. (See Table 4.12.) The black neighborhoods gave almost equal support to Beame and Badillo in the initial primary, reflecting a mix of popular sentiment for Badillo's positions and the traditional alliance with the regular organization in these neighborhoods. However, in the runoff—when turnout was at a record level and many citizens unaffiliated with regular clubs participated—the black neighborhoods gave very strong support to Badillo. Significantly, the 1973 race can be viewed as the point at which Jews shifted their political alliances to be more in line with other "white ethnics" and to withdraw support from candidates seen as favoring minority causes. Whereas upper-income Jews (as reflected in the Forest Hills vote) initially divided their support between Beame and Blumenthal, the Jewish neighborhoods' votes clearly favored Beame in the runoff. And in neither the initial primary nor the runoff, particularly the runoff, were Jewish voters giving their support to Badillo.

Although in 1973 race relations was apparently the dominant issue, other concerns were present. Traditional ethnic politics, as manifested in a balanced Democratic ticket, virtually disappeared; in the general election the Demo-

Table 4.12 Voting Distribution Index for Democratic Mayoral Primary Elections, 1973

Neighborhood	Initial Primary				Runoff	
	Beame	Blumenthal	Biaggi	Badillo	Beame	Badillo
Williamsburg	1.84	0.30	0.73	0.57	1.30	0.53
Forest Hills	1.23	1.34	0.97	0.56	1.27	0.58
Bedford-Stuyvesant	1.32	0.33	0.14	1.59	0.51	1.77
Harlem	1.35	0.60	0.32	1.28	0.65	1.54
Bushwick	0.24	0.81	0.41	2.42	NA	NA
Lower East Side	0.31	0.49	0.19	2.67	0.21	2.24
Bensonhurst	0.38	0.26	3.75	0.20	1.41	0.37
Citywide percentage	34.5%	15.8%	20.5%	29.1%	60.9%	39.1%

Source: New York City Board of Elections.

Note: NA, not available. See appendix for definition of Voting Distribution Index.

cratic mayoral and comptroller candidates both were Jewish. But voters still showed ethnic loyalties, with Italians voting relatively strongly for Biaggi, Jews for Beame and Blumenthal, and Hispanics for Badillo.

The division between service-demanders and money-providers was also relevant in the 1973 election. In the primary Biaggi aligned himself with the more conservative side, and in the general election both Marchi and Biaggi sought to represent the money-providers.

The 1977 Election

Reflecting the policies of his service-demanding constituency, Mayor Beame led the city into its infamous 1975 fiscal crisis. Unable to balance the budget and unable to convince financial institutions to continue their lending practices, Beame had to turn to specially created state agencies to finance the city's operations. In exchange, he sacrificed much control over municipal budgeting; an Emergency Financial Control Board dominated by gubernatorial appointees began to make basic financial decisions. By early 1977 Beame's reputation was tarnished; Democratic rivals saw him as vulnerable, and the Democratic governor Hugh Carey wanted a new mayor with whom he could work more constructively.

Beame was challenged in the 1977 primary by six candidates. Two were former rivals: Congressman Koch had run a brief and unsuccessful campaign in 1973; Badillo had lost a bitter primary runoff in 1973. Borough President Percy Sutton entered the race with strong support in his Manhattan organization and among blacks. Congresswoman Bella Abzug had a reputation as a combative, outspoken liberal with potential to draw media attention and feminist support. Mario Cuomo, the New York State secretary of the state, was Governor Carey's favored candidate. He was a Queens Democrat who had gained a reputation as a skilled negotiator in racial conflicts surrounding the construction of a public housing project in Forest Hills. Joel Harnett was a wealthy publisher and civic-group leader with few conventional sources of support and an admittedly limited chance of victory. Finally, Edward Costikyan, a Manhattan attorney with ties both to regulars and reformers, briefly campaigned but withdrew to join forces with Koch.

The major issue in the primary campaign was Beame's handling of the fiscal crisis. Beame was defensive, while the others focused their criticism on him. Beame suffered a setback when the Securities and Exchange Commission issued a report accusing him of misleading investors about the city's finances in the period before the fiscal crisis; Beame responded by arguing that "outsiders" were trying to replace him as mayor. Aside from their views of Beame, the other candidates evidenced few philosophical differences. Personal characteristics (for example, Abzug's style, Koch's relationship with former Miss America Bess Myerson, and Badillo and Sutton's minority status) provided the interested voters a way to distinguish among the crowded pack.

Most of the candidates were able to attract significant support, and campaign spending rose sharply over previous years. Beame was reported to have spent about $500,000 in 1973; for the 1977 primary and runoff election he spent $1,036,426. Koch spent $1,087,853, Cuomo $1,510,522, Abzug $802,129, Sutton $385,140, and Badillo $192,376. Together, spending by all candidates in the primary contests was about $5,583,000. Another approximately $1 million was spent for the general election, including $639,427 by Koch.[19] Much of the funds came from large individual loans and contributions.

The hotly contested primary drew a record number of voters, more than 916,000 compared to about 783,000 four years earlier. (See Table 4.13.) And the candidates (except Harnett) divided the votes relatively evenly. The leading candidate (Koch) gained 20 percent, second-place Cuomo had 19 percent, and sixth-place Badillo gained 11 percent. A runoff between Koch and Cuomo was scheduled for ten days later.

In the brief runoff campaign the candidates did not separate themselves with comprehensive platforms. Koch attacked Cuomo as being a "creature of the establishment" being foisted on New York City by the governor and business leaders.[20] Cuomo attacked Koch for his support of capital punishment, charging that the previously liberal Koch had "read the polls and seen a fear."[21] Meanwhile the candidates scrambled for support from the various losing camps in the initial primary. Koch gained the support of Badillo and many black politicians, including Congressman Charles Rangel, Basil Patterson, Shirley Chisholm, and David Dinkins. (Badillo and Patterson later were made deputy mayors by Koch.) Koch also quietly obtained the support of the regular political clubs in Brooklyn and the Bronx and the endorsement of Beame. Cuomo won the endorsement of Abzug and the support of most labor unions.

Election turnout fell to under 788,000, and Koch won the runoff with 55 percent. But the Koch–Cuomo rivalry was not over, because Cuomo had earlier been nominated by the Liberal party. This endorsement at a nominating convention without a primary contest had been accomplished with the support of Governor Carey earlier in the spring.

Table 4.13   Votes in the 1977 Democratic Primary Elections

County	Bella Abzug	Herman Badillo	Abraham Beame	Mario Cuomo	Joel Harnett	Edward Koch	Percy Sutton	Total	Total Votes as a Percentage of Registered Democrats
Initial Primary									
New York	56,045	27,193	23,758	25,331	3,390	50,806	35,012	221,535	51.7%
Bronx	20,435	35,007	25,747	23,028	1,860	23,453	24,861	154,391	46.7
Kings	37,236	28,909	63,304	54,845	4,032	49,470	42,903	280,699	46.1
Queens	33,883	9,051	44,607	56,698	3,912	52,002	28,525	228,678	45.2
Richmond	4,314	876	7,337	10,430	593	5,813	1,399	30,762	43.6
Total	151,913	101,036	164,753	170,332	13,787	181,544	132,700	916,065	47.1%
Runoff									
New York				61,505		115,378		176,883	41.3%
Bronx				55,355		69,612		124,967	37.8
Kings				112,587		131,271		243,858	40.1
Queens				105,522		107,033		212,555	42.0
Richmond				19,799		9,835		29,634	42.0
Total				354,768		433,129		787,897	40.5%

Source: New York City Board of Elections.

Table 4.14   Votes in the 1977 Mayoral Election

Candidate	Number	Percent
Koch	717,376	50.0%
Cuomo		
Total	587,913	41.0
Liberal	522,942	36.4
Neighborhood Preservation	64,971	4.5
Goodman	58,606	4.1
Farber	57,437	4.0
Other candidates*a*	13,822	1.0
Total	1,435,154	100.0%

Source: New York City Board of Elections.

*a*Includes Louis Wein of the City Independents, Vito Battista of United Taxpayers, Elijah Boyd of the Labor party, William Lawry of the Free Libertarians, and scattered other votes.

In addition to Koch and Cuomo, the general election included Republican and Conservative candidates. Roy Goodman, a state senator known as a moderate Republican, sought his party's nomination but was challenged by the more conservative radio personality Barry Farber. Goodman won the primary with 57 percent of the 76,399 votes, but Farber remained in the general election by winning the uncontested nomination of the Conservative party.

In the general election Koch and Cuomo seemed to reverse roles. In the primary runoff Cuomo had been the establishment candidate and Koch the insurgent; now Koch was the candidate supported by most of the regular political organizations and leading national and state Democratic figures, including President Jimmy Carter and Governor Carey. Koch also won some union support from civil service workers, but his opposition to Westway (a large highway construction project) led the AFL-CIO and the Building and Construction Trades Council to support Cuomo.

Koch won the general election with just under 50 percent of the vote. (See Table 4.14.) Cuomo gained 41 percent; Goodman and Farber each received about 4 percent, and numerous other minor candidates divided the rest. Koch outpolled Cuomo in every borough but Queens.

With respect to the four basic issues of urban politics, the 1977 election is an anomaly. The performance of Beame in the fiscal crisis displaced other issues, and candidates opposing Beame in the primary distinguished themselves by personal traits rather than policy stands. The division between regulars and reformers became virtually meaningless. Beame, who in 1961 ran on Wagner's "reform" ticket, was truly a regular with a strong base in the Brooklyn county organization. Koch, once a reformer who fought De-Sapio, ran initially with the support of some reform clubs, but he also made alliances with the regular county leaders in Brooklyn and the Bronx for the runoff. Cuomo was backed by the governor and Queens regulars, but he sought to present a reformer image. Sutton was a product of the Manhattan regular organization and Badillo was a Bronx reformer, but it was their

Table 4.15 Voting Distribution Index for Mayoral Elections, 1977

Neighborhood	Initial Primary						Runoff		General	
	Koch	Sutton	Abzug	Badillo	Beame	Cuomo	Koch	Cuomo	Koch	Cuomo
Williamsburg	0.77	0.12	0.19	1.49	3.91	0.13	1.34	0.55	1.64	0.22
Forest Hills	1.56	0.04	1.19	0.23	1.43	0.50	NA	NA	1.51	0.45
Bedford-Stuyvesant	0.29	5.46	0.39	0.16	0.22	0.16	0.77	1.28	1.24	0.75
Harlem	0.79	3.30	0.97	0.81	0.29	0.28	1.03	0.97	1.32	0.60
Bushwick	0.16	0.88	0.32	6.06	0.37	0.27	1.95	1.06	1.32	0.63
Lower East Side	0.33	0.71	1.54	4.56	0.17	0.16	1.21	0.74	1.46	0.34
Bensonhurst	0.39	0.03	0.41	0.14	0.77	3.68	0.13	2.06	0.18	2.07
Citywide percentage	19.8%	14.5%	16.6%	11.0%	18.0%	18.6%	55.0%	45.0%	48.3%	39.5%

Source: New York City Board of Elections.

Note: NA, not available. See appendix for definition of Voting Distribution Index.

98

ethnic or racial origins rather than their stand on reformism that distinguished them.

Traces of traditional ethnic politics were evident in the relatively strong support Sutton received in black neighborhoods and Badillo received in Hispanic neighborhoods (see Table 4.15), but the practice of assembling balanced tickets remained a historical artifact. The candidates in the primary ran on their own without running mates for other offices, and the primary contests provided a Democratic slate consisting of Jewish candidates for mayor (Koch) and comptroller (Harrison "Jay" Goldin) and a white woman (Carol Bellamy) for council president.

Interestingly, racial conflicts, which were present in the two previous city-wide elections, were subdued in 1977. Although Koch's emphasis on his support of the death penalty could be interpreted as an effort to appeal to some antiblack sentiment, it was not highly effective. Koch drew heavy support in Jewish neighborhoods, but Cuomo drew support in the Italian neighborhood. (See Table 4.15.) Black neighborhoods, after initially supporting Sutton, divided their votes almost evenly in the runoff and then gave their support to Koch on the Democratic line in the general election.

Finally, although fiscal matters were prominent in this election, none of the Democratic candidates presented themselves as champions of the traditional money-provider interests. All sought union support (and the unions had, ironically, become the new money-providers in the fiscal crisis), and none presented comprehensive plans for fiscal recovery. In the general election, Goodman and Farber presented philosophically conservative positions, but they won only a small minority of the votes. Even in this fiscally oriented period, New Yorkers remained overwhelmingly supportive of service-demanding candidates.

The 1981 Elections

Koch's successful collaboration with state officials in handling the city's financial problems, a turnaround in the city's economic fortunes, and his skillful use of mass media made him a popular mayor. The major point his critics raised was his failure to develop harmonious relations with minority groups in the city. The senior minority appointees in his administration left after relatively brief tenures, and Koch's rhetoric before the media was seen by some as pandering to white biases or as unnecessarily unsympathetic to minority concerns.

Koch seemed sure to win the Democratic nomination in 1981, and any opposition would likely come from the liberal end of the party. In anticipation of a potential liberal fusion campaign, Koch decided to seek the nomination of both the Democratic and Republican parties.[22] In exchange for a pledge not to run for governor in the next year (which he violated), Koch obtained the support of four of the five Republican county leaders and was given their nomination without a primary contest.

Koch was challenged in the Democratic primary. The candidate was As-

Table 4.16   Votes in the 1981 Democratic Primary

County	Edward Koch	Frank Barbaro	Melvin Klenetsky	Total	Total Votes as a Percentage of Registered Democrats
New York	78,686	67,630	5,648	151,964	37.8%
Bronx	51,420	31,949	5,298	88,667	29.2
Kings	115,150	63,861	8,183	187,194	35.2
Queens	89,304	40,686	4,706	134,696	27.1
Richmond	12,791	5,243	517	18,551	24.0
Total	347,351	209,369	24,352	581,072	32.1%

Source: New York City Board of Elections.

semblyman Frank Barbaro, relatively unknown and with liberal views. Barbaro also sought the Liberal party nomination but lost at the nominating convention to Mary Codd.

Barbaro received support from some minority group leaders and segments of the labor movement, but Koch remained the clear favorite. He won the primary with 60 percent of the vote. (See Table 4.16.) Koch had strong majorities in every borough, including the reformers' usual stronghold of Manhattan. But turnout for the election was just 581,072, a decline of more than one-third from the figure in the 1977 primary.

With both the Democratic and Republican nominations, Koch had little difficulty in the general election. Barbaro remained in the race with a line on the newly formed Unity party, ultimately receiving only about 13 percent of the vote. (See Table 4.17.) Koch triumphed with fully 75 percent of the vote, including 60 percent on the Democratic line and nearly 15 percent as a Republican.

Koch's landslide victory was aided by a lopsided distribution of campaign contributions. He had amassed about $450,000 in a campaign fund before the primary contest began in earnest; he received $913,000 in contributions during the primary period and another $321,000 during the general elections.

Table 4.17   Votes in the 1981 Mayoral Election

Candidate	Number	Percent
Koch		
Total	912,622	74.6%
Democrat	738,288	60.4
Republican	174,334	14.3
Barbaro	162,719	13.3
Esposito	60,100	4.9
Codd	41,718	3.4
Other candidates[a]	45,489	3.7
Total	1,222,648	100.0%

Source: New York City Board of Elections.

[a]Includes Jeronimo Dominguez of Right-to-Life party, Judith Jones of Free Libertarians, Wells Tobb of Socialist Workers, and 4 write-in votes.

Table 4.18 Voting Distribution Index for Primary
Election, 1981

Neighborhood	Koch	Barbaro
Williamsburg	1.16	0.80
Forest Hills	1.27	0.32
Bedford-Stuyvesant	0.49	1.83
Harlem	0.39	1.96
Bushwick	0.92	1.16
Lower East Side	0.69	1.50
Bensonhurst	0.86	1.25
Citywide percentage	59.80%	36.00%

Source: New York City Board of Elections.
Note: See appendix for definition of Voting Distribution Index.

Koch was able to spend over $1.5 million during the campaign and ended it
with cash in the bank. In contrast, Barbaro spent about $168,000 during the
primary and $58,000 during the general election, and he ended about
$13,000 in debt.

Although the 1981 election was far less competitive than the 1977 contest,
it resembled the earlier campaign in the small role played by the conventional
issues. Koch, who initially established a reputation as a reformer, was now
strongly backed by the Democratic county leaders as well as the Republican
party. While ethnic loyalties probably helped Koch in Jewish neighborhoods
and Barbaro in Italian ones (see Table 4.18), the Democratic "balanced"
ticket was the same combination of two Jewish men and a white woman as in
1977.

The only basic issue affecting voter behavior in 1981 seems to be the
division over matters of race relations. As the data in Table 4.18 reveal,
minority neighborhoods (and especially the black neighborhoods) gave strong
support to Barbaro over Koch. Koch's symbolic positions on race issues were
drawing support from a majority of those who voted, although blacks began
to register their dissent.

The 1985 Election

After being elected mayor in 1981, Koch ran an unsuccessful campaign for
governor in 1982. He lost in the Democratic primary to Mario Cuomo, his
former rival for the mayoralty.[23] Supporting Koch in his campaign was City
Council President Carol Bellamy, who would become mayor if Koch were
elevated to governor.

Despite the loss in the gubernatorial contest, Koch remained a popular
mayor. His critics were limited to the Republicans, who objected to his broken
promise and candidacy for governor, and those who felt he continued to
neglect the building of harmonious race relations as an important municipal
priority.

In 1985, Koch faced a challenge in the Democratic primary from two
credible candidates. Herman Farrell, the Manhattan Democratic leader of

Table 4.19   Votes in the 1985 Democratic Primary

County	Edward Koch	Carol Bellamy	Herman Farrell	Other Candidates[a]	Total	Total Votes as a Percentage of Registered Democrats
New York	97,993	49,993	24,832	7,033	179,851	36.3%
Bronx	75,965	15,944	20,297	6,583	118,789	32.3
Kings	131,465	36,190	27,158	9,470	204,283	31.2
Queens	113,401	22,976	16,540	4,644	157,561	30.8
Richmond	17,327	2,647	1,018	538	21,530	24.9
Total	436,151	127,750	89,845	28,268	682,014	32.2%

Source: New York City Board of Elections.

[a]Includes Frederick Newman, Gilbert DiLucia, and Judith Rubinstein.

African-American heritage, raised questions about Koch's ability to serve all New Yorkers. Carol Bellamy, a two-term city council president, also criticized Koch's performance. Her position was compromised in some observers' views, however, by her earlier support of the mayor's gubernatorial race.

Koch won in the primary with 64 percent of the votes. (See Table 4.19.) Bellamy and Farrell gained only 19 and 13 percent, respectively. Koch won a clear majority of votes in every borough. The total number of votes, 682,014, was 17 percent above the low turnout primary of 1981.

In the general election, Koch was opposed by Bellamy, who won the nomination of the Liberal party, and Diane McGrath, nominee of both the Republican and Conservative parties. (See Table 4.20.) Koch won with 74 percent of the vote compared to Bellamy's 10 percent and McGrath's 9 percent. Turnout in this election was under 1.2 million, down 4 percent from the very low figure of 1981.

The 1985 election was similar to the 1981 contest in the issues raised and

Table 4.20   Votes in the 1985 Mayoral Election

Candidate	Number	Percent
Koch		
Total	868,260	74.2%
Democrat	862,226	73.6
Independent	6,034	0.5
Bellamy	113,471	9.7
McGrath		
Total	101,668	8.7
Republican	79,508	6.8
Conservative	22,160	1.9
Other candidates[a]	87,505	7.5
Total	1,170,904	100.0%

Source: New York City Board of Elections.

[a]Includes Lew Y. Levin of Right-to-Life party, Leonara Fulani of New Alliance, Marjorie Stambers of Separatists, Jarvis Turner of People Before Profits, Andrea Gonzalez of Socialist Workers, and Gilbert DiLucia of Coalition.

Table 4.21 Voting Distribution Index for Primary Election, 1985

Neighborhood	Koch	Farrell	Bellamy
Williamsburg	0.44	0.26	3.47
Forest Hills	1.38	0.09	0.58
Bedford-Stuyvesant	0.56	2.52	1.24
Harlem	0.57	3.00	0.98
Bushwick	1.02	1.21	0.76
Lower East Side	0.93	1.27	0.48
Bensonhurst	1.27	0.18	0.60
Citywide percentage	64.00%	13.20%	18.70%

Source: New York City Board of Elections.

Note: See appendix for definition of Voting Distribution Index.

not raised. Again reform and regular divisions were virtually irrelevant. With support from the county leaders outside Manhattan, Koch was clearly a regular. But Farrell was himself Manhattan county leader, so their battle was not over this issue. In this year the traditional concern for a "balanced" ticket also was ignored. With City Council President Bellamy a mayoral candidate, the Democrats ran three Jewish men for the three citywide offices—Koch, Goldin, and Andrew Stein to replace Bellamy.

As in 1981, the only serious issue before the voters was Koch's handling of race relations, and the presence of a black candidate intensified the issue. Farrell drew very strong support in black neighborhoods (see Table 4.21), but Koch's style continued to draw support from the majority of voters.

Finally, the financial advantage Koch enjoyed in the 1981 elections became even greater during the 1985 campaign. Koch had started rebuilding his war chest shortly after the 1981 elections and was successful to an unprecedented degree. He raised and spent $6.4 million for the 1985 primary election. In contrast, Bellamy was able to spend only about $800,000 and ended the campaign in debt. Farrell raised even less, about $130,000.[24]

The 1989 Election

The popularity evident in Koch's one-sided 1985 election victory soon began to unravel in his third term. A major cause was a series of corruption scandals involving many of his close associates.[25] Although few believed Koch himself was "on the take," the dishonesty evident among many of his supporters and friends tarnished the mayor's image.

The epidemic of corruption began with a seemingly mysterious, unsuccessful suicide attempt by Queens Borough President Donald Manes early on the morning of January 10, 1986. It soon became apparent that Manes's suicide attempt was in response to an FBI investigation that was leading his way. On January 28 Manes took a self-designated "leave of absence" from his position as borough president and county leader; three weeks later he formally resigned. Manes eventually committed suicide on March 13, 1986. Subsequent investigations revealed extensive corruption in Manes's county organization, much of it made possible by people appointed to city positions by Koch at Manes's request.

Similar, if less melodramatic events surrounded Bronx county leader Stanley Friedman. He was indicted in March 1986 on charges of corruption that resulted in state and federal criminal convictions and a sentence of 12 years in federal prison. Friedman's support for Koch and his close dealings with Koch appointees further harmed the mayor's reputation.

Another county leader who supported Koch, Brooklyn's Meade Esposito, suffered a similar fate. In March 1987 he was indicted along with Representative Mario Biaggi for bribery and fraud in connection with the awarding of a federal contract. The investigation leading to the indictment also yielded numerous taped phone conversations linking Esposito to organized crime figures. In September he was found guilty and sentenced to a two-year prison term, which was suspended in consideration of his advanced age.

Esposito's link to Koch was highlighted by the case of Anthony Ameruso. Esposito had recommended Ameruso as transportation commissioner to Koch at the start of his administration in 1978. Koch appointed Ameruso despite the finding of a Koch-appointed screening panel that he was unfit. Ameruso subsequently was responsible for appointing to the Parking Violations Bureau officials who became involved with Manes and Friedman in corrupt activities. Ameruso's admitted responsibility for these poor appointments led him to resign in early 1986. His dishonesty before a commission investigating the matter led to his conviction for lying under oath in July 1987. In October of that year he was sentenced to 16 weekends in jail, 1,000 hours of community service, and 5 years' probation.

Evidence of bad character was prevalent among Koch's personal as well as public associates. Bess Myerson, who staged a romance with Koch during the 1977 campaign to kill rumors of his homosexuality, had been rewarded with an appointment as commissioner of consumer affairs. In 1987 she was charged with appointing a judge's daughter to a city position in order to get a favorable divorce settlement for her lover (a construction contractor who did significant work for the city and who later was found guilty of income tax evasion).

Initially Koch defended Myerson, giving her a leave of absence during the initial investigation. Finally, in April 1987, he accepted her resignation. After a highly publicized trial spanning more than three months, Myerson was acquitted, but the trial revealed her to be a commissioner with poor judgment offset by strong mayoral support.

Similarly, a longtime and loyal Koch staffer, Victor Botnick, had been rewarded with appointment to the chairmanship of the New York City Health and Hospitals Corporation. Both Botnick and Koch were subsequently embarrassed by revelations that Botnick had lied about his qualifications by claiming a college degree he had never earned. Koch was obliged to accept Botnick's resignation too.

The perception that patronage was endemic to the Koch administration was reinforced by investigations in early 1989 focusing on the "Talent Bank." Initially established years earlier as an effort to recruit well-qualified minority group members to public service, it had been transformed to a patronage-dispensing operation. Its head was a special mayoral assistant, Joseph DeVincenzo, with an office in the basement of City Hall. "Joe D.," as he was called, resigned (or more accurately retired, after artfully arranging for the most generous pension arrangement possible) and was subsequently indicted for perjury during the Talent Bank investigation.

These and other scandals captured headlines through much of Koch's third term as indictments were followed with court proceedings and, in most cases, with sentencing. Despite the almost ceaseless bad news and what many saw as a concomitant personal depression, Koch decided to seek an unprecedented fourth term.

Three candidates challenged Koch in the Democratic primary. Comptroller Harrison Goldin decided to run for mayor rather than seek a fifth term. However, his service as comptroller throughout Koch's mayoralty made him closely attached to Koch in many voters eyes, and he found few issues with which to distinguish himself. Richard Ravitch was a businessman who had never sought elected office before but had a distinguished public service record. He had been appointed by Governor Hugh Carey to chair the Metropolitan Transportation Authority, and he had served as Koch's appointee to chair a charter revision commission immediately prior to his candidacy. Ravitch, widely respected by many business and civic leaders, had a campaign style that excited few voters. He avoided direct personal criticism of Koch and found no issue that dramatically distinguished him from his rivals.

Koch's most formidable challenger was Manhattan Borough President David N. Dinkins. Dinkins entered the campaign after being urged to do so by black, Hispanic, and labor leaders. His labor support included the largest municipal employee union, District Council 37, and the union representing voluntary hospital workers. Both had large proportions of minority workers.

In the wake of the scandals, which caused several county leaders to lose their positions, and faced with viable opposition, Koch was not able to retain the support of the Democratic party leadership. Dinkins was endorsed by the Manhattan county leader and most of the borough's local club leaders; Dinkins also was endorsed by the recently elected Bronx Borough President Fernando Ferrer, who had replaced the incarcerated Stanley Friedman as the most powerful party figure in that borough. In Queens, where Claire Shulman had replaced Manes as borough president, the county leaders gave their support to Ravitch. With Esposito's departure, political splits in the Brooklyn organizations grew deeper; Borough President Howard Golden endorsed Jay Goldin, but numerous local club leaders in heavily minority portions of Brooklyn supported Dinkins.

The most significant issue dividing Koch and Dinkins was race relations.[26] Koch's self-proclaimed "feisty" style remained popular with some whites, but Dinkins presented a more soft-spoken approach that emphasized conciliation. Events worked to highlight the potential of Dinkins's alternative style.

The almost disastrous condition of race relations in the city was dramatized by events before and during the primary campaign. In 1987 a group of white youths with baseball bats chased two black men from the Howard

Table 4.22   Votes in the 1989 Democratic Primary

County	David Dinkins	Harrison Goldin	Edward Koch	Richard Ravitch	Total	Total Votes as a Percentage of Registered Democrats
New York	151,113	6,889	96,923	17,499	272,424	52.2%
Bronx	101,274	4,951	66,600	5,946	178,771	49.5
Kings	170,440	9,619	139,268	13,214	332,541	51.7
Queens	113,952	5,857	129,262	9,443	258,514	52.8
Richmond	11,122	1,493	24,260	1,432	38,307	44.3
Total	547,901	28,809	456,313	47,534	1,080,557	51.4%

Source: New York City Board of Elections.

Beach neighborhood in Queens, causing one to be killed on a busy highway while trying to escape. Then Koch antagonized many whites as well as blacks by his sharp criticism of candidate Jesse Jackson during the 1988 presidential primary campaign. Finally, just a few days before the September primary, a group of white men in Bensonhurst shot and killed a young black man who had entered the neighborhood to examine a used car for sale.

In this context of troubled race relations, New Yorkers held their primary election. In the Democratic contest, turnout was a record high of nearly 1.1 million. Dinkins won with just over half the total; Koch gained 42 percent, and Goldin and Ravitch divided the remainder. (See Table 4.22.)

The Republicans had a primary contest between Rudolph Giuliani and Ronald Lauder. Giuliani was a federal prosecutor who had been instrumental in the indictment of several of Koch's associates. He emphasized his integrity and campaigned primarily against Koch rather than the other candidates. Lauder was a member of a wealthy family whose parents owned a large cosmetics firm. He had been appointed ambassador to Austria by President Ronald Reagan and was now seeking to establish himself as an important political figure. His campaign emphasized his business knowledge and his concern for stimulating economic growth in New York City. Giuliani emerged as a decisive victor with 77,150, or 67 percent, of the 115,110 votes cast.

In the general election, Dinkins was a clear favorite. All his primary opponents, including Koch, pledged their support and the full party organization backed him. The civil service employee unions also campaigned strongly. In contrast, Giuliani had only a small and often ineffective Republican party base. Moreover, his campaign had been aimed primarily against Koch with an emphasis on Giuliani's strong record fighting corruption.

Dinkins waged an essentially defensive campaign. He sought to undermine Giuliani's law enforcement background by pledging to be the toughest mayor on crime the city ever had. Giuliani questioned Dinkins's integrity by revitalizing previous inquiries into Dinkins's personal finances. Dinkins had failed to file income tax returns for several years in the early 1970s and as a result was obliged to withdraw from consideration as a deputy mayor under Beame, although he continued to serve as city clerk and was never charged

Table 4.23 Votes in the 1989 Mayoral Election

Candidate	Number	Percent
Dinkins	917,544	48.3%
Giuliani		
Total	870,464	45.8
Republican	815,387	42.9
Liberal	55,077	2.9
Other*a*	111,837	5.9
Total	1,899,845	100.0%

Source: New York City Board of Elections.

*a*Includes Henry Hewes receiving 17,460 votes as the Right-to-Life party candidate; Ronald Lauder receiving 9,271 votes as the Conservative party candidate; and 85,106 other votes cast for candidates of the New Alliance, Socialist Workers party, Workers League, Independent Fusion, Liberation party, and write-in candidates.

with a criminal offense. More recently, while Manhattan borough president, Dinkins had sought to avoid conflict of interest charges on some Board of Estimate votes on cable TV franchises by transferring his stock in a cable TV company to his son. Giuliani supporters raised questions about the legality of the transfer and the propriety of votes on the matter cast by Dinkins's representative on the board.

The result of the campaign was a very close general election. (See Table 4.23.) Turnout reached nearly 1.9 million, up 62 percent from 1985. Dinkins was victorious with a bare 48 percent of the total, defeating Giuliani by just 47,080 votes. Giuliani's total of 870,464 included more than 55,000 votes on the Liberal party line.

The nature of both Dinkins's primary victory and his close general election contest suggest that race relations was the dominant issue in 1989. He defeated Koch with a large turnout and strong support among black people. As Table 4.24 shows, Dinkins won almost unanimously in black neighborhoods in the primary. But for similar reasons, his contest with Giuliani was surpris-

Table 4.24 Voting Distribution Index for Mayoral Elections, 1989

	Primary				General	
Neighborhood	Dinkins	Goldin	Koch	Ravitch	Dinkins	Giuliani
Williamsburg	0.66	2.26	1.34	0.36	0.84	1.11
Forest Hills	0.18	0.78	2.01	0.77	0.50	1.55
Bedford-Stuyvesant	1.85	0.30	0.06	0.68	1.99	0.02
Harlem	1.78	0.37	0.09	1.20	1.91	0.03
Bushwick	1.26	1.30	0.65	1.11	1.52	0.45
Lower East Side	1.13	2.78	0.72	1.16	1.66	0.28
Bensonhurst	0.27	1.30	1.86	0.95	0.14	1.96
Citywide percentage	50.70%	2.70%	42.20%	4.40%	48.30%	45.82%

Source: New York City Board of Elections.

Note: See appendix for definition of Voting Distribution Index.

ingly close. Despite the fact that nearly 70 percent of New Yorkers are registered Democrats, the Republican received almost half the votes. Obviously, many white Democrats cast their votes for Giuliani.

Conclusion

This chapter began by identifying four issues or concerns that potentially divide voters in mayoral elections: the economic conflict between service-demanders versus money-providers, party conflicts between regulars and reformers, disputes over ethnicity, and, finally, conflicts over the extent to which efforts should be made to incorporate black people into local political and social institutions. The last eight mayoral elections support some general conclusions about each of these issues.

First, although conflict between service-seeking interests and money-providing interests exists in New York City, it is not a significant conflict in electoral politics. Simply put, the overwhelming majority of New York voters sympathize with service-demanders; representatives of money-providing interests stand little chance of gaining a majority of votes. Fiscal conservatives, when they proclaim themselves, get few votes. Consequently, elections are rarely contests between these opposing points of view. However, this is not to say that money-providers are without political influence—only that it is wielded in other arenas than elections.

Second, the significance of battles between regulars and reformers is on the wane. In the 1960s mayoral contests were, foremost, decisions about the role of reform clubs and principles versus party bosses and their supporters in the running of municipal government. And in three successive contests, the regulars lost. But the bosses made a comeback with Beame's 1973 victory, and they enjoyed easy access to City Hall during the Koch years. Dinkins too was groomed in a regular clubhouse environment. But by 1989 divisions within the party were not a key electoral issue. All the major Democratic candidates sought party organization support; none were campaigning against the bosses.

Finally, traditional ethnic politics seems to have faded. Coalitions of county leaders no longer focus on assembling a balanced ticket for citywide offices. Candidates finance and organize campaigns largely outside the structure of county party organizations, and they do so primarily as self-promoting individuals rather than as part of a balanced ticket. Voters may still tend to favor a candidate with a similar ethnic background, but using this propensity to maximize the party's appeal is no longer a dominant concern among party leaders.

In recent elections race relations has become the critical issue. Koch's 1985 victory was rooted in his appeal to a majority of whites, who supported his symbolic actions and rhetoric in opposing claims for favorable actions by blacks; Koch's black opponent, Farrell, failed to mobilize his constituency, and his liberal white opponent, Bellamy, suffered from having supported Koch for governor and from running against a candidate who was black. Koch's 1989 primary defeat reflected shifts in white views brought about by unprovoked violence against blacks by racist white youths and the ability of Dinkins to mobilize black voters. The significance of race endured through the general campaign. Dinkins continued to draw strong support from black voters, but white Democrats who supported Koch shifted to Giuliani in large numbers. Dinkins's victory placed control of City Hall in the hands of a man whose supporters gave him a mandate to pursue positive measures to enhance the integration of minorities into the local political structure, but this constituency consisted of only a plurality of voters. Many, if not most of the New York City electorate did not support Dinkins because they did not share his views on race relations; this suggests the issue will remain a critical dividing line in future contests.

APPENDIX

The most direct way to explore the relations among ethnic identity, racial attitudes, and voting behavior is through individual survey data obtained at the time of elections. Unfortunately, comprehensive and historically consistent data of this sort are not available. In the absence of individual survey data social scientists have turned to a combination of census data and Board of Elections administrative data. Election results typically are published by assembly districts (and are available by subunits known as election districts); census data relating to ethnic and other characteristics are available for small geographic units known as census tracts. For a given election it is possible to link assembly district and census tract boundaries; this permits comparisons of the racial and ethnic composition of a district with its share of votes for a given candidate. However, this approach has two important limitations. First, assembly districts are relatively large units and variations within the group may outweigh similarities. Second, due to reapportionment, assembly district boundaries have changed significantly between elections; this makes longitudinal comparisons of voting behavior in an assembly district either impossible or misleading.

To cope with these substantial problems, another approach was used for this study. Specific neighborhoods whose racial and ethnic character are believed to have remained *relatively* stable in the post-1960 period were identified. These neighborhoods were defined in terms of specific election districts for each mayoral election. In addition, data for the census tracts most closely overlapping the election districts were taken from the 1960, 1970, and 1980 censuses to determine the extent to which the neighborhood's population characteristics had remained stable over the period.

Seven neighborhoods were selected to represent four groups. Two predominantly Jewish neighborhoods are Forest Hills and Williamsburg; two predominantly Hispanic neighborhoods are Bushwick and the Lower East Side; two predominantly black neighborhoods are Bedford-Stuyvesant and Harlem; a predominantly Italian neighborhood is Bensonhurst. Relevant data from the census tracts comprising these neighborhoods are summarized in Table A.1.

The significance of the ethnic character of a neighborhood for voting behavior is gauged by a "voting distribution index" (VDI). This number is calculated by dividing the actual share of the neighborhood's votes a candidate received by the share of the total votes that candidate received citywide. If all neighborhoods (and hence presumably all ethnic groups) voted in the same way, then the VDI for all candidates in all neighborhoods would be 1.0. To the extent a neighborhood favors a candidate, the VDI for that candidate in the area will exceed 1.0; to the extent a neighborhood disapproves a candidate, the VDI for that candidate in the area will fall below 1.0. The VDI for a neighborhood whose ethnic composition is relatively homogeneous can be used to gauge that ethnic group's relative support for a given candidate.

Table A.1   Characteristics of Selected New York City Neighborhoods, 1960, 1970, and 1980

Neighborhood	1960	1970	1980
Williamsburg			
Total population	16,709	15,206	15,996
East European population	11,176	9,523	10,755
East European as a percentage of total population	66.9%	62.6%	67.2%
Median income	$4,454	$5,863	$8,389
Median income as a percentage of a citywide median	73.1%	59.1%	49.4%
Forest Hills			
Total population	42,711	51,714	45,880
East European population	20,419	22,212	17,849
East European as a percentage of total population	47.8%	43.0%	38.9%
Median income	$9,621	$14,716	$24,220
Median income as a percentage of citywide median	158.0%	148.3%	144.0%
Harlem			
Total population	29,808	18,800	10,998
Black population	29,422	18,583	10,755
Blacks as a percentage of total population	98.7%	98.9%	97.8%
Median income	$3,687	$5,167	$8,471
Median income as a percentage of citywide median	60.5%	52.1%	50.4%
Bedford-Stuyvesant			
Total population	39,606	36,253	30,001
Black population	38,207	35,553	29,413
Blacks as a percentage of total population	96.5%	98.1%	98.0%
Median income	$4,685	$6,810	$9,601
Median income as a percentage of citywide median	76.9%	68.6%	57.1%
Bushwick			
Total population	12,543	12,121	9,124
Hispanic population	5,217	6,573	7,267
Hispanic as a percentage of total population	41.6%	54.2%	79.7%
Median income	$4,498	$5,981	$7,831
Median income as a percentage of citywide median	73.8%	60.3%	46.6%
Lower East Side			
Total population	32,954	28,761	17,407
Hispanic population	11,134	15,892	13,026
Hispanic as a percentage of total population	33.8%	55.3%	74.8%
Median income	$3,828	$5,260	$6,117
Median income as a percentage of citywide median	62.9%	53.0%	36.4%

(*continued*)

Neighborhood	1960	1970	1980
Bensonhurst			
Total population	15,386	14,447	12,469
Population of Italian ancestry	8,840	8,293	10,107
Italian ancestry as a percentage of total population	57.5%	57.4%	81.1%
Median income	$6,372	$10,201	$17,627
Median income as a percentage of citywide median	104.6%	102.8%	104.8%

Source: U.S. Department of Commerce, Bureau of the Census.

PUBLIC FINANCING
OF CAMPAIGNS

The November 1989 election was a milestone in New York City's political history. For the first time the campaigns of candidates for municipal offices were financed partly by public funds. With this historic election, New York City joined a small number of other cities and states that provide partial public financing of campaigns. The campaign financing program was created under the New York City Campaign Finance Act, signed into law in March 1988.

This chapter provides background on the city's program and examines its efficacy in achieving its goals. The program's goals are to reduce the influence of large contributors, to slow campaign expenditure growth, to encourage more candidates to run for office, and to educate the public about electoral issues.

The remainder of this chapter consists of four parts. The first describes the types of campaign finance reform pursued at the federal, state, and local levels in areas other than New York City and New York State. The second part analyzes the nature of campaign finance regulations in New York State and how the city's new program altered the situation. The third considers how well the program achieved its objectives in the 1989 election. The final section summarizes changes made in 1990 and presents recommendations to make the city's program more effective.

Strategies for Campaign Finance Reform

The New York City program should be assessed in the broader context of national campaign finance reform. Efforts to improve this aspect of the electoral process have pursued four types of action, which are largely complementary rather than mutually exclusive. They are disclosure of finances, limits on contributions, limits on expenditures, and public funding.

The purpose of disclosure is to "deter actual corruption and avoid the appearance of corruption by exposing large contributions and expenditures to the light of publicity."[1] Such disclosure allows the public to judge a candidate on the basis of sources of financial support. Typically, the amount of each significant contribution and the name, address, and occupation of the contributor are required to be disclosed in public reports. Campaign-related spending by type also typically must be reported.

Disclosure requirements are most effective when they specify that detailed information be provided on a timely basis, and when they are well enforced. Poorly enforced disclosure laws put candidates who abide by the requirements at a disadvantage since they risk public censure for activities that less diligent candidates fail to report. Consequently, poor enforcement discourages compliance with the law. Timely disclosure requires that contributions, especially large ones, be reported prior to an election to allow for public dissemination. However, detailed disclosure often makes timely reporting difficult by complicating the expeditious processing of disclosure reports. Because of these problems, public disclosure alone is the weakest type of campaign finance reform.

The purpose of contribution limits is to enjoin candidates from receiving large contributions, contributions from special interests, or both. Restrictions on the amount or sources of donations are designed to reduce the influence of big contributors, or the appearance of such influence, on elected officials.

The effectiveness of contribution limits depends largely on strong enforcement and the absence of loopholes in the law. Contribution restrictions that are not well enforced or contain serious loopholes, as is generally the case, diminish the impact of this type of reform.

The purpose of expenditure limits is to lower campaign costs and reduce any advantage that wealthy or especially well-funded candidates might enjoy. However, since 1976 a U.S. Supreme Court ruling has held that expenditure limits, if not accompanied by public funding of campaigns, are unconstitutional on grounds that they limit freedom of expression. As a consequence, any federal, state, or local laws imposing expenditure limits must be accompanied by public financing programs.

Determining appropriate expenditure limits is a significant problem. If spending ceilings are set high, well-funded candidates tend to spend up to the limit. In such circumstances the limits do little or nothing to control escalating costs or limit advantages of the well funded. If the limits are set too low, incumbents and well-known candidates are favored because their opponents can compensate for lack of public recognition only by spending more. Thus, in order to be effective, expenditure limits should strike a balance between being irrelevant because they are too high and favoring incumbents because they are too low.

Proponents of public funding of campaigns argue that it reduces the influence of special interests on elected officials, encourages nonwealthy individuals to run for office, and restores public confidence in the political system. Public funding programs vary in the number of offices covered, type of elections funded, and whether they fund parties or candidates exclusively.

Some programs provide financing of campaigns for a wide range of elected offices; others fund only a small number of races. Because public funds are typically tightly rationed, the decision to concentrate a program's limited resources on only a few offices increases the amount of public money participating candidates may receive. Nevertheless, the ideal for many reformers remains to extend public financing to as many elections as possible.

The decision to fund only general election campaigns or both primary and general election campaigns also involves a tradeoff between program cost and impact. Funding both types of campaigns increases the cost of a program. However, because primaries are the only meaningful elections in many areas and in all cases determine who runs in the general election, many reformers urge public funding for both types of elections.

Public funding programs also differ with respect to who receives the funds, party organizations or individual candidate organizations. Programs that exclusively fund political parties may do so only in general elections because primaries are intraparty matters. Programs that fund candidates may do so in both the primary and general elections. Proponents of funding parties argue that it strengthens party organizations while the alternative method weakens them. Supporters of funding candidates contend that it encourages greater candidate independence from party leaders and special interests.

Each of these four general approaches has been adopted by one or more of the nation's governments. New York City's 1988 reform should be placed in the context of this history of reform at the federal, state, and local level.

Federal Reforms

Campaign finance reform was on the federal agenda as early as 1961. In that year, newly elected President John F. Kennedy appointed a President's Commission on Campaign Costs to examine the causes of increased political expenditures and recommend solutions. In 1962 the commission proposed that taxpayers be allowed to deduct from their income taxes up to $1,000 for political contributions. However, this proposal never left the Congress.

In 1966 the Congress authorized an income tax checkoff plan which allowed individuals to designate $1 for a special fund for financing presidential campaigns. The plan was shelved in 1967 when no satisfactory method was found for distributing the funds to the candidates.

Spurred by the tremendous costs of the 1968 presidential and the 1970 congressional campaigns, Congress passed two significant pieces of campaign finance legislation in 1971. The Revenue Act created a public funding program for presidential elections financed by individual income tax checkoffs. The Congress, however, agreed to delay the program's start until the 1976 election in order to obtain President Richard Nixon's approval.

The Federal Election Campaign Act (FECA) was more comprehensive. It applied to all federal elections and sought to increase disclosure requirements and control spending on media advertising. The first goal was accomplished by extending contribution and expenditure reporting to the primaries. The second goal was achieved by limiting total spending on media advertising by candidates for the House and the Senate. The legislators thought that placing a cap on media expenditures would curtail the growth in campaign costs.

In the 1972 presidential election campaign spending continued to increase rapidly. President Nixon spent $61.4 million to defeat Senator George McGovern, who spent $30 million. The newly expanded disclosure laws revealed that 1,254 individuals made large contributions totaling more than $51 million to both candidates.[2]

As a consequence of the high expenditures in 1972 and the unraveling of the Watergate cover-up, Congress moved to strengthen the FECA. In 1974 amendments replaced previous contribution and expenditure limits with considerably stiffer ones, expanded the public funding provisions, and established the Federal Election Commission (FEC) to administer and enforce the FECA.

The amended FECA was challenged in the Supreme Court. In January 1976, the Court ruled important parts of the law unconstitutional in the *Buckley v. Valeo* decision. The major provisions of the FECA and the effect of the Court's decision on them warrant discussion.

Expenditure Limits

The previous limits on media advertising were removed by the 1974 amendments. Instead, the FECA limited three different types of spending. First, the act limited the total amount that presidential and congressional candidates could spend. Second, it limited the amount of their own resources candidates could spend. Third, the law restricted the amount other organizations and individuals could spend independently to elect or defeat a candidate.

The Supreme Court found all of these restrictions unconstitutional. They placed campaign spending under the protection of the First Amendment. However, the Court ruled that candidates who accepted public funds could be obliged to abide by overall limits on spending.

Contribution Limits

The FECA set limits on both single and total contribution amounts. Individual contributions to candidates could not exceed $1,000 per election. Political action committees (PACs) formed by corporations, unions, and other groups could not contribute in excess of $5,000 per election. Finally, political party committees could not contribute more than $5,000 to a candidate in each election. The act also set a $25,000 ceiling on the total contributions an individual could make in an election year. Total PAC contributions were not limited. The Supreme Court ruled that contribution limits did not interfere with free speech and upheld the FECA's provisions in this area.

Enforcement

The FECA created the FEC to receive and publicize candidates' public disclosure reports and to enforce the act. However, the Supreme Court found the FEC unconstitutional on grounds that it violated the Constitution's separation of powers clause. This violation occurred as a result of Congress's power to appoint some of the FEC's members. Shortly afterwards, the commission was reconstituted by the Congress to conform with the Court's ruling. In the new arrangement, the president appointed members subject to approval by the Senate.

Public Funding

The federal public funding program was created by the 1971 Revenue Act, but the 1974 FECA amendments altered the initial plan in significant ways. The amendments created two pubic financing programs for presidential campaigns. The first provided partial public financing for candidates during the primary election campaign. The second provided full funding for presidential candidates in the general election. To qualify for matching funds in the pre-nomination period, candidates must receive a total of $5,000, in each of at least 20 states, and the individual contributions that make up this amount may not exceed $250 each. In the general election, the nominees of both major parties are entitled to full public funding. The Supreme Court upheld both public funding programs in its 1976 decision.

The combination of the 1974 FECA amendments and the 1976 Supreme Court decision (plus some additional FECA amendments in 1979) have, in effect, created two separate federal campaign finance systems. For presidential campaigns there is public funding for candidates who accept the expenditure limits. For congressional candidates there are contribution limits and disclosure requirements, but no public funding or expenditure limits.

The nearly 14 years of experience under these two federal systems yields some important lessons about the different campaign finance strategies. The results of the publicly funded presidential system are more encouraging than that of the congressional system.

Changes in Presidential Elections

FECA has effected three major changes in presidential elections: (1) it slowed the growth of campaign spending in the general election; (2) it increased the

Table 5.1 Total Prenomination and General Election Expenditures in Presidential Elections, 1960–1988 (dollars in millions)

Year	Actual Spending	Constant-Dollar (1960) Spending
1960	$30.0	$30.0
1964	60.0	57.3
1968	100.0	85.1
1972	138.0	97.7
1976	160.0	83.2
1980	275.0	98.9
1984	325.0	93.7
1988	500.0	126.5

Source: Herbert E. Alexander, "Financing the Presidential Elections, 1988," paper presented at the International Political Science Association Mid-Term Roundtable, September 8–10, 1989.

importance of small, individual contributors; and (3) it put the two major political parties on a more equal footing in funding their campaigns.

Table 5.1 shows total spending for each presidential election since 1960. Adjusting for inflation, in the period before FECA (1960–1972) expenditures rose a total of 225 percent. In an equal time period after FECA (1976–1988) expenditures grew much less—52 percent. Most of this increase occurred in 1988, when an extensive primary campaign in both parties pushed up the total.

The FECA provision matching individual contributions with public funds during the primary campaign has increased the importance of the small, individual donor. Before 1974, it was not uncommon for a tiny number of big contributors to account for a large portion of a candidate's campaign resources. For example, 28 percent of President Nixon's total contributions in 1972 came from just 124 individuals.[3] As a result of the FECA, candidates now seek a large number of smaller contributions, which can be matched by public funds. For example, in the 1976 elections a total of 975,493 individuals contributed to the candidates in the presidential primaries, and their contributions yielded $24.3 million in matching public funds. The comparable figures for 1980 are 694,077 individuals and $30.9 million; figures for 1984 are 793,565 individuals and $34.9 million. In 1988 fully $65.7 million was paid in matching funds, but the number of individual contributions is not yet available.[4]

FECA also has established parity in general election campaign spending between the two major parties. The costs of presidential general elections since 1968 are shown in Table 5.2. Before 1976, the Republicans outspent the Democrats by a large margin. From 1976 on, however, the public grants to both parties have been the same. Proponents of public funding argue that this record justifies expanding the program to congressional campaigns. However, the presidential system is not without problems. The two most significant problems are independent expenditures and "soft money."

Independent expenditures refer to spending for or against a candidate

Table 5.2 Expenditures in Presidential
General Elections, 1968–1988

Year	Republican	Democrat
1968	$25,402,000	$11,594,000
1972	61,400,000	30,000,000
1976	21,800,000	21,800,000
1980	29,440,000	29,440,000
1984	40,400,000	40,400,000
1988	46,100,000	46,100,000

Sources: Figures for 1968 to 1976 are from Herbert E.
Alexander, *Financing Politics: Money, Elections, and Political Reform* (Washington, DC: Congressional Quarterly, 1984). Figures for 1980 election are from Herbert
E. Alexander, *Financing the 1980 Election* (Lexington,
MA: Lexington Books, 1983). Figures for 1984 and
1988 elections are from Citizens Research Foundation.
These figures do not include "soft money" or independent expenditures.

which is not coordinated with that candidate's campaign organization. This
spending was ruled a form of free speech by the Supreme Court, and such
spending is not regulated. In theory, such spending occurs independently of a
candidate on whose behalf it is done. However, much evidence exists to the
contrary.[5] As a result, this violation of the spirit, if not the letter of the law has
proved an attractive means of channeling large, otherwise illegal contributions
to candidates. For example, independent spending by PACs grew from $2.2
million to $3.3 million between the 1980 and 1988 presidential elections (and
the 1988 figure is for the prenomination period alone).[6]

In 1979 Congress amended FECA to establish another category of unregu-
lated contributions, which became known as "soft money." This refers to
contributions made to a political party for uses other than a federal election
campaign. The purpose of the amendment was to encourage state and local
"party-building" activities, such as voter registration drives, which were increasingly pushed aside by candidate media advertising expenditures. In practice, however, soft money often is used indirectly to aid presidential candidates.

The use of soft money expanded greatly during the 1980s. In 1980, both
parties raised a total of $19 million in soft money; by 1988, the figure had
risen to $45 million.[7]

In addition to independent expenditures and soft money, there are two
loopholes that allow contributors to skirt the FECA's limits. First, prospective
presidential candidates may form PACs to fund their political activities before
they officially declare their candidacies. For example, Walter Mondale, the
Democratic nominee in 1984, created the Committee for the Future of America shortly after he vacated the vice president's office in 1980. This PAC paid
for Mondale's travel expenses in 1981 and 1982 and provided employment
for people who later became senior staffers in his presidential campaign organization. Second, the law places no ceiling on costs related to internal commu-

nications by labor unions, companies, and other groups that support or oppose a candidate. In the 1984 election, a total of $6.2 million was spent on such communications.[8]

Scandals in Congressional Elections

Although achieving an equitable system of presidential elections remains problematic, that system compares favorably to the one established for congressional campaigns. Despite FECA, congressional campaigns have become highly expensive, with candidates heavily dependent on contributions from PACs.

Campaign spending for congressional races has soared. In 1976 the average cost of winning a seat in the House was $87,200, while a seat in the Senate cost $609,100. In 1986, candidates for the House spent $355,000 on the average, and candidates for the Senate averaged $3,099,554 in spending.[9] The FECA has curbed large, individual contributions to congressional candidates. However, contributions by PACs have grown considerably. In the 1974 election PACs gave a total of $12.5 million to congressional candidates. By 1986 this figure had risen to $132.2 million.[10]

Dissatisfaction with the congressional system is now widespread. Members of Congress feel constant pressure to raise funds for the next election in order to protect themselves from challenges by well-funded candidates. This makes the sitting Congress heavily dependent on PAC contributions, a situation which threatens the integrity of the legislature.[11]

State Reforms

Federal election reform during the early 1970s stimulated similar legislative activity at the state level. During this period, nearly every state passed laws that affected campaign financing. Most states simply tightened their current laws to prevent the worst abuses, but some states altered their laws in major ways. In the 1980s state reform activity slowed considerably, but recently campaign finance has returned to the top of a few states' legislative agendas.

The renewed interest in reform results from growing disenchantment with the present system in many states. Campaign spending in the states has grown as rapidly as congressional spending. Expenditures for state legislative races now approximate those for House races, and expenditures for gubernatorial campaigns are similar to those for Senate campaigns.[12] Information on total PAC spending at the state level is unavailable, but data from several states suggest that much of this increased spending has been fueled by growing PAC contributions, mostly to incumbents.[13]

Although every state changed its campaign finance laws during the 1970s, the extent of regulation varies greatly. Every state requires some form of campaign finance reporting from candidates, but only 22 states publish these data in an effort to make disclosure more effective.[14] Twenty states prohibit

Table 5.3 Major Provisions of State Public Campaign Financing Laws

State	Financing	Recipient	Elections Covered	Offices Covered
Alabama	Add-on	Parties	General	NA
Florida	Appropriation	Candidates	P/G	Statewide
Hawaii	Checkoff	Candidates	General	Statewide, legislative, local
Idaho	Checkoff	Parties	General	NA
Indiana	Special fee	Parties	General	NA
Iowa	Checkoff[a]	Parties	General	NA
Kentucky	Checkoff	Parties	General	NA
Maine	Checkoff	Parties	General	NA
Maryland	Appropriation	Candidates	General	Statewide, legislative
Massachusetts	Add-on	Candidates	P/G	Statewide
Michigan	Checkoff	Candidates	P/G	Governor, lieutenant governor
Minnesota	Checkoff	Candidates	General	Statewide, legislative
Montana	Add-on	Candidates	P/G	Statewide
New Jersey	Checkoff	Candidates	General	Governor
North Carolina	Checkoff	Parties	General	NA
Texas	Checkoff	Parties	General	NA
Utah	Checkoff	Parties	General	NA
Virginia	Checkoff	Parties	General	NA
Wisconsin	Checkoff	Candidates	General	Statewide, legislative

Source: The Council of State Governments, *Campaign Finance Ethics and Lobby Law: Blue Book, 1988–1989* (Lexington, KY: Council of State Governments, 1988), Table 16.

Note: NA, Not applicable; funds go to parties for general purposes, not individual campaigns. P/G, primary and general elections.

[a]Since 1984, Iowa taxpayers are allowed to add $1 to their tax forms along with, or instead of, the checkoff.

direct corporate contributions, and 10 proscribe direct union contributions. Nineteen states place limitations on both corporate and union PAC contributions; the remainder do not limit contributions from these sources. Fully 26 states place no limit on the amount an individual may contribute to a candidate, while the maximum permissible contribution in the other 24 states ranges from $800 to $60,000 for a gubernatorial election.[15]

At the end of the 1980s, 20 states had public campaign funding programs. The state programs differ in their financing, scope of elections covered, and whether they provide funds to political parties or directly to candidates. (See Table 5.3).

In general, the states use one of two different financing methods: the income tax checkoff or the income tax "add-on." The checkoff permits the taxpayer to divert a dollar or two of tax liability to a special fund for candidates or parties. The add-on allows the taxpayer to add to his liability a dollar or two for a campaign fund. Thirteen states raise money through the checkoff and four through the add-on. (Two states make appropriations from their general fund and one diverts revenues from special fees.) The checkoff method has achieved considerably more success in generating funds than the add-on.

In nine states, candidates directly receive public money; in the other 11 states political parties receive the public funds. Parties that receive public funds are prohibited from using the money in primary campaigns. In most states where parties receive funds, the organizations are restricted to using the money for their general operating expenses rather than specific campaigns.

States that finance candidates directly vary in the offices for which funds are available. Four of the nine states assist candidates for both legislative and statewide positions; four provide support for statewide candidates only; and New Jersey funds only gubernatorial candidates. Five states provide public funds to candidates in both the primary and general elections; four finance only general election candidates.

The 20 states with public campaign financing can be classified according to the strength of their program's effect on elections. Impact may be measured by the share of total campaign expenditures derived from public funds. The weak programs use tax add-ons and/or give funds only to parties. The add-ons generate relatively small amounts of money; funds given to parties—when they are restricted to administrative costs—are usually spread thinly among a large number of candidates. Fully 15 of the 20 state programs have limited impact because they follow one or both of these approaches.

The stronger programs use the checkoff and provide funds to candidates directly. There are five such state programs: Hawaii, Michigan, Minnesota, New Jersey, and Wisconsin. New Jersey finances only gubernatorial races; Michigan funds candidates only for governor and lieutenant governor. The taxpayer participation rates in both states have proved sufficient to finance these elections; in each state public funds account for nearly 60 percent of the total campaign receipts in the general election.[16] Since both states' programs were started, the Republican and Democratic candidates for governor have accepted public funds in every election. The other three states in this group cover more elections in their programs (for example, Hawaii gives money to candidates for local, legislative, and statewide races) and have lower rates of taxpayer participation.

Local Public Campaign Financing

Before New York City established a public campaign financing program, only two other municipalities had such a program—Seattle, Washington, and Tucson, Arizona. In January 1990 the Los Angeles City Council enacted a public campaign financing program, which was approved by a referendum in June 1990.

The city of Seattle adopted its public financing system in 1978. The program operated in the 1979 and 1981 municipal elections. In 1982 the program terminated under a sunset clause. The program was reenacted with some modifications in 1985.

The Seattle program consists of contribution limits, expenditure limits, and public financing. Candidates who accept public funds must limit contributions to $350 per individual. Candidates for mayor are subject to expenditure limits of $250,000; the limit for other municipal officials is $75,000. Since Seattle does not have a municipal income tax, the fund is supported by an annual $4 checkoff on the city's electrical bills. In 1988, the fund collected $153,944 in this manner.[17]

The Tucson program was created under an amendment to the city's charter in November 1985. All candidates, whether or not they receive public funds, may accept no more than $500 in contributions from individuals and PACs. (This local limit, however, was superseded by a 1986 state law which lowered the limit to $200). Candidates for mayor who accept public funds may not spend more than 40 cents per voter, or $77,000 in the 1987 election. Such candidates for the city council may not spend more than 20 cents per voter, or $38,000 in 1987. Since Tucson does not have an income tax, it uses the municipal water bill to collect contributions to the fund. In the 1987 primary and general elections, the public matching funds totaled $94,900.[18]

An important part of a public financing program is the eligibility requirements that serve the dual purposes of preventing frivolous candidates from running and keeping program costs down. In both Seattle and Tucson candidates for mayor who seek public funding must raise $30,000 in 300 contributions of at least $10, and candidates for the city council must raise $20,000 in 200 contributions of at least $10.

The Los Angeles program was authorized by both local legislation and a referendum in 1990. Like a similar program passed for Sacramento County in 1986, implementation of the Los Angeles program is subject to court action brought by opponents challenging the program on grounds that it conflicts with state law prohibiting public funding. If implemented, the Los Angeles program would apply to candidates for mayor, comptroller, city attorney, and the 15-member city council. It would provide matching funds for eligible candidates in exchange for the imposition of spending limits. The limits range from $2.0 million in the primary and $1.6 million in the general election for mayor to $300,000 in the primary and $250,000 in the general election for council members. Contribution limits are $500 for council candidates and $1,000 for candidates for citywide office. To be eligible for public funds a candidate must raise privately a threshold amount that ranges from $25,000 for council members to $150,000 for mayoral candidates. If the program is not invalidated by the courts, it will apply to the next municipal elections.

Reform in New York State and New York City

The city's creation of a public financing program in 1989 should be viewed in the context of failed efforts at reform in the state legislature. Inaction at the state level led to initiatives within the city when municipal scandals emerged.

Inaction in the State Legislature

New York State last significantly changed its campaign finance law in 1974, in the wake of Watergate and a national wave of reforms. The principal 1974 changes were a tightening of contribution limits and disclosure requirements. Responsibility for enforcing the law was given to the state Board of Elections.

The law requires a candidate to file three disclosure reports during an election campaign. In addition, a candidate must file three reports a year until all the campaign committee's assets have been liquidated. Candidates must itemize contributions of $100 or more and expenditures of $50 or more in these disclosure statements.

The state's contribution limits are determined by a formula which includes two factors. First, the limits differ for primary and general elections. Second, the limit increases with the number of registered voters in the candidate's district, with the most generous limits for candidates for statewide office. No limits are placed on contributions by candidates and their spouses to their campaigns. Finally, an individual is limited to $150,000 a year in overall contributions.

The contribution limits for candidates for governor illustrate how the formula works. In the 1986 gubernatorial election, the maximum allowable contribution to a candidate was $20,030 in the Democratic primary and $13,377 in the Republican primary. In the general election, both candidates could receive the same maximum contribution of $45,221.

The state has fewer restrictions on contributions from PACs and to political party committees. Corporate and labor union PACs have the same limits as individuals, but without the annual $150,000 ceiling. Labor unions, as distinct from their PACs, may give without any restrictions. Corporations may make contributions of no more than $5,000 per year, per candidate. There are no limits on contributions to political parties.

The state's law was criticized by a New York State ethics panel as a "public embarrassment."[19] The three principal criticisms are (1) inadequate disclosure requirements, (2) lax enforcement practices, and (3) ineffective contribution limits.

The disclosure requirements are defective in two respects. First, candidates need not fully disclose their corporate sources of support. Individual contributors do not have to indicate their business affiliation on disclosure statements; this means corporate giving can be channeled through employees and officers. In addition, corporations can make contributions through subsidiary units without identifying them as such. Thus the complete contributions of corporations, many of which do extensive business with the state, remain unknown to voters.

Reporting of campaign expenditures is also deficient. Investigations by the New York State Commission on Government Integrity revealed that campaign organizations often made large payments to consultants, who used the funds to pay other firms and individuals. These latter recipients of campaign funds are not required to be identified. Thus a large number of individuals and entities who receive campaign money are hidden from public view.

Lack of enforcement has exacerbated the law's weaknesses. The New York State Board of Elections delegates responsibility for enforcing the election laws to local election boards. However, these boards are not given resources adequate to ensure compliance and to make the data available to the public.

For the most part, these offices serve only as storage places for the candidates' filings. Summaries of the data are nonexistent and computerization of the statements is rare. This lax enforcement essentially negates the law's public disclosure requirements.

The state's contribution limits are, in effect, limitations in name only. Individuals and organizations can legally contribute amounts in excess of the limits through the "housekeeping" exemption and the exemption for contributions to political party committees. The first provision excludes the costs of party operations from regulation; contributors can give unlimited money for these "housekeeping" purposes. But this money can be distributed according to the discretion of the county political chairman. The second provision allows contributors to donate without limit to political party committees. As is the case with federal soft money, the distinction between money used strictly for party purposes and money for promoting candidates has become increasingly blurred. Combined with the high limits, these provisions erode public confidence in the law and encourage the practices the law was designed to prevent.

Governor Mario Cuomo created the New York State Commission on Government Integrity (also known as the Feerick Commission, after its chairman, John D. Feerick, dean of the Fordham Law School) in 1987 to examine the campaign finance law and recommend changes to strengthen it. The commission issued its recommendations in December 1988. These proposals included (1) reducing the contribution limits, (2) tightening disclosure requirements, (3) establishing an independent enforcement agency, and (4) establishing a public funding program.[20]

Despite the commission's findings, the legislature failed to revise the law. The Democratic leadership, including Governor Mario Cuomo and assembly Speaker Melvin Miller, supported the recommendations. A public campaign financing bill passed the assembly but was defeated in the senate. It was the sixth time since 1979 that a public financing bill lost in the senate after passage by the assembly. Lawmakers, especially in the assembly, criticized the Republican-controlled senate for letting another reform opportunity pass. For example, Assemblyman Steven Sanders accused state senators of being concerned that the reforms would prevent incumbents from amassing large war chests to frighten off their opponents.[21]

Legislators opposed to the reforms argue that the commission revealed no illegal activities and that the voters were indifferent to change. With respect to public opinion, the commission polled registered voters statewide on their attitudes toward campaign finance reform in June 1988. The commission found that although a majority of the voters favored reform, they were opposed to public funding because of its cost. However, some critics felt that the public funding questions were confusing to the respondents and may have led to misleading answers.

The Feerick Commission was terminated in April 1990. After three years of existence, the panel had little impact on the state's campaign finance system. Chairman Feerick could claim only the following accomplishments in summing up the commission's work: (1) public disclosure of the ways political parties finance their operations, (2) personnel changes in the state Board of Elections, and (3) computerization of some candidates' financial statements.[22]

Reform in New York City

Campaign finance reform in New York City received little attention until 1985. In the 1985 mayoral election, incumbent Edward I. Koch spent nearly $6.3 million to win his third term.[23] City Council President Andrew Stein spent nearly $3.0 million, and Comptroller Harrison J. Goldin spent $1.3 million. Neither Koch nor Goldin faced serious opposition in either the primary or general election. Stein spent most of his money in the primary to defeat wealthy challenger Kenneth Lipper, who spent more than $2 million on his losing campaign.

The tremendous expenditures were fueled by large contributions. For example, six individuals and corporations gave more than $600,000 in total contributions to the Koch campaign. One contributor, a vice president of a real estate firm, gave $115,000. Other candidates were also beneficiaries of big gifts. Comptroller Goldin, for example, received $80,000 from one financial firm between 1982 and 1985.

Throughout the campaign, the news media and a few elected officials criticized Koch and other candidates for accepting large donations. State Senator Franz S. Leichter released a report after the election showing the top corporate contributors to the members of the Board of Estimate and stated that "the line between a bribe and a contribution is almost invisible."[24] Koch repeatedly brushed aside calls for reform, saying that he found nothing "immoral" in the city's system of campaign financing.[25]

In 1986, Queens Borough President Donald Manes committed suicide and a wave of corruption scandals followed. In their wake, Koch and other municipal officials changed their views with respect to campaign finance reform. Early in the year, before the scandals peaked, several reform-minded council members introduced a bill that would impose contribution and expenditure limits on candidates who agreed to public financing. The bill was not passed in that session largely because the city council felt that the state legislature would approve similar legislation. However, the state senate failed to do so.

The legislature did, however, pass the "Goodman Law," named for its principal sponsor, State Senator Roy Goodman. Under the law, individuals who had business items before the Board of Estimate were prohibited from making donations exceeding $3,000 to board members either 6 months before or 12 months after the board's consideration of the item. The law soon proved ineffective, due to weak enforcement by the city's Board of Elections.

In its spring 1987 session, the state legislature considered legislation creating a public campaign financing program in New York City. This measure had the support of both Mayor Koch and Governor Cuomo, but it failed in the senate. City leaders concluded they could not rely on the state legislature to reform the system; the city council would have to act independently.

In mid-1987 the city's corporation counsel prepared an opinion arguing that a local public financing program was possible under local law if a candidate's acceptance of public funds and spending limits were voluntary. In that way, the city would avoid passing a local statute inconsistent with state law. Independently, the recently formed Charter Revision Commission's staff found that the city had authority under the "home rule" provision of the state constitution to establish a local public funding program.

On the basis of these two opinions, the city moved ahead. In September 1987 Mayor Koch sent a draft bill to the city council. The council passed a revised bill in February 1988, and Mayor Koch subsequently signed Local Law 8. To test public support for public financing, the Charter Revision Commission placed a question on the November 1988 ballot which authorized public funding in the 1989 municipal elections. The proposal passed by a four-to-one margin.

The city's law has four principal objectives: (1) eliminate the appearance of undue influence by prohibiting large contributions, (2) control campaign spending, (3) encourage more candidates to run for office, and (4) educate the public on political issues. To achieve these goals the law provides for partial public funding for candidates who agree to abide by its relatively strict contribution and spending limits. The law established an independent Campaign Finance Board to enforce the statute. The law's major provisions are described more fully next.

Contribution Limits

New York City's contribution limitations are considerably stricter than the state's. Under the state law, individual contributors can give up to $50,000 per election to candidates for mayor, comptroller, and city council president. The new law lowered the limit to $3,000 per election for citywide candidates who participate in the public financing program.

Under state law, contribution limits for other city offices, including borough president and city council member, vary according to the formula described earlier. The city's campaign finance law places a ceiling of $2,500 per election on contributions to candidates for borough president, and $2,000 per election to candidates for the city council.

According to state regulations, candidates can make unlimited contributions to their own campaigns. However, the city's law prohibits candidates who accept public funding from contributing more to their own campaigns than the appropriate limit for others. For example, if Ronald Lauder (a 1989 candidate for mayor, who spent millions of his own dollars) had participated in the public financing plan he could have used only $6,000 of his own money to fund his election bid. The same limitations also apply to a candidate's spouse and children.

The city's individual contribution limits apply to corporations as well. In addition, regulations promulgated by the Campaign Finance Board require contributions from corporate subsidiaries and affiliates to be counted toward the parent corporations' contribution limits. This provision was designed to stop circumvention of the contribution limits by corporations making donations through their subsidiaries. For example, before this ruling, Prudential-Bache funneled $10,000 into Mayor Koch's 1989 reelection campaign through four subsidiaries: Bache Energy gave $3,000, Prudential-Bache Leasing gave $3,000, Prudential-Bache Minerals gave $3,000, and Bache PAC gave $1,000.[26]

Loans are not considered contributions, so a candidate may borrow an unlimited amount for a campaign. However, if a loan is not repaid in full before the election, it is considered a contribution.

Spending Limits

Candidates accepting public funding must agree to expenditure limits. The same limits apply to primary and general elections for a given office, but the limits vary among offices. Mayoral candidates may spend up to $3 million per election; city council president and comptroller candidates may spend up to $1,750,000 per election; borough president candidates up to $625,000; and city council candidates up to $105,000. If a runoff primary election is held, an expenditure limit equal to half these amounts is imposed. As with contribution limits, the spending limits will be adjusted for inflation for elections after 1989.

Certain types of expenditures are not included in the limits. These are the costs of compliance with the law, the costs of challenging or defending petitions, and repayment of debts from earlier campaigns (before February 1988) or from campaigns not covered by the program. A portion of fund-raising costs also are excluded from the limits.

Disclosure Requirements

Candidates who receive public funds are required to submit periodic reports to the Campaign Finance Board. (Nonparticipating candidates file their disclosure statements with the Board of Elections.) The city's law, in contrast to the state's, provides for full disclosure of a contributor's name, address, occupation, employer, and employer's address. In addition, "intermediaries," or individuals who collect contributions from others, must submit the same information. This provision allows disclosure of the names of individuals and organizations who engage in "bundling."

The law also requires that participating candidates report their expenditures to the Campaign Finance Board. All expenditures, regardless of whether they fall within the expenditure limits, must be reported.

Public Financing

The city's law provides for partial public financing of campaigns. To receive public funds, a candidate must meet certain threshold requirements. (See Table 5.4.) The requirements vary depending upon the office sought, but the common approach is a total dollar amount composed of a minimum number

Table 5.4 Threshold Requirements for Public Funding for
Candidates for Municipal Offices in New York City

Office	Threshold Amount	Minimum Number of Contributors Donating Between $10 and $500
Mayor	$250,000	1,000 residents of NYC
City council president	125,000	500 residents of NYC
Comptroller	125,000	500 residents of NYC
Borough president[a]		100 residents of borough
Bronx	23,379	
Brooklyn	44,619	
Manhattan	25,566	
Queens	37,927	
Staten Island	10,000	
City council member	7,500	50 district residents

Source: New York City Campaign Finance Board.

[a]Computed at 2 cents per borough resident or $10,000, whichever is greater.

of contributions of between $10 and $500. Contributions used to reach the threshold are not matched with public funds.

Candidates matching the threshold then may receive $1 in matching funds for each $1 of individual contributions (that is, those not from corporations or political committees) to a maximum of $500 per individual contribution. This provision encourages candidates to seek smaller contributions because more matching funds can thus be generated. For example, a mayoral candidate who receives a $3,000 contribution from an individual would have only $500 of it matched by public funds. However, six contributions of $500 would yield $3,000 in public matching money.

The expenditure limits and matching formula are altered in a contest where a candidate who opts into the public financing program is opposed by a nonparticipating candidate. In such a case, the applicable limits may be waived and the matching rate may be raised to $2 for every $1 in matchable contributions. However, a candidate may not receive more than half the applicable limit in matching funds. For example, a mayoral candidate in this situation could spend more than the $3,000,000 ceiling but could not receive more than $1.5 million in public funds.

The law restricts the manner in which public funds may be spent. The money is to be used primarily for educating the public about the issues and the candidates. This function typically is fulfilled through radio and television advertising, although public funds also may be spent on voter registration drives and campaign literature. The law prohibits using public funds to pay for campaign workers. However, it does not prohibit paying consultant fees.

The Campaign Finance Board

The Campaign Finance Board has responsibility for enforcing the law. The board consists of five members who are appointed to staggered five-year terms by either the mayor or speaker of the city council. The board maintains a staff of 39 employees; its fiscal year 1990 budget was nearly $9 million.[27]

Results of the City's Program

The benefits of the city's new program can be assessed in terms of each of the law's objectives. In pursuit of these objectives $4.5 million of public funds was given to candidates in the 1989 election. How did this investment improve the electoral process?

Eliminating Large Contributions

In earlier elections, candidates relied heavily on a few well-to-do contributors. For example, fully $3.3 million, or nearly half (47 percent) of the total monetary contributions received by Mayor Koch for his 1985 campaign, came from just 453 contributors who gave at least $5,000. The average contribution for these donors was $7,217, more than twice the largest allowable contribution in 1989. Similarly, in 1985 contributors giving at least $5,000 accounted for over $1.3 million, or 64 percent of the total contributions to Comptroller Goldin, and for nearly $1.5 million, or 66 percent of City Council President Stein's total contributions.[28] Due to the new law's limits, such contributors necessarily played a smaller role in the 1989 election.

Not only did the new law eliminate large individual contributions; it also lowered the total amount of contributions to candidates. In general, the winning candidates for citywide office in 1989 had considerably lower total contributions than their counterparts in 1985. (See Table 5.5.) The three winners in 1985 raised more in campaign donations than their 1989 counterparts, although none of them faced serious challenges in either the primary or

Table 5.5 Total Contributions to Successful Candidates for Mayor, Comptoller, and City Council President, 1985 and 1989 Elections

Name	Office	Total Monetary Contributions	Total Contributions (1989 $)
Edward I. Koch	Mayor—1985	$6,962,333	$8,051,242
David N. Dinkins	Mayor—1989	7,462,514	7,462,514
Harrison J. Goldin	Comptroller—1985	2,045,222	2,365,095
Elizabeth Holtzman	Comptroller—1989	1,642,817	1,642,817
Andrew Stein	City council president—1985	2,204,415	2,549,186
Andrew Stein	City council president—1989	1,768,443	1,768,443

Sources: New York State Commission on Government Integrity, "Unfinished Business," September 28, 1988; New York City Campaign Finance Board, unpublished data; and New York City Board of Elections.

Table 5.6 Total Contributions for Mayor, Comptroller, and City
Council President Candidates in 1989 Primary Elections

Office	Party Primary	Total Monetary Contributions	Total Contributions[a]
Mayor			
Dinkins	D	$3,223,021	$3,234,140
Goldin	D	1,749,672	1,726,642
Koch	D	3,459,293	3,424,173
Ravitch	D	1,572,560	1,574,134
Giuliani	R	2,350,481	2,355,170
Lauder	R	12,283,746	NA
Comptroller			
Holtzman	D	1,243,376	1,259,531
Hevesi	D	682,401	757,041
Macchiarola	D	698,864	715,714
City council president			
Stein	D	1,508,863	NA

Sources: New York City Campaign Finance Board, except for Andrew Stein's figure,
which is from the New York City Board of Elections.

Note: NA, not available.

[a]Net of refunds. Includes in-kind contributions.

general election that year. On the other hand, the 1989 mayoral contest was
the most competitive in many years. David N. Dinkins, the eventual winner,
encountered tough opposition in both the primary and general elections. In
order to win both elections, Dinkins raised about $7.5 million, 93 percent of
Mayor Koch's $8.1 million in total contributions in 1985.

Elizabeth Holtzman had to defeat four rivals for the Democratic nomination for comptroller, before winning the general election with less opposition.
In doing so, she raised more than $1.6 million, only 69 percent of the aggre-
gate contributions raised by Comptroller Goldin in the 1985 election when he
faced virtually no opposition. Andrew Stein, who refused public funds in his
reelection as city council president, received more than $2.5 million in total
contributions, in 1985, but the figure dropped to $1.8 million in 1989. Stein
apparently collected less in 1989 because he wanted to avoid the adverse
publicity from accumulating a large war chest in the first year of the city's
experiment with campaign finance reform.

Total contributions to candidates in the 1989 Democratic primary for
mayor, comptroller, and city council president and the 1989 Republican primary for mayor are shown in Table 5.6. Mayor Koch had the largest amount
of contributions—$3.4 million. The winner of the Democratic party's nomi-
nation, David N. Dinkins, had the next highest total—$3.2 million.

In the race for the Democratic nomination for comptroller, Elizabeth
Holtzman drew the largest amount of contributions. Her nearly $1.3 million
in total contributions far exceeded those of her primary rivals.

City Council President Stein, in his bid for reelection, did not face a serious
challenge in the Democratic primary. Nevertheless, he collected more than

$1.5 million, a larger amount than any of the candidates in the Democratic primary for comptroller where a competitive race took place.

In the Republican mayoral primary, Ronald Lauder, a wealthy businessman and former ambassador, raised almost $12.3 million, mainly from his own family's financial resources. He received more contributions than his opponent, Rudolph Giuliani, by a margin of more than five to one, but still lost his party's nomination.

Neither Lauder nor Stein opted into the city's public financing program; therefore they were free to raise and spend funds according to the state limits. Their totals are indicative of what might have been raised by the other candidates had the new campaign finance law not been in effect. Clearly, the law succeeded in capping the growth of contributions for participating candidates.

The goal of limiting the possible influence of large contributors was in some way hindered by the practice of "bundling." This refers to the use of intermediaries to collect contributions from people with similar interests and present it to the candidate in a single large amount.

In the 1989 election, all of the major candidates benefited from bundling. However, the principal beneficiary appears to have been Giuliani. For example, one intermediary, Edward Cloonan, collected nearly $75,000 for the candidate. Two other bundlers, William Koeppel and Lawrence Reinhard, brought in $66,000 and $56,000, respectively. Many intermediaries collected contributions from multiple individuals in a single firm. Victor Ganzi pooled $25,000 mainly from employees of the law firm Rogers and Wells; James Hurlock raised $20,000 from White and Case employees.[29]

Dinkins also used intermediaries early in his campaign, but he later sought to avoid reliance on intermediaries. Instead of accepting bundled contributions with their negative connotations, Dinkins used staff members, who are not required to be identified in disclosure reports, to gather donations. Nevertheless, several bundlers collected large sums for Dinkins. Elizabeth Gotbaum, who later became commissioner of parks and recreation, raised $63,000 from 69 taxi companies and other businesses. Percy Sutton served as an intermediary for $14,000. Stanley Hill, leader of District Council 37, assembled nearly $12,000 in contributions, mostly from union members.

In sum, the law partially succeeded in curtailing large contributions and in slowing the growth of total contributions. It is no longer possible for corporations to give $100,000 to candidates, as happened in earlier elections. However, bundling allows candidates to bend the law without breaking it. Voters must rely on public disclosure to determine whether the use of intermediaries creates possible conflicts of interest.

Controlling Expenditures

City officials enacted reforms in 1988 partly because they sensed that campaign spending was out of control. In 1985 the major candidates spent enormous sums in largely uncompetitive races. The new program has reversed the earlier, troublesome trend.

Table 5.7 Total Expenditures and Cost Per Vote for Winning Candidates for Citywide Office in 1985 and 1989 Primary and General Elections

Candidate	Total Expenditures (1989 $)	Number of Votes	Cost Per Vote (1989 $)
1985 Elections			
Edward I. Koch	$7,284,878	1,304,411	$5.58
Harrison J. Goldin	1,481,777	1,203,642	1.23
Andrew Stein	3,462,958	1,085,902	3.19
1989 Elections			
David N. Dinkins	7,243,591	1,436,787	5.04
Elizabeth Holtzman	1,639,579	1,577,266	1.04
Andrew Stein	1,602,451	1,800,594	0.89

Sources: See Table 5.6.

Campaign spending may be measured two ways, total expenditures and cost per vote. Cost per vote tends to underestimate the candidates' expenses because their computation gives equal weight to both the primary and general election, although much of the spending occurs in the primary. Nevertheless, by either measure, campaign spending leveled off in 1989. Since relevant costs, especially television advertising, rose during the 1980s, the city's new law seems to be an important factor in the reversal.

Total expenditures and cost per vote for the winning citywide candidates in 1985 and 1989 are shown in Table 5.7. Adjusting for inflation, Koch, Goldin, and Stein spent $7.3 million, $1.4 million, and $3.5 million, respectively, to win office in 1985. In 1989, only Elizabeth Holtzman exceeded her 1985 counterpart's total expenditures, $1.6 to $1.5 million. However, Holtzman faced a primary battle, whereas Goldin did not. Each of the winning candidates in 1989 spent less per vote than the winning candidates in 1985.

The costs of the 1989 campaign were inflated considerably by hotly contested primaries for mayor and comptroller. (See Table 5.8.) In the Republican mayoral primary, Lauder spent a record $14 million while Giuliani spent $3.2 million. Because Lauder did not accept public financing his spending was unlimited.

In the Democratic primary for mayor, Koch faced three challengers. Koch spent the most, $4.0 million, while Dinkins spent $3.4 million. Goldin and Richard Ravitch each spent about $1.8 million.

The Democratic primary for comptroller attracted more contestants in 1989 because Goldin, the four-term incumbent, ran for mayor. Five candidates sought the nomination. Holtzman, the eventual nominee, outspent the other four.

Spending in the primary, as measured by costs per vote, is usually greater than spending in the general election. Voter turnout is smaller in the primaries and candidates use television advertising extensively to become better known to the public. Goldin, fourth among the mayoral candidates in votes, led the

Table 5.8 Total Expenditures and Cost Per Vote for Major Candidates for Citywide Office in 1989 Primary Elections

Candidate	Total Expenditures	Number of Votes	Cost Per Vote
Democratic Mayor			
David N. Dinkins	$3,383,493	537,887	$6.29
Harrison J. Goldin	1,805,895	28,792	62.72
Edward I. Koch	4,036,800	445,941	9.05
Richard Ravitch	1,815,517	48,284	37.60
Republican Mayor			
Rudolph Giuliani	3,171,390	77,150	41.11
Ronald Lauder	13,789,889	37,960	363.27
Democratic Comptroller[a]			
Alan Hevesi	831,743	224,047	3.71
Elizabeth Holtzman	1,337,950	431,490	3.10
Frank Macchiarola	846,090	192,744	4.39
Democratic City Council President			
Andrew Stein	472,393	593,101	0.80

Sources: See Table 5.6. Ronald Lauder's figure is from New York City Board of Elections.

[a]Two other candidates, Jerrold Nadler and Stephen Rose, each received less than 4 percent of the vote.

others in expenses per vote—$63 on average. Ravitch finished behind both Dinkins and Koch, but his $38 per vote led both front-runners. Koch spent heavily on television, especially in the final weeks of the campaign, but as the three-term incumbent his name recognition was the highest of the candidates. As a result, he spent only $9.05 per vote. The eventual nominee, Dinkins, relied heavily on a large field operation to keep his campaign costs to $6.29 per vote.

In the Republican primary, costs per vote are high because of the small number of registered Republicans in the city. Both candidates waged expensive media campaigns. To win his party's nomination, Giuliani had to spend $41 for each vote. Lauder's cost per vote was an astronomical $363.

Clearly, the law put a brake on campaign costs. The costs of elections had risen steadily through the 1980s because of the increasing use of expensive television advertising. The trend of rising expenditures peaked in 1985 when the citywide candidates spent large sums in noncompetitive races. Without the campaign finance law, this trend was likely to have continued in the 1989 elections. Nevertheless, the costs of getting elected in New York City are still high, especially in the important primary elections.

Encouraging Candidates to Run

An important goal of public financing is to increase the number and diversity of candidates for municipal offices. Table 5.9 shows the number of candidates for mayor, comptroller, city council president, and city council in the last three

Table 5.9 Number of Candidates for Mayor, Comptroller, City Council President, and City Council in Democratic Primary and General Elections, 1981, 1985, and 1989

Election	Mayoral	Comptroller	City Council President	City Council
		Candidates		
Democratic primary				
1981	3	2	2	47[a]
1985	3	3	6	59
1989	4	5	2	30
General election				
1981	4	3	3	96[a]
1985	3	3	3	85
1989	4	4	3	74

Sources: Data derived from election results printed in *The New York Times* on the following dates: September 23, 1981, II, p. 4; November 15, 1981, p. 8; September 25, 1982, p. 33; November 4, 1982, II, p. 9; September 11, 1985, II, p. 4; November 7, 1985, II, p. 6; September 14, 1989, II, p. 2; November 9, 1989, II, p. 6.
[a]City council figures from elections held in 1982 after the U.S. Justice Department rejected the city council's 1981 reapportionment plan.

elections. The data reveal that the new law has not increased the number of office seekers. In fact, the 1989 election witnessed a decline from earlier years in the number of candidates for city council.

The high cost of campaigning and the difficulty in defeating incumbents are two major obstacles facing potential candidates. Public financing addresses the first one, but it does little to reduce an incumbent's advantage. In fact, some critics argue that the spending limits are too low, especially for council members. Low limits serve to protect incumbents from serious challenges. In addition, the law's provisions may deter potential candidates who cannot afford to hire the lawyers and accountants needed to follow its regulations.

In all, 48 candidates participated in the public financing program. Most of the candidates for citywide office received pubic money; Lauder and Stein were the two exceptions. However, only slightly more than half (18) of the city council members running for reelection (34) chose to participate in the program. The council members who did not agree to public funding thought that the program was too complicated and required too much additional staff. Since some incumbents felt this way, potential challengers with fewer resources might have reached a similar conclusion and decided not to participate.

Educating the Public

Increasing the public's understanding of important issues is another major objective of the city's Campaign Finance Law. To pursue this goal, the Campaign Finance Board mailed voter information pamphlets to every registered voter in the city and included them in the Sunday editions of the major daily newspapers.

Since the likely consequence of greater public knowledge of the issues and candidates is a larger number of voters, turnout may be used as a surrogate measure for increased public awareness. The 1989 election witnessed a sizable increase in voter participation. After declining turnout in the last two elections, the trend reversed in 1989 with 56 percent and 34 percent increases in the number of voters in the mayoral primary and general elections, respectively.[30]

Few proponents of campaign finance reform, however, would be willing to attribute the 1989 increase solely to the efforts of the board. Large turnouts are common in competitive elections (for example, the 1977 mayoral election and the 1982 Democratic primary for governor). It is not possible to disentangle the effects of the new law from the competitive nature of the 1989 mayoral contest.

Toward a Better Program

The four goals of the city's Campaign Finance Law were partially met in the 1989 elections, but the public financing program could be made more effective by changes in the law. In light of this need for improvement, in March 1990 the Campaign Finance Board recommended amendments aimed at stimulating competition in the elections for city council in 1991. The city council incorporated many of these suggested changes in Local Law 69, which was signed by Mayor Dinkins on November 17, 1990.

For the longer run, changes should be sought to make the 1993 elections more effective in educating the public and less subject to public skepticism regarding the influence of large contributors. The Campaign Finance Board addressed some of these long-term issues in its March recommendations but none of the proposed changes for the 1993 elections were acted upon by the city council.

Changes for the 1991 City Council Elections

The revised New York City Charter required elections for council members in 1991. The members will serve in a newly structured council with an increased membership (from 35 to 51 seats) and with district lines redrawn based on 1990 census results. Since a weakness of the public financing program in 1989 was the low participation of city council candidates and the lack of challengers in council races, revising the program to address these shortcomings was a priority concern.

In response to these concerns, the Campaign Finance Board proposed significant revisions to the law in March 1990.[31] Not all of these changes, however, were adopted by the council. The board's recommended changes included:

1. Lowering the threshold for eligibility for public funds from $7,500 to $5,000 in contributions.

2. Altering the threshold contribution requirements to permit any city resident, rather than only council district residents, to make qualifying contributions. This reflects the possibility that district lines will not be drawn when fund-raising begins.
3. Making threshold contributions eligible for matching.
4. Lowering contribution limits from $2,000 per election (or $4,000 for a primary and general election) to a total of $3,000 for both elections.
5. Applying contribution and expenditure limits to the combined primary and general elections, rather than having separate limits for each election. This requires candidates to raise and use funds within an overall limit, but to use the money disproportionately in the contest in which they face the greatest challenge.
6. Simplifying reporting requirements.
7. Removing restrictions on how public funds are spent. This includes removing the prohibition on using public funds to pay salaries of campaign workers.
8. Matching contributions of up to $500 at a two-for-one rate.
9. Providing greater bonuses for participants who are opposed by high-spending nonparticipants.
10. Allowing candidates more time to opt into the public financing program.

The city council's amendments to Local Law 8 include most of the board's recommended changes with no or slight modifications. However, the council rejected two of the board's proposed changes, matching contributions at a two-for-one rate and providing greater bonuses for participants faced by high-spending nonparticipants.

The amendments have two related goals. First, they seek to encourage interested challengers to enter contests. Second, they seek to encourage candidates, especially incumbents, to participate in the programs.

With respect to encouraging challenges, the impact of the program is difficult to isolate because the 1991 races were held under new conditions besides the amended program. Because the number of districts was increased from 35 to 51, there were at least 16 districts in which no incumbent was running. This did stimulate new challenges. Fully 38 of the districts had Democratic primary contests and 3 districts had Republican primaries. There was a total of 164 Democratic primary candidates and 6 Republican candidates.

The 1991 primaries also witnessed increased participation in the public funding program. Fully 108 of the 164 Democratic candidates (66 percent) participated, as did 3 of the 6 Republican candidates. A total of $978,511 of public funds was paid to the candidates, including those who received the allowable maximum of $40,000.[32]

Changes for the 1993 Elections

The amendments passed in November 1990 are directed toward the 1991 expanded city council races. However, the program's experience in the 1989 election suggests improvements that should be considered for the 1993 city-wide elections. Three directions for further reform can be identified.

Eliminate Large Contributions

The law places restrictions on individual and corporate contributions. However, it does not restrict bundling. As a result, firms and other special interests may present candidates with large contributions that violate the spirit of the law.

An attempt to prohibit bundling probably would infringe on First Amendment freedoms. The law, however, could be amended to allow candidates to voluntarily restrict bundling in return for certain benefits. For example, in exchange for limiting collections by intermediaries a candidate might have a greater percentage of fund-raising costs exempted from the expenditure limits.

Lower Campaign Expenditures

The law limits campaign expenditures, but they are still high, especially in the primaries. Television and radio advertising account for a large portion of campaign expenditures. Media costs continue to rise rapidly. Consequently, the best way to reduce campaign spending may be to grant eligible candidates free time on commercial radio and television stations.

There are two ways this might be done. First, as a condition for federal licensure, radio and television stations could be required to devote a percentage of their air time to public service broadcasting. The definition of this type of broadcasting might be modified to include candidates' messages. Second, the Campaign Finance Board might purchase large blocks of air time and allocate them to the candidates.

Educate the Public About Electoral Issues

During the Campaign Finance Board hearings following the 1989 elections, several candidates and the spokespersons of numerous civic groups argued that participating candidates should be required to hold public debates. Such a provision would serve the public education function of the law.

Who would sponsor the debates remains a sticky point. The Campaign Finance Board maintains that in order to remain outside politics it should not be the sponsor. Board members prefer that another nonpartisan organization play that role. Such an arrangement exists in New Jersey, where the League of Women Voters runs the debates. Given the widespread agreement in principle on staging debates, the issue of sponsorship should be amenable to resolution by the next citywide elections.

Another important issue is who should be allowed to debate. Some argue that only participating candidates should be given the opportunity. However, this approach excludes other viewpoints and negates the law's public education role. But too many debators sharing a stage could confuse more than inform the public. One solution to this dilemma is to allow only those candidates who have reached the contribution threshold of eligibility to join the debate, whether or not they actually participate in the public funding program.

III

BUDGETARY POLITICS AND POLICY

6

IMPROVING THE OPERATING BUDGET PROCESS

The city of New York has hailed its recovery from the 1975 fiscal crisis with pride and relief, and it reserved its fullest celebration for the "sunset" of the state's Financial Control Board (FCB) on June 30, 1986. In attendance at the plenary meeting of the board—which was held in open air on the steps of City Hall—were most of the dignitaries who had played powerful and public roles in the early structuring of the fiscal recovery. The recovery period, originally expected to take three years, was redefined in 1978, and in the end it took over ten years for the city to demonstrate, as required by law, that it had achieved recurring budget balance, recovery of market access, and repayment of debt guaranteed by the federal government in the years following the crisis.

The event at City Hall marked the lapsing of the FCB's power to approve the city's four-year financial plans. Through this function the state of New York had been involved in enforcing long-range fiscal planning by the city and could ultimately control the aggregate expenditure levels of the locality. Thus the justifiably congratulatory and self-congratulatory speakers on the steps of City Hall celebrated the hard-won return of "home rule" to the city of New York, amid some nostalgia for the challenging if problematic days that lay behind them.

There were many reasons for pride and relief at the reduction of the FCB's oversight powers, particularly in light of the magnitude of the problems the city faced in 1975. Based on unaudited data, the city estimated that its operating deficit for fiscal year 1976 was approximately $1.87 billion, had it been reported in accordance with Generally Accepted Accounting Principles (GAAP). But after initial years of cutbacks, services were improved; and beginning in fiscal year 1981 the city's independently audited operating results showed surpluses on a GAAP basis. The city also has estimated that at the time it lost its ability to borrow unassisted in the public credit markets, it had approximately $6 billion of short-term debt outstanding. That debt was either repaid or refinanced while the city gradually built back its ability to access the public credit markets for all its capital and cash needs. At the same time the city greatly revised its financial systems and internal control practices, also cause for celebration.

But an occasion for celebration can also provide a basis for subsequent reflection. With major accomplishments behind it, it is important that the city take stock of its fiscal practices and policies as it exercises sole responsibility for its budget matters. Is the operating budget process, revamped following the loss of market access in 1975, working well? Will financial planning—projecting the effect of today's revenue and expenditure decisions into upcoming budget years—prove to be a realistic and effective tool for protecting the city's fiscal integrity? Answers to these questions could help the city in its efforts to preserve its newfound bottom line during the 1990s.

Background

In April 1975, the public credit markets closed to New York City. This cataclysmic event shook Wall Street and the shocks reverberated in Albany and Washington. It brought with it, at first, the temporary imposition of state controls over the city's fiscal and financing activities, an unprecedented intrusion upon home rule that was expected to last for only three years. In November 1978, however, following acknowledgment that the original recovery plan had been too optimistic, the city closed its deal with the federal government to provide guarantees of long-term city debt over the next four years. Federal assistance, and the commitment of financial institutions to participate in the four-year financing program, came with many strings attached, including increased state and federal oversight of local fiscal affairs. Thus, at both the beginning and the end of the 1975–1978 crisis period, substantial changes were made in the regulations governing the city's budgetary systems, making them among the most respected of those of any major city. Most of the legal changes were accomplished through revisions to the City Charter and the state's Local Finance Law, enactment of statutory provisions creating the constellation of fiscal monitors, and agreement with the federal government to guarantee city paper.

Many of those legal changes terminated when the FCB entered its sunset period and the federal guarantees were removed from city debt. Although the postsunset roles of the oversight monitors have never been clearly spelled out in state legislation, it is clear that, lacking prior approval powers, their influence on city budget decisions must now be exerted through suasion rather than authority. The city administration is now required, under state and local law, to develop and present a preliminary Executive Budget, accompanied by four-year financial plan projections, in January of each year. Following review by the city council and the oversight monitors, the administration presents the final Executive Budget, accompanied by revised four-year plan projections, for amendment and adoption by the city council prior to the commencement of the new fiscal year on July 1. The budget must be prepared and balanced on a GAAP basis, must provide funding for all mandated expenditures as well as a $100 million general reserve and must provide for all cash needs of the city.

The current-year budget projections must be extrapolated into the next three years based on reasonable assumptions, in order that adjustments can be made to maintain budget balance over time. Significant modifications to the budget during the fiscal year must receive city council approval; modification of the financial plan, however, has become essentially voluntary, although the FCB must still "reexamine" city forecasts every quarter. Actual city operating results must be presented in accordance with GAAP, audited by independent certified public accountants, and made available to the public within four months of the close of the fiscal year. Should the city's financial condition deteriorate—that is, should it incur an operating deficit of more than $100 million in any year—the FCB would by law reemerge from sunset with its full garb of control powers.

Apart from these general legal strictures, development and implementation of the budget is left entirely to the professionalism of city managers in the postsunset period. Over the period of recovery since the fiscal crisis, an admirable body of forecasting and control practices has been developed that includes provision for discretionary reserves such as the delinquency, disallowance, and collective bargaining reserves; recognition of categorical aid after commitment for the funds has been received; and the "surplus-needs assessment," which pinpoints rates of agency spending against budget.

Although it is possible, subject to certain restrictions, for the state legislature to alter the legal requirements that currently govern the city's budgetary process, it is unlikely, in the near-term at least, that this will happen. As a matter of pride and of market perception, it is likely that the city would resist any visible weakening of the systems and standards that are considered by the public to have helped it achieve and maintain its enviable fiscal bottom line. On the other hand, because much of the city's budgetary system is now a matter of voluntary procedures that are little understood and receive little public attention, and because the legal requirements that remain govern primarily beginning-of-the-year budget activity, the distinction between legal requirement and practice or custom becomes an important one when considering the possibilities for slippage or deterioration in the system and an agenda for change.

Agenda for Change

It is important to review the city's operating budget and planning process to determine what systems remain in place following the restoration of home rule to the city, and to ask how well these systems are suited to the task of maintaining fiscal health. It is clear that these systems are good, but they must be maintained, even improved, in order to ensure continued accuracy and accountability on the fiscal front.

Three contemporary pressures on the city budget complicate the situation and add urgency to the task of improving the city's budget and financial planning process. The first is the recurring wave of federal budget cutbacks that crested in the Reagan era but continues as Washington seeks to manage its own budget problems. The second is the need for new and improved municipal services, given new urgency by the emergence of epidemics of social pathology related to drug abuse and the tragedy of AIDS. The third is the deterioration in the local economy since the October 1987 stock market crash that has caused tax revenues to evaporate and obliged new efforts to cut spending. This chapter presents a set of recommended actions the city should consider taking in order to preserve and enhance the viability of its fiscal systems for the years ahead.

Safeguard the Legacy of Fiscal Recovery

As mentioned, the fiscal recovery has left the city with a skeleton of legal standards, procedures, and institutions that continues to govern the preparation of the city's operating budget and four-year financial plan and that determines the method of presentation of the city's operating results at year end. Over the years, professional city staffs have put meat on the skeleton's bones, creating a body of practices resulting in reasonably accurate budget forecasting, disclosure, and controlled budget implementation.

With the state's approval power over the financial plan terminated and budget autonomy restored, however, it becomes even more important that the city maintain the practices that it has so carefully developed and that have contributed to its positive bottom line. Because these practices now are voluntary, every effort should be made to avoid any deterioration in their observance.

Certainly the GAAP-balance and outside audit requirements have brought a tremendous degree of order and conservatism to the city's financial picture since 1978. With these requirements in place it should be virtually impossible for the city to return to the pre-fiscal crisis days of massive borrowing to meet compounding operating costs. All this is not to say, however, that the GAAP-balance and audit requirements guarantee sound budgeting practices. There is always a possibility that there will be overconfidence or slippage in fiscal controls, or that overemphasis on short-term gains and the use of so-called budget gimmicks, even though permitted under GAAP, could rise to a level that jeopardizes budget balance and a strong credit rating. Because balanced budgets and good credit are critical goals, it is essential at this juncture for the city to underscore its commitment to keep on doing what it has done so well up to this point. This will not always be easy in the high-tax, high-spending environment that is New York.

Assuming, nonetheless, a continuing city commitment to prevent backsliding in its budget and planning process, is the system nevertheless well suited to the task ahead, or could the system be strengthened? With the advantage of hindsight, careful analysis indicates that still more could by done to enhance the realism of the city's financial planning process, and the remaining agenda items warrant consideration with that goal in mind.

Restore the Quarterly Plan Modification Requirement

Under state law, the city must continue, in the postsunset period, to submit its monthly unaudited Financial Plan Statements (FPSs) to the FCB. These reports are obtainable by the public and set forth actual operating results and revised forecasts based on changing events. While the FPS reporting system has provided a useful updating of city projections, and is relied upon by the investment community among others, with sunset it has become a "standardsless" process due to the termination of the certification requirement. Complete and current information about implementation of the city's budget and the effect of developing events on financial plan projections is vital to the accountability and efficiency of the budget system, but an updating and reporting process requires standards if it is to be meaningful to the city and to the public.

To ensure public access to realistic revisions of the city's revenue and expenditure estimates on a periodic basis, there should be an amendment to the Memorandum of Understanding signed in June 1986 concerning the FCB's activities during the sunset period. This would secure agreement that the city must conform its financial plan projections on a quarterly basis to the standards of the New York State Financial Emergency Act, that is, modify its financial plan in October and May as well as in June and January. More to the point, application of these standards would impose a legal requirement that the city's projections be current and realistic; that is, projections must be "based on reasonable and appropriate assumptions and methods of estimation."[1]

Such an agreement would restore to the process the quarterly plan modification requirement that lapsed with the sunset of the FCB. This requirement helped to ensure the achievement of budget balance by maintaining the currency and realism of the city's numbers throughout the fiscal year, and it should have been continued as part of the city's postsunset responsibilities. Although the timing of the quarterly updating requirement can be awkward during negotiations with legislative or labor leaders, it nonetheless worked relatively well for the city in the past. Rigorous updating of the financial plan on a periodic basis during the fiscal year would mean that the plan would play a role in keeping city operations on course for budget balance at year end.

Under current procedures the state monitors reexamine the city's plan projections on a quarterly basis using modifications that the city voluntarily prepares. But the monitors are handicapped in that they are at least one step removed from the city's numbers and lack the staffing capacity to do as thorough a reassessment and update as the city can. Nor do they have the power to change the city's estimates. A legal requirement that the city regularly conform its projections to sound statutory standards would greatly enhance the reliability of the budget implementation and control process.

Terminate the Use of Budget Gaps

The use of budget "gaps," and the related gap-closing program customarily specified in the city's January plan, has become an outdated practice that is detrimental to the operations of a fiscally healthy municipality. Budget gaps, or excesses of estimated expenditures over estimated revenues, are essential for a governmental entity in financial trouble to identify and eliminate over time. A governmental entity that is in financial balance, however, should not be projecting budget gaps at all; or, if it does, the out-year gaps should be only as large as the tax and fee increases being proposed for those years.

When the city's first four-year financial plan was developed in 1978, it showed that expenditures (exclusive of new labor costs) would exceed revenues by more than $1 billion by fiscal year 1982, the final year of the plan. This "gap" between anticipated revenues and expenditures was a legacy of the fiscal crisis. As such, it was "real," and it represented a potential operating deficit unless the city could initiate new revenue or expenditure measures to avert it. Although the extrapolation of base-year revenue and expenditure projections into the succeeding three fiscal years indicated that the city was operating in the red, the recently revised Financial Emergency Act required that the city achieve a GAAP-balanced budget by fiscal year 1982 and demonstrate "substantial progress" toward achievement of this goal in each year prior to fiscal 1982. Thus the convention of gap-closing programs was born.

The early gap-closing programs, or so-called Programs to Eliminate the Gap (PEGs), were "below-the-line" measures designed to restructure the city's "above-the-line" finances beyond the current budget year so that it could move from a deficit position into the black. Productivity measures, program and personnel reductions, and fee and tax increases made up the city actions component of the PEG. The state and federal action components involved new programs that were outside the city's control and needed to be put in place at other levels of government. Here the city was lobbying for additional sources of revenue to fund its constrained but still-growing expenditure base. In addition to runaway inflation and an improved local economy, the period of fiscal recovery in fact saw an invigorated real property tax assessment program at both the state and local levels, a variety of tax and fee increases, steady state aid growth, and state assumption of responsibility for a variety of city programs, culminating in the takeover of the local share of long-term care Medicaid costs.

The city actually achieved GAAP-balance in fiscal year 1981, one year earlier than required by state law. This achievement marked the elimination of the budget deficit that had led to the fiscal crisis, but the question remained: Had the city's finances been sufficiently restructured so that it could maintain budget balance over time? That is, was the achievement of GAAP-balance a one-time success, or had the deficit condition, as well as the deficit, been eliminated?

Since fiscal year 1981, the city has realized an impressive string of GAAP-balanced budgets and has demonstrated that it can make timely adjustments to its financial plans in order to stay on course for budget balance in the face of pending fiscal problems. In the process, the original point of the gap convention—identification and elimination of a deficit condition—has been lost. Budget imbalance is no longer a legacy, but it has become in recent years a choice. PEG programs—such as the productivity program, tax enforcement effort, and state education aid increases—are no longer extraordinary actions but actions that recur every year and can be measured and forecast at reasonable levels. Thus it is reasonable to recommend that the city begin to wean itself from "deficit budgeting" and to specify PEG programs in its baseline estimates in order to bring estimated expenditures in line with estimated revenues for all four years of the plan. It is only the extraordinary actions such as proposed tax increases (or reductions) or major new intergovernmental aid programs that deserve to remain below the line. A fiscally healthy jurisdiction should not have gaps between revenues and expenditures unless tax changes or new aid programs are seriously contemplated. Traditional PEG programs should be specified in the baseline projections at reasonable levels so that either the financial plan shows budget balance in all four years or the hard, or "true," gaps are identified and dealt with.

There are at least three problems with the process as it currently operates. First, the city's budget gaps have lost credibility in recent years because they have sounded impossibly large but have eventually disappeared. In March 1985, for example, the city was projecting a budget gap for fiscal year 1987 of $889 million. By June 1985 that gap had been reduced to $370 million. By June 1986 the city was projecting budget balance; and at the end of June 1987 it closed the year with a modest surplus. To a large extent, such gaps have been closed through normal revenue and expenditure adjustments and state education aid growth; thus, they did not represent true gaps. The size of the hard, bottom-line gaps has been obscured and as a result their importance has been downplayed.

To some extent, work, new programs, and new dollars have been necessary to maintain fiscal stability, but these resources were necessary primarily to fund discretionary hiring of new municipal employees. Continued use of gaps in the out years has actually become detrimental to the process, serving only to allow the administration to have gaps; that is to say, under the current system the city is allowed to raise expenditures to a level where funding to pay for them need not be identified beyond the current year. Unspecified estimates of revenue increases or expenditure decreases are used to offset, or "plug," and it is only six months before the year in which it is to be implemented that the

PEG is specified and included in the agency budgets. As a consequence, this system is producing an unrealistic financial plan and is allowing a lack of the long-term planning and articulation of policy it was originally intended to foster.

Some will argue that it is necessary to preserve the gap convention in order to create pressure for unrestricted state aid increases, to lower collective bargaining settlements, and to reduce city council add-ons to the executive budget. These arguments would be more persuasive if the gaps had more credibility. The time has now come to conduct such negotiations on their merits, without beating the horse with the same stick of oversized deficits used in the aftermath of the fiscal crisis. Recent statements by officials from both the executive and legislative branches of state government lend support to this position. They are urging city officials to change their well-worn approach to Albany and base their future lobbying efforts for increased state aid on arguments of "need" rather than financial emergency. Dall Forsythe, then state budget director, was quoted in 1987:

> The City's finances are stabilized and, in some recent years, the
> City has been a good deal better off than the State. The City's tax
> base is broader, more stable, less subject to economic impact than
> the State, in part, because of the property tax . . . The City has
> come to Albany on a regular basis to ask for money—primarily
> based on the need to fill its fiscal gap. For the last decade the
> City's argument has been that its finances are in trouble, they are
> always in trouble, and it needs gap-closing aid. At this stage in
> our existence, this is clearly an artifact of an earlier age.[2]

The second problem is that increasing expenditures in Year 1 to a level where they are not being paid for in Year 2 almost guarantees some underspending of the budget in both years. In fact, one almost automatic component of the city's January revisions has been to achieve expenditure savings for Year 2 through reductions, productivity savings, reestimates, and reduced reserves. Some argue that there is no point in not increasing expenditures in Year 1 because by the time the city gets to Year 2 it may be able to fund the increases through unanticipated resources—including a surplus roll—and the citizens of the city will not have had to forgo the service enhancements. This argument could be acceptable if there existed some limit on the size of the out-year gaps allowed to be created (covering both mandated and discretionary increases), or if the city were not involved in a recurring seesaw process of planned expenditure increases in June with expenditure reductions or underspending in the following January through June. Although it may be impossible to match every spending increase with a specific expenditure decrease or revenue increase, it is reasonable to believe that the process would be more effective if, along with spending increases, the city would build its productivity and expenditure reduction programs for Year 2 into the baselines of its financial plan in June prior to Year 1. They could always be modified at a later date if they became unnecessary as a result of either unanticipated revenue increases or a developing surplus.

The third problem is that because the administration must present both a preliminary (January) and a final (April) executive budget, this almost institutionally requires several increases in city spending per year to satisfy political constituents. In theory, the January presentation is necessary so that both the city council and the state government have adequate time to consider the full panoply of the administration's program proposals and estimates. Thereafter, it is appropriate that the mayor finalize the budget based on input from city and state officials, on the results of state budget adoption (scheduled for April 1), and on current information concerning the state of the local economy and tax collections. The city council then considers the final executive budget and adopts an amended version in June. In practice, the process is more complicated. Once the preliminary budget is presented, the city council produces a list of service enhancements for inclusion in the final executive budget, to which it then adds again during the post-executive budget period. This multistep process has perforce put significant expansionary pressure on the budget.

One way to reduce this pressure would be for the administration to consolidate the steps by presenting its service enhancement program in its preliminary budget presentation in January, along with its other major budget revisions. A serious effort would then have to be made to turn finalization of the executive budget into more of a technical exercise in which no major new spending initiatives were announced unless there had been an improvement in the city's fiscal condition since January.

The paramount recommendation in this area, however, is that the city eliminate the use of budget gaps in its financial plan on a phased-in basis. It would be appropriate for the city to start the process by projecting GAAP-balance in the second (as well as the first) year of its financial plan, with gaps and unspecified gap-closing programs permitted in only the final two years of the plan. After sufficient experience with this new format, the city might then implement a format that dispensed with the below-the-line PEG programs altogether and projected GAAP-balance in all four years of the financial plan.

Internalize the Monitoring Function

The state legislature has never spelled out the postsunset roles of the oversight monitors. To give virtually no guidance or direction to these state agencies was the easiest road politically, but it leaves both city and state officials, and the public as well, with an unclear sense as to the current extent of the state's responsibility for the city's financial condition and the importance of long-range fiscal planning for the city.

Such planning continues to be important for the city. If it is well done, it leads the city to identify and address fiscal problems over time, and it constrains spending that is affordable now but not in future years. Whether or not the state monitors continue to serve as objective and effective critics of city financial management, it is essential that the city assert itself in the planning function. While financial plans change more than they remain the same, they nevertheless provide coordinates for the city's revenue and expenditure decisions, indicating what today's spending activity will cost tomorrow's taxpayers and whether or not the city's revenue base can bear the pressure of expansionary expenditure policies. Now that the city has won back fiscal autonomy, it should avoid the mistake of leaving it to the state monitors to worry about the reasonableness of the four-year financial plan and its implications for the city. Even worse would be for the city to point to the monitors as a fiscal backup system, if that should appear useful from time to time, but to pay little attention to the results of their work.

One solution to this situation is for the city to institutionalize the monitoring process by creating a financial planning function within OMB. Although officials operating in complex environments tend to emphasize crisis management, these are just the people who also need the overview and perspective of personnel trained in the longer view. It is those people who can, if allowed, exercise a conservative influence on budget making and help to prevent the kind of expense buildup that causes budget deficits and the kind of tax and fee buildup that undermines the economy.

The citizenry benefits from forthright discussion of the city's longer-range taxing and spending positions, and the city's financial plans would benefit if they were to reflect those positions fully. A major flaw in the process to date is that city work-force levels have been held almost flat in the out-year projections of the financial plan. Instead, realistic staffing targets for each agency for the full four years should be projected in the city's financial plan in order to make total city expenditure projections, and thus the plan itself, more realistic.

What are the future work force plans for New York City? What is the justification for the current size of the city's work force? Can the city afford its employment base over time, given its taxing and wage policies? The public does not at present know the answer to these questions.

A more realistic staffing plan would serve the public better in both good and hard times. In peaks of rising revenues it would constrain political leaders' tendencies to use money to expand the payroll; in periods of retrenchment it would preclude periodic announcements of "emergency" hiring freezes and layoffs. At the least, the public should be provided with sufficient information to reassure itself that the city has considered all aspects of the long-term budgetary equation and that it has the competing demands on the budget under control. The city should act as its own "financial monitor" and assume full responsibility for the realism of its financial plans and articulation of its long-term fiscal strategies.

Scale Down the Use of Budget Gimmicks

Budget gimmicks come in a variety of packages, but they are usually a technical means to find short-term funding ("one-shots") for ongoing expenditures in order to delay the longer-term problem of finding permanent funding—such as tax increases—to support them. The use of budget gimmicks is not bad per se, but becomes an unsound practice when it renders the financial plan unrealistic and jeopardizes budget balance.

One obvious example of a budget gimmick is the overestimation of revenues to "fund" new or improved services. Another gimmick is to shift revenues and expenditures between fiscal years. One way to save pension costs (which lag salaries by a year) on a one-time basis, for example, is to delay a police class from June 30 of a given fiscal year to July 1 of the next. One way to increase revenues is for the state to take advantage of the "magic window" between the two budget years and to advance the payment schedule of revenue sharing, for example, so that there is no effect on the state's budget but the city gets a one-time benefit. (This was done, in essence, in fiscal year 1985.)

Indirect capitalization of operating expenditures is another gimmick, legitimate under GAAP, but questionable as a sound budgeting practice because it delays the need to address basic funding problems and can sometimes add to the total costs that the taxpayers must ultimately pay. An illustration is the city's proposal in 1987 that it match, as required by law, an increase in the annual state operating subsidy to the New York City Transit Authority not with city operating funds but with city capital funds; this would be given to the Metropolitan Transportation Authority for use in its capital program in order to free MTA funds to be used to help balance the Transit Authority's operating budget.

The overuse of budget gimmicks can lead to budget deficits. Nonrecurring resources are used on a temporary basis to fill the gap between the levels of recurring revenues and planned expenditures. If the level of recurring revenues fails to grow fast enough to cover the gap on a permanent basis, or if it becomes difficult to find new one-shots year after year to cover it, then the gap can suddenly become too great to cope with by using budget management techniques such as year-end underspending.

Another budget gimmick which drew criticism from fiscal observers was the city's use of $240 million from its share of the proceeds from the planned sale of the New York Coliseum—a one-shot revenue—to fund recurring expenditures first in its fiscal year 1987 budget, and then in subsequent years. Not only was this risky because the timing of the closing was delayed by lawsuits, but it was not a sound budgeting practice because the amount of the one-shot revenue was so large. The city budget is large, but $240 million of Coliseum proceeds represented over 1 percent of the fiscal year 1987 budget; its nonrecurrence was a serious matter. A one-time revenue item as large as this asset sale should have been dedicated to one-time usage, such as the deferred maintenance program at the Board of Education, or at least spread out to cover ongoing expenditures over a two- or three-year period. This would have minimized the risk of permanent loss of the Coliseum funds due to litigation or other contingencies. Without reserves, a sudden loss of a quarter-billion dollars in city funds could result in the layoff of as many as 8,500 to 10,000 city employees, depending on when and where pink slips were delivered. Given this kind of risk, the use of the Coliseum proceeds to fund recurring expenditures did not represent sound budgeting practice.

A related matter is the decreasing size of the city's annual operating sur-

Table 6.1 City of New York Operating Budget Surpluses and Discretionary Adjustments, Fiscal Years 1981–1990 (dollars in millions)

Budget Item	1981	1982	1983	1984	1985	1986	1987	1988	1989	1990
Initial surplus	$486	$379	$507	$517	$570	$423	$567	$225	$409	$253
Discretionary adjustments	358	338	473	494	558	416	559	215	403	248
Transfer to capital projects fund	147	—	—	—	—	—	—	—	—	—
Revocation of MAC debt service	137	251	192	183	170	158	146	138	130	123
Transfer to debt service fund	36	47	62	30	12	23	88	33	30	36
Advance cash subsidies[a]	—	30	219	216	215	142	238	27	183	54
Prepayment of wage deferral	—	—	—	65	50	46	40	—	41	35
Rescheduling of debt service	—	—	—	—	111	47	47	17	19	—
Offset of federal education funds	38	10	—	—	—	—	—	—	—	—
Reported surplus	$128	$41	$34	$23	$12	$7	$8	$10	$6	$5

Sources: City of New York, Comprehensive Annual Financial Report of the Comptroller, fiscal years 1981–1990 editions.

[a]1982: Transit Authority. 1983: TA, Housing Authority, libraries, and others. 1984: TA, libraries, and others. 1985: TA, Health and Hospitals Corporation, and Legal Aid Society. 1986: TA, HHC, and LAS. 1987: TA and HHC. 1988: TA. 1989: TA, HA, LAS, libraries, and Metropolitan Transportation Authority. 1990: TA, HA, LAS, and libraries.

plus. Much favorable publicity has been generated by the fact that each year since 1981 the city has ended its fiscal year with a surplus. How can a surplus condition be a problem?

The city has approached the close of each fiscal year with a potential surplus of substantial proportions, most of which has been "rolled" forward to help balance the next year's budget through devices such as prepayments of debt service and of authority subsidies. (See Table 6.1.) This surplus carryforward has given the appearance of a recurring and sizable resource for the city, growing from $358 million in fiscal year 1981 to $558 million in fiscal year 1985. In any given year, however, a potential surplus is only a one-shot resource. Surpluses become a recurring resource that can be relied upon to supplement current revenues and fund recurring expenditures only to the extent that the factors causing the surplus can be sustained. However, in most recent years the surplus has been a shrinking resource that may soon disappear.

The fiscal year 1986 surplus carryforward ($416 million) was for the first time since 1982 smaller than the prior year's ($558 million), indicating that the city's current expenditures were suddenly exceeding current revenues and that its capacity to continue to generate year-end surpluses to help balance subsequent budgets had diminished. In effect, the city had been carrying the earlier years' surpluses as a sort of reserve through fiscal year 1985, but it then began depleting this reserve fund to support recurring expenditures.

Since fiscal year 1985 the city has unevenly, but almost completely, exhausted the surplus carryforward. In fiscal years 1986, 1988, and 1990 the size of the carryforward was less than in the previous year. As a result, the amount available fell from $558 million in fiscal year 1985 to $248 million in fiscal year 1990. In fiscal year 1991 the carryforward fell to $22 million, and this equivalent of a reserve fund was exhausted. In effect, rather than having a true surplus, the city actually had greater true "current" expenditures than "current" revenues in four of the six fiscal years from 1986 to 1991.

Conclusion

The proposed agenda—procedural safeguarding, rigorous updating, true-gap projection, internalized monitoring, and reduced gimmickry—is intended to make the city's financial plan more realistic, and therefore more credible and useful as an instrument for preserving fiscal health. As long as it is important to citizens and to potential creditors that the city achieve balanced budgets, it is unlikely to return to the monstrous deficit spending of the past. But it would be a mistake to keep looking to the past and forget to look to the future. As a fiscally healthy jurisdiction, the city's goals become at once more modest and more difficult than avoiding a return to the practices of the pre-fiscal crisis days. Maintaining balanced budgets, and thus a strong credit position, is not as easy as the city made it seem during the reign of the fiscal monitors. Now that the city has regained full control over its finances, it should be careful to exercise that control by maintaining and improving its current budget and financial planning systems.

BARGAINING AND BUDGETING

This chapter addresses issues involving two of the most important aspects of New York City government, municipal budgeting and collective bargaining. The issues are highlighted by the repeated failure of collective bargaining to resolve municipal wage policy in time for adoption of a realistic annual operating budget. The delays in resolving labor settlements mean that city officials must allocate resources and determine related policy issues without having the benefit of knowing what labor costs will be in a given year. This threatens the integrity of the city's budgeting and financial planning processes.

This chapter also presents options for reform of the city's Collective Bargaining Law that would strengthen both the budgeting and bargaining processes. The first section describes the nature of the problem. The second section illustrates the problem by examining the fiscal year 1985 round of collective bargaining when the problems were particularly acute. The third section discusses the policy options.

The Budgeting–Bargaining Relationship

Municipal budgeting and collective bargaining perform functions of signal importance. The budgeting process determines how much money the city will spend in a given year and for what purpose. The city's fiscal year 1991 expense budget allocated $28 billion of local public expenditure. The collective bargaining process provides unionized municipal employees a bilateral process for determining how much money they will earn for their labors. For fiscal year 1991 it was estimated that the city's nearly quarter-million workers would earn almost $15 billion.

Neither process can be considered in a vacuum. Collective bargaining has a major impact on the city's budgetary process, and vice versa. This is particularly so when budgets are formulated, considered, and even adopted without being informed by wage settlements. Having, in essence, to guess the cost of compensating municipal employees makes it all the more difficult for public officials to resolve intelligently certain important questions that are inherent in the budget process: Are revenues adequate to sustain planned work-force expansion, or will taxes have to be increased and/or other programs cut? What service goals are to be established for managers to meet, and how many employees will be available to help realize these goals? Is the share of the city's resources to be devoted to municipal workers fair relative to other groups affected by spending and taxing decisions reached in the budget process?

Admittedly, the elimination of budgetary uncertainty is not possible. Certain budget components inevitably resist precise specification (estimating local revenues, for example, because of inadequate forecasting techniques or unanticipated changes in local economic performance—or both). Nevertheless, the reduction of uncertainty is desirable. This presumption is supported by the experience before the New York City fiscal crisis, when uncertainty about revenues and expenditures was the rule rather than the exception, and by the experience since, when many outstanding reforms in budgeting and financial planning practice have occurred.

Assuming that integration of bargaining and budgeting would contribute to more informed budgeting, how would that affect the collective bargaining process? For more than two decades the city of New York has committed itself to the proposition that good labor–management relations depend on the ability of the city and municipal union leaders to resolve their disagreements over wage policy and many other issues through the bilateral process of collective bargaining. It would ill behoove the city to sacrifice collective bargaining on the altar of better budgeting if, in fact, requiring integration of bargaining and budgeting would endanger the integrity of collective bargaining. To gain a better understanding of these issues it is useful to review the changing nature of collective bargaining and budgeting as illustrated by events during the fiscal year 1985 round of negotiations.

The Fiscal Year 1985 Round of Bargaining

The immediate background for the fiscal year 1985 round of collective bargaining is the labor contracts for fiscal years 1983 and 1984, that is, for the period beginning July 1, 1982, and ending June 30, 1984. The fiscal year 1985 round of bargaining formally began in April 1984, less than three months before expiration of these labor contracts. This suggests that the negotiators were not intent on resolving municipal wage policy prior to the expiration of labor contracts at the end of fiscal year 1984. If achieving timely settlements had been the intent of the parties, then negotiations would have begun earlier or, once begun, would have proceeded more resolutely.

Whereas the first formal contract talks began in April 1984, the actual beginning of the bargaining dates back to January 1984, when the city proposed its 1985–1988 financial plan and estimated successive annual wage increases of 2 percent. Financial planning requirements force the city to so estimate its wage policy when existing contracts do not already specify wages. This requirement is thought by some to put the city in a Hobson's choice. On the one hand, it must convince the Financial Control Board (FCB) that its financial plans are reasonable in order to obtain the FCB's approval. On the other hand, stating a truly reasonable estimate of wage outcomes is considered by some to give union leaders a bargaining advantage since they are presumed able to use such an estimate as a floor upon which to negotiate higher settlements. True or not, the city's financial plan estimate of 2 percent wage increases contributed little to moving negotiations toward a reasonable or prompt outcome. Nor did the initial demands of the city's municipal union leaders for annual salary increases in the 12–15 percent range.

After adoption of the 1985 budget the city increased its wage offer to 3 percent, but bargaining proceeded only intermittently throughout the summer and fall of 1984. In November, the city abruptly petitioned the Office of Collective Bargaining, which is responsible for administering the city's collective bargaining system, to declare negotiations at an impasse as a prelude to arbitration. This represented a significant policy departure for the city since arbitration had been eschewed by labor and management in the period after the fiscal crisis.

Thus none of the outstanding contracts was settled halfway through fiscal year 1985. For budgeting purposes, the city clung to its unrealistic estimate of 3 percent wage increases for fiscal year 1985. Not having to pay any salary increases in the interim produced a windfall "profit" for the city in the form of interest on the banked funds set aside for collective bargaining. The delay was not without its costs, however. Municipal employees did not receive wage increases and lost the use of their money. Moreover, positions whose salaries already were too low to attract enough qualified applicants—entry-level teachers are the outstanding example—had to be filled with persons willing to work at 1984 wages.

In January 1985 a three-year settlement with the Uniformed Firefighters' Association (UFA) was reached providing successive 6 percent wage increases that were not compounded (that is, based on the 1984 rate) for fiscal years 1985, 1986, and 1987. As a result the city changed its financial planning estimates from 3 percent for all workers to 6 percent for uniformed workers and 4.5 percent for civilian workers, a significant change since it signaled that the city wanted to negotiate more favorable settlements for uniformed workers than civilians. However, the delegates of the UFA, at the urging of leaders of other uniformed unions, rejected the contract in February. As a result, the city revised its estimate of labor costs for each of the three years to 5.5 percent, 5.5 percent, and 5.0 percent for uniformed employees, and a percentage point lower for civilians.

In April, the city finally was able to negotiate a three-year settlement with District Council 37 (DC 37), the largest civilian employee union, calling for wage increases of 5 percent, 5 percent, and 6 percent for the 1985–1987 period. As a result, the city changed its budget plans again, this time estimating that the "5–5–6" agreement with DC 37 would become the pattern for both uniformed unions and the remaining civilian unions. The fiscal year 1986 budget, adopted in June 1985, reflected these assumptions—except that on the day the budget was adopted a three-year, 6 percent (compounded) settlement was announced with a group of uniformed unions. Thus the new budget had to be modified once again to reflect 5 percent increases for civilian employees (including managers, whose pay is established by the civilian pattern) and 6 percent increases for uniformed employees. The United Federation of Teachers and the city subsequently prepared to submit their wage dispute to final-offer arbitration (discussed later).

The failure to reach negotiated settlements in a timely fashion was caused by two major factors that are apparent from the foregoing chronology. The primary cause was the breakdown of union bargaining coalitions that, after 1975, had helped reduce competition within the ranks of municipal union officials. With the fiscal crisis a thing of the past and the key unions increasingly going their own way, city officials had trouble identifying a union to strike what they hoped would be a precedent-setting agreement for the remaining unions. The city tried hardest with the UFA, but the tentative settlement reached with the UFA in January 1985 was repudiated by delegates to that union. The city then turned to DC 37 but discovered that the 5–5–6 contract was no precedent but a floor for other union leaders to construct better contracts for their members.

A related factor underlying the delay was the city's inability to maintain a consistent position on the vexing issue of "parity" between civilian and uniformed unions. Throughout most of the city's early experience with collective bargaining, uniformed employees received higher wage increases than civilian workers. Between 1977 and 1979, however, wages were frozen across the board; and between 1979 and 1984, civilian salaries actually increased faster than uniformed salaries because lump-sum payments of equal amounts were added to the base pay of all workers for the purpose of computing their negotiated salary increases. In the fiscal year 1985 round, the city began by offering all employees the same percentage increase regardless of their uniformed or civilian status; it changed its tactics early in 1985 by offering higher settlements to uniformed employees; then it reverted back to a position that would have tied all employees to the DC 37 settlement. Finally, the uniformed settlement seemed to settle the issue by providing larger increases for uniformed employees than at least those civilians represented by District Council 37. However, the leadership of the teachers' union was unwilling to settle for what the leaders of either DC 37 or the uniformed unions negotiated for their members.

Options to Improve Bargaining and Budgeting

The issue examined in this section may be stated as follows: Would the practice of municipal budgeting and collective bargaining in the city be improved by requiring that labor contracts be settled before adoption of the budget, if necessary by final-offer arbitration rather than conventional arbitration?

Final Offer Versus Conventional Arbitration

Conventional arbitration, whereby arbitrators are free to impose any wage settlement on the parties (subject to vague standards that permit loose construction), has been in effect in New York City since 1972. Although conventional arbitration appears on the face of things to permit arbitrators substantial discretion in making awards, arbitrators under conventional rules in fact find their behavior bounded in an important way that, in turn, reduces the incentives for parties to reach negotiated settlements.

The constraint on the discretion of arbitrators under conventional arbitration is self-imposed, resulting from their fear that a party too disappointed by their award will "blackball" them from future arbitration assignments. To minimize this risk, arbitrators in conventional arbitration respond by seeking a compromise award acceptable to both parties—the ultimate manifestation of which is awards that split the difference equally. Negotiators, anticipating this behavior by arbitrators, thus have fewer incentives to compromise their positions while bargaining. A "compromiser" whose worst fears are met— that is, the other party compromises less or not at all—would experience a worse arbitration award for actually having tried to bargain. Experience shows that bargained settlements occur less frequently in governments with conventional arbitration; that is, conventional arbitration has a "chilling" effect on collective bargaining.[1]

Under the final-offer variant, arbitrators must choose the last-best offer of one party *or* the other. In short, they are prohibited from splitting the difference. This increases the incentives for negotiators to bargain because of the fear that their opponent's last-best offer may be perceived in final-offer arbitration as being more reasonable than their own. After striving in negotiations for the "last-most-reasonable" offer, the parties frequently find that they are able to negotiate settlements and do not need the services of arbitrators.

Final-offer arbitration is preferable to the conventional system if, in fact, negotiated settlements are preferred over arbitrated settlements. The strongest argument that can be made for the conventional arbitration system is that it might be "safer" than final-offer arbitration under certain circumstances (that is, where one side or the other resisted the logic of compromise under final-offer arbitration and ended the negotiation phase with an "unreasonable" position *and* where the arbitrator selected the unreasonable position as the last-best offer). To the extent this defense of conventional arbitration has any validity, it is probably in jurisdictions where negotiators are inexperienced in collective bargaining. This is not the case in the city of New York.

Nationally, final-offer arbitration is gaining support as the preferred method of arbitration in those states that permit collective bargaining for public employees. Almost one-half of the states have public sector bargaining laws that include one form or the other of compulsory arbitration. A few states, including New Jersey, Wisconsin, and Nevada, permit either conventional arbitration or final-offer arbitration. The remaining states are divided about equally between final-offer arbitration and conventional arbitration, though as noted the trend is for final-offer arbitration to replace the conventional form.[2]

Assuming that the purpose of the city's collective bargaining system is to encourage the incidence of negotiated settlements, then final-offer arbitration would be more consistent with that purpose than conventional arbitration. However, whereas final-offer arbitration indeed may induce faster negotiated settlements, it would not necessarily ensure timely resolution.

Requiring Timeliness

State and local laws regulate the budgetary process in a temporal sense because of its importance. The city's first public definition of the parameters of its next budget occurs in January when the mayor's financial plan for the next four fiscal years is made public. As noted earlier, this document includes an estimated wage settlement, usually unrealistically low, when contracts do not already specify salaries. The next key date in the budget cycle is April 26, when the mayor is required to submit the executive budget for the next fiscal year (along with a new financial plan modified to reflect the proposed budget). After that, the city council has until June 5 to adopt a budget (or until June 20 if agreement is not reached with the mayor).[3] The budget goes into effect July 1.

Timeliness for resolution of labor contracts within this sequence would fall in the period between submission of the financial plan in January and presentation of the mayor's executive budget on April 26. If certainty of information is to be a guiding principle, then the period should be narrowed to between April 1, when the state budget is supposed to be adopted, and the April 26 submission of the executive budget. Negotiations not completed by early April should be resolved by arbitration prior to April 26, in order to permit the key policy issues that must be resolved by the time the executive budget is submitted to be reached with the benefit of knowing what costs are involved. (Arguably, the date for final resolution of labor disputes could be extended into early May since that still would leave the administration some time to revise its executive budget prior to legislative consideration, which involves public hearings in May.)

The major argument against the timeliness requirement rests on the proposition that collective bargaining, to be successful, cannot be forced into too short or too rigid a time frame. Most proponents of the current, open-ended system recognize the problems that delay causes those with budgetary responsibilities but conclude nevertheless that collective bargaining should not be so restricted. A partial answer to that objection is simply to begin bargaining earlier. Remember that negotiations in the fiscal year 1985 round did not begin until less than three months before contract expiration, and then in serious fashion with only one union. There is no apparent reason why bargaining could not have begun well before April 1984.

A second argument sometimes advanced in opposition to the timeliness requirement is that it might work consistently to the advantage of one or the other party. Union leaders might fear that having to meet a statutory timetable determined by presentation, consideration, and adoption of the budget would permit management to engage in "take it or leave it" offers, known as "boulwarism." Management negotiators might fear that requiring timely settlements would exert pressure on them to settle at any cost. Institution of the timeliness rule would require that some form of arbitration be available in the event either party sought to exploit impending budget deadlines to its advantage. For reasons discussed earlier, the final-offer system would be preferable to the existing system of conventional arbitration.

Conclusion

The fiscal year 1985 round of bargaining and budget highlights the issues raised in this chapter. Collective bargaining failed in the sense that delay meant two successive budgets had to be adopted without knowing municipal wage policy. Analysis of the reasons for the delay in this round, particularly the decline of union bargaining coalitions, suggests that the issues of timeliness and reliance on arbitration would continue to be salient in future rounds. This, in fact, has been the case. The contracts for the period beginning at the start of fiscal year 1988 (July 1, 1987) were agreed to in August and October 1987, causing the previously adopted budgets to be modified midstream. These contracts extended to June 30, 1990,[4] and new agreements were not reached in time for preparation of the fiscal year 1991 budget or for the November 1990 modification of that budget.

City and union negotiators have the capacity to negotiate settlements in a timely fashion, but they do not always have the incentives to do so. The structural reforms proposed in this chapter—final-offer arbitration and the requirement for final resolution of labor contracts prior to budget adoption—would increase the likelihood that contracts would be negotiated in time to inform the budgeting process without giving either side an undue bargaining advantage.

_____8

THE CAPITAL BUDGET
AND CAPITAL
PROJECTS

A major challenge for the leaders of the city of New York is to rebuild municipal infrastructure and enhance the physical facilities that support service delivery. Since emerging from the fiscal crisis of 1975, the city has regained access to credit markets and developed an ambitious capital investment program. A key issue is how quickly these capital projects can be completed. Delays postpone improvements and add to project costs.

This chapter is organized into four sections. The first provides background on the city's ten-year capital plans, its annual capital budgets, and the information systems used to track the progress of capital projects authorized in the budget. The second part assesses the progress on 1,084 projects initiated in fiscal years 1983 through 1989. The third section presents case studies of 22 projects scheduled for completion in fiscal year 1988 to illustrate the reasons for delays. The final section presents recommendations for change in managing capital projects.

Capital Plans and Capital Budgeting

Capital investments by the city of New York are guided by a ten-year capital plan and implemented through an annual capital budget process. The long-run plan evolved in the aftermath of the city's fiscal crisis; the annual process is shaped by the city charter.

165

The Ten-Year Strategy

The 1975 fiscal crisis prevented the city from selling its bonds in public credit markets and halted all capital construction except that funded by intergovernmental aid. Capital spending plummeted from an estimated $1.1 billion in fiscal year 1973 to $257 million in 1977.[1] As a precondition of the federal loan guarantees which subsequently allowed the city to reenter the markets, the city had to assess its capital needs and develop a capacity for long-term capital planning.

The Office of Management and Budget (OMB) was assigned the task of preparing this capital plan. In May 1983, Mayor Edward I. Koch released the first ten-year plan covering the fiscal years 1983–1992 period. Since then, the plan has been revised biennially. The fourth ten-year plan appeared in May 1988 and covered the fiscal years 1989–1998 period.

The 1989 charter reforms mandated a modified form of long-term capital planning. It requires the mayor in cooperation with the City Planning Commission to prepare a Ten-Year Capital Strategy, which is then reviewed and approved by the city council. The first such document was presented by Mayor Dinkins in December 1990 and was approved in a modified form by the city council in June 1991. It covers the period fiscal years 1992–2001.

With each revision, planned capital spending over the ten-year period has increased significantly. (See Table 8.1.) From the first plan to the current strategy, the total increased 93 percent from $34.7 billion to $67.0 billion.

Table 8.1 Summary of City of New York Ten-Year Capital Plans (dollars in millions)

Type of Project	Fiscal Year 1983–92 Plan	Fiscal Year 1985–94 Plan	Fiscal Year 1987–96 Plan	Fiscal Year 1989–98 Plan	Fiscal Year 1992–2001 Strategy
Bridges	$1,491	$1,616	$1,376	$2,705	$3,285
Water supply	1,173	2,512	2,856	2,261	2,126
Water mains	887	1,238	1,515	1,771	1,244
Streets and highways	3,986	4,747	4,245	5,430	3,666
Sewers	1,109	1,762	2,034	1,830	1,644
Water pollution control	3,143	2,499	1,845	2,588	5,310
Waste disposal	1,242	3,361	4,338	3,130	2,971
Public schools	1,415	1,862	2,123	5,189	8,511
Hospitals	1,072	1,508	1,873	2,582	2,731
Parks	744	1,392	1,308	1,837	1,059
Service vehicles and facilities	1,643	1,813	2,067	2,451	3,220
Housing	141	180	4,223	5,114	4,951
Other	2,688	2,485	2,811	5,139	7,203[a]
Subtotal	$20,734	$26,975	$32,614	$42,027	$47,921
Transit	13,988	13,644	13,061	15,279	19,062
Total	$34,722	$40,619	$45,675	$57,306	$66,983

Sources: City of New York, *Ten-Year Capital Plan*, fiscal years 1983–92, 1985–94, 1987–96, and 1989–98 editions, and *Ten-Year Capital Strategy*, fiscal years 1992–2001, May 10, 1991.

[a]Includes borough presidents' allocation.

The most recent revision in June 1991 increased planned spending $9.7 billion, or 17 percent over the 1988 plan.

The periodic revisions of the plan have included significant changes in programmatic emphasis as well as increased funds. Most notably, the May 1986 revision included the addition of more than $4 billion for housing, committing the city to a major new initiative in this area. Similarly, the May 1988 revision increased planned spending for public schools nearly $3 billion, launching a significant effort to upgrade the facilities of the Board of Education. This was expanded further to exceed $8.5 billion in the 1991 strategy. Finally, in 1988 the city nearly doubled the commitment to bridges to more than $2.7 billion, in an effort to speed repair of these facilities. In contrast, planned funding for streets and highways, parks, and water mains was cut significantly in the latest plan.

The Capital Budget

Projects included in the ten-year plan become a reality through the city's capital budget. This involves four stages: (1) the *authorization* of a project; (2) the *appropriation* of funds for the project; (3) the *commitment* of funds for the project; and (4) the *expenditure* of funds for work completed on the project.

Before a project can be funded, it must be authorized by the city council. A project is authorized on the basis of information provided by OMB and the responsible line agency. Formal authority to begin a project is its listing in the annual capital budget. Each project's line in the budget includes OMB's estimate of its completion date and of its total cost. This information is supposed to be revised annually.

An appropriation makes funds available to implement a project. An initial appropriation is made at the same time the project is authorized. Usually the first appropriation for a project is for an amount that is only a portion of the project's estimated total cost. The appropriation for a given year represents the amount expected to be required to carry the project forward that year. As a project progresses, its cumulative appropriation increases. Funds are appropriated by the city council as part of the annual capital budget.

After a project receives an appropriation, the next stage is defining a project scope and developing a design and then undertaking the construction work. While the city has some in-house capacity, most of this work is done through outside contractors. A commitment of funds is made by the city for each contract. Contracts are entered into separately for design of the project and for each phase of construction such as foundation work, structural components, electrical work, and plumbing. Total contract commitments for a project legally cannot exceed the cumulative appropriation for the project.

Funds appropriated for a project that are not committed at the end of the fiscal year are generally carried forward into the next year. It is not uncommon for appropriations to be made for a project, but for the responsible agency to make no commitments in the same fiscal year. Sometimes agencies do not commit funds for a project until a few years after the initial appropriation.

Table 8.2 Indicators of Capital Budget Activity, Fiscal Years 1983–1991 (dollars in millions)

Activity Measure	1983	1984	1985	1986	1987	1988	1989	1990	1991
Appropriations	$2,010	$1,540	$2,298	$2,725	$3,859	$4,453	$5,251	$9,472	$4,460
Planned commitments	1,631	2,111	2,019	2,171	2,496	3,042	4,349	4,662	3,556
Actual commitments	1,643	1,861	1,917	2,024	2,165	3,042	4,349	4,662	3,556
Accrued expenditures	1,293	1,524	1,688	1,724	1,907	2,231	3,142	3,751	4,233
Cash expenditures	1,352	1,459	1,651	1,723	1,805	2,265	2,993	3,580	4,100

Sources: Appropriations are from City of New York, *Capital Budget as Adopted*, fiscal years 1983–1991 editions. Planned commitments for fiscal years 1983–1987 are unpublished figures supplied by New York City Office of Management and Budget. Planned commitments for fiscal years 1988–1991 are from City of New York, "Capital Commitment Plan," September editions for fiscal years 1991 and 1992. Actual commitments and cash expenditures for fiscal years 1983–1991 are from City of New York, "Monthly Transaction Analysis, Year End," fiscal years 1983–1991 editions. Accrued expenditures are from City of New York, *Comprehensive Annual Financial Report of the Comptroller*, fiscal years 1983–1991 editions.

The city measures commitments three different ways. Authorized commitments are the amount of contract awards OMB anticipates based on targets established for each agency. Planned, or "target," commitments refers to a lesser aggregate target OMB establishes after making an adjustment for the fact that historically all authorized commitments are not used by the agencies. Actual commitments represent the value of contracts actually awarded during the year.

The city pays firms for work competed under a contract. These expenditures are tracked in two ways. Accrued expenditures represent the obligations incurred by the city based on work performed by contractors. Cash expenditures are the cash outlays to the firms. The city comptroller reports accrued expenditures; OMB reports cash outlays.

Consistent with the increase in the size of the ten-year plans, appropriations have grown rapidly. (See Table 8.2.) During the fiscal years 1983–1990 period, appropriations rose from $2.0 billion to nearly $9.5 billion, or 375 percent. Appropriations grew 80 percent in 1990 alone because of a $4.3 billion appropriation for the new School Construction Authority (SCA). Appropriations fell back to $4.5 billion in 1991. Planned commitments rose from about $1.6 billion in fiscal year 1983 to almost $4.7 billion in fiscal year 1990. Actual commitments increased 182 percent from $1.6 billion in fiscal year 1983 to $4.7 billion in fiscal year 1990. Commitments then declined to $3.6 billion in 1991. Cash expenditures increased from $1.4 billion to $4.2 billion during the fiscal years 1983–1991 period.

The budgetary and spending process described here applies to specific capital projects. However, there are two major types of capital investments by the city that do not follow this process, lump sum capital appropriations and so-called continuing projects.

Lump sum appropriations are funds raised through the capital budget that are transferred to other agencies for capital purposes. The major examples are lump sum appropriations for the Metropolitan Transportation Authority (MTA) and for the recently created New York City School Construction Authority. These funds are used, along with revenues received from other sources, to fund projects identified and implemented by the respective authorities. City agencies are not responsible for implementing the projects.

Continuing projects are those for which there is a recurring need or for which it is not appropriate to establish an estimated completion date. Examples of such continuing projects include the purchase of computer equipment for municipal agencies, regular replacement of vehicles for the Fire Department, and emergency repairs to water mains. Appropriations for continuing projects also supply funds for numerous projects that are not detailed as part of the capital budget. These include, for example, repairs to individual school buildings or park facilities. Instead of detailing these items in the budget, lump sum appropriations are made for continuing projects (titled, for example, repairs to school buildings in the Bronx). After the budget is adopted, OMB and the agency identify specific projects to be initiated as part of the annual commitment plan.

The portion of the capital budget consisting of lump sum appropriations

Table 8.3 Appropriations for Continuing Projects, Fiscal Years 1983, 1987, 1988, 1989, and 1990 (dollars in millions)

Budget Item	1983	1987	1988	1989	1990
Total appropriations for continuing projects	$806.4	$1,967.0	$2,763.9	$3,238.3	$8,153.9
Total appropriations for mass transit continuing projects	158.0	452.6	565.1	531.8	123.1
Total appropriations for public schools continuing projects	67.4	102.9	86.3	187.3	4,300.6
Total appropriations for sanitation continuing projects	114.9	99.4	124.5	216.3	318.7
Total appropriations for correction continuing projects	23.5	54.7	142.7	30.2	214.8
Total appropriations for housing continuing projects	20.5	177.5	689.2	727.1	893.6
Total appropriations for human resources continuing projects	0.8	28.4	264.2	8.6	330.6
Total appropriations for all other continuing projects	421.3	1,051.5	891.9	1,537.1	1,972.6
Total appropriations for entire capital budget	$2,009.9	$3,858.9	$4,453.1	$5,251.4	$9,471.5
Continuing projects as a share of capital budget	40.1%	51.0%	62.1%	61.7%	86.1%

Sources: City of New York, *Capital Budget as Adopted*, fiscal years 1983, 1987–1990 editions.

and continuing projects has grown significantly. (See Table 8.3.) In fiscal year 1983, the combined appropriation for all continuing projects was $806 million, or two–fifths of total annual appropriations. By fiscal year 1988, the figure had increased to almost $2.8 billion, or 62 percent of the total, in part because the new housing initiatives in that year took the form of some large appropriations for continuing projects such as the renovation of abandoned buildings at unspecified sites. By the time of the 1990 capital budget, the conversion by state legislation of public school projects to a lump sum appropriation for the SCA increased the share of the capital budget to nearly 85 percent.[2]

The information available in public reports on the progress of authorized projects is fragmented and incomplete. As previously noted, the annual capital budget contains for each line item project an estimated completion date, an estimated total cost, an annual appropriation, and a summary of the total appropriation from the current and previous budgets. For continuing projects, the budget presents no expected completion date or total cost; it provides simply an annual appropriation.

After the budget is authorized, OMB prepares a Commitment Plan and revises it twice during the year. The Commitment Plan provides information relating to all capital projects for which some activity is planned during the year. (Projects with an appropriation, but for which OMB anticipates no commitments or other activity during the year, are omitted.) For line item projects, the Commitment Plan indicates the type of contract expected to be awarded during the year and the expected amount of the contract. For continuing projects, the Commitment Plan provides an itemization of the specific activities (called subprojects) that will be undertaken and the planned types and amounts of contracts to be awarded for each subproject.

Actual commitments and cash expenditures under each line item project and each continuing project are reported monthly with a year-to-date total by OMB in a set of reports called the Monthly Transaction Analysis. The Monthly Transaction Analysis for June of each year contains the fiscal-year total of commitments and cash expenditures for each line item project and for each continuing project. However, the Monthly Transaction Analysis does not provide information on specific subprojects within a continuing project. This is a significant shortcoming because so large a portion of the capital budget takes the form of continuing projects. The annual report of the comptroller presents accrued expenditures for each line item project and for each continuing project (but, again, information on subprojects within a continuing project is not reported).

Another source of limited information on capital projects is the annual *Mayor's Management Report* (*MMR*). The city began to include selected indicators of progress in implementing its capital plan in the 1987 edition of the *MMR*. The indicators included have expanded somewhat since 1987 but still remain inadequate for assessing timely performance. For most agencies with large capital programs, the only indicators reported (beside expenditures) are the number of contracts awarded and the number of projects (defined to include subprojects under continuing projects) completed. For a few agencies indicators of the volume of work completed are also reported. For example, the Department of Transportation now reports the number of highway lane-miles reconstructed and resurfaced, and the Department of Correction reports the number of new beds added to its facilities.

In sum, the information available on capital project implementation is fragmented and incomplete. Even when the data reported by separate agencies in separate reports are combined, they do not permit citizens to know whether projects are completed on time or whether their implementation is proceeding in accord with a reasonable schedule.

The OMB has recognized the shortcomings of current information systems and has designed a more comprehensive management information system for tracking capital projects. The new system—called Design, Award and Construction Project Tracking System, or DACS—was approved by the mayor and all agencies were advised to implement it in accord with OMB's instructions on July 19, 1989.[3]

New Capital Projects and Their Implementation

Between fiscal years 1983 and 1990, fully 1,084 new line item projects were authorized by the city council and Board of Estimate.[4] The initial estimated total cost of this work was nearly $7.9 billion. (See Table 8.4.) The function with the largest number of projects (259) is streets and highways; another 201 new projects involved work on public schools. Relatively large numbers of new projects also were initiated for sewers (150), parks (138), and bridges (98).

The initial planned duration of the 1,084 new projects is shown in Table 8.5. Some projects (62) originally authorized as separate line projects became continuing projects. A smaller number of projects (40) were authorized without an estimated date of completion. These two types of projects were excluded from the remainder of the analysis.

Of the remaining 982 new specific capital projects, 219 were scheduled for completion after seven or more years. None of these projects, therefore, were expected to be completed by the end of the fiscal year 1989. Another 255 projects were expected to be completed in six years; this group includes 22 projects initiated in 1983 and therefore expected to be completed by the end of fiscal year 1989. The remaining 508 projects were scheduled for completion in five years or less; this group includes 320 projects which were scheduled for completion before fiscal year 1990. Thus, of the total of 1,084 new projects, 342 were scheduled for completion by the end of fiscal year 1989.

What actually has happened to this group of projects? To answer this question, information was gathered on each project for each calendar year since it was authorized. This information is derived from three sources. The construction status as of May 1989 is as reported in the Commitment Plan prepared by OMB. Financial information was collected and aggregated from the year-end Monthly Transaction Analysis prepared by OMB at the end of each fiscal year. These figures are compared to the estimated total cost of the

Table 8.4 Number of New Capital Budget Projects and Their Initial Estimated Total Cost, Fiscal Years 1983–1990 (dollars in millions)

Type of Project	1983	1984	1985	1986	1987	1988	1989	1990	Total
Public schools	12	6	16	34	35	25	73	0	201
Streets and highways	15	66	21	31	37	28	33	28	259
Service facilities	12	8	7	5	8	4	2	4	50
Water mains	0	0	0	1	0	1	0	0	2
Water supply	1	0	0	0	0	0	0	1	2
Bridges	9	18	4	18	10	4	12	23	98
Sewers	8	11	12	8	26	29	37	19	150
Parks	14	28	18	10	21	14	24	9	138
Sanitation	4	2	2	2	7	3	1	0	21
Hospitals	2	0	1	0	0	2	0	0	5
Other	27	26	27	20	23	10	13	12	158
Total	104	165	108	129	167	120	195	96	1,084
Initial estimated total cost	$797.6	$677.1	$660.3	$943.0	$1,166.3	$1,630.6	$1,382.6	$639.0	$7,896.5

Sources: City of New York, *Capital Budget as Adopted*, fiscal years 1983–1990 editions.

Table 8.5 Number of New Capital Projects by Initial Planned Duration and Start Year, Fiscal Years 1983–1990

Initial Planned Duration	Start Year								Total
	1983	1984	1985	1986	1987	1988	1989	1990	
Two years or less	15	8	18	14	4	8	20	13	100
Three years	8	16	10	11	17	8	12	6	88
Four years	14	13	13	25	16	18	22	6	127
Five years	22	38	14	22	35	22	30	10	193
Six years	22	45	21	28	44	35	42	18	255
Seven years or more	11	26	8	8	27	27	69	43	219
Subtotal	92	146	84	108	143	118	195	96	982
Continuing projects	8	11	18	10	13	2	0	0	62
Unknown duration	4	8	6	11	11	0	0	0	40
Total	104	165	108	129	167	120	195	96	1,084

Sources: City of New York, *Capital Budget as Adopted*, fiscal years 1983–1990 editions.

project as presented in the annual capital budget to yield quantitative measure of progress on the project.

Only 29, or under 9 percent, of the projects scheduled for completion by June 30, 1989, were actually finished at that time. (See Table 8.6.) Moreover, only 68, or about 20 percent, of the projects were even in construction. The majority of the projects, 188, or 55 percent, were still in a preconstruction phase at the time they were supposed to be completed. Another 22 projects, or 6 percent, had no action taken on them since they were initiated (that is, no funds were committed) even though they were initially scheduled for completion by that time. Another 33 projects, or about 10 percent, were dropped from the capital budget, indicating the city had changed its mind about doing the work after it was initially approved.

A more quantitative approach to assessing the pace of implementation is summarized in Table 8.7. This analysis focuses on the 258 projects that were not completed but had some action since being authorized. In this group were 11 projects initially scheduled for completion by the end of fiscal year 1984; commitments for those projects at the end of fiscal year 1989 were only 61 percent of the estimated total cost. Cash expenditures for these projects equaled only 44 percent of their estimated total cost. In other words, the projects initially scheduled for completion in fiscal year 1984 were about halfway to completion by the end of fiscal year 1989.

The record for projects scheduled for completion in fiscal year 1985 was somewhat better. For these nine projects, commitments equaled 87 percent of estimated total cost at the end of fiscal year 1989. In other words, four years after they were scheduled for completion they were in a late stage of construction.

For the projects scheduled for completion in later years, the record is particularly discouraging. The commitments ranged from 61 to 28 percent of the estimated total cost for the group of projects scheduled for completion in the four most recent years. Cash expenditures on these projects equaled between 18 and 43 percent of the total cost. In other words, most of these

Status	Number	Percent
Dropped from capital budget[a]	33	9.6%
No action since authorized[b]	22	6.4
In preconstruction phase[c]	188	55.0
In construction[d]	68	19.9
Completed[e]	29	8.5
No status available or applicable[f]	2	0.6
Total	342	100.0%

Sources: City of New York, *Capital Budget as Adopted*, fiscal year 1990; City of New York, "Monthly Transaction Analysis," Year End, fiscal year 1989; and City of New York, *Executive Budget Fiscal Year 1990*, "Capital Commitment Plan," May 1989.

[a]Projects with no commitments and not listed in the *Capital Budget as Adopted for Fiscal Year 1990*.

[b]Projects with no commitments, but listed in the *Capital Budget as Adopted for Fiscal Year 1990*.

[c]Projects identified as predesign, final design, prescope, scope, bid and award, select consultant, or state and federal selection in the "Capital Commitment Plan," May 1989, or not listed in that plan but with cumulative commitments equal to less than 60 percent of the latest estimated total cost and with expenditures equal to less than 35 percent of the latest estimated total cost. The commitment and expenditure criteria were derived from comparable figures for projects whose status was reported in the "Capital Commitment Plan," and the criteria were used to classify 36 projects in this group.

[d]Projects identified as construction or finishing in the "Capital Commitment Plan," May 1989, or not listed in that plan but with commitments equal to at least 60 percent of the latest estimated total cost and with expenditures equal to at least 35 percent of the latest estimated total cost. The commitment and expenditure criteria were derived from comparable figures for projects whose status was reported in the "Capital Commitment Plan," and the criteria were used to classify 46 projects in this group.

[e]Projects identified as completed by the New York City Office of Management and Budget and projects classified as completed based on cumulative expenditures equaling at least 90 percent of the latest estimated total cost and project not listed in the *Capital Budget as Adopted for Fiscal Year 1990*.

[f]Status reported as not applicable in "Capital Commitment Plan," May 1989, and project is either an equipment purchase or a land acquisition.

projects were less than one-half completed as long as three years after they were scheduled for completion.

Interestingly, the departments or functions with the greatest number of projects are also those whose projects are furthest behind schedule. (See Table 8.8.) Highway improvements comprised 69 projects, or 27 percent of the total; for these projects only 27 percent of the total cost was committed and 20 percent spent. Parks improvements included 53 projects; for these projects only 31 percent of the total cost was committed and 14 percent spent.

The slow pace of implementation has serious cost consequences. Due to

Table 8.7 Cumulative Commitments and Expenditures at End of Fiscal Year 1989 as a Share of Most Recent Total Estimated Cost for Capital Projects Scheduled for Completion by the End of Fiscal Year 1989

Initial Estimated Completion Date	Number of Projects	Cumulative Commitments as a Share of Total Cost	Cumulative Expenditures as a Share of Total Cost
1984	11	61.4%	44.2%
1985	9	87.0	79.9
1986	29	38.7	17.7
1987	43	60.9	42.7
1988	70	30.0	22.1
1989	96	28.2	18.4
Total	258	38.4%	26.5%

Sources: Latest estimated total cost from City of New York, *Capital Budget as Adopted*, fiscal years 1983–1990 editions; cumulative expenditures and commitments compiled from City of New York, "Monthly Transaction Analysis," Year End, fiscal years 1983–1989 editions.

Table 8.8 Cumulative Commitments and Expenditures at End of Fiscal Year 1989 as a Share of Most Recent Total Estimated Cost for Capital Projects Scheduled for Completion by the End of Fiscal Year 1989 by Function

Function	Number of Projects	Cumulative Commitments as a Share of Total Cost	Cumulative Expenditures as a Share of Total Cost
Waterway bridges	2	9.8%	1.3%
Correction	5	61.1	44.9
Education, Board of	41	54.1	32.7
Economic development	4	57.5	36.6
Fire department	2	80.2	71.8
Highway bridges	24	16.3	12.4
Housing preservation and development	3	41.9	39.1
Human resources	1	4.3	1.2
Highways	69	27.0	19.9
Libraries	2	65.3	59.8
Parks and recreation	53	31.0	14.3
Police	6	32.7	10.2
Ports, international trade, and commerce	4	51.4	41.3
Cultural affairs	5	1.8	0.3
Public buildings	7	19.8	10.0
Real property	1	2.5	0.4
Sanitation	1	1.2	0.0
Sewers	27	47.5	39.9
Traffic	1	73.1	31.6
Total	258	38.4%	26.5%

Sources: See Table 8.7.

Table 8.9 Average Percentage Change in Estimated Total Cost for Projects Scheduled for Completion Before the End of Fiscal Year 1989 but Not Completed

| Start Year | With Outliers[a] | | Without Outliers[a] | |
	Number of Projects	Average Percentage Change in Total Cost	Number of Projects	Average Percentage Change in Total Cost
1983	56	522%	46	116%
1984	99	127	91	85
1985	36	77	36	77
1986	44	51	41	46
1987	17	38	15	31
1988	5	205	4	50
1989	1	0	1	0
Total	258	94%	234	62%

Sources: City of New York, *Capital Budget as Adopted,* fiscal years 1983–1990 editions.
[a]Outliers defined as projects with a change in total estimated cost exceeding 500 percent.

increased prices and other factors, the longer a project's completion is delayed, the more it is likely to cost. This is documented in Table 8.9. For 56 projects begun in fiscal year 1983 and not yet completed by fiscal year 1989, the increase in the estimated total cost averaged 522 percent by fiscal year 1989. The comparable rate of cost increase for projects begun in fiscal years 1984 and 1985 were 127 and 77 percent, respectively. Projects begun in fiscal year 1986 had an average cost increase of 51 percent. However, in each case the average increases are especially high because of a small number of projects that had unusually high increases that may be related to changes in project scope or other special factors. Excluding these "outliers" reduced the average cost increases to 116 and 85 percent for projects begun in the first two years, and 46 percent for those begun in fiscal year 1986. These significant cost increases, even after allowance for the unusual projects, indicate the serious fiscal consequences of delays.

What Causes the Delays? Illustrative Case Studies

The previous sections document but do not explain the extensive and expensive delays that characterize the city's implementation of capital projects. To gain some insight into how and why projects are delayed, the 22 projects started in the 1983 capital budget and scheduled for completion in fiscal year 1988 were examined in greater detail. In addition to the data described previously for all new projects, the case studies also reflect interviews with personnel from OMB, the responsible line agency, the Office of Construction, and the Office of Operations in order to determine the nature of the progress (or lack thereof) on each project. These 22 projects are instructive because they are typical of new capital projects in that their planned duration is six years (see Table 8.4) and because longer projects experience more extensive delays.

Table 8.10 Description and Initial Estimated Cost of Projects Begun in Fiscal Year 1983 and Planned for Completion in Fiscal Year 1988

Highway Projects

1. Construction of entrance to Pelham Parkway with ancillary street work, $2,159,000
2. Reconstruction of Classon Avenue and other streets near Fulton Avenue, $5,250,000
3. Reconstruction of streets in a part of Astoria, $9,400,000
4. Reconstruction of part of Roosevelt Avenue, $4,950,000
5. Reconstruction of part of Almeda Avenue and adjacent streets, $3,300,000
6. Paving part of Rockaway Boulevard and ancillary street work, $2,700,000

Bridge Projects

7. Reconstruction of bridge at Faile Street between Bruckner Boulevard and Garrison Avenue, $1,848,000
8. Reconstruction of bridge at 221st Street between 41st and 43rd Avenues, $2,156,000
9. Reconstruction of bridge at Bell Boulevard between 41st Street and 42nd Avenue, $2,310,000
10. Reconstruction of bridge at Hannah Street and Staten Island Rapid Transit, $2,757,000
11. Reconstruction of bridge at Tompkins Avenue and Staten Island Rapid Transit, $1,654,000

Recreation Projects

12. Reconstruction of Marcy Houses playground, $1,600,000
13. Reconstruction of Downing Stadium, $3,595,000
14. Reconstruction of Dyker Beach Park, $1,400,000

Other Projects

15. Modernization of A. Philip Randolph High School, $11,560,000
16. Construction of West Queens High School, $1,200,000
17. Storm sewers at part of Linden Boulevard, $6,210,000
18. Sanitary sewers at part of Linden Boulevard, $1,861,000
19. Rehabilitation and addition to St. George Branch Library, $1,604,000[a]
20. Conversion of Spofford Juvenile Center to adult facility, $19,850,000
21. New 66th Precinct house, $8,160,000
22. New 107th Precinct station house, $420,000[b]

[a]No estimated cost given in fiscal year 1983; figure shown is from fiscal year 1984 budget.
[b]Estimated cost was increased to $7,570,000 in fiscal year 1984 budget.

Each of the projects is summarized in Table 8.10. Fully half the projects were related to either highway reconstruction (six projects) or bridge reconstruction (five projects). Another three projects were reconstruction of recreational facilities, two were new police precinct houses, two were related projects involving storm and sanitary sewers in an area of Queens, two were public school projects, one was modification of a branch library, and one was conversion of a correctional facility from youth to adult usage. The initial estimated cost of the projects ranged from $420,000 to $19.9 million.

A first observation about the delays is that they do not seem to arise from unrealistic expectations about how quickly a project could be built. Projects such as street reconstruction (project numbers 2 through 5 in Table 8.10), school modernization (number 15), and the building of a police station (numbers 21 and 22) should, on the face of things, be achievable in less than six years.

What actually happened on these 22 projects? In the beginning of fiscal

Table 8.11 Selected Characteristics of Projects Begun in Fiscal Year 1983 and Scheduled for Completion in Fiscal Year 1988

Projects[a]	Reported Status in September 1987	Percentage Change in Estimated Total Cost	Commitments as a Percentage of Total Cost
Highway Projects			
1	In design	−0.24%	3%
2	Near completion	+78	93
3	Design completed	−52[b]	15
4	Near completion	−41[c]	64
5	In design	+424	1
6	Merged with other projects	NAP	NAP
Bridge Projects			
7	Near completion	68	84
8	Near completion	−22	77
9	Design completed	+25	NA
10	Near completion	−33	NA
11	Design completed	+87[d]	NA
Recreation Projects			
12	In design	+31	6
13	Dropped from budget	NAP	0
14	In design	+42	61
Other Projects			
15	In design	+33	4
16	Postponed	+4,450	0
17	Design completed	+6	2
18	Design completed	+49	4
19	In construction	+1[e]	54
20	Dropped from budget	NAP	0
21	Postponed	+43	0
22	In design	+42[f]	0

Sources: Status and commitment figures from data supplied by the New York City Office of Management and Budget; changes in total cost based on FY 1983 and FY 1988 *Capital Budget as Adopted,* unless otherwise noted.

Note: NA, not available; NAP, not applicable.

[a]Project numbers correspond to those in Table 8.10. See Table 8.10 for a complete description.

[b]Project changed from reconstruction to resurfacing.

[c]Project reduced in scope.

[d]Project expanded in scope.

[e]Based on figures in FY 1984 and FY 1987 budgets; no estimated total cost given in FY 1983 and FY 1988 budgets.

[f]Based on initial cost in FY 1984 budget; the figure shown in the FY 1983 budget seems inapplicable.

year 1988 only four of these projects were nearing completion in the form originally intended. (See Table 8.11.) The highway work on Classon Avenue (project number 2) was virtually completed, though at a cost 78 percent above that originally estimated. Three of the bridge projects—Hannah Street (number 10), 221st Street (number 8), and Faile Street (number 7)—also are reported to be substantially near completion. However, it is important to note that these bridge projects are implemented by the New York State Department of Transportation, not the city. These projects appear in the city's capital budget only because a fraction (about 6 percent) of the cost is funded by the city; the design and construction work is undertaken by the state agency. Thus, of the four projects nearly completed as initially planned only one was implemented by the city.

Another project was near completion, but this was accomplished after significant scaling down of the scope of the construction work. The highway work on Roosevelt Avenue in Queens (project number 4) was reduced to only a portion of the originally planned reconstruction.

Of the remaining 17 projects, only two had reached the construction phase: the library project (number 19) and the repaving of Rockaway Boulevard (number 6). It took three years to finish the design work for the branch library, and large construction contracts were not awarded until the fourth year. Meanwhile the estimated total cost doubled from about $1.6 million to $3.2 million. At the end of fiscal year 1987 commitments equaled 54 percent of the new estimated total cost, and only 15 percent of the total cost had been expended. A phone call to the librarian revealed they expected the work to be done in "about two years."

The repaving of Rockaway Boulevard was in construction in a modified form. The initial portion of the road to be repaved was incorporated with other portions of the road scheduled for repaving as a new and larger separate capital project. It was this new project that was in construction and scheduled for completion in 1989.

The remaining 15 projects include 11 in a design stage, 2 of which were still scheduled for implementation but for which no funds had yet been committed, and 2 which had been dropped from the capital budget. The projects dropped from the budget are the reconstruction of Downing Stadium (number 13) and the conversion of Spofford Juvenile Center (number 20). The former project was put in the capital budget at a time when city officials believed Olympic trials would be held there. When this failed to materialize, the total reconstruction plans were dropped. However, a rebuilding of the track at the stadium was funded and completed as part of a continuing project budget line. The conversion of Spofford was initially planned as part of a master plan for building new, decentralized juvenile detention centers. This would have relocated the children from Spofford and freed the center for conversion. However, the decentralization plans were significantly revised and were themselves subject to delayed implementation. Consequently, the conversion of the existing and still-needed juvenile center was dropped from the capital budget.

The construction of a new West Queens High School and a new 66th Precinct station house were postponed because of changed priorities within the line agencies and the OMB. The high school project was initially put in the capital budget on condition that it be funded largely as part of a special program under which private developers put up a building and include school space in it. This sharply limits the amount of city funds required. However, for several years no cooperative builder could be found and no action was taken on the project. Finally, in 1987 the city agreed to fund the full cost, raising the cost to the city from the initial $1.2 million to $54.6 million. The new estimated completion data was 1995, or seven years behind the initial plan.

The new police station house was shifted from a high- to a low-priority item by the Police Department in order to favor progress on other planned station houses. The OMB and the Police Department agreed to build station houses in sets of four over a four-year period. This project was one of the priority four in fiscal year 1983, but it subsequently was shifted to a lower priority in favor of another project. It was placed among the group of new station houses scheduled for completion in 1995. The delay largely explains the increase in estimated total cost from $8.2 to $11.7 million.

The remaining 11 projects had not entered construction by early fiscal year 1988, indicating *major* delays. This group included 6 projects on which the design work had been completed, suggesting possible delays in the awarding of construction contracts as well as delays in design work; the remaining 5 projects were still in design, indicating the delays were all encountered in that stage.

The reasons for these delays can be divided into three categories: (1) problems with site identification and approval; (2) problems with the public letting of design or construction contracts; and (3) problems related to changes in the scope of the work to be completed. Problems over site acquisition were expected to delay the construction of the 107th Precinct station house until four years beyond the original completion date. Delays stemmed from protracted negotiations with the landowner and the community board over the proposed site. In addition, new consultant selection procedures introduced in 1986 in response to the Parking Violations Bureau scandals further delayed the design of the station.

Problems in the awarding of contracts led to delays in the reconstruction of the 41st Street bridge (number 9), one highway project (number 3), and the construction of storm and sanitary sewers at Linden Boulevard (numbers 17 and 18). Design work for the bridge had been completed by the state's Department of Transportation in 1985, but when the state asked for bids there were no bidders. The state then turned the project over to the city, and it was combined with other city bridge contracts to establish a project large enough to generate competitive bids. This revised project was put up for bid in January 1987. The bids were 55 percent higher than the estimate, and all bids were rejected. The project was then scheduled to be rebid pending approval of the revised design by federal agencies.

The resurfacing of 95th Street in Astoria was delayed because of both design problems and public letting problems. During design work it was decided to change the project from street reconstruction to "engineered resurfacing," a new approach to road rebuilding adopted by the city in order to save money. This delayed completion of design work until early in fiscal year 1987. The project was then put up for bid, but the low bidder was rejected by the city officials, causing a further six-month delay to allow for rebidding. A contract to begin construction was finally awarded in the first half of fiscal year 1988. Completion of the modified project was not expected until 1989.

The initial change in scope from reconstruction reduced the estimated cost from its initial $9.4 million to $2.5 million at the start of fiscal year 1988, but the rebidding delay raised the new estimated cost to $4.5 million.

Design work for the storm and sewer projects was completed by 1986 and the work was put up for competitive bid then. However, the low bidder was found to be under criminal investigation. The city delayed awarding the contract until he eventually withdrew the bid. The project was rebid in the summer of 1987 and work then commenced. Completion was expected in 1989.

Scope changes or other design problems delayed the remaining projects. The scope of the modernization of A. Philip Randolph High School was expanded somewhat during its initial design to reflect changes in the expected student body and the addition of items such as window requirements. This delayed completion of the final design until late in 1986. The project was set for competitive bidding in the end of fiscal year 1987 and contract awards were made early in fiscal year 1988. The delays and modifications increased the estimated total cost from $11.5 to $15.4 million, and completion was not planned until 1990.

The design work for the Tompkins Avenue Bridge, which was conducted by the state's Transportation Department, was delayed by a decision to expand the scope of the project to include an adjoining bridge. The modified design was expected to be completed in fiscal year 1988. The expanded scope raised the estimated total cost from $1.8 to $3.1 million, and construction had not yet begun.

The reconstruction of Dyker Beach Park was divided into several stages, with some of the work under way and some still in design. Plans for the playground and a comfort station were completed in 1986 and these parts of the project were to be completed in fiscal year 1988. Design contracts for a softball field and beach playground were let in fiscal year 1987, and additional design work was scheduled for future years for the fieldhouse and basketball and handball courts. The complete reconstruction will not be finished until 1993.

Two highway projects—Almeda Avenue and Pelham Parkway—were delayed in the design stage. The former project required unanticipated drainage studies and was leading to plans for a large coordinated highway and sewer project. The Pelham Parkway project, which involves part of the road running through Pelham Bay Park, was caught in a dispute between the Highway and Parks departments (neither seeks responsibility). The project encountered difficulties in design because it intersects with a stream, and it was complicated by the need to meet federal highway standards because federal funding was sought as part of the renegotiation of the use of federal funds initially allocated to Westway, an abandoned limited-access highway project. The project was still in a preliminary design stage and was not likely to be completed for several years.

Finally, the delays in the design of the Marcy Houses playground were largely planned by the Department of Parks and Recreation. Although the project was put in the budget in fiscal year 1983, the department's priorities postponed its initiation until fiscal year 1988. It then was being designed and was expected to be ready for construction bidding in fiscal year 1989.

In sum, these case studies suggest that the most serious delays in implementing projects were not due to problems such as strikes or specification changes that occur during the construction phases. Many serious delays occurred during the early design phases and others derived from problems in the letting of contracts. In some cases the city's political leaders did not agree upon—or changed their minds about—the scope of the project. This led to delays in design. The connection between scope decisions and subsequent design work was sometimes unnecessarily politicized because virtually all design work was performed under noncompetitive contracts that were required to go before the Board of Estimate. A design contract could be delayed by board members when they questioned or sought a new decision about a project's scope.

In other cases, city agencies simply failed to initiate work on authorized projects promptly, sometimes because the city council and Board of Estimate decided to launch new projects that exceeded the agency's capacity to design and finance the new projects without sacrificing progress on other projects the agency leadership favors. In still other cases, design work was permitted to extend for seemingly excessive periods and then was not translated into bidding specifications and awards speedily. Finally, awarding a construction contract may have been delayed because municipal rules require rebidding or other special procedures if agency leaders want to reject the lowest bidder. Moreover, reviews of noncompetitive contracts were intensified, and consequently made more time-consuming, following the outbreak of corruption scandals in 1986. The result was that typically it took more than five years for an authorized project of a relatively modest scale to have an approved design and for construction to begin.

Recommendations

Both the aggregate data and the case studies reveal that most capital projects are not completed in a timely fashion. Five measures can be identified to help overcome the more serious obstacles to speedy implementation.

First, the mayor should take advantage of recently approved charter changes to reduce repeated, politicized reviews of capital projects. Charter revisions effective in September 1989 eliminated the Board of Estimate. Delays arising from the board's participation in capital budget approval and approval of scope and design contracts were unavoidable. The mayor should move aggressively to exercise new executive powers to expedite capital project implementation.

Second, an improved information system for tracking capital projects should be maintained and used effectively. The OMB's DACS now provides the information essential for improved management of capital projects.

Third, this new information system should be used as the basis for greater accountability in managing capital projects. The mayor should designate a senior official, such as a deputy mayor, to be responsible for the city's capital program. The newly designated head of the capital program should take a proactive role. The responsible official should track progress on major projects and intervene with agencies and OMB when projects begin to fall behind schedule; the role of the responsible deputy mayor should not be limited to dealing with problems in their latest stages after long delays already have occurred.

The deputy mayor should oversee project management activities that are conducted at the agency level. The recommendation of the Mayor's Private Sector Survey to create well-staffed project management teams within municipal agencies would speed the pace of construction,[5] but high-level monitoring and a clear line of accountability should complement these project management teams.

Fourth, the mayor should report regularly to the public on progress in implementing the capital plan. The mayor should expand the information included in the *Mayor's Management Report* to cover more fully each agency's accomplishments with its capital funds.

Fifth, the activities of the comptroller's office in providing review and oversight of capital project activities should be expanded. The comptroller should expand reporting on capital projects to include whether projects are proceeding on schedule and in accord with initial cost estimates. The comptroller also should use the new information systems and other sources to study the reasons for delay and to identify ways to speed capital project implementation.

9

TAX POLICY

This chapter presents a framework for evaluating the tax policies of the city of New York.[1] It is divided into five sections. The first examines the central but contested issue of the extent to which municipal tax policy affects local economic performance. The second section reviews how municipal tax revenues and the local economy have changed since the 1960s. A discussion of the standards that may be used in evaluating tax policy is found in the third section. The fourth section applies the standards to the major local taxes. The final section discusses the implications for New York City's municipal tax system.

The Importance of Local Taxes

Discussions about the role of tax policy in stimulating or stifling economic growth often are polarized by extreme positions. Some instinctively reject any tax increase proposals out of hand, pointing out that New York City's municipal taxes already are the highest among U.S. cities and claiming that any increase will erode the city's economic competitiveness. On the issue's other side usually are the recipients of local services, often in alliance with the municipal employees who deliver them, who maintain that the city's economy is strong enough to withstand the current level of taxes as well as tax increases designed to finance better services.

The views of taxpayer and service groups clash because often they have different interests in local tax policy. However, analysts with no immediate self-interest are divided on the extent to which local taxes and economic

185

performance are correlated. The view that higher taxes diminish economic activity has logical appeal because local taxes represent a cost of doing business. To the extent that taxes in one jurisdiction exceed those in another, firms in the high-tax community may experience reduced profitability vis-à-vis competitors located in lower-tax communities. If firms relocate to reduce their tax costs, the employment and income will fall in the high-tax community.[2] Evidence in New York City (discussed in the next section) provides some support for the proposition that high taxes contributed to local economic decline in the 1969–1977 period.

The view of those who minimize the economic effects of local taxes is buttressed by research finding that the correlation between local economic growth and local taxes is statistically insignificant, though such findings are contested by other scholars.[3] According to this view, other factors such as wages and various costs of production, access to markets, technological change, and quality of life preferences, are more powerful locational determinants than local taxes. That New York City's economy grew significantly from 1977 through 1989, despite comparatively high municipal taxes, may be interpreted as supporting the view that taxes are relatively unimportant. Proponents of this view also note that the impact of local taxes is mitigated somewhat by their deductibility from federal income taxes.

The differences among analysts over the extent to which local taxes affect economic performance is not surprising. The complexity of urban areas, particularly one as large, diverse, and dynamic as New York City, makes it difficult to construct economic models designed to separate cause and effect between local taxes and local economic behavior. Two major complicating factors stand out in such research. One involves the extent to which local businesses are able to pass on, or "export," taxes to regional, national, and international consumers of the goods and services they produce. By way of illustration, severance taxes on oil make the per capita taxes of Alaskans higher than those in any other state, but their oil taxes are passed on to consumers outside Alaska. An analogy, though clearly weaker, is New York City's advanced services sector, which sells a substantial share of its financial, legal, accounting, advertising, educational, health, and other services to non–New Yorkers. However, the producers of these services still compete with others producing similar services elsewhere. The ability of local businesses to so shift the burden of taxes, while hard to measure, assumedly declines as competition with businesses in other cities increases.

A second evaluative problem is that some city governments provide more or better services than others. The consumer-taxpayers of local government services, who are presumed to "vote with their feet" in search of the most favorable location to live and do business, take into account not only what local government costs them in the form of taxes but also what they receive in the form of a "bundle" of local public services. High taxes do not inhibit local economic growth if the public service benefits purchased by taxes outweigh the costs. Again, however, the relationship between taxes and services is not captured easily in models testing the relationship between local taxes and economic performance.

The impact of local taxes on the local economy is difficult to demonstrate conclusively, but it is reasonable to assume that municipal taxes affect local economic performance. However, the impact can vary over time if the quality of services or the city's economic advantages change. A locality with unique attributes (for example, oil in the ground, legalized gambling, specialized financial markets in which it assumes a national or international role) can export or shift local taxes more easily than other communities. But if changing economic circumstances reduce a city's economic advantage, the differentials in taxes become more significant. In the case of New York City's financial services, changes in technology, government regulations, and the attractiveness of other areas may be weakening the city's competitive advantages for some of the functions of financial firms. Therefore, high local taxes may well pose a greater economic threat than they have in the past.

Even if no market forces are weakening a city's locational advantages, changes in the level and quality of public services may affect the importance of taxes for economic development. The experience in New York City attests to the fact that the quality of public management over time is not constant; moreover, the mix of public services may vary over time as a result of changes in municipal priorities as well as intergovernmental mandates. A city that provides poorer and poorer services (either for the community as a whole or for its most mobile individuals and firms) will find the economic effects of its taxes increasingly burdensome compared to a city whose taxpayers perceive that local government provides a fair return in the form of local public services.

Local Taxes and Economic Performance

Discussion of taxes and economic performance should recognize their historical and comparative context. Local taxes may increase by appreciable amounts without deterring economic development if other localities experience more rapid tax increases. Conversely, local tax burdens can decrease without yielding positive economic effects if taxes in competing areas fall more rapidly. This section begins by describing aggregate trends in New York City taxes historically and comparatively and then examines changes in the mix of local taxes and in the performance of the city's economy.

Aggregate Tax Trends

Tax revenues of the city rose nearly tenfold in the last three decades, increasing steadily from about $1.6 billion in fiscal year 1960 to $15.1 billion in fiscal year 1990. (See Table 9.1.) However, a different picture emerges after adjusting these figures for inflation. Real or inflation-adjusted taxes nearly doubled between 1960 and 1977, fell in four of the next five years, and then began to increase again in 1983. Real tax revenues in 1989 were 13 percent above their earlier 1977 high point, but then fell slightly in 1990.

Table 9.1 Local Tax Revenues of the City of New York
in Current and Constant Dollars, Fiscal Years
1960–1990 (dollars in millions)

Fiscal Year	Current Dollars	Constant Dollars[a]
1960	$1,551	$6,571
1965	2,203	8,669
1970	3,283	10,511
1975	5,189	11,819
1976	5,451	11,644
1977	6,298	12,787
1978	6,416	12,393
1979	6,409	11,571
1980	6,959	11,354
1981	7,708	11,392
1982	8,261	11,302
1983	8,757	11,357
1984	9,575	11,885
1985	10,582	12,593
1986	11,238	12,915
1987	12,725	14,101
1988	13,326	14,009
1989	14,397	14,397
1990	15,056	14,249

Sources: City of New York, *Comprehensive Annual Financial Report of the Comptroller,* fiscal years 1960–1990 editions. Constant-dollar adjustments based on U.S. Department of Labor, Bureau of Labor Statistics, Middle Atlantic Regional Office, "Consumer Price Index for All Urban Consumers (CPI-U) in the New York–Northeastern New Jersey Area" (fiscal-year average).

[a]Constant dollars are fiscal year 1989 dollars.

Other measures of the level of aggregate taxes take into account changes in the city's population, employment, and economic output. Local taxes per capita were $2,056 in fiscal year 1990, more than ten times higher than in 1960. (See Table 9.2.) Adjusted for inflation, per capita taxes more than doubled in the 1960–1990 period. In real terms, per capita taxes fell from $1,717 in 1978 to a recent low of $1,575 in 1983 before increasing again to the 1989 high of $1,952. Somewhat similar trends obtain for local taxes per employee. These doubled in constant dollars between 1960 and 1978, rising to a peak of $3,793, declined to $3,357 in 1982, and then rose to $3,977 in 1989 and $3,991 in 1990.

A final tax burden measure relates aggregate local taxes to local personal income. Personal income is a broad measure that includes the earnings of proprietors and employees as well as dividends, interest, and rent and transfer payments like social security and public assistance. It measures income received by New York City residents rather than New York City's output, but it is the most comprehensive economic measure officially reported for New York City and for other urban areas. As Table 9.2 shows, local taxes as a share of local personal income rose from 8.1 percent in 1970 to 9.6 percent in 1978. Between 1978 and 1984, taxes as a share of personal income declined to 8.7

Table 9.2 Local Taxes Per Capita, Per Employee, and as a Share of Personal Income, Fiscal Years 1960–1990

	Per Capita		Per Employee		
Fiscal Year	Current Dollars	Constant Dollars[a]	Current Dollars	Constant Dollars[a]	As a Share of Personal Income
1960	$201	$850	$441	$1,869	NA
1965	283	1,112	619	2,438	NA
1970	423	1,355	892	2,857	8.1%
1975	705	1,606	1,604	3,653	9.5
1978	889	1,717	1,964	3,793	9.6
1980	975	1,591	2,088	3,407	8.9
1981	1,080	1,596	2,279	3,367	8.9
1982	1,156	1,581	2,454	3,357	8.9
1983	1,214	1,575	2,594	3,364	8.8
1984	1,319	1,638	2,775	3,445	8.7
1985	1,451	1,727	3,021	3,595	9.1
1986	1,529	1,757	3,162	3,633	9.1
1987	1,726	1,913	3,531	3,913	9.7
1988	1,805	1,897	3,681	3,870	9.4
1989	1,952[b]	1,952	3,977	3,977	9.6[c]
1990	2,056	1,946	4,217	3,991	9.8[c]

Sources: Local taxes data from City of New York, *Comprehensive Annual Financial Report of the Comptroller,* fiscal years 1960–1990 editions. Population data from U.S. Department of Commerce, Bureau of the Census. Employment data from U.S. Department of Labor, Bureau of Labor Statistics. Personal income data from U.S. Department of Commerce, Bureau of Economic Analysis. Constant-dollar adjustments based on U.S. Department of Labor, Bureau of Labor Statistics, Middle Atlantic Regional Office, "Consumer Price Index for All Urban Consumers (CPI-U) in the New York–Northeastern New Jersey Area" (fiscal-year average).

Note: NA, not available.

[a]Constant dollars are fiscal year 1989 dollars.

[b]The Bureau of the Census has not estimated New York City Population for 1989. The population figure used is that for 1988.

[c]Personal income figure is estimated.

percent because income grew more rapidly than tax revenues; however, in 1989 the share was again 9.6 percent and was estimated at 9.8 percent in 1990.

In summary, taxes were substantially higher in 1990 than in 1960. Tax burdens fell after the mid- to late 1970s, but in the late 1980s they increased again.

Comparisons with Other Urban Areas

The significance of these trends in New York City's aggregate taxes depends in part on how they compare with other areas—and how these relationships have changed over time. As noted earlier, a city's tax burden may decline over time but have no positive effect if taxes in other cities fall even more.

Comparisons of New York City taxes with those in other cities are difficult to make for two reasons. First, in other areas municipal taxes cover only a portion of taxes that are paid locally. Indeed, the taxes levied by county governments, school districts, and other special authorities may exceed municipal taxes for functions such as police, fire, and sanitation. The distribution of taxes among the various governments of urban areas varies widely, reflecting the diversity of public functions performed by local governments, as well as the extent to which state governments and the federal government finance local government activities. New York is unique among the nation's cities in the fiscal responsibilities that it carries, particularly for public assistance and medical care.

One method of adjusting for such differences, albeit not a perfect method, is to compare New York City's aggregate taxes with those of all local governments in the counties within which other large cities are located. For example, under this approach taxes in New York City are compared to taxes in all local jurisdictions within Cook County, Illinois, which include taxes of the city of Chicago as well as those of other local governments, including Cook County, that contribute to the financing of local services in Chicago. Data from the U.S. Bureau of the Census permit such comparisons to be made among New York City and the 19 next largest cities (as defined above) and all metropolitan areas in the United States in 1962, 1972, and 1983, the last year for which such data are available.

Both on a per capita basis and measured as a share of income, local taxes in New York City were more than twice the average for all metropolitan areas and for the counties containing the 20 largest American cities in 1983. (See Table 9.3.) Per capita taxes (by the Census Bureau's accounting) were $1,214 in New York City in 1983 compared to the average of $603 for the 20 largest cities and $608 for the metropolitan average. As a share of local income, taxes in New York City in 1983 were 9.2 percent compared to 4.7 percent for the large cities and 4.5 percent for all metropolitan areas.

Moreover, Table 9.3 shows that New York City's comparative position worsened both in the overall 1962–1983 period and between 1972 and 1983. In 1962, the city's local taxes per capita were 59 percent higher than the average for all metropolitan areas, and its tax–income ratio was 38 percent higher. By 1972, the corresponding figures were 74 and 56 percent; by 1983, both measures were more than two times the metropolitan average. In contrast, per capita taxes and taxes as a share of income in the 20 largest cities fell relative to the metropolitan average between 1972 and 1983.

These differentials may have narrowed somewhat since 1983 but municipal taxes in New York City almost certainly remain substantially higher than in any other major U.S. city. San Francisco was New York City's closest competitor in 1983; however, its per capita taxes were only 62 percent of New York City's, and its tax–income ratio stood at less than 50 percent.[4]

Comparisons of New York City taxes with those in the immediate New York region (Table 9.4) show that municipal taxes also are high, particularly relative to suburban counties in Connecticut and New Jersey. In 1983, New York City's per capita local tax level of $1,224 exceeded by substantial amounts those in all but Nassau County ($1,230) and Westchester County ($1,205). The differences were greatest between New York City and New Jersey suburban counties, where per capita local taxes ranged from only $620

Table 9.3 Taxes Per Capita and as a Share of Income in New York City, the Central County of the 20 Largest U.S. Cities, and All Metropolitan Areas, 1962, 1972, and 1983

Taxes	1962	1972	1983
Per Capita			
New York City	$220	$485	$1,214
Central county of 20 largest cities	$143	$302	$603
All metropolitan areas	$138	$279	$608
Per capita index[a]			
New York City	159	174	200
Central county of 20 largest cities	104	108	99
As a share of income			
New York City	7.2%	8.9%	9.2%
Central county of 20 largest cities	5.2%	6.0%	4.7%
All metropolitan areas	5.4%	5.7%	4.5%
Share-of-income index[a]			
New York City	138	156	204
Central county of 20 largest cities	96	105	104

Sources: 1962 and 1972 from U.S. Department of Commerce, Bureau of the Census, *Census of Governments*, 1961–62, 1971–72; 1983 from Bureau of the Census, *Local Government Finances in Selected Metropolitan Areas*, 1982–83. Local area personal income used in calculations from U.S. Department of Commerce, Bureau of Economic Analysis.
[a]All metropolitan areas = 100.

in Essex to $829 in Somerset. The same general pattern prevailed for the measure of local taxes as a share of income. New York City's 9.2 percent share was at least twice the levels in the New Jersey and Connecticut counties and exceeded by substantial amounts those in Nassau (6.8 percent) and West-chester (6.4 percent) counties.

In summary, New York City is—and has been for many years—a high-tax jurisdiction compared with metropolitan areas as a whole, other large U.S. cities, and the surrounding New York metropolitan area. The disparities be-

Table 9.4 Taxes Per Capita and as a Share of Income, New York City and Selected Counties in the New York Region, 1983

Area	Taxes Per Capita	Taxes as a Share of Income
New York City	$1,224	9.2%
Nassau, NY	1,230	6.8
Westchester, NY	1,205	6.4
Somerset, NJ	829	4.6
Fairfield, CT	814	4.4
Bergen, NJ	780	4.1
Middlesex, NJ	686	4.7
Essex, NJ	620	4.6

Sources: U.S. Department of Commerce, Bureau of the Census, *Local Government Finances in Selected Metropolitan Areas*, 1982–83. Personal income data used in calculations from U.S. Department of Commerce, Bureau of Economic Analysis.

tween New York City's local taxes—measured on a per capita basis and as a share of local income—and those of American cities increased steadily between the early 1960s and early 1980s, notwithstanding the declines in local tax burden that occurred in New York City in the second half of the 1970s. Part of the explanation for New York City's high local taxes relative to other cities is that they are not required to finance as large a share of local public assistance and medical assistance costs. The city's relative tax burden may not have deteriorated further in recent years, but it is doubtful that its position of being the local tax capital of American cities is under serious challenge.

The Changing Composition of Local Taxes

The changes in the aggregate level of taxation just analyzed have been accompanied by substantial changes in the mix of local taxes. If New York City's aggregate level of taxation is atypical, so too is the mix or composition of its taxes—particularly in its greater reliance on revenue sources other than the property tax.

As Table 9.5 shows, the city relies primarily on real property, sales, and personal and business income taxes. In 1990, these tax sources accounted, respectively, for 44 percent, 16 percent, and 29 percent of total local taxes, with the latter comprised of business income taxes (12 percent) and personal income taxes (17 percent). The share of taxes derived from sales has fallen somewhat since 1965; the major changes have been in the reduced reliance on property taxes, which contributed 63 percent of revenues in 1960, and the increased contribution of the personal income tax following its introduction in 1966. The other major local tax—the commercial occupancy tax—accounts for less than 5 percent of the total.

Comparative data on local taxes in other large cities and all metropolitan areas are most readily available for real estate taxes, and they establish that New York City's reliance on property taxes is atypically low. (See Table 9.6.) In 1962, New York City received 63 percent of its local taxes from real

Table 9.5 Selected Local Taxes as a Percentage of Total Local Taxes, Fiscal Years 1960, 1965, 1970, 1975, 1980, 1985, and 1990

Fiscal Year	Real Estate	Sales	Personal Income	Business Income[a]	Commercial Occupancy	Other
1960	62.7%	19.0%	—	12.9%	—	5.4%
1965	59.0	20.4	—	11.4	3.2%	6.0
1970	56.8	14.5	6.4%	11.5	2.9	7.9
1975	53.6	16.0	9.4	10.8	3.9	6.3
1980	45.9	16.4	12.6	13.6	3.1	8.4
1985	39.9	17.3	16.5	15.3	4.1	6.9
1990	43.5	16.1	17.0	12.3	4.5	6.6

Sources: City of New York, *Comprehensive Annual Financial Report of the Comptroller*, fiscal years 1960–1990 editions.

[a]Includes general corporation tax, financial corporation tax, unincorporated business tax, and utilities tax.

Table 9.6 Real Property Taxes as a Share of Total Local Taxes, New York City, the Central County of the 20 Largest U.S. Cities, and All Metropolitan Areas, 1962, 1972, and 1983

Category	1962	1972	1983
As a share of total local taxes			
New York City	63.3%	51.6%	43.3%
Central county of 20 largest cities	87.1%	79.4%	68.9%
All metropolitan areas	85.9%	82.1%	72.3%
Property tax share index[a]			
New York City	74	63	60
Central county of 20 largest cities	101	97	95

Sources: 1962 and 1972 from U.S. Department of Commerce, Bureau of the Census, *Census of Governments*, 1961–62, 1971–72; 1983 from Bureau of the Census, *Local Government Finances in Selected Metropolitan Areas*, 1982–83.

[a]All metropolitan areas = 100.

property levies compared to 87 percent for the 20 largest cities and 86 percent for metropolitan areas as a whole. Using the metropolitan average as a base, New York City's property tax index stood at 74 compared to 101 for the average of the 20 largest cities. Since then, urban areas increasingly have turned to other sources than the property tax, but not as rapidly as New York City. Accordingly, New York City's property tax index was only 60 in 1983 compared to 95 for the other large cities.

The contrast with suburban governments in the New York City area is also striking. In 1983, Nassau and Westchester counties' real property taxes contributed 83 percent and 87 percent, respectively, of their total local taxes— compared to 43 percent in New York City. Suburban counties in Connecticut and New Jersey relied almost entirely on property taxes.

Local Taxes and the Local Economy

The transformation of the New York City economy since 1960 is striking in several respects. However, the linkage between the major changes in the scale and mix of its economic functions, on the one hand, and changes in the level and mix of local taxes, on the other, is difficult to specify for reasons noted earlier. Nevertheless, it is possible to suggest some ways in which municipal tax policy may have affected the local economy—both negatively and positively.

Table 9.7 summarizes changes in the city's employment base in the 1960– 1989 period. In the overall period total local employment grew 2 percent, from 3,538,000 to 3,609,000. This net growth masks a dramatic job loss of 610,000, one of every six jobs, in the 1969–1977 period. Fortunately, the 1960–1969 and 1977–1989 periods bracketing this sharp retrenchment were growth periods—7.3 percent in the period before retrenchment and 13.2 percent in the period after. By 1989, the city's job total was above its 1960 level and 95 percent of the high-water mark in 1969. However, employment decline followed in 1990.

Table 9.7 Employment by Sector in New York City, Selected Years, 1960–1989 (in thousands)

Sector	1960	1969	1977	1989	Percentage Change			
					1960–69	1969–77	1977–89	1960–89
Total employment	3,538	3,798	3,188	3,609	7.3%	(16.1%)	13.2%	2.0%
Private employment	3,130	3,251	2,680	3,008	3.9	(17.6)	12.2	(3.9)
Manufacturing	947	826	539	361	(12.8)	(34.7)	(33.0)	(61.9)
Services	609	782	785	1,150	28.4	0.4	46.5	88.8
Wholesale/retail trade	745	749	620	633	0.5	(17.2)	2.1	(15.0)
FIRE	384	466	414	531	21.4	(11.2)	28.3	38.3
Transportation/utilities	318	324	258	213	1.9	(20.4)	(17.4)	(33.0)
Construction	127	104	64	120	(18.1)	(38.5)	87.5	(5.5)
Public employment	408	547	508	601	34.1	(7.1)	18.3	47.3

Sources: 1960 from U.S. Department of Labor, Bureau of Labor Statistics, Middle Atlantic Regional Office; 1969–1989 from State of New York, Department of Labor, Division of Research and Statistics.

Even more striking are the changes in the mix of local economic activities during this period. The most profound is the loss of nearly two-thirds (62 percent) of all manufacturing jobs in the period; employment in the transportation and utilities sector fell by one-third; jobs in wholesale and retail trade fell by almost one-sixth. In all, these three declining sectors lost over 800,000 jobs in the 1960–1989 period, about 586,000 in manufacturing alone.

Fortunately, there were growth sectors whose employment gains during the overall period were large enough to offset the losses in manufacturing, trade, and transportation and utilities. The general service sector and its more specialized components of finance, insurance, and real estate (FIRE) and government grew rapidly (except between 1969 and 1977). In the overall 1960–1989 period, service employment rose 89 percent, FIRE 38 percent, and government 47 percent. These three sectors added 811,000 jobs. The FIRE and service sectors, particularly the latter, have been the linchpins of economic activity throughout the period; between 1969 and 1977, the service sector was the only one that held its own.

Without attempting to relate specific changes in local tax revenues to these changes in local economic function, what can be said more broadly about the relationship between taxes and economic development? As discussed earlier in this section, the city's aggregate local tax burden, variously measured, rose sharply in the 1960s, continued to increase (though at slower rates) through the mid-1970s, then declined until the early 1980s. That the performance of the local economy is affected by factors in addition to local taxes is suggested by the fact that the local economy grew throughout most of the 1960s, when local tax burdens were rising rapidly, and the recovery continued for more than a decade after the 1977 employment low despite the city's comparatively high taxes. Nevertheless, the relevance of local taxes should not be discounted entirely. A case can be made that the city's tax policies contributed both to economic decline between 1969 and 1977 and to the subsequent recovery.

By the late 1960s, the costs associated with doing business in New York City had grown far out of line in comparison with other U.S. cities. The costs of local government were one ingredient in the untoward price increases, but wage, space, energy, and other factor costs also were important. The significance of the tax variable was increased, however, by the fact that an increasing share of local public expenditure was directed not toward general service improvements but to debt service, public employee retirement costs, and meeting the mandated costs of social welfare programs.[5] This is indicated by the fact that total municipal employment rose only 4 percent in the 1970–1975 period while local tax revenues grew 14 percent in real terms; moreover, municipal employment in police, fire, sanitation, and education actually fell 9 percent while employment in welfare, hospitals, and higher education grew 18 percent.[6] These data suggest that basic municipal services were not growing as rapidly as local taxes and that the city was changing the mix of local public services at the same time; apparently many mobile individuals and businesses found this combination of events not to their liking. Then, immediately after the fiscal crisis in 1975, the city was forced to raise taxes even higher and, at the same time, to reduce municipal employment and diminish local services—

another deleterious admixture of policies, at least in the short run. If the local government's fiscal policies did not "cause" the city's economic decline in the 1969–1977 period, they contributed to it.

The city's economy began to recover in 1977.[7] The city's wage and space costs fell relative to other areas during the decline, eventually creating more advantageous locational opportunities than had prevailed earlier. But in addition, the city froze certain local taxes, principally the real property tax, and reduced some others in the 1976–1978 period.[8] This promoted the decline in aggregate tax burdens noted earlier and contributed to the perception as well as the reality that New York City was regaining certain advantages as a site for economic activity. And as the economy began to recover and local tax revenues grew, improvements in municipal services eventually followed, beginning in the early 1980s.[9] Once again, tax policy impacted on the performance of the local economy, but this time in a positive fashion.

Standards for Evaluation

Whether or not New York City's aggregate municipal tax burden is too high is difficult to determine. Scholarly research offers a divided view on the economic effects of high local taxes. One standard—the city's tax burden compared to other major cities—suggests they are too high; yet the city's economic performance in recent years suggests local businesses are able to "afford" relatively high taxes—partly because of other comparative advantages the city offers and partly because local taxes are reduced by federal deductibility. It may be, too, that the local government provides a comparatively rich mix of local public services. Thus, parity with other jurisdictions is not a realistic goal, but narrowing the disparities between New York City and its principal competitors is an appropriate objective.

A second standard for determining whether local taxes are too high involves comparing the share of local income represented by local taxes to some earlier benchmark figure. As Table 9.2 shows, local taxes grew as a share of local income, reaching 9.6 percent in 1978. The city reduced the tax burden to 8.7 percent in the early 1980s, but in the latter part of the decade it climbed back to 9.6 percent and reached 9.8 percent in 1990. Since public service needs change over time, a benchmark such as the earlier ratio may be an inappropriate measure for today. Still, reducing the city's aggregate tax burden so that it is more in line with the past is a worthwhile economic development strategy. However, even if a precise standard is set as an objective, the city would still face the challenge of determining which taxes to change and on what basis.

The standards for evaluating individual taxes, drawn from the theory and literature of public finance, include efficiency, equity, revenue-generating capacity, and feasibility.[10] The nature of these standards is such that they may be employed in considering whether to raise, reduce, or simply maintain the level of revenues flowing from a given tax.

Efficiency

The principle of efficiency has two components. First, a tax in one jurisdiction should not be so high relative to other jurisdictions that it reduces local economic activity; this may be referred to as external efficiency. Second, a tax should not cause some economic activities within a jurisdiction to suffer at the expense of others. This standard is internal efficiency.

The efficiency standards are related closely to the concept of choice. If taxes are higher in one jurisdiction than another, then taxpaying firms and individuals will "vote with their feet" and relocate if all other considerations are equal. The high-tax jurisdiction may benefit in the short run from being able to provide better services than its less-taxing competitor, but in the long run its tax base will be reduced and, with that, the tax revenues necessary to maintain services of acceptable level and quality. The same principle applies with respect to economic activity within a jurisdiction. If one form of local economic activity is taxed more than others, then otherwise rational investment decisions will not be made in order to capitalize on the tax advantage accorded by local tax policy. In the short run, again, this may produce positive benefits—politically or perhaps even with respect to economic activity—but in the long run the local economy will suffer because of the inefficient use of resources.

Virtually all forms of local taxation affect economic efficiency by violating this "neutrality" principle either in its external or internal dimension. Moreover, a tax that is efficient may not be equitable, which raises the problem of determining which standard should be accorded primary consideration. Nevertheless, some taxes are worse than others with respect to their impacts on economic efficiency.

Equity

Like efficiency, the equity standard can be applied in two dimensions: horizontal equity requires that taxpayers in like situations should be taxed on the same basis; vertical equity requires that those with more wealth pay more taxes than those with less wealth.

The principle of horizontal equity can be illustrated by a simple example with relatively small fiscal and economic consequences that, nevertheless, is commonplace in New York City. If an individual with a taste for prepared food purchases a take-out meal in a supermarket or delicatessen, he or she pays no tax under New York City's retail sales tax; a person who consumes the same meal in a restaurant does. The tax thus treats the consumers (and the sellers) differently, despite their similar circumstances. (This example also illustrates that the equity and efficiency criteria do not always conflict. The sales tax exclusion for prepared food purchased in a grocery store violates the principle of internal efficiency noted earlier by, in effect, subsidizing grocery stores and delicatessens in their competition with restaurants for the business of those who prefer to purchase prepared food rather than prepare it themselves.)

Vertical equity is a more complex standard to apply. Taxes may be classified on the basis of their income effects. A tax that causes the share of income absorbed by it to rise with the income of the taxpayer is known as a progressive tax; one that absorbs a larger share of the income of lower-income taxpayers is a regressive tax; a third category is a proportional, or "flat," tax, so named because it absorbs the same share of income regardless of income amount. Generally speaking, American society accepts the view that taxes should be progressive (though some view proportional taxes as inherently fairer).

The equity standard is easier to define than to employ analytically, however. One reason, noted earlier, is that some taxpayers are able to shift the burden of taxes to others because of their market power. Thus two commercial sectors paying the same business income tax rate may feel the impact of taxes quite differently based on their different abilities to shift the burden. Another uncertainty involves the distorting effect of state and federal taxes and, in particular, tax deductions. A seemingly progressive local tax, like a graduated income tax, may be less progressive because deductions from state and federal income taxes provide high-income taxpayers a larger benefit than low-income taxpayers. Finally, the use or expenditure of tax revenues may be such that an inequitable tax promotes income equality; for example, the proceeds of a regressive sales tax could be used to transfer income to the poor, in which case the indirect effect of the tax would be progressive.

By applying the vertical equity concept to different taxes its analytic strengths and weaknesses can be illustrated better. The sales tax generally is considered to be regressive because low-income persons must allocate a larger share of their income for consumption than high-income persons (who save or invest relatively larger shares of theirs). In light of this, most governments that employ a sales tax exempt certain purchases, usually "necessities" like food, shelter, hospital care and prescription drugs, and sometimes clothing.

The property tax raises similar issues. On the face of things, one might assume that poor people generally pay a larger share of their income for housing than wealthier persons, and that renters ultimately bear the actual cost of residential property taxes. Although estimating the overall income effects of property taxes is difficult, the evidence suggests that they are regressive in New York City.[11]

Income taxes, particularly personal income taxes, in theory are easier to evaluate from the perspective of vertical equity. If tax rates are graduated, that is, increase with income, the system may be said to be progressive. However, the exemptions, deductions, and credits permitted by a locality may be such that its apparent progressivity is reduced or even eliminated. Moreover, since local income taxes are deductible from federal taxes, high-income taxpayers in essence receive a federal rebate that reduces the overall progressivity of the local tax.

The Advisory Commission on Intergovernmental Relations, using 1982 data, attempted to analyze the vertical equity of New York City's tax system, including the effect of state and federal taxes.[12] The commission found that the local system was slightly regressive, but that state and federal taxes made the overall system progressive. The local sales and property tax systems were both regressive for families of four with incomes ranging from $17,500 to $100,000, so much so that their impact was not offset by the progressive local income tax. The three major local taxes consumed 5.4 percent of the income of those families with incomes of $17,500, but only 5 percent for those with $100,000 income. After including taxes of the state of New York and the federal government, however, the overall system became progressive. Tax policy changes since then, particularly in the federal income tax, probably have made the overall system in New York City somewhat less progressive.

Another study, using 1986 tax data, focused only on the local personal income tax, local sales tax, and property tax on residential property.[13] It found these municipal taxes to be highly regressive for families with incomes below $25,000, proportional for families with incomes between $25,000 and $50,000, and mildly regressive for families above $50,000. The generally regressive character was due primarily to the incidence of the property tax; the income tax was mildly progressive and the sales tax generally proportional.

Studies by the government of the District of Columbia provide more recent data and a comparative perspective. (See Table 9.8.) Their analysis indicates

Table 9.8 State and Local Tax Liability for a Family of Four, New York City and Other Areas, 1975, 1980, and 1990 (Sales, Income, Property, and Auto Taxes as a Share of Income)

Area	1975	1980	1990
New York City			
Low-income family[a]	18.1%	12.4%	10.6%
Low–middle-income family[b]	18.5	15.4	12.6
High–middle-income family[c]	19.1	16.4	14.1
High-income family[d]	20.1	17.3	14.5
Large-city average[e]			
Low-income family[a]	9.1%	7.0%	8.7%
Low–middle-income family[b]	9.0	7.4	8.9
High–middle-income family[c]	8.8	7.4	9.8
High-income family[d]	8.7	7.4	9.8

Sources: Government of the District of Columbia, Department of Finance and Revenue, Office of Fiscal Planning and Research, *Tax Burdens in Washington D.C. Compared with Those in the Nation's Thirty Largest Cities, 1975* (February 1977); Government of the District of Columbia, Department of Finance and Revenue, Office of Economic and Tax Policy, *Tax Burdens in Washington D.C. Compared with Those in the Nation's Thirty Largest Cities, 1980* (May 1982); Government of the District of Columbia, Department of Finance and Revenue, Office of Economic and Tax Policy, *Tax Rates and Tax Burdens in the District of Columbia: A Nationwide Comparison* (June 1991).

[a]Income level is $10,000 in 1975, $17,000 in 1980, and $25,000 in 1990.

[b]Income level is $20,000 in 1975, $35,000 in 1980, and $50,000 in 1990.

[c]Income level is $30,000 in 1975, $50,000 in 1980, and $75,000 in 1990.

[d]Income level is $40,000 in 1975, $75,000 in 1980, and $100,000 in 1990.

[e]In 1975 and 1980 refers to the 30 largest cities in the United States; in 1990 refers to the largest city in each of the 50 states and the District of Columbia.

the share of a four-person family's income assumed by state and local sales, income, property, and auto taxes. In 1990 this tax burden for New York City residents was modestly progressive. The taxes accounted for 10.6 percent of a $25,000 income, 12.6 percent of a $50,000 income, 14.1 percent of a $75,000 income, and 14.5 percent of a $100,000 income. This was a far more progressive pattern than in the average large American city. Trend data from these studies also indicate the city's tax burden continued to fall in the 1980s, while in other areas it typically rose.

Revenue Capacity

A more practical standard for evaluating a tax is its ability to contribute to the revenues necessary to sustain government activities. An optimal tax system from the perspectives of efficiency and equity simply may not generate enough revenues to finance desired public services, in which case public policy may (and, arguably, frequently does) place a higher value on the revenue capacity of a tax than on its efficiency and equity effects.

The capacity of a tax to generate revenues is a function of many variables. The effectiveness of a single tax, or of a tax system, as a revenue generator may be measured by its elasticity—that is, the rate of change in the revenues produced by the tax compared to the rate of change in economic activity.[14] Some taxes "pull their own" better than others, perhaps because of public policy decisions involving tax rates, bases, and administration and perhaps because of market forces that exert differential impacts on the kinds of economic activity that are taxed.

Feasibility

Assuming that a review of municipal tax policy based on the standards surveyed here suggests that one or another existing law should be changed, the final question to be considered is whether or not the indicated change is politically acceptable. If change is not possible, the consideration of alternatives is wasteful; sometimes, however, the examination of policy alternatives, particularly if joined with some other stimuli, leads to change. In any event, feasibility ultimately is determined by politics more than analysis.

A related issue involves the administration of a tax. In order to be effective, a tax must be collectible. Moreover, the extent to which taxes legally owed are collected affects the equity of the local tax system. The costs of administration should be weighed against the presumed benefits of compliance in evaluating tax policy, but there is no basis for defending a system in which compliance efforts lag and some taxpayers end up paying their taxes in full while others do not.

The City's Tax System and the Evaluative Standards

A better tax structure might be created locally if the current system and proposals to change it were analyzed from the perspectives of efficiency, equity, revenue capacity, and administrative feasibility. This section undertakes such an analysis for the five most important municipal taxes. These five taxes accounted for more than 93 percent of the $15 billion the city collected in fiscal year 1990 from its local taxes. The taxes are the property tax (44 percent of the local tax revenues in fiscal year 1990); the personal income tax (17 percent); the sales tax (16 percent); business income taxes, including the general corporation and financial corporation taxes (12 percent); and the commercial rent tax (4 percent).

Real Property Taxes

Despite its long-term decline in importance, the real property tax remains the backbone of the municipal tax system. Because of its importance, a separate chapter in this book is devoted to it. Nonetheless, it is an appropriate starting point of the present analysis, not only because it is the largest municipal revenue source but because it raises issues involving each of the evaluative criteria. The state constitution limits the amount of real estate taxes that can be levied for operating purposes to 2.5 percent of the average full value of taxable property for the last five years (including the current year); however, property taxes may be levied without limit to pay the principal and interest on the city's long-term debt. In the past the constitutional limit accounted in part for the declining role of the property tax in local public finance, but in recent years the city has not used its full taxing authority (discussed later).

New York City's property tax is inefficient because it taxes various property classes at different rates. However, inefficient local practice is in conformance with a state law passed in 1981 dividing real property in New York City into four classes and permitting them to be taxed at different nominal rates. The four types are Class I, consisting of residential properties housing up to three families; Class II, comprising all other residential property; Class III, consisting of real property owned by utility companies; and Class IV, which covers all other real property and includes what may be termed the city's "commercial" real estate.

Prior to 1981, all property was taxed at a single rate, but tax discrimination was practiced nonetheless by assessing different classes of property at different percentages of full market value. In 1979, for example, assessment (to full market value) ratios by some common property types were as follows: one- and two-family houses, 24.6 percent; other housing, 59.3 percent; non-residential (generally commercial) property, 63.4 percent. These differential assessment practices when applied to the uniform nominal tax rate yielded effective (based on full market value) tax rates of $2.15 per $100 of assessed value for one- and two-family homes, $5.19 for other residential housing, and $5.55 for commercial property.[15]

The state law passed in 1981 required consistent assessment ratios for each class and permitted localities to tax various properties at different nominal rates if they chose to do so. In fiscal year 1982 the city taxed its four property classes at the same nominal rate, $8.95 per $100 of assessed value. Since then, however, the tax rate for commercial property has been increased much faster than the rate for residential properties. The problems associated with this new system, and its misuse, are discussed in the next chapter.

New York City's property tax system is also inequitable in that properties within the same class are taxed differently because of nonuniform assessment practices, an administrative failure. City officials have increased their efforts to address this problem, but the system still is riddled with intraclass inequities. In general, three-family residential properties are assessed closer to market value than are one- and two-family properties, which means higher effective tax rates for the former group of Class I properties.[16] Similar discrimination exists among Class II apartment buildings and Class IV commercial properties, particularly for new buildings or recently acquired buildings where reassessments tend to be concentrated,[17] although the problem has been mitigated somewhat by municipal policies lowering the assessment for these properties from 60 percent to 45 percent.

Additional inequities arise under the property tax due to an extensive system of exemptions and abatements that lower the burden for some owners. These "tax expenditure" programs typically were passed to stimulate economic development and housing improvements, but their limited applicability creates inequities; individuals or firms receiving the benefits pay less property tax then their neighbors or competitors who have not received the exemption.

In fiscal year 1991 city-authorized tax expenditure programs under the property tax granted $655 million in tax expenditures.[18] The largest category was housing programs, totaling $409 million; economic development programs totaled $172 million. The other smaller programs were exemptions for senior citizens and veterans. The housing and economic development programs have been criticized for subsidizing projects that would have been built without the tax exemptions. In such cases the tax subsidy only enriches the developers without yielding broader social benefits.

Although it is the largest source of municipal revenues for New York City, the real property tax system contributes less than it might to municipal revenues. The aforementioned constitutional limitation sets an upper bound on the amounts the city can raise from real property taxes for operating purposes, but that limit has not been reached in recent years. (See Table 9.9.) In the most recent fiscal year for which data are available, the revenue potentially available from the real property tax that was not levied totaled almost $3.0 billion. Increasing the yield to the constitutionally permissible maximum would raise substantial sums but, it should be remembered, would also exacerbate the efficiency and equity problems noted earlier unless the differences in effective tax rates for various classes were narrowed and assessment practices were standardized within property classes.

The local real property tax system, based on the standards employed in this report, provides opportunities for reform. The critical policy issues in-

Table 9.9 City of New York Real Property Tax Levy and Limit, Fiscal Years 1975–1991 (dollars in millions)

Fiscal Year	Operating Limit[a]	Levy Within Operating Limit[b,c]	Unused Operating Margin[d]
1975	$1,851.7	$1,707.2	$ 144.5
1976	1,858.8	1,793.6	65.2
1977	1,897.3	1,896.6	0.7
1978	2,006.7	1,909.3	97.4
1979	2,074.6	1,936.1	138.5
1980	2,020.2	1,918.7	101.5
1981	2,070.6	2,065.3	5.3
1982	2,399.8	2,396.4	3.4
1983	2,718.1	2,703.0	15.1
1984	3,181.6	2,971.9	209.7
1985	3,589.1	3,181.5	407.6
1986	4,010.5	3,648.9	361.7
1987	4,432.0	3,956.0	476.0
1988	4,969.5	4,432.3	537.2
1989	6,808.5	4,996.3	1,812.2
1990	7,789.1	5,401.3	2,387.8
1991	9,109.3	6,154.7	2,954.6

Source: City of New York, Department of Finance, *Annual Report on the New York City Real Property Tax*, fiscal year 1991 (January 1991).

[a]As determined by the New York State Board of Equalization and Assessment.

[b]Represents that portion of the real property tax levy that is subject to the constitutional limitation.

[c]Based on total assessed valuation data not shown in table.

[d]Derived by subtracting the levy within the operating limit from the operating limit.

volve choices about the rates at which different property classes should be taxed, the extent to which properties are fairly assessed, the effectiveness of tax expenditure programs, and the extent to which property taxes should contribute to the overall revenue system. A system that narrowed effective tax rates among the four property classes, moved faster toward uniform assessment ratios within classes, granted fewer tax exemptions, and approached the maximum yield permitted by the state constitution would be more efficient, more equitable, and more productive than the current system.

The Sales Tax

Since its introduction in the 1930s, the local sales tax has played an important role in local government finances. The city's sales tax of 4 percent is levied on sales (or in some cases use) of personal property, utilities, restaurant meals and hotel occupancy, and selected admissions. The major exemptions are for rents, food (for home consumption), mass transit usage, hospital services, and prescription drugs.

From an efficiency perspective the New York City sales tax can be faulted.

Its total rate of 8.25 percent, which includes 4 percent for the city, 4 percent for the state, and 0.25 percent for the Metropolitan Transportation Authority, generally is higher than in surrounding jurisdictions. Connecticut had a 7.5 percent state sales tax that was lowered to 6.0 percent in 1991, and New Jersey has a 7.0 percent state sales tax. The rates in adjoining New York counties are 8.25 percent in Nassau and 5.75 percent in Westchester (except for select Westchester municipalities, where rates range from 8.25 percent in Mount Vernon and Yonkers to 7.25 percent in New Rochelle and White Plains). Moreover, neighboring jurisdictions exempt certain sales that are taxed in New York City. Although the sales tax doubtlessly causes some consumption to be shifted from New York City (and encourages some illegal tax avoidance on local sales), the scope of such tax-avoiding behavior probably has declined over time as surrounding jurisdictions have increased their rates relative to New York City's.

With respect to the principle of internal efficiency, the local exemptions for rent, food, mass transit, hospital services, and prescription drugs no doubt shift some consumption toward these products and away from others. Despite the exemptions noted previously, low-income persons apparently still spend a higher percentage of their incomes on taxable goods than wealthier persons. This is suggested by the ACIR study discussed earlier.

One of the virtues of the sales tax is its sensitivity to local economic conditions. Its elasticity, as measured by the change in sales tax revenues compared to changes in local economic output, was nearly 1.0 in the 1977–1984 period.[19] Unless significant changes in local markets occur, it is reasonable to assume that sales tax revenues will continue to grow at least as fast as the local economy. The greater volatility of other taxes, expressed either in terms of slow or fast growth relative to economic performance, makes the stability of the sales tax attractive.

In summary, the local sales tax raises some clear-cut issues. It invites some tax-avoidance behavior (both legal and illegal) by being higher than in surrounding jurisdictions; due to its exemptions, it doubtlessly alters consumer behavior in ways that the efficiency standard would deem undesirable; and the tax remains regressive, despite the exemptions in its coverage. However, the sales tax represents a stable, economically sensitive source of revenues.

The Personal Income Tax

The city imposes an income tax on the net income of its residents and a tax on nonresident earnings from wages and salaries or self-employment (commonly known as the "commuter income tax"). As shown earlier (Table 9.5), growth in personal income tax revenue represents one of the major changes in the local tax system in recent decades. Introduced in 1966, its rate has been increased or subject to surcharge on several occasions. As of early 1991, the tax rate for New Yorkers begins at 2.2 percent for the first $8,000 of taxable income for a single individual (and $14,400 for joint filers); the rate tops at

3.91 percent on taxable income over $60,000 for individuals (and $108,000 for joint filers). These rates include a temporary surcharge of about 0.5 percent that is scheduled to end in 1993. In contrast, wage and salary earnings of nonresidents are taxed at a flat 0.45 percent, and their self-employment income is taxed at a flat rate of 0.65 percent.

The municipal income tax for New Yorkers is high relative to other American cities and, in particular, to surrounding metropolitan communities, which typically do not have such taxes. The local tax, coupled with the state personal income tax, provides substantial incentives for New Yorkers to avoid the tax by moving to suburban areas, particularly outside of the state. Federal deductibility, the presence of the commuter income tax, and the recent increases in standard deductions and personal exemptions for New Yorkers all reduce these relocation incentives somewhat, but the tax remains high in absolute and relative terms.

The New York City personal income tax is progressive, but only to a point—specifically, $60,000 for individuals and $108,000 for couples. Above these levels, it is a flat (proportional) tax of 3.91 percent.

From an equity perspective the most troublesome feature is the wide difference in the taxation of resident and nonresident income. The current nonresident tax on wages and salaries earned in New York City, which carries a $3,000 exclusion, is a flat 0.45 percent regardless of income. Thus, for New York City residents the minimum tax rate is five times that of a commuter and the maximum nearly nine times higher. Effective tax rate differences are not as pronounced as these numbers suggest, but they are large at all income levels and grow more pronounced for those with higher incomes. Although it may be unfair to tax nonresidents at rates comparable to New Yorkers, present commuter rates are unreasonably low.

Without the increase in personal income tax proceeds experienced in New York City, other revenue sources, primarily the property and sales taxes, would have had to play a more prominent role in financing the city of New York. One of the most striking indicia of its revenue-producing effectiveness is its high elasticity, estimated at 2.3 in the 1977–1984 period.[20]

Questions about the city's personal income tax are raised in varied quarters. New Yorkers who believe the city's high-income residents do not pay their fair share can fault its proportional quality for persons with taxable incomes above $60,000 or $108,000. Persons with taxable incomes up to these figures, particularly those at the lower range, might join in this position but also believe that the low-income allowance exempts too many persons with incomes close to their own. High-income persons may argue with some validity, despite its proportional character for them, that the tax encourages migration to suburban locations and should be reduced.

However, the clearest problem with the local personal income tax remains the discrimination between resident and nonresident taxes. Tax rates on nonresidents have been frozen since 1971 due to the influence of suburban legislators in the state legislature and appear unlikely to be increased in the near future.

Business Income Taxes

Business income taxes levied by the city of New York take several forms, including a general corporation tax, a financial corporation tax, an unincorporated business tax, and a utilities tax. The rates vary from tax to tax, and the bases for determining tax liability are multiple.

The general corporation tax is the major business income tax. In fiscal year 1990 its revenues were $1,123 million, or 7 percent of total tax revenues. Generally speaking, the tax rate is 9 percent of allocated net income, but alternative means of computing liabilities not based on business income may be applicable—in which case the highest liability applies. The tax is imposed on all corporations that do business in the city, with the exception of financial corporations, transportation corporations, utilities, and various specialized investment companies. All of the corporate forms that are exempt from the general corporation tax, except insurance companies, are subject to other business income taxes.

The financial corporation tax produced $196 million in fiscal year 1990. It covers both commercial banks and thrift associations. The basic tax rate is 9 percent of net income allocated to New York City activities.

The unincorporated business tax is levied at 4 percent of taxable income on activities carried on in New York City. This tax, which covers almost all noncorporate firms, is paid in addition to the personal income tax (or the self-employed earnings tax of nonresidents). In fiscal year 1990 the unincorporated business tax yielded $356 million.

The last major business tax is the utilities tax, which is set at 2.35 percent of gross receipts for most of the city's utility firms. Fiscal year 1990 revenues from this tax were $184 million.

The city's business income taxes raise efficiency issues. Their high levels relative to other areas can be cited as an economic deterrent. Utility companies do not relocate to avoid taxes, but they pass on their tax liabilities to local consumers of their products, including other businesses, whose operating costs are raised accordingly.

The city's business income tax policies once violated norms of horizontal equity (and internal efficiency) in that they taxed businesses essentially alike at different rates. This was particularly true with respect to differences in tax treatment between general corporations, including security and commodity firms on the one hand, and commercial banks, on the other. The latter paid a rate of nearly 14 percent of their net income, whereas the former were taxed at a 9 percent rate. Whatever justification for such differential rates that once existed certainly was reduced as the line between "financial" and "nonfinancial" institutions became blurred. However, the changes in state and local tax policies enacted in 1985 equalized tax rates.

Concern over the city's business income taxes is warranted, particularly from the perspective of potential locational effects related to their high levels. The 9 percent rate of local taxation, when coupled with the similarly high state business income taxes, represents a substantial cost of doing business in New York City.

Commercial Occupancy Tax

This tax, originally passed in 1963 when the city was bumping up against the constitutional limit on property taxes, imposes a 6 percent levy on commercial rents. The $685 million it yielded in fiscal year 1990 comprised about 4 percent of the tax total.

The commercial occupancy or rent tax adds appreciably to the cost of doing business in New York City, a burden (it has been argued) that falls disproportionately on the city's marginal businesses, particularly manufacturing firms. Its effects on the local economy in general and on certain functions are difficult to evaluate, however, since it is not clear whether the tenant or the property owner bears the actual as opposed to the nominal burden of the tax. Arguably, the cost is borne by property owners, not renters, in markets where vacancies are high; if so, the argument that the commercial rent tax has worked to the general disadvantage of marginal manufacturing enterprises is wrong. In areas where rental space is in short supply, however, it is reasonable to conclude that tenants, not owners, bear all or much of its burden.[21]

In one major respect the commercial rent tax violates the principle that like taxpayers should be treated alike. Commercial tenants of office buildings pay the occupancy tax as renters; their neighbors on an adjoining floor do not pay the tax if they own the building they occupy (though they pay real estate taxes, which, in certain circumstances, they are not able to pass on to tenants).

The commercial occupancy tax is not an ideal tax given the efficiency and equity issues noted in this chapter. However, it is a proven "moneymaker" for the city, particularly in a period of rising rents.

Conclusion

The multiple, and sometimes conflicting, criteria that distinguish better from worse taxes make it difficult to identify a clearly desirable case for tax reform. But at least three general directives are clear.

First, there are notable ways in which the current system violates the standards of efficiency and economic neutrality. The current municipal tax system favors some activities over others and thereby harms the local economy. The unincorporated business tax and the commercial rent tax epitomize these problems. Both are priority targets for reductions and eventual elimination.

The unincorporated business tax is a form of double taxation (along with the personal income tax) on small businesses and many professional services that are provided by partnerships. A progressive and effectively administered personal income tax could serve the same purpose without promoting local disincentives for such activity.

The commercial rent tax is another form of double taxation. It was created to tax commercial property at a time when the property was near its constitutional limit. It has become economically harmful because it adds to some businesses' tax burdens and favors ownership of property over rental of property. Since it is now possible to raise property tax rates within the constitutional limit, it would be preferable to replace this tax with higher, and more broadly based, property tax rates or another more economically neutral tax.

Second, the current system contains significant violations of the equity principle. The tax system is generally regressive, due primarily to the incidence of property tax on residential property. The system would be made less regressive by relying more on the personal income tax and by offsetting property tax burdens on low-income families with a refundable credit on the personal income tax.[22]

Equity principles are also violated by the nature of the property tax system. The setting of different nominal and effective rates for rented versus owner-occupied residential property treats otherwise similar families differently for tax purposes. Richer-than-average homeowners are taxed less heavily than poorer-than-average renters. In addition, city administrative practices in the assessment rolls leave many inequities among properties in the same class. That is, homeowners in different neighborhoods have different effective tax rates because the basis of their assessment is not uniform. Eliminating the substantial inequities in the property tax is a key component of policies designed to alleviate inequities.

Finally, municipal taxes are too high relative to other areas. To become more economically competitive, the city should lower its aggregate tax burden. But pressures for expanded services make this almost impossible politically. The major opportunity for lower taxes will arise from shifting some city responsibilities to higher levels of government. The leading opportunity is in the financing of Medicaid and public assistance. The share of these activities financed locally is higher in New York than any other state. Shifting more of this financial responsibility to the state and federal levels would spread the burden more equitably and thereby permit tax reductions in New York City. Until the federal and state governments remove the oppressive burden of aiding poor families from local shoulders, significant tax reductions will prove an elusive goal.

_____10

THE PROPERTY TAX

Over the past decade, real estate taxes consistently have accounted for almost one-fourth of the city of New York's revenues. From fiscal year 1980 to 1990, the increase in property taxes slightly outpaced growth in the operating budget, rising 105 percent while total revenues grew 97 percent.[1] This growth in property tax revenues, however, came largely at the expense of the owners of commercial and industrial property.

The number one priority of New York City property tax policy has been to protect the interests of owners of small residential property. The city has decreased the small residential owners' share of the property tax burden and increased that of commercial and industrial property owners. City policy has pronounced as anathema equal taxation among different types of property. The result has been a growing "interclass" inequity, in which commercial and industrial properties provide a disproportionate share of property tax revenues.

This inequity has been implemented through two types of decisions. First, the nominal tax rate for residential properties has been set below that for other types of property. Before fiscal year 1983, all local property was taxed at the same nominal rate, $8.95 per $100 of assessed value in 1982. A state law permitted different rates for four different types of property (small residential, other residential, utility property, and commercial and industrial property) beginning in 1983. The city established separate rates and the disparity has grown; in fiscal year 1990 the rates varied from $9.23 and $9.45 for the two classes of residential property to $9.54 for most commercial property and $12.90 for utility property.

Second, and even more significant, is a disparity in the way in which these classes of property are assessed. In fiscal year 1990 the average small residential property was assessed at only about 9 percent of its market value; in contrast, larger residential property and commercial property were assessed at about 45 percent of market value and utility property at about 50 percent.

The combination of different nominal tax rates and differential assessment practices creates tremendous variations in the real or effective tax rates among types of property. One-, two-, and three-family home owners paid only about 84 cents in tax for every $100 of property value in 1990; the comparable figures for apartment house owners, commercial property owners, and utilities were $4.15, $4.29, and $6.45, respectively.

This inequitable property tax policy has been molded primarily by political concerns. Elected officials are wary of tax increases that directly affect the purses of their constituents. To please their constituents, and thereby protect their incumbencies, elected officials in New York City have protected home owners in favor of burdening businesses and apartment dwellers. In effect, businesses and residential renters are subsidizing the home owners' inequitably small share of the tax burden. By placing the onus of revenue production on apartments and on commercial property, the mayor and the city council have created a disincentive to doing business in New York City and to new investment in rental housing.

The pursuit of these short-sighted political goals placed the mayor and the city council in potential conflict with state laws as fiscal year 1989 neared an end. The law required increases in home owners' taxes and relief for other types of owners. Instead of complying with the law, city officials sought to change it. The result was new legislation perpetuating the inequities.

This chapter relates the history of the New York City property tax system and presents some recommendations for future directions. The history is told in four parts: the situation before the classification system was established, the city's procedures under this system from fiscal years 1983 to 1989, the dilemma of 1989, and city tax policy for fiscal year 1990 and beyond.

Before Classification

Until 1981, New York State Real Property Tax Law (RPTL) required that all properties be assessed at full market value. However, New York City and many other localities violated this law. In New York City, there was no standard procedure for the routine assessment of real estate. As a result, for the 20 years leading up to fiscal year 1981, the assessed value of real estate in the city rose 40 percent while its market value increased more than 200 percent.[2] Increases in assessment were primarily made for new and high-priced commercial properties; assessments of small residential properties remained virtually stable.

In 1975, the New York State Court of Appeals ruled that property assessments on the basis of a percentage of market value were in violation of the RPTL.[3] The court required that all localities in New York State conform with the full market value provision of the RPTL.

Institution of full market value assessments in New York City would have led to a major redistribution of the property tax burden. The tax burden for small residential properties would have increased greatly, while that of other residential and nonresidential properties would have decreased substantially. One study, commissioned by the city's Department of Finance, estimated that instituting full-value assessment and a uniform tax levy would have doubled the tax burden of New York City small-home owners.[4] The study further estimated that the nonresidential tax burden would have decreased by 25 percent. However, the city did not move immediately to conform with the court's ruling. Instead, the state legislature enacted a series of moratoria which postponed any necessary action until the end of 1981.

The state's response to the *Hellerstein* decision came in December 1981, when the legislature amended the RPTL with S-7000A. This statute brought New York City and other localities into compliance by eliminating the law they were violating. S-7000A repealed the full market value law and created four property classes: Class I property, consisting of one-, two-, and three-family homes; Class II, all other residential properties, including apartment houses, cooperatives, and condominiums; Class III, utility real property; and Class IV, all other property, including office buildings, factories, stores, and other commercial property.[5] The new law divided the tax burden among the four classes according to their assessed value in fiscal year 1981, rather than their market value, thus solidifying the then-current distribution.

Each succeeding year, the city would be required to adjust the distribution of the tax burden to reflect changes in the value of property in each class. That is, each class's share would grow in proportion to changes in its share of total market value. The city was, however, given discretionary authority to increase or decrease a class's share of the total tax burden by up to 5 percent annually. The intent of this provision was not specified, but some observers expected it would be used gradually to bring the burdens of small-home owners closer to that of owners of other types of property (or at least not to widen the gap if property values grew at different rates among classes).

The new law called for the allocation of the property tax burden to be reviewed every three years based on market surveys by the State Board of Equalization and Assessment (SBEA). The shares of total market value for the four property classes in 1981 were designated as "base percentages" to which future shares of market value would be compared. In the future the SBEA would periodically survey market value and compute the current percentage for each property class and the change in share from the 1981 base percentages. The SBEA-calculated rates of increase or decrease in market value would then be applied to the *assessed* value shares for each class of property in the 1981 base year (called base proportions) to create new class shares of assessed value, called adjusted base proportions. The SBEA's adjusted base proportions would be the basis on which the city would have to levy its property tax in the period following the SBEA review.

The new law became effective in fiscal year 1983, with the first SBEA market value adjustment scheduled for fiscal year 1987. However, a 1984 amendment postponed the first SBEA adjustment until fiscal year 1990, and the base year for the adjustment was changed to fiscal year 1984.

S-7000A also addressed some assessment problems. It attempted to remedy "intraclass" inequality by requiring that all properties within each class be assessed uniformly.[6] However, the new law also put a limit on the size of any individual owner's assessment increase. Class I properties were limited to no more than a 6 percent increase per year, and 20 percent over five years. Class II properties of four to ten units were limited to 8 percent per year and 30 percent over five years. Assessment increases for Class IV and other Class II properties must be phased in over five years, using a formula set forth in the RPTL. These provisions limited the city's ability to achieve intraclass equity because previously underassessed properties could be brought to a fair assessment level only gradually.

Property Taxes After S-7000A

With the disparity in tax burdens firmly entrenched by the passage of S-7000A, city tax policy in subsequent years widened the gap. Market values for real property in the city rose sharply after the enactment of S-7000A, with Class I property values outpacing the other three classes. From 1983 to 1989, Class I taxable market value increased 175 percent. (See Table 10.1.) Classes IV and II grew 132 and 95 percent, respectively, while Class III lagged far behind at 4 percent.[7] The larger growth in Class I property values should have led to a shifting of the tax levy burden toward Class I from the other classes.

However, city policy decisions had the opposite effect; the Class I share of the tax burden actually decreased. The Class I properties represented 14.1 percent of the tax levy in 1983 but only 11.7 percent in 1989. (See Table 10.2.) This occurred despite the fact that the share of market value for Class I property increased from 32.3 to 40.8 percent of the total. During the same period, Class IV properties' share of the tax levy grew from 41.6 to 47.8 percent, although its share of market value grew at a slower pace than one-, two-, and three-family homes (122 percent versus 175 percent).

The limitations on assessment increases under S-7000A played a part in keeping the Class I tax levy share down. Although the market value of Class I property increased 174.8 percent between fiscal years 1983 and 1989, its assessed value grew only 22.1 percent. This reflects both the statutory limitations on assessment growth and a city policy of underassessing these properties. For the same period, Class IV assessed value increased 73.6 percent and Class II assessments grew 46.1 percent, while Class III assessments grew only 4.2 percent.

If the city had applied the full assessment increase allowed by S-7000A, Class I assessments could have grown 20 percent over the first five years, through fiscal year 1988, and then an additional 6 percent in fiscal year 1989. Thus the maximum assessment increase permitted by law was 27.2 percent. The actual increase in total assessed value for Class I property from fiscal year 1983 to fiscal year 1989 was only 22.1 percent, 5.1 percentage points short of

Table 10.1 Taxable Assessed Value, Tax Levy, and Taxable Market Value, Fiscal Years 1983 and 1989 (dollars in millions)

Property Class	Fiscal Year 1983	Fiscal Year 1989	Percentage Change 1983–89
Taxable Assessed Value			
Class I	$6,217.2	$7,591.9	22.1%
Class II	11,774.1	17.197.4	46.1
Class III	7,927.8	8,261.2	4.2
Class IV	17,905.7	31,091.1	73.6
Total	$43,824.8	$64,141.6	46.4
Tax Levy			
Class I	$556.4	$717.6	29.0
Class II	1,053.8	1,594.5	51.3
Class III	722.1	932.6	29.1
Class IV	1,664.2	2,979.1	79.0
Total	$3,996.5	$6,223.9	55.7
Taxable Market Value			
Class I	$31,086.0	$85,427.0	174.8
Class II	19,623.5	38,238.4	94.9
Class III	15,836.5	16,535.6	4.4
Class IV	29,823.6	69,121.8	131.8
Total	$96,369.6	$209,322.8	117.2

Sources: Taxable assessed value and tax levy from City of New York, Department of Finance, *Annual Report on the New York City Real Property Tax,* fiscal year 1990. Taxable market value derived by dividing the tax levy by the effective tax rate. Effective tax rates from City of New York, Office of Management and Budget, *Executive Budget for Fiscal Year 1990: Message of the Mayor,* May 18, 1989.

the city's legal authority. The 22.1 percent increase represents a growth in assessed value of $1.4 billion, from $6.2 billion in fiscal year 1983 to $7.6 billion in fiscal year 1989. If the full 27.2 percent legal authority had been applied, the growth in assessed value would have been almost $1.7 billion, a difference of $316 million in taxable assessed value. At the fiscal year 1989 tax rate of $9.45 per $100 of assessed value, the shortfall in assessment growth accounted for a loss of nearly $30 million of tax revenue for fiscal year 1989.

Table 10.2 Class Tax Levy Shares, Fiscal Years 1983–1989 (percent of total)

Property Class	Fiscal Year							Percentage Change 1983–89
	1983	1984	1985	1986	1987	1988	1989	
Class I	14.1%	13.9%	13.4%	12.9%	12.5%	12.2%	11.7%	(17.2%)
Class II	26.3	26.0	25.9	25.5	25.4	25.5	25.6	(2.8)
Class III	18.0	18.0	17.8	18.2	16.6	15.7	15.0	(17.0)
Class IV	41.6	42.1	42.9	43.4	45.5	46.6	47.8	15.0

Source: City of New York, Department of Finance, *Annual Report on the New York City Real Property Tax,* fiscal year 1991, January 1991.

However, 22.1 percent is most likely greater than the actions actually taken by the city to increase individual assessments. The 22.1 percent increase also reflects additions of new property and restoration of existing property to the Class I tax rolls, as well as additions or improvements to existing property, all of which are exempt from the RPTL's assessment limitations. Considering the effects of the adjustments in assessed value for additions, improvements, and similar items suggests the actual city actions to increase assessments on typical Class I properties are far less than 22.1 percent. Thus, the city's unused assessment authority is probably greater than 5.1 percentage points, the understatement of assessed value most likely larger than $316 million, and the loss of revenue greater than $30 million. Therefore, the entire blame for slow assessment growth for Class I cannot be placed on the state's RPTL; the city has not exercised its full power to raise assessments.

Another aspect of the city policy that has contributed to the growing inequity is differential nominal tax rates. The tax levy share for a class of property is a factor of both its level of assessment and its nominal tax rate. And city policy has also favored small home owners in terms of these rates.

As shown in Table 10.3, when S-7000A came into effect in 1983 the city shifted from a single rate ($8.95 in 1982) to differential tax rates for each class. The rate for residential property in both Class I and Class II was set lower than that for utility property, which in turn was less than for all other property. This pattern has generally been maintained, although rates on utility property were revised notably in 1988 (in part related to reductions in the base due to changed legal definitions of utility property).

The continued impact of differential tax rates and widening gaps in assessment practices is the vastly different effective tax rates among the classes of property. As noted earlier, home owners pay only 84 cents per $100 of property value while the equivalent figure for Class II is $4.17, for Class IV is $4.31, and for Class III is $5.64.

Table 10.3 Nominal and Effective Tax Rates, Fiscal Years 1983–1989

Property Class	Fiscal Year							Percentage Change 1983–89
	1983	1984	1985	1986	1987	1988	1989	
Nominal Tax Rate								
Class I	$8.950	$9.100	$9.100	$9.100	$9.330	$9.330	$9.452	5.6%
Class II	8.950	9.057	9.150	9.150	9.150	9.150	9.272	3.6
Class III	9.109	9.237	9.051	9.051	9.172	9.942	11.289	23.9
Class IV	9.294	9.323	9.460	9.460	9.460	9.460	9.582	3.1
Total	$9.120	$9.206	$9.255	$9.256	$9.315	$9.434	$9.704	6.4%
Effective Tax Rate								
Class I	$1.790	$1.820	$1.680	$1.550	$1.210	$1.210	$0.840	(53.1%)
Class II	5.370	5.430	4.120	4.120	4.120	4.120	4.170	(22.3)
Class III	4.560	4.620	4.530	4.530	4.590	4.970	5.640	23.7
Class IV	5.580	5.590	4.260	4.260	4.260	4.260	4.310	(22.8)
Total	$4.807	$4.850	$3.926	$3.924	$3.898	$3.964	$4.071	(15.3%)

Source: See Tables 10.1 and 10.2.

The Dilemma of 1989

The city's use of its discretionary power came in conflict with state law in 1989. The first step in the drama was the SBEA's market survey of the 1984 tax roll to establish the base percentages. Another survey was conducted for the 1986 tax roll to determine market value trends between 1984 and 1986. These trends determined the adjusted proportions that the city would have to live under in fiscal year 1990.

The SBEA's analysis of market trends and its calculation of adjusted base proportions of assessed value would have obliged the city to alter drastically its tax policy for fiscal year 1990.[8] Whereas the city had decreased the Class I share, the state-mandated procedure required increases in the Class I share. Whereas the city's policy had increased the burden for Class IV, the state law required reductions for that class. More modest adjustments upward were required for Class II and Class IV shares.

Specifically, based on the SBEA's findings, the city's Tax Study Commission estimated that in fiscal year 1990 the Class I nominal tax rate would have to rise 34.5 percent to $12.71 per $100 of assessed value; the average one-, two-, and three-family home owner's tax bill would increase by $410.[9] Combined with assessment increases, the total bill increase would be $506, or 42 percent. The nominal tax rates for Class II and Class III properties would rise 2.5 percent to $9.50 and 9.6 percent to $12.37, respectively. The nominal tax rate for Class IV property, however, would decline 9.7 percent to $8.65 per $100 of assessed value, 30 cents lower than the tax rate prior to S-7000A. The typical factory would save more than $800 on its tax bill; a prime Manhattan office building would save 48 cents per square foot.

Faced with the prospect of large increases in the tax bills of small-home owners, city officials took a predictable course. Although the means proffered differed from one politician to another, the ends were the same: Amend the property tax law. The legislative history of property taxes in New York City and New York State has been one not of tailoring taxing practices to meet statutory requirements but of amending and repealing parts of the RPTL to further the city's inequitable property tax policy.

Instead of searching for a method of efficiently bringing the city's tax levy shares up to the SBEA's standards, Mayor Edward I. Koch and City Council Majority Leader Peter Vallone sought a two-year moratorium on the implementation of any SBEA adjustments. Although Koch and Vallone stated that the moratorium would "allow the Legislature ample opportunity to find a way to make sure that Class I homeowners pay a fair share of the property tax bill," it is more likely that they sought a method of avoiding Class I tax increases altogether. The mayor and the majority leader were plain in their desire to protect small-home owners, pointing out that, unlike other classes of property, one-, two-, and three-family homes are more often owner-occupied, and thus not income-producing. That fact is evidence enough, they said, "why Class I owners deserve special protection and consideration when it comes to apportioning property class shares."[10]

City officials blamed the assessment limitations of the RPTL for the prospect of sudden, large tax increases for home owners. The law's cap on assessments was pointed to as the sole explanation for the Class I tax burden falling below the 1983 proportion, while the city's use or misuse of its discretionary authority was dubbed a "policy of attempting to stabilize rates."[11] However, as demonstrated previously, the city did not exercise the full assessment powers accorded by the RPTL, and its discretionary authority to set differential rates contributed to the problem.

Organizations representing owners of commercial property were alarmed by the political leaders' recommendations to eliminate their legally mandated (and economically sensible) decrease in tax burden. One group called on the state legislature not only to allow the SBEA adjustment to occur for fiscal year 1990 but also to eliminate the city council's discretionary authority.[12]

As with the passage of S-7000A in 1981, the property tax crisis was not resolved so much as it was removed by changing the RPTL. An amendment to the RPTL was passed on June 12, 1989. It has two major provisions. The first is a moratorium on any adjustments to the class shares of the tax burden—other than the 5 percent discretionary authority and the annual adjustment for additions and changes to the tax roll—for fiscal years 1990 and 1991. This removed the immediate threat of the mandated tax increase for Class I property and set the stage for the institution of the second, more sweeping provision.

The second major provision is a redefinition of the fair shares of the tax burden for each class. The base year is shifted from 1984 to 1990, thus implicitly endorsing the city's discretionary adjustments in the 1984–1990 period. In addition, adjustments for growth in market value in 1992 and subsequent years are limited to 5 percent. That is, a class share cannot increase by more than 5 percent annually regardless of trends in market value. Finally, this new adjustment process will be administered primarily by the city rather than the SBEA.

The overall effect of the amendment is to legitimize and lock in place the city's inequitable tax system. Whereas S-7000A implicitly defined as fair the inequitable distribution of the tax burden in place in 1981, the new amendment solidifies a distribution which the city has made even less equitable during a period when it was supposed to be moving in the opposite direction. There is little prospect that interclass inequality will ever be addressed under the current RPTL.

Tax Policy for Fiscal Years 1990 and 1991

Given the state legislature's willingness to legitimize the short-sighted and politically motivated behavior of city officials, it is not surprising that the city council followed the well-established path for fiscal years 1990 and 1991. The city again used its discretionary authority to reduce the Class I share and increase the Class IV share. As shown in Table 10.4, the city used the full 5 percent of its discretionary authority in each year to reduce the Class I tax levy share to 10.9 percent, down from 14.1 percent in fiscal year 1983 despite a 4

Table 10.4 Discretionary Adjustment, Tax Levy Share, and Nominal Tax Rate, Fiscal Years 1990 and 1991

Property Class	Discretionary Adjustment		Tax Levy Share		Nominal Tax Rate	
	1990	1991	1990	1991	1990	1991
Class I	(5.00%)	(5.00%)	11.1%	10.9%	$9.452	$9.840
Class II	0.23	(2.18)	25.7	25.8	9.229	9.154
Class III	(4.49)	(4.50)	13.8	10.3	12.903	15.079
Class IV	2.44	3.19	49.3	53.0	9.539	9.924

Sources: Resolution of the Council of the City of New York Fixing the Tax Rate for Fiscal Year 1990, adopted June 30, 1989; Resolution of the Council of the City of New York Fixing the Tax Rate for Fiscal Year 1991, adopted June 30, 1990.

percent increase in the Class I tax rate. Class III received almost a 9 percent decrease, and Class II dropped nearly 2 percent. Class IV bore the brunt of the Class I and III decreases, rising to a tax levy share of 53 percent, up from 41.6 percent in fiscal year 1983.

Conclusion

Is there any hope for redressing the interclass inequality of the New York City property tax? Unless the RPTL is drastically revised, and city officials have a 180 degree change of heart, the answer is an emphatic "No." The latest amendments legitimized the status quo. No change is likely primarily because city leaders believe the system is fair. They don't believe it is broken, so they don't want to fix it.

But the city's property tax system *is* broken. It unfairly burdens businesses as it subsidizes small-home owners. The result is serious adverse economic pressures that could lead to business relocation out of the city.

Short-sighted politicians see this issue as a choice between reelection and revenues. Protecting the small-home owner garners votes. Injuring businesses could decimate the tax base, not only for the property tax but for other taxes such as the corporate income tax and the commercial occupancy tax. New York City's leaders have chosen reelection, but eventually they may not have much of a tax base to support their government.

What should be done? Ideally, barriers to assessment growth should be removed, and assessments should follow market conditions. That is, the new law should be abandoned and replaced with one following the earlier principle that the tax levy share for a class or property should rise or fall based on trends in the value of that property. The current commitment to keeping home owner bills extremely low regardless of the cost to others should be reconsidered.

IV
SERVICE DELIVERY

───11

EXPENDITURES AND SERVICES

The relationship between what local government spends in money and produces in services has important effects on the local economy and resident
welfare. Municipal officials who are able to produce "acceptable services at
acceptable costs" contribute to the economic fortunes of their communities
and the living standards of their citizens. In return, they can expect to receive
support from campaign contributors and voters. Municipal officials who are
unsuccessful at managing the spending–service relationship are likely to elicit
challenges to their policies, perhaps even to their positions; more important
from a community perspective, their behavior reduces local living standards
and employment opportunities and encourages outmigration of those for
whom "exit" appears a more appropriate response than "voice."[1]

The spending–service relationship is particularly important in big-city
governments. They devote a large share of their financial resources to direct
service delivery, and they are surrounded by governments whose propinquity
offers footloose consumers the opportunity to savor the city's attractions while
avoiding some of its taxes and services. One respected student of urban development, an economist mindful of the fact that municipalities are not monopo-
lies, went so far as to identify public management as *the* scarce resource of
cities like New York.[2]

Its importance helps explain why the relationship between spending and
service is a recurring theme in New York City politics and policy. Pursuing
this line of inquiry offers two important opportunities: first, it provides a basis

for evaluating the performance of elected and appointed officials; second, it helps identify options to alter the spending–service relationship in ways that enhance the prosperity of the city and its people. These goals are related; the policy analyst presumes that however political leaders are doing, they—or others—could do better.

The first section of this chapter reviews the spending–service literature on New York City, discusses the theoretical assumptions and analytic tools underlying that line of research, and identifies the major obstacles to its development. The second section evaluates the management of one municipal service—refuse collection—using an approach that modifies earlier efforts in an attempt to deal with some of the obstacles. The utility of this revised approach is considered in the last section.

Earlier Spending–Service Studies

The New York City fiscal crisis was viewed with alarm for many reasons, not the least of which was the fear that retrenchment or spending cuts would seriously diminish municipal services. Frequently, public voicing of such alarm is guileful, a tactic municipal officials use to pressure the sources of municipal funds—including local taxpayers as well as officials of the state and federal governments—to contribute more to the city's treasury. During the fiscal crisis, however, such expressions were more than simple posturing. Serious students of the municipal government with no apparent axes to grind, including a former New York City budget director writing in the pages of *Daedalus,* warned that retrenchment would precipitate a general service crisis.[3] The presumption underlying these concerns was that service levels are positively (and closely) correlated with spending levels. Long a theorem of advocates of increased public expenditure, the spending–service hypothesis was applied to retrenchment with equal conviction.

The New York City Studies

A few studies dating back to the mid-1960s provide evidence to contradict the popular proposition that "what you spend is what you get." These include a national study finding no strong relationship between spending and student achievement and studies showing low correlations between state government spending and selected services.[4] In addition, a study of spending in selected agencies of the city of New York over the 1961–1971 period found widely differing relationships between spending increases and improvements in services.[5]

The first study of spending–service relationships in a period of retrenchment is found in *Setting Municipal Priorities, 1981.*[6] It compared the experience of five local functions (police, fire, sanitation, education, and mass transit) in periods of spending growth (1970–1975) and decline (1975–1979). During the first period, major spending increases were associated with modest improvements in some services and with reductions in others; during the fiscal crisis period, major spending cuts were associated with reductions in some services but with improvements in others. Sometimes, though not usually, service levels were correlated with spending changes.

If changes in spending explain only some of the variation in municipal services, what accounts for the rest? Dennis C. Smith's subsequent analysis of New York City police services demonstrated that management behavior affects the extent to which changes in expenditure translate into changes in services.[7] During growth periods managers do not fully utilize the resources at their disposal to produce services; when retrenchment occurs, they mitigate service cuts by drawing down these "slack" resources (for example, by cutting "frills" or redirecting staff resources to line purposes).

Another variable that affects the spending–service relationship—consumer behavior—was subsequently identified in *Setting Municipal Priorities, 1983*.[8] In that study the authors revisited the 1981 chapter, using more detailed data and extending the analysis through 1982. Their study confirmed the spending–service hypothesis in several services, but it revealed two important exceptions suggesting that the volume and quality with which the citizenry consumed services had an independent effect on service levels (including both volume and quality). In refuse collection and firefighting, particularly the latter, declining consumer "demand" mitigated the service effects of retrenchment. The study concluded by recommending that city officials focus more attention on altering managerial and consumer behavior in those services where one or the other held the most potential to affect the spending–service relationship.

Subsequently, the locus of research in this general area shifted to the Citizens Budget Commission (CBC), but the focus also changed. For the most part, the series of annual reports published by CBC measured changes in the level and quality of the major municipal services to determine whether they were getting "better" or "worse."[9] The first two reports, covering the 1978–1981 and 1981–1982 periods, respectively, found declines in the volume and quality of several important services. Initially, city officials differed with CBC's interpretation of the data, but continuing development of the city's reporting system and resulting changes in CBC's methodology narrowed these differences.

The next two CBC reports found a general reversal of the trend toward "worse" services. Indeed, CBC's 1985 report, published in the midst of the mayoral campaign, was cited approvingly by Mayor Edward I. Koch as evidence that he had delivered on his 1981 campaign promises to improve municipal services in his second term.[10]

Of course, there is no necessary connection between improved services, on the one hand, and good management, on the other. Spending more money and employing more workers is not necessarily good management, even though a "resource-intensive" strategy may yield improved services for a time. The challenge, assuming that the demand for municipal services is not price-inelastic, is to produce acceptable services at acceptable costs.

In light of this, CBC altered its approach in its 1986 review of municipal services. Instead of examining whether services continued to improve in 1986, it analyzed changes in services *relative* to changes in the resources consumed in providing them during the 1983–1986 period. In this period, retrenchment was replaced by growth. Real spending rose 17 percent, and employment increased 14 percent.[11] After comparing trends in services and resources (primarily employment, because spending data for individual service functions were not available), the report grouped eight municipal services into three categories: well-managed, where service improvements clearly outpaced increases in resources (refuse collection and administration of income maintenance); routinely managed, where service improvements approximated spending gains (crime fighting, elementary education, and street cleaning); and poorly managed, where service improvements did not occur or were small relative to increased resources (probation investigation, high school education, and fire fighting). Eight other services, the report concluded, could not be evaluated because either resource or service data (and sometimes both) were insufficient.[12]

City officials greeted this report less enthusiastically than its immediate predecessor. Mayor Koch dismissed it as "ivory towered" in a statement to the press.[13] In a more formal response, the director of the Office of Operations argued that some of the data CBC used were inadequate and where the data were adequate, they supported a different conclusion.[14] Other city officials claimed that public service delivery was too complex a process to be studied from the "outside," particularly by comparing resource and service trends.[15]

To summarize, the New York City studies began by testing the spending–service hypothesis then reformulated the relationship to include other independent variables, management and consumer behavior. A second, narrower line of research grew out of the Setting Municipal Priorities studies, a series of Citizens Budget Commission reports monitoring changes in the level (volume and quality) of municipal services. These research strands were brought together in the 1986 CBC study, which argued that the performance of the city's managers should not be evaluated without considering the resources used in providing services. That study, which added "acceptable costs" to the "acceptable services" standard, drew critical responses from city officials, though on a number of different grounds.

Assumptions and Tools

A core assumption of the studies just reviewed is that city governments are subject to competition, albeit not perfect competition. For this reason municipal leaders must manage the resources at their disposal in a way that yields taxpayers an "acceptable return" in services. The standard is difficult to specify, because neither the benefit of services nor the cost of taxes has a constant value. In a period of local economic growth, for example, the benefits of a New York City location may be so substantial that employers and residents are willing to pay high taxes for a given level of municipal services. Other periods and conditions, however, may make them less blase about the "money's worth" issue. Although the concept of acceptable return is hard to measure, the logic of competition suggests that some spending–service relationships are better than others.

Given this assumption, input–output, or "production function," analysis is an appropriate analytic tool.[16] The key concepts of the input–output model are resources and services. Their relationship defines productivity. When inputs decline relative to outputs, productivity increases; when inputs grow in relation to outputs, productivity declines. Increased productivity is not the only goal of municipal government, nor should it be. But it is an important goal because of competitive threats and because productivity gains narrow the gap between the service needs of urbanites and their ability to pay.

The logic and implications of the input–output model may be illustrated by borrowing an example from business management education. Consider manufacturers who produce this standard good—the widget—in a competitive market. Competition, the theory goes, forces the managers of firms to engage in an unceasing effort to increase productivity in order to reduce the unit cost (and price) of a widget. Managers increase productivity through innovation, either by altering the mix of resources between labor and capital or by using the same mix of resources differently. Those managers who make the right choices among competing policy options contribute to the firm's profitability and are rewarded by grateful owners. Managers who make the wrong policy decisions will be forced to seek employment elsewhere. And if the inefficient firm is unable to respond in time, consumers will buy elsewhere and eventually drive the inefficient firm from the market.

This scenario exists only in theory. Most organizations, particularly large and important ones, do not operate under such harsh conditions. The experiences of organizations like Chrysler and, more to the point, the city of New York suggest that the "market" will not shut them down. However, this does not mean that the city of New York is not subject to competitive pressures. When the city's managers are unable to produce acceptable services at acceptable prices, the short-run effect is a reduction in the living standard of New Yorkers. If the problem is not corrected, the longer-run effect will include net outmigration. These are significant problems which competitive pressures create but do not always resolve.

Research Problems

Application of the input–output model to municipal services is difficult. Both inputs and outputs are hard to measure. And if one or the other cannot be measured, then their relationship cannot be understood. And if the relationship between a given set of inputs and outputs cannot be evaluated, then neither can alternative relationships. Each of these obstacles requires further discussion.

Output Measurement

Efforts to measure public output lag those in the private sector. This is not because public product is an unmeasurable "black hole," as some maintain, but because services are harder to measure than goods. The education of children in private schools is no easier to measure than the education of public school youth; widgets produced in a prison would be no harder to measure than those produced in a private factory. That the primary measurement problem reflects the nature of the product more than the ownership of the producer does not lighten the load of measuring public services, although it does remove a conceptual barrier to trying.

There is a substantial literature devoted to measuring public services.[17] And in New York City there is a substantial governmental effort dedicated to this purpose. The focal point of that effort is the Office of Operations, which has a budget of approximately $7 million and a staff of 144. One of its primary responsibilities is to prepare the biannual *Mayor's Management Report (MMR)*, which includes about 3,000 different performance measures for municipal agencies. The literature and the *MMR* suggest that most municipal services can be measured on the dimensions of volume and quality, and that volume generally is easier to measure than quality.

The conceptual and empirical problems encountered in the measurement of service volume and quality have been discussed in detail elsewhere, and for this reason are treated in very abridged form here.[18] With respect to most services a ready measure of volume exists, including refuse collection (tons of refuse collected). For example, the number of children who attend public schools indicates the volume of service provided by the New York City Board of Education; the number of inmates in the city's jails serves the same purpose for the Department of Correction.

The greater difficulty in measuring service quality also is evident in the analysis of refuse collection, as we will see, but the same is true generally. The problem is not the impossibility of collecting information about the quality of service as much as it is the lack of consensus about what data should be collected. This reflects underlying ambiguities about the purposes of many public services. For example, is the purpose of education to help young people become good citizens? Productive workers? Both and more?

Despite these ambiguities, there is room for common sense in measuring service quality. To again use the education example, lack of agreement on its ultimate purposes does not mean that educational quality is beyond measurement.[19] The results of standardized tests measuring the ability of students to read and perform mathematics are reasonable measures because these skills are required to become a good citizen, a productive worker, or virtually any other goal of schools. Similarly, the security of municipal jails is a reasonable, though not necessarily exclusive, measure of the quality of correctional services, because incarceration, not rehabilitation, is the basic purpose of municipal jails.

Most available indicators of public service quality are imperfect. This means they should be used and interpreted carefully, not that they should be ignored. The act of measuring and interpreting will lead to improved measurement and interpretation, as is attested by the development of the literature and the city's repeated efforts in the *MMR*.

Input Measurement

Input measurement often seems less challenging than output measurement because money provides a common and quantifiable standard. For municipal services in New York City, however, input measurement is a major obstacle to input–output analysis. The reason is simple: The city of New York does not tally its expenditures for a given service. City officials generally relate resources and services by counting labor inputs with measures ranging from simple "head counts" to somewhat more sophisticated measures such as "person days" or "person hours." Beyond this, there is little to say except that input–output analysis requires a different conceptualization and fuller accounting of inputs.

The Relationship Between Inputs and Outputs

It is time now to address the last major problem of applying input–output analysis to study of the relationship between public expenditure and public service. Required is a formal statement of the linkages between resource inputs and service outputs, beyond that which was presented in discussing the manufacture of widgets.

Let us begin considering the relational issue by returning for a moment to the spending–service hypothesis. That hypothesis and the input–output model each begin with the act of public expenditure. According to the hypothesis, the dependent variable, service, is correlated closely with the independent variable, spending. The review of the spending–service studies indicated that this relationship was more complex; thinking of the sequence by which resource inputs become service outputs helps understand why.

The input–output model provides a different conception of the budgetary process than the conception underlying the original spending–service hypothesis. If changes in the level of public expenditure drive changes in public services, then budget decisions are critical to determining service levels. This perspective leads many executives to present their budgets by detailing incremental spending changes for various agencies, usually accompanied by a budget message heralding the prospect of improved services in those agencies where spending is to rise (or lamenting decline in service if retrenchment is necessary). While the average citizen may not read the budget, the media can be counted on to make the official information available. The "budget-is-everything" perspective is shared by other political participants, including legislators and the leaders of pressure groups who lobby on behalf of a particular public service. For them, the budget signals whether their efforts during budget adoption have "improved education" or "made the streets safer."

Now, consider the budget as merely a technical document that authorizes officials to spend money for specific purposes. From this perspective, all the budget does is permit officials to write checks in order to pay for the factors of production—labor, machines, space, and supplies and materials—which are needed to produce services. However, budget authority or money does not provide services, at least not directly. (Income transfer programs are the major exception.)

When public expenditure is conceived thus, it is easier to understand why the correlations between spending and service are not stronger. The initial use of money, the product of public finance, is to acquire the factors of production. Then, policy decisions less visible than those in the highly publicized process of budget adoption determine how the raw materials of services are to be assembled and utilized, acquired and managed. How are available funds to be divided between capital and labor? How are available funds for labor to be divided between expanding (or contracting) the work force and expanding (or contracting) the compensation of the work force? What machines are to be introduced in the production process? What rules are to direct the efforts of the work force? The way in which these types of questions are answered—that is, the policies governing the acquisition and use of the factors of production—affect the nature of public services independently of the amounts appropriated in the budget.

These decisions are not reached in a "command post" where a small set of senior officials assemble on a regular basis to resolve competing municipal priorities and then devise the most appropriate means of accomplishing them. The policy-making process is much more complicated. The many officials responsible for securing and utilizing the factors of production do not all have the same goals, and reconciling them is difficult because their decisions are separated in time and space. Nonetheless, they choose among competing policy options, just as the managers of widgets do, and their choices make a difference. In the first instance, their decisions affect the fortunes of those who control the factors of production, including those with money to lend and those who arrange the lendings, the suppliers of paper spreadsheets and of Lotus 1-2-3, and most of all current and would-be municipal workers. Ultimately, and of more immediate concern, these decisions affect the volume and quality of municipal services and their cost.

The Case of Refuse Collection

Refuse collection is one of many services provided by the city of New York. Why single it out for analysis? The answer is that it is a relatively simple service. This makes it a convenient threshold case for the underlying purpose of the chapter, which is to explore the utility of the input–output mode of analysis.

The Conventional Approach

One of the major challenges to systematic analysis of municipal services is that the agencies formally responsible for providing them typically deliver more than one service. This complicates the task of tying resources to a given service and it complicates the measurement of services. There are tradeoffs between the volume and quality of a given service and among the related services an agency provides.

This is the case in the Department of Sanitation (DOS). Refuse collection is but one of its responsibilities. The department also disposes of the refuse it collects, cleans streets, and removes snow when accumulation interferes with transportaton. These services are interdependent. For example, if waste is not disposed of satisfactorily, then refuse collection will be altered. The department will have to redirect its priorities from collecting refuse efficiently to reducing the amount of refuse it must collect. This implies that the management of "consumer" behavior will become more important.[20]

The interdependence of services explains why administrators try to group related services in a single agency. This "administrative design," in theory, facilitates the adjustment of organizational priorities and corresponding alterations in organizational behavior. Ideally, the resources available to an agency like the DOS are fungible. However, many factors conspire to reduce the fungibility of public resources in an agency setting. In large part, the performance of the DOS in the last decade reflects the ability of its managers to utilize differently the resources at their disposal. This record has been analyzed in detail elsewhere,[21] but it is summarized next as a prelude to evaluating the record from conventional and new perspectives.

Sanitation Management Since the Fiscal Crisis

Before the fiscal crisis, the DOS was not viewed as a well-managed agency. Its work force was organized by a strong union, the Uniformed Sanitationmen's Association, which had the reputation of controlling the agency. The union was seen as having clout in electoral politics, and occasionally it demonstrated its power directly by interrupting services. Evidence of its influence is that sanitation workers, whose jobs lack some of the status of other titles in the uniformed ranks, long have earned base pay equal to 90 percent of police and fire personnel. In most other American cities, the differential is much greater.[22] The work force also had a reputation for being idle much of the working day, a charge that was periodically reinforced by journalists who tailed sanitation workers and reported their unauthorized breaks and abridged schedules. (However, when one examines the tons of refuse collected by an average employee, even before the fiscal crisis, it is apparent that their work was not all play.)

The control over the "workplace" exercised by the work force and their union extended to the tools of the trade. The refuse collectors worked on trucks with relatively small capacity, which meant that they were able to hold down the amount of "hard" work (picking up and loading refuse) they were required to perform, while maximizing the "easy" side of their jobs (driving trucks to dump sites and cleaning streets). When collection trucks were loaded, the driver left for the dump site; the remaining two collectors assigned to the truck became street sweepers armed with old-fashioned brooms.

As might be surmised from this description, the management of DOS was not strong. Commissioners took their major duty to be maintaining stable relations with the workers and their union leaders. If mayors did not make their peacekeeping function clear to commissioners, their deputies in the agency did. Many of the latter had risen through the ranks and had difficulty thinking of themselves as managers.

Not surprisingly, the operations of DOS came under periodic attack by outside critics and sometimes, though not frequently, even by officials of other municipal agencies. Reforms ranging from privatization (or, as it was known then, contracting out) to technological innovation to closer field supervision were urged. But innovation foundered because the political costs of change were thought to be prohibitive. The Department of Sanitation fit the profile of a bureaucracy that had achieved a high degree of immunity from the outside world.[23]

The fiscal crisis changed the department. First, it simply reduced its size. Between 1975 and 1978, departmental spending fell 20 percent in real terms, and employment declined 19 percent.[24] In response, the department's managers began to allocate and utilize their resources somewhat differently. They shifted employees from street cleaning to refuse collection and initiated new supervisory and disciplinary policies (the "stick" approach to management). Nevertheless, their innovations were insufficient to make up for the sharp reductions in employment. The quality of sanitation services declined in the remainder of the 1970s. And worker productivity in collections, which one might assume would increase greatly because the decline in collection personnel substantially exceeded the decline in the volume of refuse, rose 0.1 percent between 1974 and 1980.

In the 1980s, however, the department's managers and workers finally addressed the issue of low productivity. The centerpiece of their efforts was the so-called gainsharing agreement between the city and the Uniformed Sanitationmen's Association. The essentials of the agreement involved the work force dropping its opposition to the introduction of collection trucks that could be operated by two rather than three persons in return for payment of a productivity bonus above and beyond their basic salary to collectors working on the new trucks. This initiative had been under discussion for years, but the city's continuing fiscal problems (and a threat by the department's leadership to contract out some refuse collection) moved the proposal off the drawing board.

Introduced on a limited basis in 1981, the two-worker truck program was extended to the entire city by 1985. Even with payment of the bonuses, the "carrot" in the plan, the city realized considerable savings. Higher productivity in the collections function enabled DOS to redirect resources to other functions, street cleaning in particular. The result was that refuse collection and street cleaning services both improved despite continued reductions in spending.

The City's Method of Evaluating Refuse Collection

These improvements in refuse collection during the 1980s are documented in the reports prepared by the Office of Operations. Created during the fiscal crisis, that office has evolved into one of the city's important staff organs. Its biannual *MMR* is the primary source of public information on municipal services.

Table 11.1 is a selective listing of the major indicators used in the *MMR* to monitor refuse collection during the 1980–1986 period. More recent versions of these reports contains 45 indicators for DOS as a whole, but the 8 shown in Table 11.1 are the most important.[25]

The first indicator seen in Table 11.1, total expenditures, introduces virtually all of the empirical sections of the *MMR*, which is organized on an agency basis. In addition to showing expenditures for the prior fiscal year, the *MMR* presents planned and actual expenditures for the current year and preliminary spending estimates for the next. However, the data are not reported on an inflation-adjusted basis; nor do they include all expenditures (such as pensions, fringe benefits, and debt service) that would be included under a full cost-accounting method. As reported in the *MMR*, expenditures of the Department of Sanitation rose 60 percent in the 1980–1986 fiscal period.

In addition to departmental spending, the *MMR* typically includes full-time employment agencywide (plus additional detail not shown in Table 11.1 disaggregating agency employment into categories like civilian and uniformed and funding sources for the agency's work force). Whereas the spending data do not depict accurately the real level of financial resources available to the agency, the employment series reflects the level of human resources available to perform agency functions. In the case of DOS, the work force increased 15 percent between 1980 and 1986, with the growth concentrated in 1985 and 1986. This is a reversal of the retrenchment that prevailed in the 1975–1980 period.

In addition to agencywide employment, the *MMR* provides some detail on employment by major functions in many municipal agencies. Total employment for cleaning and collections together is reported regularly (as is employment for waste disposal and for other selected programs of the department). During the 1980–1986 period, employment within the cleaning and collections function increased 13 percent, somewhat less than in the agency as a whole. Again, the pattern is not one of steady growth.

On the service as opposed to resource side, the *MMR* includes five major measures for refuse collection: (1) tons of refuse collected; (2) share of collections made at night; (3) share of loads not collected daily during "normal" weeks; (4) share of acceptably clean streets; and (5) Productivity Analyis

Table 11.1 Selected Measures Used by the City of New York as Performance Indicators for the Sanitation Department, 1980–1986

Mission and Indicators	1980	1981	1982	1983	1984	1985	1986	Percentage Change 1980–86
Total department expenditures	$298,792	$310,566	$336,332	$386,435	$411,307	$434,865	$479,024	60.3%
Total department employment	10,928	11,684	11,811	11,598	11,357	12,045	12,558	14.9
Cleaning and collections employment	8,149	8,270	8,193	7,982	7,569	8,285	8,252	12.6
Tons of refuse collected (000s)	3,325	3,183	3,217	3,320	3,420	3,512	3,488	4.9
Percentage of refuse collections made at night	14.1%	8.7%	8.8%	9.8%	14.8%	12.2%	8.5%	(39.7)
Percentage of loads uncollected daily	3.0%	2.6%	1.3%	5.4%	3.0%	1.9%	2.1%	(30.0)
Percentage of acceptably clean streets	52.0%	57.5%	62.0%	62.9%	64.8%	68.7%	74.0%	42.3
PAR index	63.2	66.2	71.7	74.7	80.0	91.4	95.9	51.7

Sources: City of New York, *The Mayor's Management Report*, final editions fiscal years 1981–1987.

232

Reporting (PAR) index. The first indicator measures the volume of refuse collected, the second, third, and fourth the quality of the service, and the fifth its productivity.

The volume measure, tons of refuse collected, is straightforward. The weighing of refuse at dump sites is not error-proof, but the measure is considered reliable. The workload of refuse collectors, while varying from year to year, increased 5 percent in the 1980–1986 period. This contrasts with the second half of the 1970s, when tons collected declined 6 percent. The determinants of refuse production by the populace are not fully understood, but the altered trends in the last decade probably are related to changes in the city's population and economy. During "bad" times, declines in population and income reduce service demands on certain agencies; in "good" times, growth increases demand.

Two of the quality measures—the percentage of collections made at night and the percentage of loads not collected daily during normal weeks ("normal" meaning when collection schedules are not interrupted by holidays or snowstorms)—reflect the assumption that refuse presented for collection by the citizenry should be picked up quickly, and particularly so as not to disturb nocturnal activities. The second of these measures is interesting because New Yorkers need their refuse collected on holidays no less than on normal days (and on some holidays, more). However, from the perspective of evaluating the department's managers the reduced standard is reasonable because they are not responsible for negotiating labor contracts or otherwise determining when refuse collectors receive holidays. In this (and in other respects discussed later) the city's service-reporting system is designed to evaluate the performance of "line" rather than "overhead" managers. In any event, each measure shows quality improvements in the 1980–1986 period. The share of night collections fluctuated in those six years, but the figure in the last two years was down sharply from 15 percent to 9 percent. The share of loads not collected during normal weeks declined from 3 percent at the beginning of the period to 2 percent at the end, reaching a low of nearly 1 percent in 1982 and a high of more than 5 percent in 1983.

The third measure of the quality of refuse collection—street cleanliness— is a hybrid in that it is used to measure street cleaning performance as well. This is sensible in that collectors who spill refuse while transferring it from can to truck contribute to dirty streets (though the major contributors are littering citizens). The city's method of measuring street cleanliness dates to 1975, when a pilot effort called Program Scorecard was developed. In brief, 6,000 sample blocks are examined regularly on a visual basis and are graded on a spectrum ranging from clean to filthy. For the city as a whole, the share of streets rated acceptably clean rose from 52 percent in 1980 to 74 percent in 1986, an increase of 42 percent. In 1975, by comparison, 73 percent of the city's streets were accorded the acceptably clean score, a proportion that declined steadily until a turnaround in 1980.

The measure of refuse collection productivity found in Table 11.1 shows a remarkable increase of 52 percent between 1980 and 1986. This measure is derived from the city's PAR system, which relates the hours of effort expended by collectors to the tons of refuse they collect adjusted for different neighborhood conditions throughout the city. The increase in the index during the 1980–1986 period reflects the gradual implementation of the gainsharing agreement between 1981 and 1985. In 1980, prior to the program, the PAR index stood at 63.2 percent. By 1985, it had reached 91.4 percent, and it rose again in 1986 to 95.9 percent.

In summary, the city's reporting system confirms what has been written repeatedly of the quality of collection service and its management: It is good and getting better. New Yorkers are receiving higher-quality service even though they are generating more refuse. Moreover, the city's reporting system shows that the work is being done much more efficiently.

A Revised Input–Output Method

What additional light, if any, does application of the input–output mode of analysis shed on refuse collection? The first requirement of the input–output model is to account for the costs of producing a given service. As noted earlier, the *MMR* does not provide a full accounting of expenditures for the DOS and, by extension, for the separate services it provides. Nor do the accounts of other municipal agencies, including the Office of Management and Budget and the Office of the Comptroller. Hence, it is necessary to estimate the costs of collecting refuse. This has been done using certain allocative assumptions, but readers should remember that the findings presented below are approximate rather than precise.[26]

Table 11.2 shows estimated total spending for refuse collection in the 1980–1986 period, adjusted for inflation. There was substantial variation within the period, but real spending for refuse collection declined nearly 10 percent overall.

How did municipal officials allocate that sum among the factors of production? Capital spending rose 60 percent from $24 million in 1980 to $40 million in 1986, bringing the share of spending for capital from 10 percent to 18 percent.[27] The category Other includes miscellaneous purchases and rentals of supplies, materials, property, and equipment. The smallest of the expenditure components, it declined in absolute and relative terms between 1980 and 1986. In 1986, spending for Other purposes was $23 million, down 23 percent from $30 million in 1980. Its share of total spending fell from 12 to 10 percent.

The same trend is evident for labor spending, the largest of the three categories. The cost of labor fell 17 percent from $198 million to $164 million. This reduced labor's share of spending (or, put differently, the labor intensity of refuse collection) from 78 to 72 percent. These trends are consistent with the previous discussion of the department's strategy of substituting capital embodying new technology (larger two-person trucks) for labor.

Table 11.2 also shows the division of labor spending between expanded number of employees and higher compensation per employee. The trade consistently has favored higher compensation. The number of workers assigned to

Table 11.2 Inputs, Outputs, and Productivity for Refuse Collection, 1980–1986

Category	1980	1981	1982	1983	1984	1985	1986	Percentage Change 1980–86
Total expenditures[a]	$251,916	$258,080	$235,649	$241,977	$250,720	$216,354	$227,681	(9.6%)
Capital	$24,242	$25,672	$19,073	$30,833	$36,025	$25,927	$40,238	66.0
Other	$30,094	$32,009	$31,188	$28,088	$26,305	$23,606	$23,125	(23.2)
Labor	$197,580	$200,399	$185,388	$183,006	$188,391	$166,821	$164,317	(16.8)
Number of employees	7,074	7,290	6,481	6,238	5,789	5,700	5,125	(27.6)
Average compensation per employee	$27,930	$27,490	$28,605	$29,337	$32,543	$29,267	$32,062	14.8
Productivity measures								
Tons per employee	470.0	436.6	496.4	532.2	590.8	616.1	680.6	44.8
Labor cost per ton	$59.4	$63.0	$57.6	$55.1	$55.1	$47.5	$47.1	20.7[b]
Total cost per ton	$75.8	$81.1	$73.3	$72.9	$73.3	$61.6	$65.3	13.8[b]

Sources: Expenditure data estimated from City of New York, Executive Budget, fiscal years 1981–1987 editions; employment and output data from City of New York, The Mayor's Management Report, final editions fiscal years 1981–1987; constant-dollar adjustments made on the basis of U.S. Department of Labor, Bureau of Labor Statistics, Middle Atlantic Regional Office, "Consumer Price Index for All Urban Consumers (CPI-U) in the New York–Northeasten New Jersey Area" (fiscal-year average).

[a]Expenditures in thousands of fiscal year 1980 dollars.

[b]Shown in positive terms since the decline indicates a productivity gain.

refuse collection was reduced from nearly 7,100 to slightly more than 5,100, a 28 percent decline. At the same time, the average constant-dollar compensation of employees rose 15 percent, from almost $28,000 at the beginning of the period to slightly more than $32,000 at the end. This increase primarily reflects the city's collective bargaining policies during the 1980–1986 period, which provided all municipal workers real-pay increases. The base pay of sanitation workers rose almost 17 percent in constant dollars during these six years.[28] In addition, the compensation data seen in Table 11.2 reflect the bonuses paid to employees for staffing the new collection trucks.

Thus, municipal officials made significant changes in the mix of production factors, turning increasingly to capital and away from labor. They also favored a smaller but better-compensated work force. In addition, as discussed earlier, they utilized capital and labor inputs differently. The presumption would be that these policy innovations in the purchase and use of the factors of production affected service outputs and productivity. The city's reports support this conclusion, showing quality improvements and a more than 50 percent increase in the productivity of refuse collectors as measured by PAR.

Table 11.2 includes three additional productivity measures, each of which is more inclusive than the city's measure. The first—tons collected per employee—is closest to the city's measure, but it includes all employees assigned to refuse collection and does not adjust for neighborhood conditions or for hours of work expended. This broader indicator shows a 45 percent employee productivity increase, somewhat less than the 52 percent increase reported by the city.

The second productivity measure is labor expenditures per ton. It reflects the price as well as the volume of labor. This measure also shows a substantial increase of 21 percent. This measure is less useful than the first (and the city's productivity measure, too) for evaluating the performance of DOS officials because their role in determining the price of labor is limited; however, the broader measure reflects the effect of other official behavior, particularly of the city's labor negotiators, on refuse collection productivity.

The third and broadest measure is total expenditures per ton of refuse collected. It reflects all management decisions concerning the mix and use of production factors. This measure of total factor productivity increased 14 percent. While the picture is not quite as rosy as the city's measures suggest, the record is still positive.

Implications of a New Approach

The purpose of the case study of refuse collection is to examine the utility of the input–output approach. The purposes of its application, from the chapter's introduction, are threefold: first, to further understanding of the relationship between public spending and public services; second, to assist in evaluating the performance of elected and appointed leaders; and third, to identify policy options that might improve services. The ways in which the method serves these purposes, and the ways in which it does not, are examined next.

Understanding the Spending–Service Relationship

The case of refuse collection shows there is no necessary link between spending and services. Spending was down during the first six years of the 1980s, but the level of service increased both in volume and quality. Clearly, other factors affected the relationship. Prior research indicated that consumer behavior may affect spending–service relationships, but in the case of refuse collection this factor seems relatively unimportant. A form of consumer behavior— the generation of refuse—changed sightly to increase the volume of refuse. This suggests that DOS faced somewhat more difficult management challenges as a result of citizen behavior. (However, consumer behavior manifests itself in several ways, including the manner in which people bag their refuse. If the "bagging" behavior of the populace improved, this would have contributed to service improvement.)

Management behavior is another determinant of the spending–service relationship, and this was evident in the case of refuse collection. However, this point does not emerge exclusively from application of input–output analysis. That management mediates the relationship between "what goes in" and "what comes out" of organizations is not a new proposition; in the case of DOS, that conclusion was reached by earlier analysts employing other approaches.

The input–output model does shed additional light on the role of the budgetary process in public service production. By distinguishing between direct and indirect consequences of public spending, the approach helps pinpoint who the immediate beneficiaries of spending are. This is an important step in pursuing Harold Lasswell's suggestion that the job of political scientists is to determine "who gets what, when, and how."[29] At the same time, the input–output approach cautions against relying too heavily on budget allocations to analyze how broad population groups like service-demanders and revenue-providers fare in political competition. Spending (and taxes) may go down while services improve; services may decline while spending (and taxes) rises. When these spending–service relationships prevail, some of the normal assumptions of political inquiry may need to be revised.

Performance Evaluation

Does the input–output model contribute to evaluation of officialdom's performance? The case study of refuse collection supports the widespread belief that management of this service improved. If judged on this service alone, city officials deserve high marks. (Whether they performed as well in the delivery of other services is addressed in Chapters 13 through 15.)

One obvious limitation of the input–output approach is its inability to formally incorporate the qualitative dimension of services, though this confounds other modes of analysis as well. In the case of refuse collection, for example, how would the performance of city officials be evaluated if the share of night collections and uncollected loads had risen during the period of analysis? The problems of measuring the quality of services argue for care in using the results of input–output analysis for evaluative purposes. Like all analytic modes, it is a tool—nothing more, nothing less. Carefully employed, it adds a dimension to performance evaluation for at least one municipal service; the extent to which it is useful generally awaits further research.

Policy Identification

The third standard for evaluating the input–output approach is its potential to specify options which, if implemented, would improve the ability of the city to provide acceptable services at acceptable costs. The product of policy analysis may be useful theoretically and may enhance the ability of citizens to evaluate the performance of public servants. Both are important goals, but so is utility to policymakers.

The policy implications of the input–output approach appear to be macro rather than micro. The distinction is not clear-cut, but it can be explained through illustration. In the case of refuse collection, managers in the Department of Sanitation (and their counterparts in the sanitation task forces of the Office of Management and Budget and the Office of Operations) have considerable knowledge of how the mix of production factors might be altered to achieve a different service outcome. They are able to compute, for example, the increased productivity that would be achieved by substituting one-person collection trucks for two-person trucks or the improvements in the quality of street cleaning that would result from further mechanization of that effort. Thinking more systematically about how various production factors might be recombined or redeployed might contribute to their understanding and performance, but personnel of the department and related agencies generally perform these tasks with a high degree of competence.

The input–output approach highlights the important role of overhead managers in determining the nature of services. Analysis of the service consequences of technological change and of innovation in human resource utilization is an important part of the process by which larger decisions are reached. However, in the final analysis officials with citywide (as opposed to agency-specific) responsibilities resolve the core issues: How much money should be spent for the system as a whole? How should that sum be divided among competing programs? Within that limit, how should spending be divided among the competing factors of production, capital, and labor in particular? Included prominently within this group of decisionmakers are the mayor, the budget director, the director of labor relations, and other overhead officials whose decisions affect the behavior of line officials.

The input–output model reconceptualizes the relationships among these actors and line managers. For example, the city's Office of Labor Relations, which is responsible for negotiating labor settlements with representatives of the organized work force, becomes a direct participant in determining the efficiency of service delivery because collective bargaining determines the price of labor, affects the number of employees the city can hire, and defines the limits of innovation for line officials in their utilization of the work force. If the city's labor negotiators are unable to obtain productivity gains in collective bargaining, then managers of line agencies will find it very difficult, particularly in the more labor-intensive agencies, to maintain service standards.

Similarly, the way in which other overhead actors manage the capital budget influences the cost and quality of municipal services. The purpose of most capital projects is to improve a given municipal service, yet the links between the capital budget and the operating budget are rarely considered explicitly. If capital funds are raised but not spent, the cost of servicing loans becomes an expenditure with no service return. A similar result obtains if capital funds are spent, but unwisely, or if capital projects are delayed and for this reason require additional borrowings.

Analyzing service delivery in a broad framework clarifies some of the relationships among municipal officials, but it does not reorder them. Reordering requires that the mayor and the mayor's senior staff adopt a broader conception of the relationship between spending and services.

In closing, one modest recommendation is proposed. The city should account for its spending on a sufficiently disaggregated basis to enable expenditures to be tied to specific services. The city already has a strong—indeed, prizewinning—financial reporting system;[30] implementation of the recommendation would make it even better. Existing information would have to be reformatted somewhat, but this is relatively easy. This initiative would be helpful to outside analysts (and is, in this sense, self-serving). But more importantly, it would help public officials achieve the municipal priorities they are responsible for setting by providing better information with which to weigh alternative uses of municipal resources and to evaluate the consequences of municipal decisions once taken. A number of municipal offices could develop and publish such information, including the Office of Operations, the Office of Management and Budget, and the Office of the Comptroller.

—————12

MUNICIPAL WAGE POLICY

On June 30, 1990, contracts between the city of New York and most of its unionized employees expired. The relatively new Dinkins administration began its first round of collective bargaining. Its initial settlements with the United Federation of Teachers in early October 1991 and two other large municipal employee unions a few weeks later were widely criticized as too generous, adding to the city's mounting fiscal woes.

This chapter presents a general framework and specific recommendations for an alternative municipal wage policy better suited to the economic and fiscal conditions of the early 1990s. Three guidelines are presented: (1) the average increase in compensation for municipal employees should be significantly below the projected regional rate of inflation; (2) there should be substantial variation among specific occupations around the average increase based on the city's ability to attract qualified workers for the job title—that is, occupations for which there are shortages should receive above-average increases, and occupations with an abundant supply of qualified applicants should receive little or no pay increase; (3) employee groups who agree to changes in work rules that yield recurring productivity gains should receive additional compensation based on a principle of gainsharing between the city and the workers.

The remainder of this chapter presents the information on which these recommendations are based. The first section describes the structure of municipal labor relations. The second section traces the pattern of settlements

241

since the mid-1970s in terms of their relationship to the cost of living, the pay of private sector workers, and the availability of municipal revenues under existing tax laws. The third section describes the variation in labor market conditions for several occupations with significant numbers of municipal employees. The final section summarizes the evidence as it relates to the three recommendations.

The Structure of Municipal Labor Relations

The structure of municipal labor relations is the context within which new contracts must be negotiated. Its elements include the actors involved in the negotiations, the "rules of the game" by which they play, and the results of recent negotiations.

The Players

In simplest terms the players in collective bargaining are management and labor. But for New York City the specific actors on each side are more complicated.

Management

The mayor, as chief executive of the city of New York, bears the ultimate responsibility for all collective bargaining agreements. However, the mayor is rarely involved directly in the bargaining. Instead, the Office of Labor Relations (OLR) acts as the city's agent in negotiations with the unions. The OLR is responsible for negotiating and drafting labor agreements, representing the city in grievance proceedings and other administrative matters, labor-related legal actions, and research, as well as for administering the city's Employee Benefits Program.[1]

The OLR was created in 1967 by Executive Order 38, which followed concurrent passage of the New York City Collective Bargaining Law (NYC-CBL) and the New York State Public Employee's Fair Employment Law (the Taylor law). That legislation prohibited strikes by public employees and granted them collective bargaining rights.

Labor

The city employs approximately 326,600 persons on a full-time basis; about 94 percent of them are represented by a union.[2] These employees can be divided into two broad categories, civilian and uniformed.

Civilians total about 265,000, or 81 percent, of all full-time employees. Of these, approximately 77 percent, or 204,000, are represented by one of two unions, District Council 37 of the American Federation of State, County and Municipal Employees (DC 37) and the United Federation of Teachers (UFT).

DC 37 is the largest municipal union, representing approximately 130,700 workers. Unlike most other municipal unions, DC 37 represents workers in job titles found in multiple agencies as well as titles found only in a particular agency. The UFT represents almost 73,400 employees of the Board of Education, of whom nearly 66,000 are teachers. The remaining 41,800 unionized civilian municipal employees are represented by 40 other unions.

The uniformed work force of more than 61,600 is employed in six agencies: the Departments of Police, Fire, Sanitation, and Correction, and the Transit and Housing authorities. Entry-level uniformed employees in those agencies are represented by six unions: the Patrolmen's Benevolent Association (PBA) represents 18,300 police officers; the Uniformed Firefighters Association (UFA), 9,200 firefighters; the Correction Officers Benevolent Association (COBA), 9,200 correction officers; the Uniformed Sanitationmen's Association (USA), 7,000 sanitation workers; the Transit Authority Patrolmen's Benevolent Association (TPBA), 3,000 transit police officers; and the Housing Authority Patrolmen's Benevolent Association (HPBA), 1,600 housing police officers. Superior officers—numbering over 13,300—are represented by 15 superior officers' unions.

The Board of Collective Bargaining

Simultaneously with the establishment of OLR, the Board of Collective Bargaining (BCB) was created to replace the city's Department of Labor. The BCB is comprised of seven members, of whom two are appointed by management (the mayor) and two by labor (the municipal unions); the remaining three are appointed jointly. The Office of Collective Bargaining (OCB) acts as the administrative branch of the BCB, and the chair of the BCB serves as its director.

The OCB is responsible for making determinations essential to the conduct of collective bargaining. It also has the authority to intervene in contract talks through factfinding, mediation, and binding arbitration. The OCB's involvement in arbitration is initiated by action of the BCB; however, actual wage arbitration is conducted by a panel drawn from a list of registered impasse panel members.

The Rules

In order to simplify bargaining, and thus avoid having to negotiate de novo more than 100 separate wage contracts, certain informal rules or customs are followed by both the city and the unions. Four such informal rules are discussed next.

Pay Parity

Among uniformed workers the most widely accepted and utilized custom is "pay parity." The salaries of uniformed employees are set in a fixed relationship horizontally across agencies and vertically within each agency. In other words, firefighters receive whatever salary increases police officers receive, and vice versa. Furthermore, once the salaries for members of the PBA or UFA are set, pay parity establishes the salaries of superior officers. From time to time, a uniformed union attempts to negotiate a more generous package than that received by the other uniformed unions, but pay parity has remained the custom in negotiating contracts for uniformed employees.

Pattern Bargaining

Among civilian employees there is a custom referred to as "pattern bargaining."[3] Most civilian employees receive the same percentage wage increase, which usually is slightly lower than, but occasionally matches, that received by uniformed employees.

However, three types of deviations from pattern bargaining have been followed. First, lower-wage employees have received salary increment "floors," or fixed-dollar amount raises. These floors increase their wages by a higher percentage than is the case for higher-salaried employees. Second, unions representing hard-to-fill occupations have occasionally negotiated higher salary raises than were granted to other civilian employees. Third, some recent settlements have included "equity funds." This refers to a fixed sum of money, which, by a joint decision of management and the union, is allocated among groups of workers who might otherwise feel they have been treated inequitably. Typically, the equity funds are granted to workers whose longevity otherwise prevents them from receiving increments under the established salary schedules. Thus, pattern bargaining among civilian employees is less strictly adhered to than is pay parity among uniformed employees.

Coalition Bargaining

During the fiscal crisis in the mid-1970s, nearly all of the municipal unions—uniformed and civilian alike—formed an alliance and bargained jointly with the city. Since then, however, the scope of coalition bargaining has steadily diminished. The disintegration of coalition bargaining in the 1988 round of settlements made coalitions among unions for wage bargaining a thing of the past. This makes bargaining more complex and time-consuming than was the case during the fiscal crisis.

Binding Arbitration

Binding arbitration is used only as a last resort, and it is used sparingly. Three major wage arbitrations have occurred since 1975, when police officers unsuccessfully attempted to break pay parity with firefighters. In 1985, the UFT entered wage arbitration with the city after being unable to reach an agreement on a new salary structure. In the 1988 round of collective bargaining, the city and the UFA entered into binding arbitration after three separate contract proposals had been rejected by the firefighters and nearly two years of the contract period had expired. In the summer of 1991 the city and the PBA went to arbitration more than one year after the previous contract had expired.

Previous Settlements

Prior to the adoption of citywide collective bargaining in 1967, wages legally were established by local legislative action based on the recommendations of the mayor and the Department of Personnel. As mentioned, the simultaneous enactment of the Taylor law and the NYCCBL granted most city employees collective bargaining rights.

From the establishment of collective bargaining until 1975, city employees received wage increases that outpaced inflation. In addition, their pension and fringe benefits became more generous in this period. As a consequence, society's general view of the relative compensation of civil servants changed markedly from one of their being "underpaid" to their being "overpaid." By the onset of the fiscal crisis in the mid-1970s, a popular perception was that city workers were overpaid in the sense that (1) their compensation was higher than that which market forces would have yielded if they applied to the public sector and (2) New York City civil servants were treated even more favorably than their counterparts in other units of government. Although the empirical evidence does not conclusively support these notions, it does support the view that for at least some important occupations New York City paid more than comparable jurisdictions. For example, an Urban Institute study at about that time revealed that the hourly compensation of police officers, firefighters, and refuse collectors in New York City was, respectively, 12, 37, and 47 percent above the average for 12 large American cities.[4]

The financial pressures of the fiscal crisis prompted a change in compensation policy. A previously negotiated 6 percent salary increase for fiscal year 1976 was deferred. In addition, during that fiscal year several thousand employees were laid off, in part as a measure to avoid absolute pay reductions for municipal employees.[5]

The city's financial plight continued to be reflected in the fiscal year 1977–1978 settlement. This agreement was negotiated between the city and a coalition that included all of the major unions except the UFT. Once again, no increases in salary were granted, and some fringe benefits were cut. Cost of living adjustments (COLAs) and bonuses were granted for fiscal years 1976, 1977, and 1978 but were not included in the salary base and thus did not affect the computation of percentage increases in future years.

The 1979–1980 settlement marked the first time municipal workers received base-pay increases since prior to the fiscal crisis. The PBA, UFA, New York State Nurses Association, and the Committee of Interns and Residents bargained individually but gained nothing extra by doing so. The unions received two successive 4 percent salary increases (with a floor of $400), effective on October 1 of each fiscal year, and some earlier cuts in fringe benefits were restored. Similar to the previous settlement, a nonpensionable cash payment (NPCP) of $750 was granted in each year. In addition, a previous COLA of $441 was "rolled into" the base pay on July 1, 1979, for the purpose of computing future wage increases.

The city negotiated the 1981–1982 settlement with two separate union coalitions: a coalition of the six unions representing entry-level uniformed employees, and a civilian coalition which also included uniformed superior officers' unions. The uniformed coalition received a 9 percent increase for fiscal year 1981 and an 8 percent increase for fiscal year 1982. The civilian coalition did not fare as well, receiving successive 8 percent increases (with floors of $900 in each year). The city continued its practice of granting $750 NPCPs in each year. It is an interesting comment on the strength of pay parity versus coalition bargaining that, despite negotiating with the civilian coalition, the superior officers received the higher uniformed coalition increases.

In negotiations over the 1983–1984 settlement, the civilian coalition did not include any uniformed unions and the uniformed coalition divided. Several uniformed unions negotiated with the city separately, including the USA (which developed the gainsharing agreement for working two- rather than three-person trucks in exchange for productivity bonuses in addition to salary increases). The other uniformed unions received successive 8 percent increases, while the civilian unions received an 8 percent increase for fiscal year 1983 and 7 percent for fiscal year 1984 (each with a floor of $900). Additionally, a previous $750 NPCP was rolled into the base pay.

The next round of collective bargaining resulted in a three-year settlement, covering fiscal years 1985–1987. Coalition bargaining continued to decline, but parity remained firmly entrenched. The city and the uniformed unions agreed to successive 6 percent annual increases. The civilian agreement called for a 5 percent increase in fiscal year 1985, a noncompounded increase of 5 percent in fiscal year 1986, and a noncompounded 6 percent in fiscal year 1987 (with floors of $675, $700, and $850, respectively). The civilian settlement also provided an additional 1.77 percent for the creation of an "equity fund" and to provide longevity pay to employees not covered by longevity awards from the equity funds. As described earlier, the equity funds are used principally to provide longevity pay to the most senior workers.

The fiscal year 1988 round of settlements also covered a three-year period ending in fiscal year 1990. By this time, coalition bargaining was dead. Teamsters Local 237 reached agreement with the city first, in August 1987, and received three annual 5 percent increases, one of which was noncompounded.

The agreement also created an equity fund equal to 1.2 percent of the previous year's wages. The UFT reached an agreement at the same time, negotiating a contract that also included state Excellence in Teaching dollars to fund additional increases to improve teacher salaries, especially at the entry and maximum levels. DC 37 reached an agreement with the city in October 1987, providing three annual 5 percent increases (all compounded). The DC 37 agreement also provided for a 1.2 percent equity fund. One distinct difference in the DC 37 contract is the agreement to a 39-month contract that did not expire until September 30, 1990, thus delaying any increases in a new contract for three months.

Negotiation of the uniformed agreements featured the application of the custom of pattern bargaining to the total cost of agreements, resulting in a net increase of 16.99 percent over the period of the contract. The uniformed contracts included three annual 6 percent increases. Each of the uniformed unions then negotiated further benefits changes and tradeoffs in order to remain within the 16.99 percent agreement. The PBA received a substantial increase in its longevity schedule in exchange for a new salary schedule for police officers hired after fiscal year 1988. The UFA was one of the last unions to come to terms with the city, having rejected three settlements—twice by the UFA's delegates, and once by its executive board. The UFA and the city eventually entered into binding arbitration, resulting in the same three annual increases of 6 percent that the other uniformed unions received, and a tradeoff of longevity increases similar to the PBA agreement, while agreeing to work more hours in exchange.

The fiscal year 1991 round of bargaining remained incomplete more than 15 months after most contracts expired. In October 1990 a one-year contract was signed, and then renegotiated, with the UFT. A few weeks later 15-month contracts were signed with DC 37 and the Teamsters. No other agreements were reached and, as noted earlier, the city and the PBA went to arbitration in August 1991.

The UFT contract granted a 5.5 percent wage increase and a $100 increase in the annual contribution to the union's welfare fund. A portion of the wage increase was conditioned on passage of state legislation reducing the annual contributions the city is required to make to the teachers retirement fund. Midway through the school year the agreement was revised in the face of severe budgetary pressures threatening to force layoffs of teachers. The UFT agreed to defer a portion of the pay increase until fiscal years 1995 and 1996, in effect giving the city an interest-free loan until 1995 (interest is paid in fiscal year 1996). When this one-year contract expired at the end of September 1991, the UFT dropped its usual "no contract, no work" policy and continued negotiations with the city.

The Teamsters and DC 37 jointly settled with the city, although the Teamsters contract had expired at the end of June 1990 and DC 37's contract at the end of September 1990. Each signed a 15-month contract granting 3.5 percent pay increases at the start of the contract and an additional 1 percent effective at the start of the thirteenth month. Both unions also received $100 annual increases in their welfare fund contributions. As with the UFT, a portion of the wage increase was conditioned on passage of state legislation reducing the city's necessary contributions to the workers retirement funds. Unlike the UFT, neither DC 37 nor the Teamsters subsequently agreed to any deferrals or other concessions during fiscal year 1991.

Criteria for Future Settlements

Parties to municipal labor negotiations generally use three criteria to justify particular wage increases: cost of living, pay comparability, and the public interest. Each can be used to assess the recent record and provide a basis for identifying a responsible agreement covering the coming years.

Cost of Living

The theory behind the cost-of-living criterion implies that wages should rise or fall at a rate equal to inflation in order to keep workers at a constant standard of living. Wage increases below the rate of inflation imply a loss of compensation in real terms; wage increases above the rate of inflation imply an increase in real pay. This criterion can be applied to each element of total compensation—wages, pensions, health insurance, and union welfare fund contributions.

Wages

The Consumer Price Index for All Urban Consumers (CPI-U) rose 126 percent from fiscal year 1976 to fiscal year 1990.[6] During the same period, annual wages for a police officer first grade rose 123 percent from $17,458 to $38,914. (See Table 12.1.) Adjusted for inflation, this position experienced a decrease in real wages of slightly more than 1 percent. This net change in real pay reflects the combination of a nearly 17 percent decline in the 1976–1982 period and a similar increase in the 1982–1990 period. In light of pay parity, essentially the same changes occurred in pay for other uniformed positions.

Civilian employees fared differently according to position and salary level. Table 12.1 includes three levels of pay for civilian employees and tracks changes in salary according to the contracts signed by DC 37; pattern bargaining suggests that these wage progressions are representative of most civilian employees.

A civilian employee making $7,500 in fiscal year 1975 would have outpaced inflation with a 145 percent increase in nominal pay, which translates to an overall 2 percent increase in real wages. The two higher salary levels did not fare as well. An employee beginning with a $15,000 salary in 1975 would have received a combined 116 percent increase in current-dollar pay by fiscal year 1991, or a 10 percent decrease in real wages. An employee at the $22,500

Table 12.1 Wage Progression of Selected Municipal Employee Groups, Fiscal Years 1976–1991

| | Police Officer 1st Grade | | Civilian Employees | | | | | | Teachers[a] | | | |
| | | | $7,500 | | $15,000 | | $22,500 | | Minimum | | Maximum | |
Period Beginning	Current Dollars	Constant Dollars[b]	Current Dollars	Constant Dollars[b]	Current Dollars	Constant Dollars[b]	Current Dollars	Constant Dollars[b]	Current Dollars	Constant Dollars[b]	Current Dollars	Constant Dollars[b]
July 1, 1975	$17,458	$37,293	$7,500	$16,021	$15,000	$32,042	$22,500	$48,063	$9,700	$20,721	$21,850	$46,675
July 1, 1976	17,458	35,446	7,500	15,228	15,000	30,455	22,500	45,683	9,700	19,694	21,850	44,363
July 1, 1977	17,458	33,722	7,500	14,487	15,000	28,974	22,500	43,461	9,700	18,737	21,850	42,206
July 1, 1978[c]	18,156	32,779	7,900	14,263	15,600	28,164	23,400	42,246	10,036	18,119	23,366	42,185
July 1, 1979[c]	19,341	31,556	8,741	14,262	16,683	27,220	24,795	40,455	10,141	16,546	24,741	40,367
July 1, 1980	21,082	31,157	9,641	14,249	18,018	26,629	26,779	39,577	10,981	16,229	26,660	39,401
July 1, 1981[d]	22,769	31,151	10,541	14,422	19,459	26,623	28,921	39,568	11,821	16,173	28,738	39,318
July 1, 1982[e]	25,401	32,944	12,194	15,815	21,825	28,306	32,045	41,560	13,577	17,609	31,847	41,304
July 1, 1983	27,433	34,050	13,094	16,252	23,353	28,986	34,288	42,559	14,527	18,031	34,076	42,296
July 1, 1984	29,079	34,606	13,769	16,386	24,521	29,182	36,002	42,845	15,500	18,446	35,807	42,613
July 1, 1985	30,824	35,423	14,469	16,628	25,689	29,521	37,716	43,343	18,500	21,260	38,050	43,727
July 1, 1986	32,673	36,205	15,319	16,975	27,090	30,019	39,773	44,073	20,000	22,162	40,700	45,100
July 1, 1987	34,633	36,409	16,085	16,910	28,445	29,904	41,762	43,904	21,650	22,760	43,142	45,354
July 1, 1988	36,711	36,711	16,889	16,889	29,867	29,867	43,850	43,850	23,000	23,000	45,800	45,800
July 1, 1989	38,914	36,828	17,733	16,782	31,360	29,679	46,043	43,575	25,000	23,660	50,000	47,319
July 1, 1990[f]	NA	NA	18,354	16,405	32,458	29,011	47,655	42,595	26,375	23,574	52,750	47,149
Percentage change												
FY 1976–91[g]	122.9%	(1.2%)	144.7%	2.4%	116.4%	(9.5%)	111.8%	(11.4%)	171.9%	13.8%	141.4%	1.0%
FY 1976–82	30.4	(16.5)	40.5	(10.0)	29.7	(16.9)	28.5	(17.7)	21.9	(21.9)	31.5	(15.8)
FY 1982–91[g]	70.9	18.2	74.1	13.7	66.8	9.0	64.8	7.7	123.1	45.8	83.6	19.9

Sources: Current-dollar salary detail provided by New York City Office of Labor Relations. Conversion to constant dollars based on U.S. Department of Labor, Bureau of Labor Statistics, Middle Atlantic Regional Office, "Consumer Price Index for All Urban Consumers (CPI-U) in the New York–Northeastern New Jersey Area" (fiscal-year average).

Note: NA, not available.

[a] Contracts effective in September of year shown.

[b] Constant dollars are fiscal year 1989 dollars.

[c] Salary increases for Police Officer 1st Grade and Civilian Employees for fiscal years 1979 and 1980 were effective on October 1, 1978, and October 1, 1979.

[d] Does not include roll-in of $750 nonpensionable cash payment on June 30, 1982.

[e] Salary increase of 8 percent for most civilian employees was effective September 1, 1982. However, Local 237 accepted a smaller increase in exchange for a wage increase effective on July 1, 1982. Salary increase for teachers was effective November 9, 1982.

[f] Salary increases for DC 37 employees effective October 1.

[g] Figures for police officer are through fiscal year 1990.

level in 1975 would have done worse, receiving only a 112 percent increase or an 11 percent decrease in real pay.

The difference between workers in the lower- and the two higher-salary categories is directly attributable to the lower-salaried employees receiving salary increment floors instead of percentage increases. Floors are flat amounts granted to employees in lieu of percentage increases when the latter increase equals a dollar amount less than the amount of the floor. The size of the salary increment floor changed from settlement to settlement, but in all years except fiscal year 1983 the floor amount was greater than the percentage increase for the lowest civilian salary level in Table 12.1. Therefore, in those years, this employee would have received percentage increases greater than those of workers at the other two salary levels.

The variation in total salary increases among the two higher-salary levels is a result of the fiscal year 1980 roll-in of the $441 COLA and fiscal year 1983 roll-in of the $750 NPCP. These amounts constitute a greater percentage of the $15,000 salary than of the $22,500 salary, thus contributing to a larger overall percentage increase in wages for the $15,000 group.

The change in salary for teachers exemplifies the variation among civilian employees created by difficulties in attracting qualified applicants for certain occupations. The minimum salary for teachers received the largest increases of any of the occupations and levels examined: 172 percent in current dollars, or 14 percent in real pay. In fiscal year 1986 alone, real pay for entry-level teachers increased more than 15 percent. The maximum salary for teachers closely mirrored growth in inflation with a 141 percent increase (a 1 percent increase in real wages).

In sum, changes in the real pay of municipal workers since the fiscal crisis have varied among groups. In fiscal year 1990 uniformed workers were paid real wages approximately equal to those at the start of the fiscal crisis and fully 18 percent above those in 1982. In fiscal year 1991 teachers were paid real wages above those at the start of the fiscal crisis, and in the case of entry-level teachers the real-pay gains were substantial; teachers' real-pay gains from 1982 to 1991 ranged from 20 to 46 percent. Lower-salary civilian workers also were paid more in real terms in 1991 than in 1975, but other civilian workers suffered a loss in real pay after the mid-1970s. However, from fiscal year 1982 to 1991, civilian workers' real-pay gains ranged from 10 to 16 percent. In addition, many municipal employees received increases in longevity pay and equity funds, which added to their overall gains in wages.

Pensions

Pension benefits are an important element in the compensation of civil servants. The city of New York provides pension benefits to its workers under a system established by state law. The system includes five different pension funds: police officers, firefighters, and pedagogical employees of the Board of Education each have a separate fund; employees of the Board of Education other than pedagogical employees have a separate fund; and all other city employees participate in the New York City Employees Retirement System (NYCERS).

For each group of workers the benefits have changed significantly in recent decades. However, because the New York State Constitution prohibits reducing pension benefits of specific workers, the changes have applied only to workers hired after each change was enacted. Consequently, there are employees in each pension fund group subject to different pension plans.

The most generous pension plan, known as Tier I, applies to workers hired before July 1, 1973. While specific provisions vary among uniformed and other workers, the Tier I plan generally was not coordinated with Social Security benefits. Tier I permitted civilian employees to retire at age 55 and provided benefits equal to at least 55 percent of the employee's final-year earnings including overtime for those with 25 years of service. For uniformed employees Tier I permitted retirement after 20 years of service with no age limit and benefits equal to 50 percent of the final-year earnings including overtime. It was, by all standards, a very generous plan.

Fiscal pressures precipitated a revision of the system for workers hired after July 1, 1973. This Tier II system changed the rules for civilian employees by setting age 62 as the retirement norm with lower benefits for those opting to retire at age 55. It also lowered the base pay on which pension benefits were calculated for most workers from the final year's earnings to a modified average (excluding some overtime pay and capping total included earnings) of the final three years' pay. For uniformed workers Tier II changed the base for benefits from the final year's pay to an average of the last three years' pay (with some limitations) but did not alter the basic 20-year period for qualification.

In the midst of the fiscal crisis, pension benefits were reduced for workers hired after July 1, 1976. The new system, known as Tier III, reduced benefits for civilians from 55 to 50 percent of average earnings and further reduced benefits to take into account Social Security benefits. The effect was a significant reduction in benefits and in the city expenditures for its share of civilian pension fund contributions.

In fiscal year 1984, when the city's finances were markedly improved, civilian employees successfully lobbied the state legislature to obtain more generous pension benefits. The Tier III system was replaced, and almost all civilian employees hired after July 1, 1976, were made eligible for a new Tier IV system with more generous benefits than those of the Tier III plan, largely because reductions are no longer made for Social Security benefits.

In sum, the originally very generous pension system was made somewhat more restrictive during the fiscal crisis, but these reductions were reversed retroactively in 1983. City workers again enjoy relatively generous pension benefits.

Health Insurance

The city's agreements with its unions require that the city provide health insurance for workers and retirees, but the contracts do not specify the nature of the insurance. Instead the city separately contracts with several insurance plans to provide coverage and offers workers a choice of plans. The cost of this coverage varies from year to year depending on the experience with claims by covered individuals and on the amounts the policy stipulates as payments to physicians and other providers for specific services.

In the aftermath of the fiscal crisis in the 1970s, the city sought to curb its health insurance costs primarily by freezing the amounts it reimbursed workers for physician services. This policy continued until fiscal year 1984, when a significant updating of reimbursement schedules was implemented. Additional enhancements of benefits have been required by federal legislation. The Tax Equity and Fiscal Responsibility Act of 1982 and the Deficit Reduction Act of 1984 combined to require that the city be the primary insurer, and Medicare the secondary insurer, for employees and their spouses from age 65 to 69. The Consolidated Omnibus Budget Reconciliation Act of 1985 extended this requirement to persons over age 70 and offered continuation of benefits to persons no longer employed by the city for up to three years.

The more generous benefits and coverage mandated or agreed to in recent years have increased the value to workers of the city's health insurance program. (See Table 12.2.) From fiscal year 1981 to 1991, the number of enrollees in the program increased 22 percent to over 524,000 employees and retirees. The constant-dollar cost per enrollee more than doubled during this period from under $850 annually to $1,875. In fiscal year 1991 the total cost to the city of health insurance was $1.1 billion.

Table 12.2   City of New York Health Insurance Benefits, Fiscal Years 1980–1991

Fiscal Year	Total Expenditures	Number of Enrollees	Average Cost Per Enrollee (current dollars)	Average Cost Per Enrollee (constant dollars)[a]
1980	$226,850,142	NA	NA	NA
1981	246,959,137	429,584	$575	$850
1982	286,874,539	439,776	652	892
1983	324,253,744	433,767	748	970
1984	418,875,980	435,309	962	1,194
1985	474,286,813	446,753	1,062	1,263
1986	557,713,657	426,035	1,309	1,504
1987	648,426,338	451,425	1,436	1,592
1988	694,342,952	451,726	1,537	1,616
1989	822,580,424	503,215	1,635	1,635
1990	946,856,513	514,817	1,839	1,740
1991[b]	1,100,045,668	524,331	2,098	1,875
Percentage change FY 1981–91	385%[c]	22%	265%	121%

Sources: New York City Office of Labor Relations. Conversion to constant dollars based on U.S. Department of Labor, Bureau of Labor Statistics, Middle Atlantic Regional Office, "Consumer Price Index for All Urban Consumers (CPI-U) in the New York–Northeastern New Jersey Area" (fiscal-year average).

[a]Constant dollars are fiscal year 1989 dollars.

[b]Estimated.

[c]Percentage change fiscal years 1980–91.

Union Welfare Funds

Welfare funds are used by the unions to provide dental coverage, free or discounted eyeglasses, prescription programs, additional health insurance coverage, death benefits, and other benefits to their members. The size of the city's contribution to the welfare funds is negotiated as part of the collective bargaining process. Separate funds are maintained by each of the larger municipal employees' unions, and the city's contribution varies among the unions. Table 12.3 shows the annual contribution to six of the large unions' funds.

For members of DC 37 and Teamsters Local 237, the contribution was frozen from fiscal year 1976 to 1980 but rose from $350 in 1980 to $925 in 1991. Over the 1976–1991 period the constant-dollar increase for these unions was nearly 10 percent, with the increase since 1983 equaling over 40 percent. For UFT members the contribution was frozen through 1978 at $420 but subsequently rose to $1,045 in fiscal year 1991. This represents a 3 percent constant-dollar increase since 1976 and a 25 percent constant-dollar increase since fiscal year 1983. For members of the PBA and UFA contributions were frozen at $400 in the 1976–1980 period but subsequently rose to $825 in 1990. This represents a constant-dollar decline of about 9 percent in the entire 1976–1990 period but a 34 percent increase since fiscal year 1983. USA members were treated the same as PBA and UFA members until fiscal year 1988; in the next three years their contribution remained $675 while the other uniformed workers' contributions were increased. USA members agreed to the freeze in welfare fund contributions as a part of their 1988–1990 contract.

Pay Comparability

The pay comparability criterion takes two forms. First, it stipulates that municipal employees in New York City should receive compensation equal to that of employees in the same occupations in comparable cities. For example, police officers in the city should receive compensation comparable to that of police officers in other large cities. Alternatively, it stipulates that city employees should receive compensation comparable to that of privately employed persons in similar occupations within the city or region.

Comparable Communities

Only very limited data are available comparing the pay of workers in the same occupation among similar jurisdictions. As noted earlier, the only systematic study of compensation among large American cities is now a decade old. Given the significant changes, up and down, in compensation in New York City since then, that study is no longer a reliable benchmark.

One available source of comparative data is figures collected by OLR for

Table 12.3 City Per Worker Contribution to Union Welfare Funds, Fiscal Years 1976–1991

Fiscal Year	PBA and UFA Current Dollars	PBA and UFA Constant Dollars[a]	USA Current Dollars	USA Constant Dollars[a]	UFT Current Dollars	UFT Constant Dollars[a]	DC 37 Current Dollars	DC 37 Constant Dollars[a]	Local 237 Current Dollars	Local 237 Constant Dollars[a]
1976	$400	$854	$400	$854	$420	$897	$350	$748	$350	$748
1977	400	812	400	812	420	853	350	711	350	711
1978	400	773	400	773	420[b]	811	350	676	350	676
1979	400	722	400	722	445	803	350	632	350	632
1980	400	653	400	653	445	726	350	571	350	571
1981	425	628	425	628	520	769	400	591	400	591
1982	450	616	450	616	570	780	450	616	450	616
1983	450	584	450	584	570	739	450	584	450	584
1984	525	652	525	652	645	801	525	652	525	652
1985	625	744	625	744	745	887	625	744	525	625
1986	675	776	675	776	795	914	675	776	575[c]	661
1987	700[d]	776	700[d]	776	795	881	700[d]	776	675	748
1988	725	762	675	710	845	888	725	762	725	762
1989	775	775	675	675	895	895	775	775	775	775
1990	825	781	675	639	945	894	825	781	825	781
1991	NA	NA	NA	NA	1,045	927	925	820	925	820
Percentage change										
FY 1976–91[e]	106.3%	(8.5%)	68.8%	(25.2%)	148.8%	3.3%	164.3%	9.6%	164.3%	9.6%
FY 1976–83	12.5	(31.6)	12.5	(31.6)	35.7	(17.6)	28.6	(21.9)	28.6	(21.9)
FY 1983–91[e]	83.3	33.7	50.0	9.4	83.3	25.4	105.6	40.4	105.6	40.4

Sources: New York City Office of Labor Relations. Conversion to constant dollars based on U.S. Department of Labor, Bureau of Labor Statistics, Middle Atlantic Regional Office, "Consumer Price Index for All Urban Consumers (CPI-U) in the New York–Northeastern New Jersey Area" (fiscal-year average).

Note: NA, not available.

[a]Constant dollars are fiscal year 1989 dollars.

[b]Increase to $470 scheduled for September 1977 was deferred. The increase was restored in two $25 installments in fiscal years 1979 and 1981.

[c]Increase to $575 effective January 1, 1986.

[d]Includes an additional $25 one-time lump sum payment.

[e]Figures for PBA, UFA, and USA are through fiscal year 1990.

Table 12.4 Salaries of Police Officers in Surrounding Jurisdictions, June 30, 1990

Jurisdiction	Entry Salary	Maximum Base Salary	Years to Maximum Base	Maximum Longevity	Years to Maximum Longevity
New York City	$25,977	$38,914	5	$4,000	20
Nassau County	28,687	46,453	5	15 years, $1,500 plus $100 for additional year with no maximum	
Suffolk County	26,616	47,294	5	6 years, $660 plus $110 for additional year with no maximum	
New York State Troopers[a]	25,009	37,144	5	$3,560	20
Jersey City	23,160	40,650	6	$5,691	24

Source: New York City Office of Labor Relations.

[a]Base salary includes a "downstate" adjustment of $701.

police officers in neighboring jurisdictions. (See Table 12.4.) As of June 30, 1990, salaries for police officers in New York City were about in the middle of the range paid by surrounding jurisdictions.

The entry-level salary of New York City police officers was $25,977. Nassau and Suffolk counties offered higher entry-level salaries, $28,687 and $26,616, respectively. However, New York State Troopers received a starting salary of $25,009, and Jersey City police officers $23,160.

For maximum base salary, New York City police officers were second lowest among the five groups, at $38,914. New York State Troopers were lower, with a maximum base salary of $37,144. Suffolk County had the largest maximum, $47, 294. The number of years of service required to reach the maximum base salary (five years) was the same for all but Jersey City (six years). The city of New York limited the amount of longevity pay a police officer can receive ($4,000 over 20 years), as did Jersey City ($5,691 in 24 years) and the New York State Troopers ($3,560 in 20 years). Nassau and Suffolk counties had unlimited longevity pay; Nassau granted only $1,500 for 15 years of service but added $100 per year thereafter with no maximum; Suffolk granted $660 for 6 years, plus an additional $110 per year thereafter with no maximum.

A questions exists, however, about the salience of pay in neighboring communities to the city's negotiations. Why should the city pay its employees based on the pay scales of neighboring communities? The traditional answer is that disparities in pay put the city at a competitive disadvantage in its attempts to attract and retain a qualified work force. According to this argument, New York City police officers will depart for the greener pastures of Nassau and Suffolk counties. Available figures on police officer hiring in Nassau and Suffolk counties do not support this argument.[7] First, Nassau and Suffolk each hired approximately 1,100 police officers between 1981 and 1991, compared with 25,000 hires by the city. Second, neither county has hired officers in the last two years, nor do they plan any hiring in the near future, whereas the city has plans to hire thousands of officers under the Safe

Streets/Safe City program. Despite its lower compensation, the city is not in danger of experiencing an exodus of qualified police officers.

Comparability with Private Sector Trends

Trends in private sector compensation are measured by the federal Bureau of Labor Statistics with the Employment Cost Index for Wages (ECI-W). It measures the change in compensation paid to a sample of private sector workers and is available for the northeast region.

During the period fiscal years 1976–1989, the ECI-W followed virtually the same path as inflation, as measured by the Consumer Price Index. The ECI-W rose 129 percent compared to 126 percent for the CPI-U. Consequently, the relationship between city employees' wages and private sector wages as reflected in the ECI-W was virtually identical to the relationship between city workers' pay and inflation. That is, uniformed workers did about as well as private sector workers; teachers did better than private sector workers; lower-wage civilians did better than private sector workers; and middle-level civilian workers did not fare as well as private sector workers.

Because the ECI-W is an index, it masks wide variation in the pay trends for different occupations. Private wages are sensitive to shortages and surpluses in the labor market, and there is more variation among occupations than the ECI-W reveals.

Table 12.5 presents trends in wages for selected private sector occupations in the New York area. The occupations were selected based on the fact that they account for large numbers of workers in the local labor market and represent a range of skill levels. Changes in real pay over the 1976–1990 period varied from a 15 percent reduction for guards to a 20 percent increase for secretaries. In between are accounting clerks, with a 4 percent real-pay increase, and janitors, with an 8 percent increase.

These data suggest that trends in private sector pay differ from those in municipal workers' pay in two important ways. First, there is greater variability among occupations in the private sector. Practices such as wage parity and pattern bargaining are less prevalent. Second, the variation is linked to labor market conditions in the private sector, whereas the more limited variation among municipal occupations is related to factors such as equity concerns (that establish floors for lower-wage workers) and interunion competition, which leads uniformed workers to seek greater percentage increases than civilian workers.

Rephrased, the comparison between municipal and private sector wage trends suggests that on average the two groups have experienced similar trends. But there is greater deviation from this average among groups of private sector workers than among groups of city workers. The private sector deviations are rooted in labor market conditions that evidently play a smaller role in shaping municipal wage decisions.

Table 12.5 Mean Salary for Selected Private Sector Occupations, 1975–1990

Fiscal Year	Secretaries		Accounting Clerks		Guards[a]		Janitors, Porters, and Cleaners[a]	
	Current Dollars	Constant Dollars	Current Dollars	Constant Dollars	Current Dollars	Constant Dollars	Current Dollars	Constant Dollars
1975	$194.50	$443.03	$167.00	$380.39	$3.49	$7.95	$4.22	$9.61
1976	207.00	442.18	178.00	380.23	3.61	7.71	4.68	10.00
1977	218.00	442.62	190.50	386.78	3.67	7.45	5.05	10.25
1978	231.00	446.20	191.50	369.90	3.82	7.38	5.26	10.16
1979	244.50	441.42	203.00	366.50	3.94	7.11	5.60	10.11
1980	261.50	426.66	216.00	352.42	4.23	6.90	5.94	9.69
1981	289.00	427.12	235.50	348.05	4.71	6.96	6.17	9.12
1982	317.50	434.38	256.00	350.24	4.94	6.76	6.79	9.29
1983	343.50	445.50	273.00	354.06	5.16	6.69	7.38	9.57
1984	362.50	449.94	288.00	357.47	5.30	6.58	7.78	9.66
1985	379.00	451.04	306.00	364.16	5.23	6.22	7.86	9.35
1986	405.00	465.42	322.50	370.61	5.42	6.23	8.24	9.47
1987	433.50	480.36	343.50	380.64	5.58	6.18	8.79	9.74
1988	454.50	477.81	367.00	385.82	5.88	6.18	9.12	9.59
1989	518.50	518.50	395.00	395.00	6.41	6.41	10.56	10.56
1990	564.00	531.83	420.00	396.04	7.16	6.75	11.02	10.39
Percentage change								
1975–90	190.0%	20.0%	151.5%	4.1%	105.2%	(15.1%)	161.1%	8.1%
1975–82	63.2	(2.0)	53.3	(7.9)	41.5	(15.0)	60.9	(3.3)
1982–90	77.6	22.4	64.1	13.1	44.9	(0.1)	62.3	11.8

Source: U.S. Department of Labor, Bureau of Labor Statistics, Middle Atlantic Regional Office.

Note: All data for May of given year except 1989, which is from June.

[a]Mean salary on an hourly basis; all other occupations on a weekly basis.

The Public Interest Criterion

The public has an interest in collective bargaining because city funds used to increase wages have alternative uses: first, the money could be used to hire additional workers, which would increase the volume of services the city could provide: second, the money could be used (more accurately, not used) by the city to permit tax reductions. That is, wage increases must be funded with tax dollars, and citizens can question whether their taxes should be used to increase the real living standard of civil servants.

To apply this criterion, it is instructive to examine two types of information. (For illustrative purposes, data relating to the situation at the start of fiscal year 1991 are used.) First, how much money is available to the city without enacting new taxes? The mayor's Executive Budget for fiscal year 1991 answers this question. The projected budget gap for that year was more than $1.8 billion, based on the assumption of a 1.5 percent pay increase for municipal workers. The cost of that pay increase was about $210 million, so without an increase the gap still approached $1.6 billion. To close the gap, the mayor proposed $859 million in new taxes and other measures to reduce expenditures. If an agreement above 1.5 percent was reached, either further tax increases would be needed or the size of the municipal work force would have to be reduced.

The second type of relevant information is the number of jobs that will be sacrificed or traded off to fund a settlement above that recommended by the mayor. The difference in cost between annual 1.5 percent increases and annual 5.0 percent increases would be nearly $1.4 billion in fiscal year 1993. If this money were used to increase services, it could provide an additional 27,960 police officers in fiscal year 1993 while still granting the 1.5 percent increase provided in the Executive Budget. Alternatively, the same funds could allow the city to hire 38,833 additional teachers in fiscal year 1993.[8] As these figures suggest, municipal wage increases are a costly use of tax dollars that sacrifice additional employment and, thereby, enhanced public services.

Productivity Enhancements

One way to ameliorate the wage–employment tradeoff is to implement measures that increase the productivity of city employees. An example of such a measure is the previously mentioned gainsharing agreement in the Sanitation Department. Several suggestions for highly valuable productivity improvements were presented in a 1989 report by the Mayor's Private Sector Survey but are yet to be acted upon in any substantive manner.[9] A recent Citizens Budget Commission report on the city's uniformed services also suggests many possible improvements in productivity such as single-officer patrol cars and single-worker refuse collections trucks.[10] Unfortunately, implementation of original, effective productivity initiatives has been rare.

Municipal Wages and the Labor Market

The previous discussion of the public interest criterion might lead readers to believe it always is in the public interest to reduce the wages of municipal workers in order to lower taxes or expand services. However, there is an economic constraint on this means of pursuing the public interest. The city should pay wages sufficient to attract qualified workers. If wages do not keep pace with trends in the private labor market, current and potential workers will not keep or take jobs with the city. Labor shortages would interfere with effective service delivery.

Alternatively, labor market behavior can also provide evidence that the public interest is not being well served because wages are well in excess of those needed to recruit and retain qualified workers. For New York City, this appears to be the case for several occupations with large numbers of workers.

The attractiveness of city employment can be gauged by examining the number of applicants for positions. Moreover, because municipal employment often requires passage of civil service exams, the results of these exams provide evidence of the attractiveness of city employment for *qualified* applicants. When qualified applicants greatly exceed the number of available positions, this suggests real pay could be lowered without jeopardizing the city's ability to secure a qualified work force.

Table 12.6 summarizes data relating to applications for positions in the uniformed services. For sanitation workers, the 1983 civil service exam yielded nearly 45,000 qualified applicants for just 534 positions available each year. That is, there were 84 qualified people available for each open position. Over 101,000 persons took the most recent Sanitation exam, yielding a ratio of more than 100 to 1. For firefighters, the equivalent ratio is nearly 37:1; for police officers and correction officers, the ratio falls to 8:1. Although this figure is well below the others, it still indicates that current wages attract an abundant supply of qualified applicants for these positions. Furthermore, waiting lists from exams are maintained for four years, and thus the ratio of qualified applicants to persons hired likely is much larger.

The attractiveness of current wages among the uniformed services also is evident in their relatively low attrition rates. Relatively few leave for better jobs. Among civilian employees, attrition ranged from 9 percent in the Fire Department to over 17 percent in the Departments of General Services and Sanitation. In recent years, civilian attrition has passed well over 20 percent in some agencies. In contrast, attrition among firefighters was 3.5 percent, police officers 6.2 percent, sanitation workers 7.5 percent, and correction officers 5.9 percent.[11]

Whereas compensation for uniformed workers appears more than adequate to ensure an abundant supply of qualified newcomers and to retain experienced workers, this is not true for all occupations required in municipal government. For other job titles the city has great difficulty attracting a sufficient number of qualified applicants and keeping its experienced workers. Precise data are not available, but positions such as engineers, attorneys,

Table 12.6 New York City Recruitment Through Civil Service Exams

Date of Exam	Number of Applications	Number Taking First Test	Number on List	Average Annual Hires[a]	Ratio of Number on List to Average Annual Hires
Police Officer					
10-24-87	39,564	25,274	15,000	1,231	12.2 : 1
10-29-88	22,997	13,905	8,995		7.3 : 1
05-20-89	25,869	16,296	11,776		9.6 : 1
06-09-90	26,208	16,187	13,597		11.0 : 1
12-15-90	25,655	18,099	15,278		12.4 : 1
03-02-91	22,524	12,044	9,419		7.7 : 1
Firefighter					
09-11-82	40,922	30,787	21,305	436	48.9 : 1
12-12-87	45,398	33,479	16,046		36.8 : 1
Sanitation Worker					
09-24-83	84,521	61,783	44,905	534	84.0 : 1
09-21-90	101,211	71,007	NA[b]		NA
Correction Officer					
04-23-88	23,000	15,174	12,853	1,615	8.0 : 1
12-09-89	21,389	15,411	13,224		8.2 : 1
02-09-91	18,039	12,157	NA[b]		NA

Source: New York City Office of Labor Relations.

Note: NA, not available.

[a]Computed from 1987–1990 hiring data.

[b]Not yet established.

computer analysts, and health professionals appear to be in this category. For these positions substantial wage increases may be necessary to attract and retain an adequate supply of qualified workers.

Conclusions and Recommendations

The previous sections described the structure of municipal labor relations and assessed previous rounds of bargaining in terms of three criteria: cost of living, pay comparability, and the public interest. The evidence assembled points to two general conclusions.

First, the coming years are a period during which it is appropriate for most municipal employees to experience modest reductions in their real wages. That is, the average percentage increase in municipal employees' wages in the next few years should be somewhat below the expected rate of inflation. This conclusion is based primarily on the cost-of-living and the public interest criteria.

With respect to cost of living, the real wages of most municipal workers have risen significantly since fiscal year 1983 and are now at levels close to or in excess of those received at the onset of the city's fiscal crisis. Since most current municipal employees joined the city's work force after the fiscal crisis, they have enjoyed real-wage gains for virtually the entire period of their public service.[12] It is appropriate for the pendulum to begin to swing in the other direction.

With respect to the public interest, the city's financial condition is now weaker than it was for most of the 1980s because the local economy has taken a downturn. Citizens cannot afford to fund wage increases at or near the projected rates of inflation without suffering large tax increases or sacrificing the availability of important services. As the city's finances worsen, citizens will have to pay higher taxes and endure service reductions; during these same adverse times, it is reasonable and equitable to expect civil servants to accept slower rates of increase in their compensation.

The pay comparability criterion provides little guidance for the next settlement. Firm evidence is not available to compare the city's pay scales with those of other large American cities, and the available evidence with respect to comparability with the private sector leads to the same conclusion as the cost-of-living data. That is, for many occupations it is an appropriate time to slow the rates of increase.

The second conclusion supported by the evidence in this chapter is that for a few occupations required by municipal government real-pay reductions would be counterproductive, because the city already experiences difficulty recruiting and retaining workers for these jobs. In these instances, which should be carefully documented in the near future, significant increases in real compensation are justified and should be negotiated.

A corollary to this conclusion is that there also exist numerous occupations in municipal government for which there is an abundant supply of qualified applicants. Entry-level positions for the uniformed services are clear examples of this situation. In these instances substantial reductions in real wages in coming years are justifed by the public interest standard and the realities of the labor market. Taxpayers should not be asked to pay for wage gains for workers to be hired into positions that already pay salaries sufficient to attract as many as 84 applicants for every opening.

Based on these general conclusions, it is possible to identify three specific recommendations:

1. *Average increases in compensation for municipal employees should be substantially below the expected rate of inflation.* The city's June 1990 financial plan anticipated rates of inflation of 5.5 percent in calendar year 1990, 4.5 percent in 1991, and 4.9 percent in 1992. For the period of fiscal years 1991–1993 the Financial Plan funded a reserve for collective bargaining sufficient to cover successive increases of 1.5 percent annually in each of the three years. Such settlements (with the exceptions noted below) would be consistent with the principle that increases should be substantially below the expected rate of inflation.

2. *The actual increases received by specific occupational groups should vary substantially from the overall average increase based on labor market conditions creating shortages and surpluses among different occupations. Settlements should vary from no increase for those job titles with an abundant*

supply of qualified applicants to significant increases in real pay for those titles for which current salaries prohibit the city from recruiting enough qualified applicants. Positions in the uniformed services which now draw far more qualified applicants than are needed for available positions should receive no general increase. In contrast, positions which have fewer qualified applicants than are needed should have their real compensation increased appropriately.

It should be recognized that this recomendation will made the task of the city's labor negotiators far more difficult. In the past, the practice of adhering closely to principles of wage parity and pattern bargaining has simplified the process of collective bargaining. But this practice is no longer serving the public interest well. To obtain the high-quality work force the city deserves without wasting taxpayers' money, the next round of settlements should treat workers far more diversely than has been the practice in the past. This is more difficult than bargaining across-the-board increases, but it is essential for promoting efficient municipal government.

3. *Exceptions to the wage policies identified above should be made based on negotiated productivity gains that yield recurring savings.* If the city and municipal unions are able to negotiate changes in work rules that yield productivity gains, then the affected employees should receive bonuses which reward them with a significant share of the recurring savings realized by such initiatives. The prototype arrangement is the gainsharing agreement reached in the early 1980s with the USA, whereby sanitation workers receive an annual bonus (which is not part of their basic salary but which is pensionable) in return for staffing collection trucks with two rather than three workers.

THE UNIFORMED SERVICES

Chapter 11 explained how an input–output approach can serve three purposes in the analysis of municipal services: it can further understanding of the expenditure–services relationship, facilitate performance evaluation, and help identify options for service improvement. This chapter applies the approach to the city of New York's four uniformed services—sanitation, fire, police, and correction—with an emphasis on evaluation and options for improvement.

This focus requires an awareness of the characteristics of municipal management and the constraints on policy innovation. Four distinguishing features can be identified.

First, like most bureaucracies, the city's agencies resist change. They may grow larger or smaller as a result of changes in the city's fiscal condition, but the way the agencies produce services remains much the same. There are a few instructive exceptions to this generalization, notably the change from three- to two-person collection trucks in the Department of Sanitation. But the exceptions are so few they prove the rule that municipal agencies are operationally conservative. The implication of this is *not* that trying to change the bureaucracies is a waste of time. To the contrary, the implication is that the potential to increase productivity is substantial.

Second, commissioners and their senior staff cannot change operations unilaterally even with mayoral support. The nature of municipal service delivery is shaped by many factors, including formal rules established by local law, state law, and collective bargaining. Changing agency operations often requires changing statutes and contracts, which is something that neither mayors nor commissioners can do on their own. They need help. By dissecting agency operations it is possible to identify specific policies that reduce productivity.

Third, the public officials who can change the structure of service delivery are far removed from daily operations. Members of the city council and state legislature can change laws, and city negotiators and union leaders can bargain new contract language—but the real work is done by civil servants in far-flung, hard-to-supervise places. They need to be brought into the process of change.

Fourth, citizen behavior is a key determinant of the efficiency and effectiveness of municipal services. Many service-delivery problems have little to do with bureaucratic failures; they result from the failure of New Yorkers to behave responsibly or intelligently.

The next four sections of this chapter examine and evaluate the operations of the Departments of Sanitation, Fire, Police, and Correction, respectively. These agencies share several characteristics. Each provides one or more essential services; each is headed by a commissioner appointed by the mayor; each is organized in hierarchical, almost paramilitary fashion. Virtually all the employees in each agency have their status defined and protected by the rules of the civil service system. In addition, virtually all are represented for purposes of collective bargaining by one of the city's uniformed unions.

The four agencies are relatively large. Together they employ 30 percent of the city's work force and account for 14 percent of the city's operating budget. (See Table 13.1.) These agencies are financed almost entirely by local revenues; in fact, they consume approximately one-fifth of all local revenues. Dollars saved by better management in these agencies affect the budget more directly than savings in agencies funded largely with intergovernmental aid.

Table 13.1 Uniformed Services Expenditures and Employees, Fiscal Year 1990 (dollars in millions)

Work-Force Sector	Employees	Total Expenditures	Locally Funded Expenditures[a]
Uniformed services—Subtotal	71,458	$3,731.9	$3,656.7
Department of Sanitation	12,726	633.5	631.4
Fire Department	12,769	721.3	716.2
Police Department	32,976	1,621.7	1,597.7
Department of Correction	12,987	755.4	711.4
City total	243,090	25,931.6	17,946.6
Uniformed services as a percentage of total	29.4%	14.4%	20.4%

Source: The City of New York, *Comprehensive Annual Financial Report of the Comptroller for the Fiscal Year Ended June 30, 1990.*

[a]Excludes state and federal aid.

Notwithstanding these similarities, the four agencies are very different from an operational perspective. By and large, they do different things. Because of this, and because each is an old agency, they have distinctive styles or cultures which bear heavily on their operations and the way they are managed.

Each of the next four sections begins with an overview of the agency's operations before examining and evaluating the agency's performance in the period from fiscal year 1987 to 1989. Where relevant, comparisons are made with their performance in earlier years.[1] The concluding section presents recommendations for improved performance and identifies the public officials responsible for their implementation.

Sanitation

The Department of Sanitation (DOS) performs three primary functions: collecting household refuse, cleaning streets, and disposing of refuse. However, these are not self-contained tasks; they are related components of a solid waste management "system."

The system "begins" when New Yorkers throw things away. At this New Yorkers are extraordinarily accomplished; per capita they discard twice as much as other Americans.[2] In addition, much of what New Yorkers throw away is difficult to dispose of. Based on local eating habits and birth rates, New Yorkers probably discard a disproportionately large amount of polystyrene food containers and disposable diapers—two of modern society's more indestructible forms of refuse. Finally, New Yorkers throw things away in a sloppy fashion. Efficient methods—securely tied garbage bags and sidewalk receptacles—are not used as often as they should be.

Enter the Department of Sanitation. Its operating expenditures neared $600 million in fiscal year 1989, and it spent an additional $210 million on capital equipment and facilities. The largest share of the department's expenditures is devoted to picking up household refuse and street litter. (Private carters pick up commercial refuse.) More than 8,000 uniformed sanitation workers spend their days picking up household garbage and cleaning the streets. (See Table 13.2.)

After the city's waste is collected, DOS must dispose of it. The department also makes its disposal facilities available at a fee to private carters, who may use the municipal facilities or develop their own disposal options. The waste disposal part of the solid waste management system is the department's Achilles' heel.

For decades, the city relied on a combination of incineration and landfill. In the 1960s, federal clean air regulations forced the city to shut down many of its aging incinerators. This required the burying of more waste, which reduced landfill capacity even more rapidly. In 1979, city officials announced a plan to build eight giant, high-temperature incinerators (known as resource recovery plants because they generate usable steam and other products). The intention was to have those plants gradually take over for the diminishing landfills, particularly the Fresh Kills facility, which absorbs the bulk of the

Table 13.2 Department of Sanitation Resource and Performance Indicators, Fiscal Years 1987–1989

Category	1987	1988	1989	Percentage Change 1987–89
Departmental resources				
Operating expenditures (millions)				
Current dollars	$529.0	$569.0	$596.3	12.7%
Constant dollars[a]	586.2	598.2	596.3	1.7
Capital expenditures (millions)				
Current dollars	$165.4	$141.0	$209.8	26.8
Constant dollars[a]	183.3	148.2	209.8	14.5
Number of employees				
Total	12,708	12,421	12,362	(2.7)
Uniformed	8,840	8,654	8,500	(3.8)
Civilian	3,868	3,767	3,862	(0.2)
Refuse collection indicators				
Tons collected (thousands)	3,553	3,483	3,524	(0.8)
Night collections (percent)	7.4%	9.2%	9.1%	23.0
Missed collections (percent)	1.9%	1.3%	1.2%	(36.8)
PAR index	97.3	96.8	95.2	(2.2)
Street cleaning indicators				
Clean streets (percent of total)	72.8%	73.1%	73.5%	
Percentage of districts with less than 50 percent of streets rated acceptably clean	1.7%	5.1%	13.6%	
Waste disposal indicators				
Tons disposed (thousands)				
Total	7,857	8,030	6,135	(21.9)
Landfill	7,367	7,548	5,693	(22.7)
Incineration	490	482	442	(9.9)
Cost per ton (1988 dollars)	$96.40	$100.72	$108.39	12.4
Recycled (percent of waste stream)	1.90%	1.9%	4.0%	110.5

Sources: Unless otherwise noted data on expenditures and employees are from City of New York, *Comprehensive Annual Financial Report of the Comptroller*, fiscal years 1987–1989 editions; other data are from City of New York, *The Mayor's Management Report*, 1987–1989 September editions. Conversion to constant dollars based on U.S. Department of Labor, Bureau of Labor Statistics, Middle Atlantic Regional Office, "Consumer Price Index (CPI-U) for the New York–Northeastern New Jersey Area" (fiscal-year average).

[a]Constant dollars are fiscal year 1989 dollars.

city's waste. The incineration plan has been a failure, to date at least. Construction of the first plant, to be located in the Brooklyn Navy Yard, was to begin in 1984, and the plant was to be operable in 1987. Its construction has not begun.[3]

Meanwhile, valuable time that could have been used to develop alternatives was lost. The alternatives are recycling—which reduces the amount of waste that must be buried or burned—and waste reduction—which reduces the amount that enters the waste stream. A recycling law eventually was passed in 1989,[4] but the city has done little about waste (or source) reduction. Fortunately, private carters have begun shipping more to other locales. Unfortunately, other locales are closing their landfills. How long Fresh Kills will last given current policies is estimated later. First, however, the performance of DOS in the 1987–1989 period is examined.

Refuse Collection

Demand for the refuse collection service can be measured by the tons of garbage sanitation workers pick up (assuming all that citizens present is eventually collected). As Table 13.2 shows, collections fell from nearly 3.6 million tons in 1987 to less than 3.5 million tons in 1988, but then rose to more than 3.5 million tons in 1989. Overall, tons collected declined less than 1 percent in the two-year period. This contrasts with the record between 1983 and 1987, when tons collected rose 7 percent.

The amount of household refuse New Yorkers produce depends on demographic factors, including population size and wealth, and the number and average size of households, as well as their behavior as buyers and discarders of goods. Whatever the amount, it is reduced by recycling. In this connection, it is worth noting that municipal recycling diverted 202,900 tons in 1989. This is a relatively small amount, most of which represents cans and bottles recycled under the state's "bottle" law.[5]

Efficiency

One of the difficulties in systematically evaluating the performance of municipal agencies is that the city does not publish or even maintain information on the cost of providing a given service. This is the case for refuse collection. However, the city measures labor productivity in collection by its PAR index.[6] In the 1987–1989 period, the PAR index fell from 97.3 to 95.2.[7] (See Table 13.2.) In contrast, between 1983 and 1987 the PAR index rose from 74.4 to 97.3 percent.

Quality

A high-quality collection service would be one where collectors waited at front doors to collect garbage from citizens and then hauled it away without spillage on sidewalks or streets. This would also be a very expensive service. Instead, DOS collects household refuse twice each week in half of the city's districts and from three to five times a week in the rest.

The city measures the quality of refuse collection in two ways. The first is the share of collections made at "night," defined as the hours from 12 p.m. to 8 a.m. A higher share of night collections means lower quality, because night collections are more disturbing than day collections. Between 1987 and 1989 the share of night collections rose from 7.4 to 9.2 percent; in contrast, between 1983 and 1987 it fell from 9.8 to 7.4 percent.

The second quality measure is the share of collections missed on a scheduled shift. The lower the share, the better the quality since collecting garbage on a later shift means it sits around longer. This measure evidenced improvement in the 1987–1989 period, continuing the earlier trend. In 1987, some 1.9 percent of collections were missed, a number that fell to 1.3 percent in 1988 and to 1.2 percent in 1989.

Street Cleaning

The Department of Sanitation cleans the streets using vehicular and manual cleaners. The city does not maintain data on the cost or productivity of this service. However, it measures the quality of cleaning operations by having trained observers look at randomly selected streets and assign them grades of clean, acceptably clean, or filthy.

During the 1987–1989 period, the share of streets assigned to the clean category rose slightly from 72.8 to 73.5 percent. However, the share of districts in which less than half the streets were rated acceptably clean increased from 1.7 percent in 1987 to 13.6 percent in 1989. Thus, the quality of this service declined.

Disposal

Once collection trucks are full, they are driven to transfer stations where the garbage is dumped and subsequently trucked to incinerators or trucked and barged to landfills. The city's disposal sites include one landfill—the gargantuan Fresh Kills site on Staten Island—and three incinerators, including two in Brooklyn and one in Queens. The incinerators produce ash, which is transported to Fresh Kills and buried. Fresh Kills also handles waste brought there by private carters, though most privately collected waste is recycled, disposed of out of town, or dumped illegally in the city.

The city disposes of more than it collects, but it does not dispose of all that is collected. The variable is how the private carters dispose of their collections. As noted, some of it is disposed of at Fresh Kills. Private carters pay a "tipping" fee when they use municipal disposal facilities. This is an important policy tool. The higher the fee, the more private carters bypass the overloaded municipal disposal system.

As Table 13.2 shows, DOS disposed of less refuse in 1989 than in previous years. In 1988, tonnage disposed rose to 8.0 million tons from 7.9 million tons in 1987. This 2.2 percent increase was less marked than but still consistent with the record in the 1983–1987 period, when tonnage disposed of increased 25 percent. In 1989, however, municipal disposal dropped 22 percent to 6.1 million tons. The explanation is that the city increased the tipping fee from $18.50 to $40.00 per cubic yard. As a result, private carters reduced their use of municipal facilities.

Efficiency

The cost of disposing of a ton of refuse in municipal facilities is a basic measure of efficiency for the disposal function. The estimates of disposal costs per ton shown in Table 13.2 were calculated on the basis of data used by the city to set its tipping fee. These data include operating and capital costs for each disposal facility. During the 1987–1989 period, the constant-dollar cost per ton increased 12 percent, from $96 to $108. Thus, efficiency declined.

Quality

The quality of the disposal system is a function of how much the facilities pollute the environment. Generally, landfill pollutes more than incineration, particularly if the landfill sites are not lined in a way that reduces leachate. Leachate is caused by rainwater filtering down through garbage and being contaminated on its way to becoming groundwater. Fresh Kills produces an average of approximately 1.5 million gallons of leachate daily, which ultimately flows into and pollutes New York Harbor.[8] (Barging refuse to Fresh Kills also pollutes New York City Harbor, as the city admitted in the summer of 1989 when it signed a consent decree requiring catches on its garbage scows.) In addition, landfilling pollutes the air by generating certain harmful gases.

Incineration also degrades the environment, particularly if incinerators employ "low-heat" fires. Resource recovery plants like the city plans to construct are "high-heat" incinerators that produce a minimum of particulate matter and gases. However, the three incinerators the city currently operates are low-heat facilities, and the city has had to invest heavily in them to bring them up to minimum federal standards.

In sum, the city's low-heat incinerators and unlined landfill comprise a low-quality waste disposal system. The most positive thing that may be said about it is that its use declined substantially in the 1987–1989 period, primarily because the city raised its tipping fees.

Evaluation

The department's problems in disposing of the city's solid wastes are so awesome that evaluating its record in collecting refuse and cleaning streets seems almost irrelevant. Nevertheless, the department devotes most of its considerable resources to these tasks, and they represent important services to the city's residents and businesses.

Refuse Collection

The department's collection service deteriorated in the 1987–1989 period. Labor productivity, as measured by the PAR index, fell for the first time since

1983. In addition, there was a sharp increase in the share of collections made at night. The DOS still does a good job collecting refuse, but it no longer does an excellent job.

Collecting refuse is a highly labor-intensive function. Accordingly, increasing labor output is essential to productivity gain. The key continues to be technological innovation and new work routines. The breakthrough in productivity gain realized by the gainsharing agreement in the early 1980s relied on these two tools—larger trucks operated by two rather than three workers. This concept should be extended.

Street Cleaning

This service is harder to evaluate than refuse collection because of the paucity of performance data. However, it is clear that quality deteriorated in the 1987–1989 period. The share of streets rated clean was maintained citywide (indeed increased slightly), but this record was achieved at the cost of dirtier streets in many more districts. The department's explanation for lower quality is cuts in the so-called Clean Team of manual cleaners. In the two-year period, their numbers declined from 1,287 to 587.

The key problem in this service, however, is not the performance of the Clean Team but the performance of New Yorkers. Street litter is not a natural phenomenon. Litter occurs because citizens discard their wastes—from hot dog wrappers to abandoned vehicles—improperly. The major tool that DOS employs to clean streets is mechanical sweepers. Their effectiveness is reduced by citizens guilty of illegal parking.

The department has tried many policies to get citizens to stop parking illegally—fines, tow-away programs, hard-to-remove stickers placed on the windows of offending vehicles, and even tapes of Mayor Koch exhorting New Yorkers to shape up. The penalties for littering need to be increased—if not by higher fines, then by tougher enforcement.

Waste Disposal

New York City's waste disposal system is a disaster, or at least a looming disaster. The steps that need to be taken to avert calamity emerge from the dynamics of the current system.

New Yorkers generate an estimated 35,000 tons of solid waste every working day.[9] As noted earlier, on a per capita basis this sum is more than twice the national average. Thus, part of the problem is excessive waste production, and part of the solution is waste reduction.

The system has many other problems, though. The city uses the worst disposal method—landfilling—to dispose of nearly all of its waste. It disposes of 18,000 tons daily in Fresh Kills. The city burns 1,500 tons a day in its three less-than-state-of-the-art incinerators. Only an estimated 670 tons daily is diverted through recycling. Even if New Yorkers generated less refuse and recycled more under the new law, the city still would have a major capacity problem in its disposal system.

The "missing" 15,000 tons a day is disposed of privately, either by recycling or by exporting to other locales. Last year, private carters are estimated to have increased their exports by more than 6,000 tons a day because of the tipping fee increase. More and more trucks that arrive each morning with the city's foodstuffs leave full of the city's commercial wastes. However, landfills are being closed at a rapid pace throughout the nation. If private carters lose their ability to export, they will dispose of more in municipal facilities. This would compound the already acute problem of dwindling landfill capacity. One reasonable estimate is that Fresh Kills's capacity, assuming current policies, could be exhausted as early as 2004.[10]

Fire

Originally, the main job of the Fire Department was to protect the lives and property of New Yorkers from fires, particularly building fires. This is no longer the case. The department's employees still race through the streets, but most of the time in response to emergencies other than fires.

The department's key operational challenge is getting personnel to fires and other emergencies as quickly as possible. Despite their willingness to put their lives on the line, firefighters resist managers' attempts to deploy them effectively. A state law, passed in 1938 at the urging of firefighters, mandates that they work in equal numbers during the day and night. Since emergencies do not occur in equal installments throughout the 24 hours, this state mandate deprives the citizenry of protection. Until recently, other constraints arose from collective bargaining decisions. The "inclement weather" clause prohibited managers from assigning firefighters to inspect buildings when the temperature/humidity index reached 78 or the wind/chill factor fell to 20. Another contract provision required a minimum of five firefighters per fire truck.

Underlying these and other inefficient policies are the values of firefighters. Their work consists largely of waiting in fire houses for alarms. Firefighters alternate between 9- and 15-hour shifts, and they frequently swap tours so they may work as many as 24 hours consecutively. During these long periods the fire house is their home, the place where they eat, sleep, and socialize while they wait to be called. Reassigning firefighters to another fire house is tantamount to evicting them from their homes. Changing their shifts, assigning them to inspectional duties, altering the way equipment is manned, and hiring women all threaten the firehouse culture.

Protecting this culture from change is a major responsibility of the firefighters' union, the Uniformed Firefighter's Association (UFA). But its watchful eye does not fully explain the department's resistance to change. The department's managers are conservative too. All but a handful are a product of the firehouse culture.

As a competitor for municipal resources, the Fire Department has not fared well. From 1987 to 1989 the city's operating budget grew 5 percent in constant dollars, but the Fire Department's increased by only 0.3 percent. In the same period the department's staff was cut 2 percent. (See Table 13.3.)

Before examining the Fire Department's performance, it is helpful to characterize urban fires. Forest fires may be started by "acts of God," but fires in cities like New York are almost always caused by people. While some fires are started on purpose, most result from negligent behavior like smoking in bed, allowing children to play with matches, stacking flammable materials near heat sources, and failing to maintain electrical equipment. In short, the city's fires are preventable. Thus, the department's prevention activities are a suitable topic to start an evaluation.

Fire Prevention

The department's prevention activities fall into two broad categories, education and inspections.

Education

The most striking fact about the department's educational activities is their low priority. The department maintains a special unit for fire safety education, but only 20 employees (or ⅙ of 1 percent of the department's staff) were assigned to it in 1989.

In addition to these headquarters staff, firefighters assigned to field units are available for education activities. Fittingly, in light of the high proportion of fires started by youth, the department focuses its educational activities on children. The department does not publish information on its educational activities, but it claims that efforts to educate the city's students about fire safety are frustrated by Board of Education policies governing instructional visits by firefighters.

Inspections

The department divides its inspection activities between two groups. The Bureau of Fire Prevention is responsible for inspecting structures that pose particular threats, like high-rise buildings and public structures. Firefighters assigned to field (or firehouse) units also are available to conduct inspections. These field inspections serve the dual purpose of identifying unsafe conditions, which helps prevent fires, and of familiarizing firefighters with the layout of buildings in the event they are called on to extinguish fires in them. It is easier, and safer, to extinguish a blaze in a building with which firefighters are familiar.

As Table 13.3 shows, the number of inspections performed by the department fell 9 percent between 1987 and 1989. Virtually all of the decline resulted from a 19 percent reduction in inspections by the field staff. While

Category	1987	1988	1989	Percentage Change 1987–89
Departmental resources				
Operating expenditures (millions)				
Current dollars	$608.3	$634.3	$675.9	11.1%
Constant dollars[a]	674.0	666.8	675.9	0.3
Capital expenditures (millions)				
Current dollars	$21.9	$19.4	$22.9	4.9
Constant dollars[a]	24.2	20.4	22.9	(5.4)
Employees				
Total	13,599	13,306	13,321	(2.0)
Uniformed	12,403	12,072	12,073	(2.7)
Civilian	1,196	1,234	1,248	4.3
Fire prevention indicators				
Employees	12,603	12,335	12,365	(1.9)
Firefighters	12,185	11,914	11,888	(2.4)
Prevention staff	418	421	477	14.1
Total inspections	308,497	334,437	279,854	(9.3)
Firefighters	153,851	158,828	125,406	(18.5)
Prevention staff	154,646	175,609[b]	154,448	(0.1)
Inspections per employee	24.5	27.1	22.6	(7.5)
Firefighters	12.6	13.3	10.5	(16.5)
Prevention staff	370.0	417.1	323.8	(12.5)
Emergency response indicators				
Employees	12,185	11,914	11,888	(2.4)
Total responses	307,736	327,034	344,220	11.9
Fires	89,088	91,890	98,475	10.5
Structural	31,105	32,171	31,165	0.2
Other	57,983	59,719	67,310	16.1
Non-fire emergencies	86,304	96,507	104,434	21.0
False alarms	132,344	138,637	141,311	6.8
Mean response time citywide (seconds)[c]	274	277	282	2.9

Sources: See Table 13.2.

[a]Constant dollars are fiscal year 1989 dollars.

[b]Number of fire prevention inspections in 1988 inflated by inclusion of "no access" visits.

[c]Calculated by the authors as a weighted average based on average response time for each borough (reported in *The Mayor's Management Report*) and the number of responses per borough (provided by the Fire Department).

there was a small (2 percent) decline in the number of firefighters during the 1987–1989 period, the basic cause of the reduced number of inspections was a decline from 13 to 11 in the average number per firefighter. Productivity also declined in the Bureau of Fire Prevention. These employees conducted an average of 324 inspections in 1989 compared to 370 in 1987, a 12 percent reduction.

The main reason for the department's limited inspectional activities is historic restrictions on the authority of managers to assign employees to conduct inspections. One restriction was the aforementioned "inclement weather" clause; another is the "two-platoon" law. Since it is difficult to conduct inspections at night, fire managers cannot utilize the mandated night shift effectively. These constraints limited inspections in the 1987–1989 period, but they were neither new nor more restrictive and thus do not explain the poorer performance in this period.

However, the dismal record should improve in the future. As a result of a collective bargaining settlement with the UFA in early 1989, managers won the right to assign firefighters to inspectional duties regardless of weather conditions. How successfully they exercise their new authority remains to be seen.

Emergency Responses

The department's major service is responding to three kinds of calls: fires, non-fire emergencies, and false alarms.

Between 1987 and 1989, the department's total responses increased 12 percent from 307,736 to 344,220. Responses to fires increased nearly 11 percent to reach 98,475. However, the number of structural fires was basically stable during the period, ranging from 31,000 to 32,000 annually. In contrast, nonstructural fires—the most common of which are vehicular and rubbish fires—increased 16.1 percent to reach 67,310. The increase in nonstructural fires is a departure from earlier trends and accounts for the growth in total fire responses.

Non-fire emergencies include true emergencies (for example, transport accidents or explosions) and "accidental" alarms (usually due to improper installation or maintenance of alarm systems in commercial office buildings). Between 1987 and 1989, the department's responses to non-fire emergencies increased 21 percent from 86,304 to 104,434. In the latter year they comprised three of every ten responses.

The third and most frequent type of response is to false alarms. False alarms are one of the department's most important managerial problems; they illustrate how the antisocial behavior of some New Yorkers can deprive others of essential services. In 1987, the 132,344 false alarms constituted 43 percent of the department's total responses. A 7 percent increase in the next two years raised the number of times that resources were wasted answering false alarms to 141,311. The false alarm in effect sends firefighters on a wild goose chase, which is particularly serious if another emergency (or second alarm) occurs in the meantime. Since firefighters cannot be in two places at once, their response to the second alarm is slowed. In emergency services, slowed response is dangerous.

For this reason, response times have been used to measure the quality of the Fire Department's emergency services. Response times deteriorated in the 1987–1989 period. In 1987, the average response time citywide was 274 seconds; it rose to 277 seconds in 1988 and to 282 seconds in 1989—a 3 percent increase overall. This two-year trend repeats the experience in the 1985–1987 period. In 1985, the citywide average was 270 seconds. It rose to 272 in 1986 and to 274 in 1987. In the four-year 1985–1989 period, the total increase was 12 seconds, or a 4 percent decline in quality.

The department attributes the slower response times to the decline in the number of firefighters and the rise in the number of responses (including false alarms). It also may be that the city's firehouses no longer are in the right place—"right" being a function of their proximity to high-incidence areas. This explanation is suggested by the fact that the average firehouse was built 61 years ago.[11] In recent years the department has had some success in closing underutilized firehouses and shifting personnel and equipment to areas of greater demand.

Evaluation

The record in fire prevention shows a sharp deterioration in service. Overall, 9 percent fewer inspections were conducted, with the field units contributing 19 percent less. As pointed out, the reduction in inspection activity cannot be attributed to a decline in the number of employees. Inspections per firefighter and per employee in the Fire Prevention Bureau declined 17 percent and 12 percent, respectively.

The quality of the department's emergency response services also deteriorated in the 1987–1989 period. Citywide, the average response time rose from 274 to 282 seconds, a 3 percent increase. In sum, the performance of the department was poor in the 1987–1989 period.

However, some positive managerial changes that have taken place should lead to improved prevention service and perhaps quicker response times. One outcome of the collective bargaining agreement between the city and the UFA in 1989 was the elimination of the inclement weather clause. This contract provision prohibited managers from assigning firefighters to inspectional activities when weather conditions did not fall within a relatively narrow range. With managers now able to order field units to conduct inspections without regard to prevailing weather conditions, the department should be able to increase the number of inspections significantly. This, in turn, should reduce the number of fires and enable firefighters to extinguish those that occur faster.

A second major opportunity arises from a recent arbitration decision that permits the department to reduce staffing on certain pieces of fire equipment. Early in the 1970s the UFA won a "minimum manning" clause, which required the department to staff all ladder trucks and pumper trucks with five firefighters. Under the new policy, the city will be able to staff pumpers with four firefighters. In addition to increasing productivity, the new policy will reduce overtime costs. Under minimum manning, a firefighter automatically had to be assigned overtime when a colleague called in sick; this created incentives to abuse overtime.

Thus, while performance declined in recent years, the management of the department and the city's labor negotiators made important progress in over-coming restrictive work rules. Follow-up action to take advantage of newly acquired managerial authority and other actions recommended in the last section could lead to notable service improvements in the future.

Police

The purpose of the city's police forces is to protect the lives, property, and sense of security of the city's residents and visitors. To do this, the city funds three separate police forces: the New York Police Department (NYPD), Transit Authority Police Department (TAPD), and Housing Authority Police Department (HAPD). Each investigates reported crimes, makes arrests, and deters crime by the presence of their officers in the city's streets, subways, and public housing projects.

How well the city's police forces perform is not clear. Unlike sanitation workers, who collect nearly all of the household refuse presented to them, and firefighters, who extinguish all of the fires to which they are called, the police do not eliminate crime. In fact, they solve only a modest share of New York City crimes.[12] However, even police states do not eliminate crime. The challenge confronting each administration in not to eliminate crime but to reduce it.

Crime in New York City

No one knows how many crimes are committed in New York City or how many criminals commit them. In 1989, as Table 13.4 shows, approximately 550,000 felonies were reported. National victimization surveys in the early 1980s found that 37 percent of felonies were reported.[13] *If* the New York City felony reporting rate equaled the national average, then the number of felonies in the city approximated 1.5 million in 1989. And *if* violations and misdemeanors are reported as often as felonies, then a total of about 4.5 million crimes were committed locally in 1989. However, these are big "ifs." The New York City reporting rate for felonies probably was below the national average when the surveys were done, probably has declined since then, and probably is lower still for misdemeanors and violations.

The incomplete and potentially misleading character of data on reported crimes is noteworthy because in recent years these data have contradicted commonsense perceptions. Reported data show a decline in crime. As Table 13.4 shows, the number of reported crimes reached 1.78 million in 1987, fell to 1.71 million in 1988, and fell again to 1.67 million in 1989—a 6 percent decline overall.

Of course, not all crimes are equally offensive. Felonies generally are worse than misdemeanors and violations. Reports of felonious behavior rose 7 percent in the 1987–1989 period, from 517,202 to 552,659. The decline in reported crime was concentrated in the more numerous misdemeanors and violations, which decreased 11 percent. This may reflect a decline in the reporting of these less serious infractions by citizens becoming increasingly hardened to criminal activity.

The City's Response

How did city officials respond to the crime problem between 1987 and 1989? Did elected public officials provide the city's three police departments additional money and staff, and did police managers deploy the staff made available to them more effectively?

Expenditures

Between 1987 and 1989, the city's elected officials increased real (or inflation-adjusted) police spending by less than 2 percent. In 1987, the combined spending for the NYPD, TAPD, and HAPD was $1,815 million. (See Table 13.4.) This sum was increased to $1,866 million in 1988 but was cut slightly to $1,850 million in 1989. In the 1987–1989 period real spending for TAPD and HAPD decreased 1.5 percent and 6.9 percent, respectively; real spending for the NYPD, the largest of the three police forces, rose 3 percent. This overall record stands in sharp contrast to the 1983–1987 experience, when total police spending jumped 36 percent in real terms.

Employment

Elected officials reduced the number of persons employed to fight crime between 1987 and 1989. Total police employment fell 2.2 percent from 40,521 in 1987 to 39,614 in 1989. The number of Housing Authority police was cut the most, 6.2 percent, followed by a cut of 5.3 percent in the Transit Authority police. The NYPD force was cut least, 1.6 percent. The policy of cutting police employment also stands in sharp contrast to the 1983–1987 period, when total police employment rose 18 percent.

Deployment

As the previous chapter emphasized, the spending of more money or the hiring of more employees is not a good predictor of the level or quality of municipal services. Spending more (and by extension, raising taxes) does not necessarily yield better services. How managers utilize the staff made available to them often is more important than the number of personnel at their disposal. Table 13.4 sheds some light on how the NYPD deployed its staff.

Enforcement strength is the daily average number of police officers as-

Table 13.4 Police Department Resource and Performance Indicators, Fiscal Years 1987–1989

Category	1987	1988	1989	Percentage Change 1987–89
Service demand				
Reported crimes	1,781,004	1,708,711	1,671,923	(6.1%)
Felonies	517,202	509,949	552,659	6.9
Misdemeanors and violations	1,263,802	1,198,762	1,119,264	(11.4)
Total resources				
Operating expenditures (constant dollars in millions)[a]				
Total	$1,815.3	$1,865.5	$1,849.6	1.9
New York Police Department	1,468.8	1,510.4	1,513.1	3.0
Transit Authority Police Department	256.3	253.0	252.4	(1.5)
Housing Authority Police Department	90.3	102.1	84.1	(6.9)
NYPD overtime expenditures (constant dollars in millions)[a]	$78.1	$81.9	$93.7	20.0
Number of full-time employees				
Total	40,521	40,608	39,614	(2.2)
New York Police Department	33,951	34,077	33,414	(1.6)
Uniformed	27,502	27,483	26,303	(4.4)
Civilian	6,449	6,594	7,111	10.3
Transit Authority Police Department[b]	4,200	4,176	3,978	(5.3)
Housing Authority Police Department[b]	2,370	2,355	2,222	(6.2)
Enforcement strength (NYPD daily average)	9,593	9,995	9,928	3.5
Specialized units	2,327	2,816	2,846	22.3
Patrol component	7,266	7,179	7,082	(2.5)
Officers on foot patrol per day (average)	1,954	1,883	1,580	(19.1)
Active radio patrol cars per day (average)	1,459	1,436	1,446	(0.9)

Service measures				
Arrests[c]	264,936	274,376	288,283	8.8
Felonies	129,506	139,393	158,511	22.4
Misdemeanors and violations	135,430	134,983	129,772	(4.2)
Drug arrests (NYPD only)	65,556	69,203	80,143	22.3
911 calls (thousands)	7,581	7,955	8,360	10.3
"Crime-in-progress" radio runs (thousands)	455	500	595	30.7
Average dispatch time for "crime-in-progress" radio runs (seconds)	192	216	210	9.4
911 radio runs (thousands)	3,933	4,052	4,256	8.2
911 call response rate (percent)	51.9%	50.9%	50.9%	
Service efficiency				
Total arrests per employee	6.5	6.8	7.3	11.3
Felony arrests per employee	3.2	3.4	4.0	25.2
Total arrests per enforcement officer[d]	23.0	23.3	25.1	8.7
Felony arrests per enforcement officer[d]	12.1	12.5	14.3	18.1
911 responses per radio patrol car				
Annually	2,696	2,822	2,943	9.2
Per day	7.4	7.7	8.1	9.2

Sources: See Table 13.2.

[a]Constant dollars are fiscal year 1989 dollars.

[b]Information provided by NYPD.

[c]Arrests data for NYPD, TAPD, and HAPD based on New York Police Department, "Complaints and Arrests Reports," 1986–1989.

[d]Based on NYPD arrests only.

signed to *direct* law enforcement duties either in specialized units (for example, Organized Crime Control, Warrant Division, and Narcotics Division) or regular patrol (which includes foot patrol and car patrol). The enforcement contingent is the "front line" in the fight against crime; these officers are assigned to positions where they can both make arrests and deter crime through their visibility on the streets.

Despite the overall decline in NYPD personnel between 1987 and 1989, the enforcement strength rose 3.5 percent from 9,593 to 9,928. The share of the department's uniformed employees assigned to enforcement duties rose from 34.9 percent in 1987 to 37.7 percent in 1989. This deployment pattern contrasts with the record in the 1983–1987 period, when enforcement strength fell from 37.7 to 34.9 percent of the total.

Two major factors explain why it requires nearly three uniformed employees to get one "on the street." First, the average police officer works only 207 of the 243 days to which he or she is assigned for the year. The difference is vacation days (27), sick days (6 on average), and various other leaves (3 days) to which a police officer is entitled under collective bargaining contracts. This means, in essence, that the NYPD must hire seven police officers to obtain the coverage of four. And this is before administrative needs.

Second, like all bureaucracies, the NYPD needs personnel to manage and support its direct service providers. The issue is whether there are too many officers in "desk" jobs and too few in "street" jobs. A related issue is whether civilians could fill more positions held by uniformed officers. In addition to freeing officers for enforcement duty, "civilianization" saves money. The yearly cost of a police officer, the lowest-paid uniformed position in the NYPD, is more than $73,000. Civilians who work in the NYPD cost about $31,000 annually.[14] Civilianization helps explain how the NYPD increased its enforcement strength despite the cut in uniformed personnel. Between 1987 and 1989, the number of civilian employees rose 10.3 percent from 6,449 to 7,111.

Police officials also redeployed the enforcement contingent in the 1987–1989 period. Officers were shifted from foot patrol to specialized crimefighting units, primarily to institute the Tactical Narcotics Team (TNT) program. The number of officers assigned to specialized enforcement units rose 22.3 percent from 2,327 to 2,846, while the number assigned to foot patrol was reduced 19 percent from 1,954 to 1,580. Precise data on the number of officers assigned to radio patrol cars are not available, but the number of active cars was approximately 1,450 throughout the period. Assuming two officers per car, approximately 2,900 officers were motorized—about twice the number on foot patrol in 1989.

To summarize, the managers of the NYPD compensated for cuts in uniformed staff by deploying personnel differently. Direct law enforcement was favored over administration, and within the enforcement contingent specialized crimefighters were favored over police officers assigned to foot patrol. In addition, civilians were substituted for uniformed officers in support jobs.

Strategy

The two primary strategies for reducing crime are (1) to make arrests and (2) to deter would-be criminals. The deterrence effect is impossible to measure, though presumably it is related to the number of officers who are deployed so as to be visible to potential criminals. Arrest data are available, however, and they provide a basis for analysis of crimefighting strategies.

The number of arrests by police officers increased 8.8 percent in the 1987–1989 period. The number of felony arrests increased 22.4 percent, and the number for less serious crimes declined 4.2 percent. Thus, police officers either were directed to focus on apprehending criminals who committed the most serious of crimes or themselves decided to eschew lesser criminals and seek felons.

Another change in the arresting behavior of police involved crimes for the possession or sale of drugs. The number of NYPD arrests for drug offenses rose 22.3 percent in the 1987–1989 period from 65,556 to 80,143. There was also a shift in the kinds of drug arrests. Felonies were charged in 55.2 percent of the drug arrests in 1989, compared to 47.2 percent in 1987. In addition, the police focused on the cocaine derivative known as crack. The share of arrests for possession or sale of crack rose between 1987 and 1989, while the share for other drugs declined.

In sum, police arrest strategies changed in the 1987–1989 period. They increased the number of arrests overall, but they increased arrests for felonies even more, particularly for the possession or sale of crack.

Evaluation

The mayor and local legislators provided police managers with fewer personnel in the 1987–1989 period. Police managers responded by redeploying personnel and by pursuing new strategies. Did these changes improve the quality and efficiency of police service?

Quality

The quality of police service is difficult to evaluate. The city uses two unsatisfactory measures: the arrest rate (the number of arrests divided by the number of reported crimes) and the felony clearance rate (the number of felonies which the police say they have solved divided by the number of reported felonies). Neither is a meaningful measure because of the disparity noted earlier between reported and actual crime.

A third quality measure used by the city is the speed with which patrol cars are dispatched in response to "crime-in-progress" calls. A more appropriate measure is the time of *response*, not just of dispatch, but the NYPD, unlike the Fire Department, does not measure the elapsed time between dispatch and arrival of officers. However, there was a 9.4 percent increase in dispatch time between 1987 and 1989, from 192 seconds to 210 seconds. (In contrast, the Fire Department's response time in 1989 was 282 seconds, which implies that, typically, firefighters are well on their way to the scene of an emergency by the time police officers are even dispatched.)

Efficiency

Police attempt to reduce crime in several ways, including investigation, apprehension, and deterrence. However, the only available data on their "output" measure the number of arrests they make. Thus, there is no basis for attempting an overall evaluation of their efficiency. However, the average number of arrests per employee represents a narrow measure.

In 1989, the 39,614 employees of the city's three police forces caused 288,283 arrests, an average of 7.3 per year. The averages in 1987 and 1988 were 6.5 and 6.8, respectively. During the same period, the average number of felony arrests per employee rose 25 percent from 3.2 to 4.0 a year. On average, then, the employees of the city's police forces averaged one arrest every 7 weeks and one felony arrest every 13 weeks.

Some police officials argue that the proper denominator for calculating the average number of arrests is not all police employees but, rather, the average number of police officers assigned to enforcement positions. The counterargument is that civilians and uniformed officers who support the enforcement contingent are essential to the latter's activities. Nevertheless, the enforcement contingent is, literally, in a position to make an arrest. Using this narrower measure of efficiency, the 1989 average was 25.1 arrests per year (roughly one every two weeks), including 14.3 felony arrests (roughly one every four weeks).

However measured, the average number of arrests per officer is low, particularly in light of the number of crimes that are committed in New York City. One explanation for the low average number of arrests is that the criminal justice system cannot accommodate more defendants and convicts. If district attorneys, defense attorneys, judges, and jails are operating at full capacity (as is the case at least for the jails), then making more arrests simply results in more persons being released either by prosecutors and judges who drop charges or by jailers who release inmates prematurely.

Given the congestion elsewhere in the criminal justice system, there is a practical limit on the number of arrests police can make. In light of this, at present the most predictable consequence of adding police is that the average number of arrests per officer would drop.

Of course, police deter crime by their presence on the streets as well as by making arrests. Under current policies, 2.6 officers are employed for every officer who is assigned to a post where he or she is able to deter crime. In addition, the daily average enforcement strength, 9,928 in 1989, is spread over three shifts. The average number of officers assigned to foot or car patrol duties during the highest-staffed 8 a.m. to 4 p.m. shift was 3,194. Between midnight and 8 a.m. only 1,163 police officers performed patrol duties.

The high average compensation for a police officer (about $73,000 including fringe benefits) combined with the low proportion of officers assigned to enforcement (38 percent) makes it very expensive to place more police on the street. Adding one officer to enforcement strength on each of the three shifts would require a total of 7.8 officers. This means the annual cost of adding one officer to street duty round-the-clock exceeds $500,000.

In sum, the performance of the Police Department is more difficult to evaluate than the Fire Department or the Department of Sanitation. The demand for its service is unknown, because most crimes go unreported. The volume of service it provides is unclear, since arrests measure but one aspect of police service. The quality of police service does not lend itself to quantitative analysis, and the Police Department makes little effort to generate relevant information. However, some indirect measures are available, notably the share of the work force deployed to apprehend and deter criminals. The department's managers did redeploy some officers to increase the share assigned to direct law enforcement; they also sharply reduced the foot patrol complement in favor of specialized units like TNT and car patrol. Based on this limited evidence, the department's performance is judged as passing, with room for significant improvement.

Correction

In theory, penal agencies represent the end of the criminal justice system. An individual enters the system by being arrested for commiting a criminal act, then is prosecuted, tried and found guilty, sentenced, "serves time" fitting the crime, and finally is released from jail; the goal is to release a rehabilitated individual who will not reenter the system. This is not how things work in New York City.

The demand for the services of Department of Correction (DOC) is derived largely from the actions of other parts of the criminal justice system. If judges impose higher bails or longer sentences, or if prosecutors drop fewer charges, or if police make more arrests, then the workload of the department increases. If growth in demand for DOC's service exceeds growth in its capacity—that is, if the number of detainees and convicts grows faster than the number of beds—then the system springs a leak. Either DOC is forced to release prisoners prematurely, or the word goes out to police, defense attorneys, prosecutors, and judges to restrict the flow of new inmates.

City officials know how the system works. Their primary response throughout the 1980s has been to increase the capacity of DOC. In the 1987–1989 period alone, spending for operations increased 30 percent, and staff increased 25 percent. (See Table 13.5.) The department's capital expenditures more than doubled from 1987 to 1988 but were cut somewhat in 1989 to 41 percent above the 1987 level. This happened because DOC housed more

Table 13.5 Department of Correction Resource and Performance Indicators, Fiscal Years 1987–1989

Category	1987	1988	1989	Percentage Change 1987–89
Departmental resources				
Operating expenditures (dollars in millions)				
Current dollars	$424.3	$523.3	$613.1	44.5%
Constant dollars[a]	470.2	550.2	613.1	30.4
Capital expenditures (dollars in millions)				
Current dollars	$119.8	$276.8	$169.1	41.1
Constant dollars[a]	132.8	291.0	169.1	27.3
Employees				
Total	9,449	11,077	11,767	24.5
Uniformed	8,089	9,437	9,851	21.8
Civilian	1,360	1,640	1,916	40.9
Service volume indicators				
Average daily inmate population	13,941	15,000	17,439	25.1
Detainees	9,239	9,629	11,213	21.4
Sentenced inmates	3,471	3,628	3,933	13.3
State inmates	1,231	1,725	2,262	83.8
INS inmates	—	18	31	

Admissions, annual total	103,609	109,044	119,558	15.4
Average length or stay, detainees (days)	41	39	41	0.0
Service efficiency indicators				
Operating cost per prisoner (constant dollars)[a]	$33,728	$36,680	$35,157	4.2
Paid overtime (millions of constant dollars)[a]	$71.7	$70.6	$71.3	(0.6)
Service quality indicators				
Escapes	4	10	3	(25.0)
Personal security (number of incidents)				
Homicides and suicides	5	5	0	—
Use of force by officers[b]	1,098	1,207	997	(9.2)
Rate per 100 inmates	7.9	8.0	6.2	(21.5)
Violent infractions by inmates[c]	13,839	15,907	14,251	3.0
Rate per 100 inmates	99.3	106.0	88.0	(11.4)
Inmates as percentage of bed capacity	105.5%	100.9%	101.7%	(3.6)
Inmates in school or work programs (percent)	44.9%	45.8%	39.1%	(12.9)
Average monthly visits per inmate	2.3	2.1	2.0	(13.0)
Inmates delivered to court on schedule (percent)	NA	78.0%	76.0%	

Sources: See Table 13.2.

Note: NA, not available.

[a]Constant dollars are fiscal year 1989 dollars.

[b]Information provided by Board of Correction.

[c]Information provided by Department of Correction.

prisoners in modular units, reconverted ships, and upstate facilities as alternatives to the more expensive option of building new jails in the city.

However, as soon as new facilities and staff are in place, still more are required. In the 1987–1989 period, the average daily inmate population rose 25 percent from 13,941 to 17,439. This expansion followed a 40 percent increase in the preceding four-year period, which means that the city's prison population nearly doubled in this six-year period. If current criminal justice policies continue, so will growth of this new municipal leviathan.

Before evaluating the department's performance in the 1987–1989 period, it is helpful to understand what goes on in the jails. The city's jails are harder to manage than state prisons because their turnover rates are much higher. Most state prisoners are sentenced for at least one year. In contrast, the average stay in the city's jails was 53 days in 1989.[15]

In addition to processing large numbers into and out of the jails, many other "transactions" occur. The first set involves sorting out the new admissions. The department segregates women from men and adults from adolescents, and it tries to segregate those who are prone to violence, those who are mentally unstable, those who are "seriously" addicted to drugs, and those who suffer from contagious diseases. In addition, the department is required to separate detainees and parole violators from city convicts. Since the number and defining characteristics of those who are admitted do not mirror those who are discharged, there is a constant scramble to find appropriate beds.

Once admitted, the jail population must be moved frequently. In part, this occurs because most of the prisoners have not been tried for the crimes they are alleged to have committed. These "detainees" are shuttled from jail to court appearances. The department also shuttles prisoners to and from municipal hospitals when its health facilities cannot meet their needs. Supervised movement within the system is also frequent, as prisoners are transported to and from visits with friends, relatives, and attorneys, recreational spaces, clinics, and dining rooms.

Another way the city's jails are unlike state prisons is that the majority of local inmates are not housed in cells for one or two inmates but in dormitory facilities with as many as 60 beds. These less secure arrangements coupled with the frequent commingling of correction officers and prisoners requires officers to make difficult judgments on a nearly continuous basis.

In carrying out their responsibilities, the DOC's managers are subject to a high degree of regulation. For a decade, a federal judge has been a "senior manager" of DOC responsible for determining and enforcing a wide range of standards. This unusual intergovernmental involvement results from a consent decree which the city entered into in 1979 in order to avoid the judge's finding that the city was violating constitutional rights of inmates. In 1983, he gave the city notice to comply with several different rulings dating back to 1981. As a result, more than 600 prisoners had to be released.

State laws also determine some of DOC's management rules. In addition, certain managerial behaviors are mandated by regulations issued by the New York State Commission of Correction. Correction officials also manage within a set of regulations set by a local Board of Correction, which sets and monitors compliance with minimum standards of care for everything from space requirements and personal hygiene to protection from discrimination. Finally, the provision of jail service requires prisoners and correction officers alike to devise informal "rules of the game" to help regulate their complicated, too-often violent, relationships. In sum, this is not an agency whose managers control their own destiny.

The Demand for Jails

As noted earlier, the average daily inmate population was 17,439 in 1989, but this measure fails to reflect the volume of transactions involved in "processing" inmates. The department admitted 119,558 persons in 1989, up 15 percent from 103,609 in 1987. The discrepancy between the number of admissions and the average daily inmate population is primarily a function of the relatively short stays of many inmates.

The jail population is comprised of four separate categories: detainees, convicted inmates sentenced to incarceration in municipal jails, convicts sentenced to state facilities or in violation of state parole, and inmates who have run afoul of the federal Immigration and Naturalization Service. The last group is relatively small in number—31 on an average day in 1989.

State inmates are the third most numerous group. These inmates should be in state facilities either because of their more-than-one-year sentences or because they have violated state parole. State inmates are the most rapidly growing category of prisoners. Their number nearly doubled from 1,231 to 2,262 in the 1987–1989 period. Parole violators now constitute more than two-thirds of the state inmates. In 1983, by contrast, the city's jails contained only 72 state inmates. The state pays the city for incarcerating state inmates, but the payment is substantially below the city's operating costs.

Inmates convicted of crimes and sentenced to serve time in the city's jails are the second largest category, but they are also the slowest growing category. Their numbers in the three-year period increased only 13 percent, from 3,471 to 3,933.

Detainees are the largest group of inmates by far, comprising about two-thirds of the total. In 1987, they numbered 9,239; they rose 21 percent in number to 11,213 in 1989. The basic reason detainees are imprisoned is their inability to make bail.

In sum, the number of inmates increased substantially between 1987 and 1989, and the mix changed as well. The changes in the composition of the population are important, because some prisoners are more difficult to manage than others. Detainees are in and out of the system frequently, and state convicts (who generally have committed a serious crime) are a relatively dangerous lot. In addition, the health status of the prisoners is declining. There are more drug abusers, more with tuberculosis, more with syphilis, and more with AIDS.[16]

The City's Resources

Did the department's resources increase along with its inmate population? Operating expenditures in real terms rose 30 percent during the 1987–1989 period, a rate of expansion higher than the 25 percent increase in the average daily population. Another relevant resource is employees. In 1987, DOC employed 9,449 workers; the number rose 25 percent to 11,767 in 1989. From the perspective of staffing, then, resources kept up with the average daily population. However, there was a change in the distribution of DOC's work force between uniformed officers and civilians. The civilian share of the total rose from 14 to 16 percent.

Capital spending jumped from $133 million in 1987 to $291 million in 1988, but it fell to $169 million in 1989. The number of beds added between 1987 and 1989 was 3,900, a 30 percent increase. In general, city officials provided DOC with enough staff and beds to keep up with the increased inmate population.

Efficiency

As noted, real operating expenditures rose 30 percent in the 1987–1989 period, while the inmate population increased 25 percent. Thus, per-inmate operating costs rose more than 4 percent from $33,728 to $35,157 annually.

Unit costs could have been lower were there not such a heavy reliance on overtime, which required payments of $71 million in 1989. Paying overtime to current officers rather than hiring more officers is not bad per se; up to a point it is cheaper to pay overtime than it is to pay the salaries and other benefits of new workers. However, the current amount is extremely high.[17] The department's inability to reduce overtime costs is a major problem.

Quality

There is a belief among some people who are familiar with the city's correctional services that the rapid expansion of the system has been accompanied by a deterioration in quality. One leg of this argument is that the new facilities used by the city—modular units, prison ships, and upstate jails—cut quality. The other leg of the argument is that rapid expansion of the staff has caused the quality of correction officers to be reduced by having to go further "down the list" in hiring and by having younger and less experienced officers.

The modular units popping up on Rikers Island are attached to the older structures. They raise bed capacity, but they also make the preexisting dining, recreational, and other facilities more congested. The floating jails, which account for approximately 750 beds, contain fewer facilities than the other enclosures, thereby reducing access of the boat prisoners to supporting services (with the exception of addiction services, which are concentrated on the prison barges). Finally, sending inmates to jails located several hundred miles from New York City makes it difficult for them to be visited by friends, relatives, and lawyers (although DOC provides bus service for are those who want to travel 14 hours round-trip).

The staff-related explanation of reduced quality is somewhat more subtle than the facilities-related explanation. As noted earlier, correction officers work in close proximity to their charges. Deciding whether to confront a tense situation solo or to call other officers for assistance is an important decision requiring judgment born of training and experience. New officers receive only ten weeks of training before assignment and may work two or three consecutive shifts when they first are assigned. Some observers believe the work force is too young and inexperienced for the demands of the job.

More quantitative indicators relate to three aspects of quality: the security with which inmates are incarcerated; the safety of jails to officers and inmates alike; and the supporting services provided inmates.

The number of escapes indicates DOC's ability to protect the public from inmates. Successful escapes are few: four in 1987, ten in 1988, and three in 1989. The DOC secures its charges in the sense that it nearly always prevents detainees and convicts from getting out of jail on their own accord.

The city's jails are more secure than safe, however. The worse breakdowns in safety involve inmates taking their own lives or killing one another. This happened five times in 1987 and in 1988, but on no occasion in 1989. Other serious safety violations include "violent infractions," which involve untoward physical contact between inmates—from rape to stabbings to fistfights. Reports of these incidents rose from 13,839 to 14,251 during the 1987–1989 period. Adjusted for the larger population, however, the rate fell.

In addition to being safe from one another, inmates should be safe from abuse by correction officers. Apparently, the jails grew safer from this perspective as well. Reports of use of force by officers declined 9 percent from 1,098 to 997 between 1987 and 1989.

The quality of the services provided to inmates is difficult to measure. One aspect of quality for inmates is the extent to which they are crowded. The crowding problem declined in the narrow sense that prisoners as a percentage of bed capacity fell from 106 percent in 1987 to 102 percent in 1989. But this aggregate measure is somewhat misleading. There are peaks during the year when the percentage is substantially higher. Moreover, this measure reflects only inmate-to-bed ratios; it does not reflect crowding in health clinics, dining rooms, recreational areas, and other facilities that have not expanded with bed capacity.

A second measure of service to inmates is the share who receive schooling or job training. This indicator shows a substantial decline in the two most recent years. While 45 percent of the inmates participated in some kind of work or school program in 1987, this was the case for only 39 percent in 1989.

While in custody, inmates are entitled to receive visits; detainees are entitled to three a week and convicts to two. Data are not available on a disaggregated basis, but the average number for both categories fell from 2.3 *per month* in 1987 to 2.0 in 1989. Again, the expansion of the jail system appears to have had a negative impact on the quality of inmate services. Visiting inmates has always been a complicated process, and the expansion of the jail population has made it more difficult. This is particularly true for those who wish to visit prisoners housed in the upstate facilities.

Another important service provided inmates in transporting them to court appearances. Inmates should not be deprived of the opportunity to make scheduled court appearances; moreover, a missed appearance may prolong an inmate's stay and contribute to jail overcrowding. The DOC measures the percentage of "scheduled transports" that arrive at court at the targeted time each morning and early afternoon. Unfortunately, this is not equivalent to the number or share of detainees who arrive in time for the processing of their case. Whatever its meaning, this indicator declined from 78 percent in 1988 to 76 percent in 1989.

Evaluation

Between 1987 and 1989, the efficiency of the city's jails declined in the sense that real operating costs per inmate rose 4 percent; this continued the trend in the 1983–1987 period.

Moreover, the quality of service to inmates declined in the most recent two-year period. More prisoners were kept in inferior facilities; a smaller share received education or job training; visitations fell; and the city's performance in transporting prisoners to court appearances deteriorated.

Admittedly, DOC operates under difficult circumstances over which its managers do not have complete control. Nevertheless, this service was poorly provided between 1987 and 1989. And as long as the city continues its policy of increasing capacity without taking other steps, it is likely that this service will continue to decline.

Recommendations

This section recommends 20 steps to increase productivity in the uniformed services. Most could be implemented promptly, and at little or no added cost.

The Department of Sanitation

The earlier evaluation of the Department of Sanitation identified this agency's problems. It does a good job collecting household refuse, though the previous trend of productivity gains in this function was reversed in the 1987–1989 period.

The DOS does not clean the city's streets as well as it collects refuse, but the fault lies more with the citizenry than with the department. New Yorkers continued to throw their litter on the streets rather than in receptacles, and they continued to interfere with cleaning activities by parking illegally.

The third function of DOS, waste disposal, is the most seriously deficient.

Again, citizen behavior is part of the problem. New Yorkers throw things away at a rate more than twice the national average, which unnecessarily burdens the department's disposal capacity.

However, the behavior of municipal officials also has been irresponsible. The Koch administration initially insisted that the future for waste disposal should be incineration and sought to build large, high-temperature incinerators. This policy failed because the members of the Board of Estimate, except Mayor Koch, were unwilling to take the political heat for siting the plants. With no recycling program and little incineration capacity, the disposal burden was placed almost entirely on the Fresh Kills landfill site during the 1980s. To make matters worse, the city invited private carters to use municipal disposal facilities by not charging them full cost. In sum, the effective, if not explicit policy of the city of New York for most of the 1980s was to encourage depletion of one of the city's most precious assets, the Fresh Kills landfill.

As a result of these policy failures, garbage is likely to begin backing up in the city's homes, businesses, and streets early in the twenty-first century *unless* there is substantial change in the city's solid waste management system. This can be achieved through the following initiatives:

1. *The city council should enact legislation to reduce the volume of waste, including nonrecyclable, nondegradable, and toxic materials entering the solid waste stream.* Waste reduction and recycling should go hand in hand. The offending materials are well known—batteries, disposable diapers, polystyrene food containers, and plastic shopping bags, to mention a few. So are the options, which range from the imposition of charges of one kind or another to outright bans. The council needs only to follow the lead of other local governments that have already embraced waste reduction as part of their solid waste management strategies.

2. *The department should establish tipping fees that further encourage private carters to reduce their reliance on municipal disposal facilities.* More of the waste generated in New York City comes from the commercial sector than households. Tipping fees for the private carters who collect commercial waste should be fixed at a level that further discourages their use of municipal disposal facilities. This initiative will add to the cost of business in New York City, but it should also stimulate increased recycling and new waste reduction measures by the private sector.

3. *The department should construct the Brooklyn Navy Yard incinerator as soon as the state permits it.* Even if demand were reduced by the foregoing recommendations, the city still would need to increase the capacity of its disposal system. There are only two alternatives, landfill and incineration. Opening new landfills is an inferior policy from every perspective—environmental pollution, cost, and political feasibility. The administration should begin construction of the Brooklyn Navy Yard incinerator as soon as the state approves it (which requires that the city develop a state-approved plan for disposing of incinerated ash as quickly as possible). The number of additional incinerators required beyond the Brooklyn plant depends on the success of the other solid waste management policies.

4. *The department, city labor negotiators, and the Uniformed Sanitationmen's Association should renegotiate refuse collection procedures to require a full day's work for a full day's pay and to permit one-person trucks.* Collection productivity is of less strategic importance than improving the waste disposal system, but productivity gains could yield significant budget savings. When a sanitation worker's collection is completed, the workday is done, even if it is completed well within a normal shift. The earlier analysis also suggests that the productivity gains from the two-person truck initiative have been fully implemented. The parties identified above should renegotiate current collection practices in order to increase the amount of work refuse collectors perform and permit the use of one-person collection trucks in those areas of the city where practical.

5. *The department, with legislative support of the city council if required, should increase the penalties for littering.* Current policy requires law-abiding citizens to subsidize the antisocial behavior of miscreants. Whether through higher fines and/or better enforcement, penalties for litterers should be greatly increased. Cities that have adopted a "get-tough" policy—Seattle is an example—have succeeded in sharply reducing street litter and cleaning costs.[18]

6. *The department and the Board of Education should begin an educational campaign to teach New Yorkers how to assist the city in its war against garbage.* Citizen behavior complicates every aspect of solid waste management. Regulation and fines are less desirable ways to modify citizen behavior than education. New Yorkers need to learn what not to buy, how to separate their wastes into streams compatible with different disposal methods, how to present waste for collection, what the cost of littering is, and what will happen to the city in the event the disposal system fails. The schools chancellor should work with DOS to develop an effective educational curriculum for schoolchildren.

The Fire Department

The Fire Department is responsible for preventing fires, extinguishing fires, and responding to non-fire emergencies. Historically, it has shirked the first responsibility, and in recent years its performance in the other two areas has declined at least as measured by response times. However, the department has begun to respond to some management problems; other public officials could make major contributions to its performance by initiating the policies recommended here.

The department's poor performance can be traced to three basic problems. First, the department's managers and workers prefer fighting fires to preventing them. This is a harsh criticism, but the facts are clear. The department assigns only $\frac{1}{6}$ of 1 percent of its staff to educational activities intended to prevent fires. The other way the department is able to prevent fires is by inspecting buildings; firefighters reduced the number of building inspections 19 percent in the 1987–1989 period.

Second, a lack of flexibility in scheduling and deployment of personnel delays emergency responses. An appropriate analogy is fast-food restaurants or other establishments that seek to provide prompt service. The owners of a McDonald's franchise would be irrational if they assigned as many employees to work in the middle of the night as during breakfast and lunch periods—or if they located their restaurant where few people lived or worked. But the Fire Department, in effect, follows these policies. Its resources are not allocated on the basis of demand for its services, and the public pays the price in slower service. People who are trapped in burning buildings or crushed vehicles need help as soon as possible.

The third problem is perhaps the most basic. Put simply, the raison d'être of the Fire Department, putting out building fires, is no longer the appropriate basis for organizing its activities. Only 9 percent of the department's responses in 1989 were to structural fires, and between 1987 and 1989 the balance tipped from firefighting to the provision of other kinds of emergency services. The organization and operations of the Fire Department have not kept pace with the changes in its basic mission.

To improve the performance of the Fire Department, public officials should pursue the following initiatives:

1. *The Fire Department should greatly expand the number of fire inspections and the resources it devotes to educating New Yorkers about fire safety.* The present commitment to fire prevention is indefensibly low. With the inclement weather clause out of the contract between the city and the UFA, the opportunity exists for firefighters to conduct many more building inspections. Expansions of fire safety education should be planned in cooperation with the Board of Education.

2. *The city council should require the Fire Department to inspect all buildings in the city, including small residential properties, on a regular basis.* In addition to enabling firefighters to identify and correct unsafe conditions in the approximately 600,000 one-, two-, and three-family residential structures, which is where the vast majority of the city's building fires occur, this initiative also would permit firefighters to enforce local laws requiring installation of smoke alarms in such buildings. Finally, it would provide an opportunity for firefighters to spend a few minutes educating people in their homes about what to do in the case of a blaze.

3. *The state legislature should repeal the "two-platoon" provision of the state constitution requiring that the Fire Department be staffed at the same level at all times.* If the employees of a McDonald's franchise petitioned the legislature to require the owner to assign as many employees to work in the middle of the night as during breakfast, lunch, and dinner hours, state legislators probably would not be very supportive. Yet this is precisely how they have required the Fire Department to staff its operations for more than five decades. This indefensible state mandate serves no public interest whatsoever and should be removed from the state constitution.

4. *The Fire Department should close underutilized fire houses and transfer personnel and equipment to locations where they could be employed more productively.* Effective redeployment of resources often requires politically unpopular actions like closing fire houses. Mayor Koch demonstrated his

willingness to begin allocating the department's resources on the basis of the public interest despite opposition from members of the city council and lawsuits by advocacy groups. Mayor Dinkins should continue the effort to deploy resources more productively.

5. *The mayor should give the Fire Department expanded responsibility for non-fire emergencies and, by extension, the Police Department less.* The Fire Department is better trained, equipped, organized, and experienced to provide emergency services than the Police Department, at least in most situations. Moreover, the NYPD has its hands full fighting crime.

The Police Department

Earlier it was estimated that between 4 million and 5 million crimes were committed in New York City during 1989, including 1.5 million felonies. The city employs almost 40,000 people to fight crime, including more than 33,400 in the NYPD. The pervasiveness of crime in New York City, particularly of drug-related crime, leads to nearly unanimous support for the proposition that more police should be hired.

There are problems with this conclusion, however. The NYPD has only two basic means to reduce crime. One is to arrest more criminals. The problem is that the rest of the criminal justice system is full. This fact helps explain why increasing the number of police is likely to result in fewer arrests per officer. The police know that the rest of the system is full. Police officers spend long hours waiting for district attorneys to arraign suspects; they spend long hours waiting to testify in trials; and when police get back on the street they frequently run into the same people they previously arrested because jails are too full to hold them for long periods.

Crime also can be reduced by deterring would-be criminals. This tactic requires police visibility. But it is not necessary to hire more police in order to gain more police presence. This can be accomplished by transferring police officers from support positions to posts where they can fight crime.

In sum, the mayor and police commissioner should focus on making better use of the NYPD's current resources. This can be accomplished through the following initiatives:

1. *The Police Department should reassign officers from administration to enforcement.* Implementing this recommendation requires that the following questions be asked about every administrative position currently staffed by a uniformed officer: Is the position essential? If so, is it essential that it be filled by a uniformed officer? If, hypothetically, 2,000 officers could be reassigned from administration to enforcement, the average daily enforcement strength could be increased approximately 1,100, or more than 10 percent over the current level.[19]

2. *Within the enforcement contingent officers should be reassigned from car patrol to foot patrol.* In recent years, the NYPD has downgraded foot patrol in favor of patrol cars and specialized units like TNT. By 1989, only one of six officers assigned to enforcement patrolled on foot. This is a serious

managerial mistake, at least with respect to patrol cars. Officers on foot patrol are better able to mobilize residents and community groups in the war against crime. Evidence in New York and other cities indicates that residents in crime-ridden neighborhoods represent an important crime-fighting resource by serving as the "eyes and ears" of officers on foot patrol.

Officers should be transferred from car patrol to foot patrol. Nearly twice as many officers are assigned to car patrol. Their contribution to crimefighting is not clear. On average, a radio patrol car makes only eight responses every 24 hours, only one of which is to a crime in progress.

3. *The police commissioner should initiate the use of one-officer patrol cars.* This initiative would minimize the tradeoff between car patrol and foot patrol explicit in the preceding recommendation. Given the level of crime in New York City and the city's inability to hire more officers for fiscal reasons it is time for the department to use every means at its disposal to employ police officers as effectively as possible, which includes one-officer cars. The department has had the authority to use one-officer cars since 1977, when an impasse panel ruled in its favor on the issue,[20] but it has exercised this authority only in very limited circumstances.

4. *The Police Department should expand its campaign to "demarket" use of the 911 system.* New Yorkers asked for police assistance through the 911 system on more than 8,000,000 occasions in 1989, and cars were dispatched 51 percent of the time. The department already is attempting to reduce demand for this service through a public service advertising campaign; this effort should be supported and expanded.

5. *The Police Department and the district attorneys should initiate changes in procedures and technology to reduce the amount of police time lost during the period between arrest and arraignment.* As stated in a recent consulting report commissioned by the city, current procedures governing arrest and arraignment are "pre-programmed for maximally inefficient operation."[21] According to that study, the average time from arrest to arraignment ranged from 32 hours to 44 hours, depending on the county. The average police time used for postarrest procedures was 17 hours in Queens (the worst example), including more than 11 hours used while police waited for prosecutors to complete their paperwork. The "best" record (in the Bronx) was 10.4 hours of police time used after each arrest, including 4.5 hours waiting for paperwork to be completed. In addition to increasing the street presence of the police, reforming postarrest procedures would cut overtime costs (which jumped 20 percent from $78 million in 1987 to $94 million in 1989). Changes in booking and arraignment procedures coupled with the introduction of new technology would permit this sorry record to be improved.

The Department of Correction

The department's basic problem is that too many people are committed to jail for the purpose of detention and too few for the purpose of punishment. The result is a congested, high-turnover enterprise that is difficult to manage either efficiently or effectively.

Rather than address the issue of who should be in jail and who should not, the basic policy response of the city has been to meet demand by building more jails and hiring more correction officers. This has been a very expensive policy. In the 1987–1989 period the city was obliged to increase departmental staff 25 percent to 11,767 and increase operating expenditures 30 percent to $613 million. To make matters worse, the quality of correction services declined.

The demand on the system should be reduced by making more use of alternatives to incarceration. The alternatives are well-known, and available evidence suggests they are effective. But these innovations are underutilized, largely because of the "Willie Horton" syndrome. Alternatives to incarceration require district attorneys and judges in particular to take risks. They are reluctant to do so because unsuccessful cases lead to severe criticism from politicians and the public. For wider use of alternatives to incarceration to become acceptable, district attorneys and judges must take some risks, and elected officials must exercise some political leadership by interpreting the policy to the public in a supportive fashion.

With respect to correction services, the following initiatives would lead to improved services:

1. *The mayor and correction commissioner should expand the use of alternatives to incarceration instead of building more jails.* Since detainees dominate the system, alternatives particularly suited to them should be given the highest priority. Most detainees are confined to jail because they cannot make the bail that is imposed in order to guarantee their appearance at trial. When they make bail, often in a matter of days, they are released. In the meantime, they have occupied a bed that could be better used. Bail requirements should be reduced. Another alternative appropriate for this group is supervised "off-premises" detention.[22]

A third alternative which is appropriate for both convicts and detainees (at least those detainees who volunteer) is work release programs. In addition to permitting convicts to pay back society by performing a useful function, such programs enable inmates to learn about the obligations and benefits of work.

Finally, and most obvious, convicts and detainees who are addicts, but not otherwise dangerous, should not be in jail but in supervised settings where they can be treated for their drug or alcohol problem. If they are not treated for their addictions, they are likely simply to end up in jail again.

2. *The state should relieve the department of the responsibility of incarcerating parole violators and convicts who have been sentenced to the state penal system.* From 1983 to 1989, the number of state prisoners in the department's facilities increased from less than 100 to more than 2,200 on an average day. The state only partially reimburses the city for this service. Full-cost reimbursement, while desirable, does not address the congestion problem. The best solution is for the state to accept responsibility for incarcerating these prisoners. When inmates are sentenced to state prisons they should be transferred immediately. With respect to parole violators, parole hearings

should be completed faster. The state can take up to 135 days to complete parole hearings. This number should be reduced to 10 days, which is the rule in those counties that have successfully sued the state for relief.

3. *The department should expand emergency health facilities on Rikers Island.* Because of inadequate facilities on Rikers Island, many inmates who require "routine" emergency medical services (suturing, x-rays, laboratory tests, for example) must be transported to Health and Hospital Corporation facilities "on the mainland." This requires that correction officers transport them and remain with them throughout their treatment. This initiative would improve the quality of health services for inmates, increase the security of the jail system, and cut costs.

4. *The city council should repeal the 1939 local law prohibiting the correction commissioner from assigning more than a certain percentage of correction officers to steady tours.* The law in question requires that no more than 15 percent of correction officers citywide may be assigned to steady tours (and no more than 25 percent in a single jail). Repeal would permit DOC to reduce overtime costs, which have consumed more than 10 percent of the department's operating expenses in recent years.

Conclusion

This chapter has emphasized that the responsibility for improving agency performance does not rest entirely with the mayor and the commissioners. For example, four of the recommendations must be approved by the city council. As a result of the recent charter reforms, the council now is the city's sole legislative body. These recommendations provide the council an opportunity to demonstrate that it can be an effective legislative body. For example, the city council could contribute to the improved delivery of correction services by simply repealing the 1939 law that prohibits the DOC from assigning more than a fixed percentage of correction officers to steady tours.

The state of New York also contributes to the city's management problems. Too often city officials focus only on the state's ability to help New York City by giving it more money. This is important, but it is not the only way the state can improve government in New York City. For example, the state legislature could help New York City's government by initiating repeal of the constitutional provision requiring the Fire Department to be staffed on a two-platoon basis.

Nevertheless, the major responsibility lies with the mayor and the commissioners. They will choose which municipal priorities to emphasize and which to eschew. They can approach their jobs in traditional ways—raising taxes or cutting services to balance budgets—or they can embrace better management as a priority.

THE DEPARTMENT OF PARKS AND RECREATION

Standing before the stony panorama of New York City's concrete skyscrapers and asphalt streets, the average New Yorker would be surprised to learn that fully one-sixth of the city is public parkland and that a larger portion of its land is reserved for parks than in any other large American city. (See Tables 14.1 and 14.2.) In fact, the average share devoted to local parks among the nation's largest cities is only about 6 percent, less than half the equivalent figure for New York City.

Like many aspects of life in New York, however, these startling facts are part of a paradox. Although the city is well endowed with parkland, the average New Yorker is short of it. New York is so densely populated that its parkland is scarce relative to population. Among the 14 large cities, New York stands next to last in parkland per resident. Six other cities have more than twice as much per resident, and only Chicago has less.

Moreover, parkland is allocated unequally among the boroughs. One-quarter of the Bronx is parkland, although that borough accounts for less than 14 percent of the city's area. Brooklyn and Queens have smaller-than-average shares of parkland. With Central Park, Manhattan has a share of parkland just above the citywide average; Staten Island has an even larger share.

Another aspect of New York's parkland paradox is that the city has gone to great lengths to create a large park system, but it has not maintained its facilities. The neglect of these valuable assets contributes to the underutilization of parks in an overcrowded city.

Table 14.1 New York City Total Land Area and Parkland, by Borough (figures in acres)

Borough	Total Land Area	Borough as a Share of Total City Land Area	Federal Parkland[a]	State Parkland	City Parkland	Parkland as a Share of Total Borough Land Area
Bronx	27,925	13.9%	0	25	6,821	24.5%
Brooklyn[b]	47,647	23.7	3,118	9	4,090	15.1
Manhattan	15,185	7.5	3	28	2,656	17.7
Queens[b]	72,210	35.9	2,647	12	7,046	13.4
Staten Island	38,437	19.1	1,218	250	5,691	18.6
Other[c]	—	—	58	—	—	—
Total	201,404	100.0%	7,043	324	26,304	16.7%

Source: The New York City Open Space Task Force, "Open Space and the Future of New York: How to Analyze Community Open Space and Recreation Needs," 1988.

[a]Comprised almost entirely by the Gateway National Recreation Area (GNRA). GNRA's total acreage is 26,640, of which approximately 17,000 is lands underwater and approximately 2,658 is in Sandy Hook, New Jersey. The remaining 6,982 acres is distributed here.

[b]Brooklyn and Queens federal parkland acreage each include half of the 3,175 acreas shared jointly by the two boroughs in the Jamaica Bay Wildlife Refuge and the North Shore.

[c]Includes Statue of Liberty and Ellis Island.

Table 14.2 Local Public Parkland in Selected Large U.S. Cities, 1986

City	Population	Local Parkland Acreage	Local Parkland as a Share of Total Land	Local Parkland Acreage Per 10,000 Residents
Phoenix	853,900	29,458	11.9%	345
Dallas	975,600	19,609	9.2	201
Indianapolis	709,900	9,300	4.1	131
Houston	1,728,900	19,000	5.3	111
Baltimore	762,400	6,480	12.3	85
San Diego	954,900	8,021	3.9	84
San Antonio	843,700	5,990	3.4	71
Philadelphia	1,642,900	9,950	11.4	60
San Jose	689,700	4,000	3.7	58
Detroit	1,086,200	5,866	6.8	54
Los Angeles	3,125,000	15,000	5.0	48
San Francisco	717,400	3,300	11.1	46
New York	7,352,700	26,138	13.5	36
Chicago	3,009,500	7,309	5.0	24
Median			6.1%	66

Sources: Parkland acreage from surveys by Fairmount (PA) Park Commission (1986). Total city acreage and population from U.S. Department of Commerce, Bureau of Census, "1984–85 City/County Government Finances."

Note: Figure for New York City is only local public parkland. Share of total parkland in Table 14.1 includes state and federal parkland in New York City.

This chapter begins with a description of the parkland assets entrusted to the municipal Department of Parks and Recreation (DPR), including their history, current status, and need for improvement. The second section examines the way DPR maintains and operates these facilities. The third section examines citizens' use, and abuse, of their parks. The final section identifies possible directions for grappling with the problems facing the parks system in a time of severe fiscal constraint.

Physical Assets

This section begins with a brief history of the municipal system because many of the city park system's unique features can best be understood in these terms. A "snapshot" of facilities is then presented, followed by an analysis of recent and planned capital investments.

Historical Development

The origin of the municipal parks department can be traced to colonial days.[1] In 1733 the Common Council governing New York used the authority granted it by royal charter to establish the first municipal park, Bowling Green Park, in a parade ground and marketplace situated at the foot of Broadway. The royal charter also transferred ownership of two other properties destined to become city parks: the southern tip of Manhattan, known as the Battery, and the "Flats," the area now comprising City Hall Park.

Following the Revolutionary War, the designation of New York City as the state and national capital aroused interest in improving its parkland. Trees and grass were planted along the sea wall and in the Flats, fences were erected to set off green areas, and landfill was deposited to extend the city's shoreline. In 1797 the acquisition of Duane Street Park marked the first municipal purchase of parkland.

During much of the nineteenth century, development of New York City (which remained separate from much of the other four boroughs until consolidation in 1898) was guided by the Commissioners' Plan, or Randel Survey, published in 1811. It set forth the grid pattern of streets and avenues and reserved some areas as open space for parks. However, the initial amount of planned open space was modest (about 470 acres), a decision justified on the grounds that "the large arms of the sea" surrounding Manhattan would satisfy the need for open space.[2] Yet even this limited acreage was reduced as development took place and the grid was filled in.

Additional parks were laid out in what are now the other boroughs during the nineteenth century. Port Richmond Park (now known as Veterans Park) was created as Staten Island's first park in 1836. By 1839, eleven new parks were being planned for Brooklyn.

The 1840s and 1850s saw an extension of the perceived purpose of public parks. Increasingly, parks were used as places of recreation and organized athletics. An official game of baseball was played in 1845 at the location that was to become Madison Square Park. Parks also became a repository for works of art. The equestrian statue of George Washington was placed in Union Square in 1856, followed in 1857 by the Worth Memorial obelisk near Madison Square.

However, by 1850, parks in Manhattan (below 42nd Street) still amounted to only 63 acres. The riverfront acreage envisioned by the Randel Survey as available for "health and pleasure" actually fell prey to rapid commercial development.[3] Public concern over the need to relieve crowded conditions with open park spaces led to the city's acquisition, between 1853 and 1856, of the land that was to become Central Park. The New York State Legislature created the Board of Commissioners of Central Park in 1857 to oversee its construction. In 1858 the board selected a plan for Central Park submitted by Frederick Law Olmsted and Calvert Vaux, who were retained as supervising architects during the construction. By the summer of 1858, the southern section of the park was opened to the public.

Parks development hit a snag during the reign of William "Boss" Tweed, the leader of the Tammany Hall Democratic Club. Tweed replaced the Board of Commissioners with a City Department of Public Parks that was firmly in his corrupt grasp. Olmsted, Vaux, and Andrew Haswell Green, the park comptroller, were fired. Vast sums subsequently were embezzled from the city's treasury through graft in a number of city agencies.

With the uncovering of the Tweed Ring in 1871, control of the city's parks was returned to the commissioners. Olmstead, Vaux, and Green were reinstated, and the construction of Central Park was completed over the next several years.

In 1888 the city made its largest acquisition of parkland—fully 3,495 acres located in the Bronx, which was annexed as part of the city of New York in two steps taking place in 1874 and 1875. At the same time that large parks were being established in the "hinterlands" of the Bronx, new attention was focused on creating smaller neighborhood parks in the crowded sections of Manhattan. In 1887 the state legislature passed the Small Parks Act, which empowered the city to acquire such parks.

In 1898 consolidation combined the city of New York with the previously separate city of Brooklyn, the area surrounding Brooklyn (including Queens), and Staten Island. Consolidation of the local governments in these areas also meant consolidation of their parks functions. This was accomplished through the creation of a Parks Board composed of three commissioners—one from Brooklyn (who also administered parks in Queens), one from the Bronx, and one from Manhattan (whose jurisdiction included Staten Island). Subsequently, the composition of the board was changed to include separate commissioners from Queens (in 1911) and from Staten Island (in 1920).

The Parks Board presided over a single Department of Parks, but this ostensibly citywide agency was highly decentralized on a borough basis, with much authority for each commissioner. In 1898 the new department possessed approximately 6,935 acres, nearly 60 percent of which was in the

Bronx. Manhattan contained almost 1,300 acres; Brooklyn and Queens 1,574 acres (mostly in Brooklyn); and Staten Island less than 3 acres. However, in the next few years Queens acquired more than 1,000 acres of parkland.

In the early part of the twentieth century development of the city's park system was influenced strongly by the "playground movement." Lillian Ward, Jacob Riis, and fellow reformers urged that parks be more than open space, that they provide recreational opportunities for children. The year of consolidation also marked the formation of the Outdoor Recreation League, an independent group which provided recreational equipment for neighborhood playgrounds. In 1902, the Department of Parks took over the nine playgrounds begun by the league, improving them with the construction of recreation pavilions, running tracks, and outdoor gymnasia. The city established the nation's first permanent playground in a municipal park in 1903, in Seward Park. The first Bureau of Recreation was established in the Department of Parks in 1910. It built 61 new playgrounds by 1915.

The increased recreational use of the parks, however, had some deleterious effects. Recreation took precedence over conservation of public green spaces. The condition of the city's parks began to deteriorate. Central Park was especially hard hit; the Merkel Report, published in 1927, documented its declining condition and suggested measures such as placing playgrounds near park entrances to protect open green spaces from overuse from recreational activities.

Acquisition of additional parklands sped forward to accommodate the economic and population booms following World War I, especially in Queens and Staten Island, where intense development was expected. Nonetheless, the condition of the city's parks continued to worsen, largely because of the Tweed-like graft drawn through the Department of Parks by the Tammany Hall–controlled government. By the early 1930s, the poor state of public parks in New York City was a scandal.[4]

Revitalization and expansion of the city's parks became possible as the city entered a reform era. The ousting of the Tammany machine with the election of Mayor Fiorello La Guardia in 1933, and the subsequent revision of the city charter, were major elements in reform. But the key ingredient for the parks was the rise to power of Robert Moses. Moses combined offices in state and city government with substantial federal funds to make himself a shaping force in New York City parks history.

In 1934 the Parks Department was reorganized with greater, centralized control given to a single commissioner, and Moses became that commissioner. During Moses's 26-year tenure, a work force reaching almost 84,000 persons at one point increased the number of playgrounds from 119 to 777. A total of 288 tennis courts and 673 baseball diamonds were carved out of fields and forests. Also among Moses's accomplishments was the building of 3 zoos, 10 golf courses, 53 recreational buildings, and 11 pools of a size and design that had never before been seen. Coney Island, Rockaway, South Beach, and Jacob Riis beaches all received substantial renovations. Orchard Beach was literally re-created, landfilling the channel between Rodman's Neck and

Hunter and Twin islands, and expanding a tiny bathing area into an immense, crescent-shaped beach. In all, Moses built 17 miles of new beaches.

Preparations for hosting the 1939 World's Fair included filling and landscaping a 1,200-acre area in Queens that would become Flushing Meadows–Corona Park. In 1954, city-owned land was combined with a recent purchase to create Jamaica Bay Park, a wildlife refuge.

The balance between the conservation of green spaces and recreation in parks tilted heavily toward recreation under Moses. He saw parks primarily as an opportunity to build recreational facilities. Moses provided New Yorkers with an enormous outlet for relaxation and recreation, but the means to that end was a depletion of the city's store of untouched, natural landscapes, despite an increase in total park acreage from 14,827 to 34,673 acres.

Moses ended his stint as parks commissioner in 1960, but new directions for the department were not set until the election of a new reform mayor in 1965. During his campaign John V. Lindsay produced a "White Paper" on parks and recreation. It advocated promotion of community involvement in parks planning and the construction of "vestpocket" parks. Vestpocket parks are small parks—normally the size of a single building lot—placed in densely populated areas. Ten of these parks were created in 1967 and others followed.

But Lindsay's policies also followed the Moses tradition of emphasizing the recreational uses of parks. Consistent with this approach, as well as his emphasis on reorganization of city government into "superagencies," Lindsay created the Parks, Recreation and Cultural Affairs Administration (PRCA). This transferred responsibility for funding libraries, museums, and performing arts groups to the same department administering the parks and operating recreational programs. As a result, the New York Philharmonic and the Metropolitan Opera began to offer free concerts in Central Park. Central Park also played host to free rock concerts attended by as many as half a million people.

The possibilities for more widespread and intensive use of the city's parks were undermined by the fiscal difficulties that began early in the 1970s and peaked after the fiscal crisis of 1975. The parks unit of the PRCA sustained staff losses through attrition beginning in the early 1970s. These losses had visible consequences for parks maintenance. In addition, ambitious citywide plans initiated in Lindsay's first term were set aside. For example, by the time a new master plan for the restoration of Central Park was developed and released in 1973, it had little prospect for prompt implementation.

During this early period of fiscal difficulty, the city saw the federal government as one means for easing its burden. In 1974 more than 13,000 acres of city-owned parkland in Staten Island, Brooklyn, and Queens were transferred to the National Parks Service, enabling the city to focus its increasingly limited resources in other areas. These new federal lands have become known as the Gateway National Recreation Area.

In the years following the fiscal crisis the parks unit, like virtually all municipal units, was cut back through layoffs and attrition. As a result of these staff cuts, the nature of parks maintenance was changed significantly. The number of facilities with fixed-post staff (workers who remain in a specific park) was curtailed, and new mobile crews were established with a mandate to cover several facilities through periodic visits. The department's responsibility for maintaining land adjoining parkways was transferred to the Transportation Department.

Structural changes also occurred. Mayor Abraham D. Beame divided the PRCA back into separate Departments of Cultural Affairs and of Parks and Recreation, and Mayor Edward I. Koch continued this organization. Koch also began to shift some of the department's operating functions to private organizations. He started by transferring responsibility for operating the zoos to the New York Zoological Society. He also granted concessions for operating a number of parks facilities, including golf courses and skating rinks, to private companies. This both gained new revenue and enabled remaining municipal workers to concentrate on parks maintenance.

The Inventory of Facilities

As the historical summary indicates, the story of municipal parks was one of expansion for more than 200 years. The growth of the city's park system was essentially completed in the 1960s, when Lindsay's vestpocket parks were added to the already extensive network of parks and playgrounds. In the 1970s the municipal system shrank when substantial acreage was transferred to the National Parks Service as a way to reduce local operating costs. Since the 1970s the major task of the Parks Department has been to operate and maintain the already established system with revenues that have proved inadequate.

What is the nature of the park system for which DPR is responsible? The latest comprehensive inventory of facilities, completed in 1982, provides the most current available snapshot of the system.[5] DPR property can be divided into two categories, parks and other properties. Of the total of 25,058 acres, fully 19,585, or 78 percent, are parks.

The Parks

As shown in Table 14.3, the 19,585 acres of parks are divided among 479 different parks. More than two-fifths of the parks acreage is accounted for by five large "flagship" parks located in each of the boroughs. The largest of these (3,910 acres) is the network of facilities in Van Cortlandt–Pelham Bay Parks, accounting for fully one-fifth of all municipal parks acreage. The network of facilities comprising the Greenbelt in Staten Island accounts for another 1,593 acres, or about 8 percent of all parks acreage. The other flagship parks are Flushing Meadows–Corona in Queens, Prospect Park in Brooklyn, and Manhattan's Central Park.

In addition to its flagship parks, DPR maintains another 34 parks of more than 100 acres each. Together these facilities comprise another two-fifths (43 percent) of all parks acreage. The remaining acreage (approximately one-sixth) is divided among 41 parks of between 20 and 100 acres and another 399 smaller parks. The group of larger parks accounts for 1,824 acres and the smaller ones for 1,248 acres.

Table 14.3   City of New York Department of Parks and Recreation Properties

Category	Number of Properties	Number of Acres	Percent of Total Acres	Percent of Category's Acres
All properties	1,533	25,058	100.0%	NA
Parks	479	19,585	78.2	100.0%
Flagship parks	5	8,127	32.4	41.5
Central Park	1	840	3.4	4.2
Flushing Meadows–Corona	1	1,258	5.0	6.4
Prospect Park	1	526	2.1	2.7
Greenbelt	1	1,593	6.4	8.1
Van Cortlandt–Pelham Bay	1	3,910	15.6	20.0
Other parks over 100 acres	34	8,385	33.5	42.8
Parks of 20–100 acres	41	1,824	7.3	9.3
Parks under 20 acres	399	1,248	5.0	6.4
Nonparks properties	1,054	5,473	21.8	100.0
Playgrounds	503	871	3.5	15.9
Expressway and parkway land	37	4,042	17.6	80.4
Malls, strips, and plots	127	71	0.3	1.3
Circles, squares, and triangles	170	40	0.2	0.7
All other	217	89	0.4	1.6

Source: City of New York, Department of Parks and Recreation, Office of Management Planning and Analysis.
Note: NA, not available.

Other Properties

In addition to its parks, DPR is responsible for another 1,054 properties of a diverse nature. The most numerous group (503) consists of playgrounds which together account for 871 acres. These playgrounds include facilities located adjacent to schools and jointly operated with the Board of Education (226), and so-called freestanding (as opposed to being located within parks) playgrounds located throughout the city (277).

In terms of acreage, the most important nonparks properties are the lands located along expressways and parkways. These lands comprise fully 4,402 acres and, as discussed later, some sections are used for recreational purposes.

Other properties include 127 malls, strips, and plots (usually located in the middle of highways), and 170 circles, squares, and triangles (usually located at highway intersections). Together these types of properties total 111 acres.

The remaining 217 properties total just 89 acres, but they include a number of important facilities. This diverse set of properties includes different types of recreational and athletic facilities that are freestanding, as well as holdings such as Yankee Stadium and Shea Stadium.

Recreational Facilities

Located within DPR's parks and other properties is a vast array of recreational facilities. Perhaps the best known of these are the playground facilities. They number 838, with the majority (503) consisting of separate freestanding and jointly operated playground facilities. Another 308 playgrounds are located within parks, with the largest group (148) located in the parks of less than 20 acres. The remaining 27 playgrounds are located in nonparks properties other than playgrounds, including 10 on land near parkways and expressways.

The most numerous types of recreational facilities are basketball courts and handball courts, numbering 2,009 and 1,885, respectively. These facilities are located predominantly in the freestanding and jointly operated playgrounds.

DPR owns 760 ball fields, most of which (469) are in parks. DPR also maintains 627 tennis courts, 13 golf courses, and 6 skating rinks. Most of the tennis courts (558), all of the golf courses, and 5 of the skating rinks are located in parks. Since the Moses era, DPR has been a large operator of pools. Its latest inventory includes 46 pools and 33 minipools.

DPR also possesses over 12 miles of running paths, 5 zoos, and numerous facilities related to its recreational mission, including 635 comfort stations and 183 recreational buildings. Finally, DPR owns 126 parking areas that account for 19,924 parking spaces.

Capital Investment

The construction and rehabilitation of DPR's properties are financed through the city's capital budget. The city's plans for capital investment are biennially prepared, the most recent covering the period fiscal years 1992–2001. (A fuller discussion of capital budgets and ten-year capital plans can be found in Chapter 8.)

Despite the enormity of its responsibility, DPR customarily receives a disproportionately small allocation of capital funds. Exacerbating that problem, the current ten-year allocation for DPR's capital program represents the largest reduction of any agency since the May 1988 plan, shrinking 42 percent from $1.8 billion to $1.1 billion.[6] The department's current allocation amounts to 1.6 percent of the total plan, down from 3.2 percent of the previous plan.

The DPR program to reconstruct parks is divided between two efforts; one focuses on the large major and regional parks, and the other is dedicated to neighborhood parks and playgrounds. The plan for the larger parks is allocated $441 million, a two-fifths drop from the last plan. The decline in funding for these parks, however, is actually larger because $200 million is designated for constructing the West Side Esplanade, which was not previously included in the plan. Thus, funding for the 235 large major and regional parks is $241 million, a two-thirds decrease. The decline is due in part to the fact that the Parks Department focused almost singularly on the larger parks during most of the 1980s and has now turned its sights on smaller parks.

The plan for the larger parks includes the redesign of landscapes and natural features, as well as recreational facilities. Work will be performed in

98 (or 42 percent) of the parks included in this category. In terms of acreage, the current plan will address 488 acres, a nearly three-fourths reduction from the 1,875 acres included in the 1988 plan.

The plan for neighborhood parks and playgrounds has been cut 47 percent to $253 million. This work is performed in two ways: traditional "straight capital" work, which involves the complete redesign and reconstruction of the park; and the Neighborhood Park Improvement Program (NPIP), which speeds improvements by contracting out the replacement of specific features in a number of parks and playgrounds, without the cost of the complete redesign of the property. The NPIP reduces the cost of reconstruction by roughly 50 percent. The 232 properties included in this program are divided almost evenly between each type of work—119 sites by NPIP and 113 by comprehensive reconstruction.

Funding for major recreational facilities has been cut 32 percent to $121 million. These funds will reconstruct 4 of the 24 year-round, multipurpose recreation centers. Ten recreation centers have already been reconstructed, leaving ten more to be addressed after the current plan. This allocation will also reconstruct six pools.

The plan for beaches and boardwalks is allocated $80 million, a decrease of 37 percent, and will fund beach nourishment programs, as well as the reconstruction of the Rockaway Boardwalk. Purchases of vehicles and equipment and the reconstruction of support facilities will receive $123 million, 38 percent less than the last plan. Reductions in the purchase of vehicles will prevent DPR from meeting recently established replacement cycles, which likely will result in increased down time for repairs.

Land acquisition and tree planting have decreased more than two-thirds to just $38 million. This portion of DPR's plan is responsible for the 700,000 street trees in the city, approximately 20,000 of which are lost each year for a number of reasons. The level of tree replacement in the last plan did not meet that demand and would have resulted in a net loss of 79,000 trees over the ten-year period. The cut in funds in the current strategy will even more substantially reduce the city's street tree population. Under the current plan, the net loss could be as high as 140,000 trees, or 20 percent of the total population.

The prospects for restoring DPR's capital program to its previous level are bleak. Even if the lost funds were replaced, the capital plan would still fall far short of properly maintaining the capital plant. For example, despite DPR's emphasis on larger parks during the 1980s, less than one-fifth of the acreage in those parks received capital work. Smaller parks were even more neglected. The likely future will be a steady decline in the condition of parks, playgrounds, and recreational facilities, to the point that many will be unusable. This consequence, although unintentional, amounts to the abandonment of significant portions of the park system.

Private Capital Investment in Parks

Perhaps the sole bright spot for DPR's capital budget has been the creation of private parks conservancies. The model for these organizations, the Central

Park Conservancy, was established in 1980. Subsequently, similar citizens' organizations have been formed to assist DPR in maintaining flagship parks including the Prospect Park Alliance, the Friends of the Greenbelt, and units serving Flushing Meadows–Corona Park and Pelham Bay and Van Cortlandt parks.

So far, only the Central Park Conservancy has been able to provide substantial assistance. Using its own staff of landscapers, horticulturalists, recreation specialists, and others, and coordinating thousands of volunteers, the conservancy spent $31 million from 1981 to 1989 to improve Central Park.[7] The conservancy spent more than $16 million on capital improvements including the restoration of Central Park's cast iron bridges, the rebuilding of the Ballplayer's House and Ranger Station, and the restoration of Playmates Arch. Work is currently under way to dredge the Harlem Meer and restore its surrounding area. An additional $15 million was spent on horticulture, landscaping and maintenance, and services to visitors. The conservancy's employees and volunteers have also removed debris from the park, as well as cleared brush, raked leaves, and swept paths. Conservancy crews also provided assistance in removing graffiti. From its services center at the Dairy, the conservancy's educational and recreational services have reached out to hundreds of thousands of visitors to Central Park.

Another recent revenue source is the Adopt-a-Park program created by Parks Commissioner Elizabeth Gotbaum in 1990. Private organizations and corporations can "adopt" a park by donating from $5,000 to $250,000 (depending on the size of the park) for the maintenance of the park. Gotbaum also started the City Parks Foundation, a nonprofit group organized to solicit donations to supplement New York City parks programs.

Maintenance and Operations

With DPR's physical assets described, it is instructive to consider the agency's day-to-day activities. The first section considers the fiscal resources allocated to DPR; the second examines how these funds are converted into human resources and how the personnel are managed to accomplish the department's mission; the third examines the data available to judge how well DPR accomplishes its tasks.

Fiscal Resources

Table 14.4 shows the department's operating expenditures for selected years from 1945 through 1990 in constant dollars. A clear pattern emerges. The resources allocated for parks operations have gone through three phases and are now in a fourth. For the first 24 of the 46 years in the period examined, real resources grew continually. In constant dollars the agency's expenditures grew more than 160 percent from under $73 million in 1945 to nearly $190 million in 1978. Expenditures continued to rise from 1975 to 1978 because of

Table 14.4 City of New York Department of Parks and Recreation Operating Expenditures in Constant Dollars, Selected Fiscal Years 1945–1990 (dollars in thousands)

Fiscal Year	Total Operating Expenditures[a]	Personal Services[b]	OTPS[c]	Other[d]
1945	$72,792.1	$61,510.9	$9,978.8	$1,302.4
1950	85,027.3	77,466.1	6,861.8	699.4
1955	113,284.3	105,644.7	7,549.2	90.4
1960	121,447.4	113,518.1	7,929.3	0.0
1965	150,652.1	142,487.8	8,164.3	0.0
1970	168,461.6	152,683.9	16,031.2	(253.6)
1975	173,174.9	148,878.4	24,296.4	0.0
1978	189,913.5	171,272.3	20,723.5	(2,082.1)
1979	176,738.4	154,324.7	22,413.5	0.0
1980	170,029.8	144,050.6	25,979.1	0.0
1981	159,672.1	133,532.7	26,139.6	0.0
1982	153,565.8	128,247.5	25,318.3	0.0
1983	150,414.6	128,083.7	22,330.8	0.0
1984	148,212.9	128,687.0	24,291.4	(4,765.6)
1985	176,384.4	153,147.2	28,908.5	(5,671.5)
1986	177,706.9	152,050.4	31,786.1	(6,129.5)
1987	181,174.2	157,316.2	30,087.1	(6,229.1)
1988	183,341.4	156,742.1	32,735.3	(6,136.0)
1989	176,279.8	153,699.5	30,790.1	(8,209.8)
1990	169,008.7	147,690.0	31,129.6	(9,810.8)

Sources: City of New York, *Comprehensive Annual Financial Report of the Comptroller,* fiscal years 1945–1990 editions. Conversions to constant fiscal year 1989 dollars based on U.S. Department of Labor, Bureau of Labor Statistics, Middle Atlantic Regional Office, "Consumer Price Index for All Urban Consumers (CPI-U) in the New York–Northeastern New Jersey Area" (fiscal-year average).

Note: Totals may not add due to rounding. Constant dollars are fiscal year 1989 dollars.

[a]Totals include intracity sales and change in estimate of prior payables.

[b]Excludes fringe benefits in all years and pensions after fiscal year 1979.

[c]Other-than-personal services.

[d]Includes miscellaneous expenditures and interfund agreements.

the Comprehensive Employment and Training Act (CETA) program. The CETA funds were targeted for public service employment opportunities for relatively low-skilled and low-wage workers; DPR was a major recipient of federal CETA funds in this period.

The next phase in DPR's budgetary cycle was a period of decline from 1978 to 1984. In these seven years the agency's constant-dollar budget fell a total of 22 percent.

The next phase was a relatively brief, but marked, period of increased resources. The agency's constant-dollar operating expenditures rose 24 percent between 1984 and 1988. In the latter year its real spending was exceeded only by the 1978 high point.

The latest phase in DPR's fiscal history began in fiscal year 1989. That year the constant-dollar budget was reduced about 4 percent. The department was then obliged to make cuts as part of a program to balance the city's fiscal year 1990 budget. That budget was reduced from $176 million to $169 million, DPR's lowest inflation-adjusted spending level since before fiscal year 1985.

The next year, 1991, was especially difficult for DPR. The department responded to several mayoral requests to cut its budget. The $164 million adopted budget for 1991 was cut to $158 million. The 1992 budget was adopted at $109 million in 1989 dollars (a one-third reduction), the smallest parks budget since the early 1950s.[8]

Comparing trends in spending for parks with total municipal spending reveals the priority assigned to parks in the competition for municipal funds. Between fiscal years 1945 and 1955, parks expenditures accounted for approximately 1.5 percent of the city budget. Then the park share declined steadily through the late 1970s, eventually dropping below 0.6 percent in fiscal year 1979. During the 1980s, the park share hovered between 0.7 and 0.8 percent. However, in fiscal years 1991 and 1992 the share drops below 0.6 percent.[9]

Human Resources

As Table 14.4 indicates, the bulk of DPR's fiscal resources are used to purchase labor. So-called personal service expenditures, which cover salaries for employees, comprised 87 percent of the operating budget in fiscal year 1990. Consequently, it is important to consider the volume of labor these appropriations have secured.

DPR has two types of employees, full-time and seasonal workers who are employed primarily during the spring and summer to help staff parks during this busy period.[10] Since 1978 the trend in full-time employment has generally followed the pattern of financial resources. (See Table 14.5.) Employment fell in the 1978–1984 period faster than expenditures (29 versus 22 percent).

Similar to the trend in real expenditures, full-time employment experienced some recovery after fiscal year 1984. However, whereas real expenditures continued to grow through fiscal year 1988, full-time employment began to fall off after fiscal year 1986. Between fiscal years 1986 and 1991, total full-time employment dropped 10 percent.

The outlook for 1992 is a dramatic acceleration of the employment cuts of the latter half of the 1980s. The projection for fiscal year 1992 is 2,628, a 45 percent reduction from fiscal year 1986.[11] The fiscal year 1992 projection is 53 percent lower than fiscal year 1975, and it represents the Parks Department's lowest level of employment since before the Moses era.

Seasonal employment has varied even more than full-time employment. For fiscal years 1978 through 1991 the peak number of seasonal employees ranged from a high of 4,154 to a low of 3,015, a swing of 27 percent.[12] But these extremes did not correspond to periods of high and low budgets. In fiscal year 1984, when DPR's real budget and full-time staff were at low points, seasonal employment was 3,700—well above the figure in most preceding years. And the resurgence in fiscal resources and full-time employment in the 1984–1988 period saw a decline in the number of seasonal employees.

Table 14.5 City of New York Department of Parks and Recreation Full-Time Employees, Fiscal Years 1978–1991

Fiscal Year	Operations	Forestry and Horticulture	Recreation	Technical Services	Capital Projects	Executive and Administration	Urban Park Service[a]	Total
1978	4,028	NA	NA	NA	NA	NA	—	5,595
1979	3,146	330	602	526	151	340	—	5,095
1980	2,385	284	460	458	128	276	—	3,991
1981	2,969	210	485	478	151	247	—	4,540
1982	2,703	191	402	435	159	299	—	4,189
1983	2,438	181	379	391	159	293	—	3,841
1984	2,287	241	343	474	170	315	135	3,965
1985	2,487	277	353	566	219	297	174	4,373
1986	2,895	264	334	554	219	312	191	4,769
1987	2,866	273	324	529	225	304	168	4,689
1988	2,926	250	286	514	248	301	131	4,656
1989	2,616	266	290	577	273	305	236	4,563
1990	2,809	192	271	453	273	290	151	4,439
1991[b]	2,447	250	317	504	322	264	237	4,341
Percentage change 1979–91	(22.2%)	(24.2%)	(47.3%)	(4.2%)	113.2%	(22.4%)	NA	(14.8%)

Sources: City of New York, Office of Operations, The Mayor's Management Report, fiscal years 1978–1990 final editions.

Note: NA, not available.

[a]The Urban Park Service, created in 1984, is comprised of the Urban Park Rangers and the Parks Enforcement Patrol. Employees in these areas were previously included under Recreation.

[b]Preliminary plan.

Apparently, seasonal employees are utilized as stopgap measures during periods of low full-time employment.

Deployment of Resources

The efficacy of the fiscal and human resources allocated to DPR is determined by more than the level of such resources; another key element is how well they are managed. Since personnel is the largest component of the budget, and a key ingredient in maintaining parks, it is appropriate to consider how DPR's managers deploy their human resources.

For budgetary and reporting purposes, DPR allocates its full-time personnel among the seven categories seen in Table 14.5. The largest category, with 2,800 workers, or about 60 percent of the staff in fiscal year 1990, was operations. (Virtually all seasonal personnel also were assigned to operations.) This refers primarily to routine maintenance of parks and other properties. The next largest category, with over 450 workers, was technical services, the more specialized mechanics and craftsmen who do maintenance work on facilities and on vehicles and other equipment. The third largest category, with almost 300 people, was executive and administrative. The nearly equal-sized category recreation includes personnel who staff recreational facilities. Next largest was capital projects, which included the engineers and designers who work on capital budget activities. The forestry and horticulture group consisted of approximately 190 people who prune trees and do planting. The smallest group was the Urban Park Service.

The net result of the ups and downs of personnel in the 1979–1990 period was an overall loss of 13 percent. However, as Table 14.5 shows, the groups did not share equally in the staff cuts. The capital projects work force expanded markedly. In contrast, recreation workers were assigned the lowest priority. The group was more than halved, dropping from over 600 to 271 in fiscal year 1990. The cuts in forestry and horticulture were also disproportionate, with more than two of every five such positions eliminated. Operations and executive and administrative staff cuts were close to the departmental average, 11 and 15 percent, respectively.

In order to understand better how DPR utilizes its personnel, it is useful to review its organizational and management structure. A major dividing line is between "the boroughs" and the central facilities. The former refers to the five offices handled by borough commissioners. They were assigned three-quarters of DPR's workers—a total of 3,407 as of November 1990. (See Table 14.6.) The borough commissioners are responsible for DPR's park maintenance functions, equipment and vehicular care, forestry and horticulture work, and provision of recreational services. Most parks maintenance personnel, recreational personnel, climbers and pruners, and mechanics are assigned to the borough offices.

The borough offices are organized hierarchically. Each borough is divided into districts corresponding to the city's 59 community districts, plus five separate districts for the flagship parks. Each district is headed by a principal

Table 14.6 City of New York Department of Parks and Recreation Full-Time Employees by Title and Location, November 1990

Title	Borough						Other				Total
	Bronx	Brooklyn	Manhattan	Queens	Staten Island	Central	Capital Projects	Five Borough	Urban Park Service	Recreation	
City park worker	343	388	356	351	84	26	0	24	1	0	1,573
Associate park service worker	85	115	110	100	34	11	1	25	1	1	483
Park supervisor	41	53	64	42	17	9	0	4	0	0	230
Technical support aide	1	12	6	6	4	139	23	4	6	2	203
Laborer	48	47	39	35	18	1	0	4	0	0	192
Principal administrative associate	13	14	7	13	9	93	20	8	3	7	187
Office associate	15	16	9	8	8	38	10	9	3	3	119
Climber and pruner	20	15	25	49	10	0	0	0	0	0	119
Urban park ranger	0	0	0	1	1	3	0	0	104	0	109
Principal park supervisor	18	29	20	22	5	4	0	1	0	0	99
Recreation director	14	23	26	10	5	0	0	0	0	11	89
Auto mechanic	9	13	0	12	4	0	0	28	0	0	66
Assistant project coordinator	0	0	0	0	0	1	54	0	0	0	55
Assistant supervisor of recreation	15	10	6	13	3	0	0	0	0	4	51
Other[a]	100	134	126	116	42	111	202	63	36	43	973
Total	722	869	794	778	244	436	310	170	154	71	4,548

Source: Department of Parks and Recreation, Office of Management Planning and Analysis.

[a] Covers 129 titles. All titles with 50 or more workers are shown separately.

park supervisor, who reports to an administrative park and recreation manager. The manager normally is responsible for three districts and reports directly to each borough commissioner's chief of operations. A park supervisor, who reports to the principal park supervisor, is responsible for either operating a specific facility or supervising a mobile crew. Under the park supervisors are one or more associate park service workers and city park workers. Mobility within the department generally follows this hierarchical path. New workers are recruited "at the bottom" as city park workers and move up the ranks on the basis of closed (i.e., open only to current employees) civil service exams.

In addition to supervising the hierarchy of maintenance workers, the borough commissioners also oversee repair work at each borough's repair shop. These shops have craftsmen who make repairs to equipment that is brought to them or are dispatched to sites to make repairs. Borough commissioners also supervise the forestry, horticulture, and recreational workers assigned to their respective boroughs.

The one-quarter of DPR's personnel not assigned to "the boroughs" work in one of five centralized activities. These are the capital projects staff, the Urban Park Service, the staff of the "five-borough shop" (a specialized repair facility on Randalls Island serving all five boroughs), a relatively small group of recreation workers assigned from the central office, and the executive and administrative central office staff.

Performance Indicators

How effectively does DPR use its financial and human resources to perform its tasks? Data relating to DPR's performance are published annually in *The Mayor's Management Report (MMR)*.[13] These indicators shed some light on DPR's activities, but they do not comprise a comprehensive report card.

Maintenance

Routine maintenance of parks and playgrounds is the task that consumes most of DPR's labor expenditures. The *MMR* indicators reveal that the share of drinking fountains in service has risen from 46 percent in fiscal year 1978 to 77 percent in 1991; the share of comfort stations in service has improved from 65 percent to 76 percent over the same period; and the share of tennis courts in service has fluctuated between 80 and 90 percent through 1990, before falling off to 78 percent in 1991. While the drinking fountain and comfort station measures have improved, it is disheartening that nearly one in four such facilities remain out of service.

In the early 1980s, when DPR staffing was at a low point, the approach to measuring maintenance performance was changed to reflect the aforementioned switch from fixed-post assignments to mobile crews. By fiscal year 1991 only 35 percent of the playgrounds and 45 percent of the parks had fixed-post staff, compared to 70 percent of the playgrounds in 1983 and 67 percent of the parks in 1984. Whereas the MMR relates the share of facilities receiving mobile crew maintenance, it does not indicate the frequency of that maintenance. Because approximately 80 percent of the parks and playgrounds fall in this category, it could be masking a devastating lack of maintenance. Furthermore, no indication is given of the adequacy of this type of maintenance.

Similarly, the full-time staffing indicator is ambiguous. It indicates the share of parks and playgrounds staffed full-time but not the number of positions. A worst-case scenario is that such parks are staffed by only one employee; certainly, that is insufficient for many parks.

The DPR initiated a more outcome-oriented indicator of maintenance in fiscal year 1987. The "ABCD" system uses inspections to rate the condition of parks as excellent, good, fair, or poor. Each site is rated at least twice a year based on the condition of fences, benches, shrubs and trees, comfort stations, play equipment, and the need for repair and maintenance. From fiscal year 1987 to fiscal year 1989, conditions improved slightly, as the share of properties rated good or excellent grew from 79 percent to 88 percent. However, in fiscal year 1990 the ABCD system was revamped to increase the emphasis on safety factors and to provide better measures of reconstruction and repair needs. Consequently, the results for fiscal year 1990 show only 60 percent of DPR properties rated good or excellent under the new standards. In 1991, the share improved to 73 percent. This new rating system holds the promise of becoming a far more meaningful performance indicator for maintenance activities.

Enforcement Indicators

Stringent enforcement of littering and loitering regulations contributes to park cleanliness; this is largely the responsibility of the enforcement agents assigned to the Urban Parks Service. DPR uses two measures of enforcement activity. The first is the number of summonses issued for violations of the parking, health, and administrative codes. Between 1982 and 1990, the total number of summonses issued dropped 56 percent from 83,273 to 36,577, but this reflected DPR's decision to focus on ecological and health violations rather than parking violations. In this period the number of summonses for parking violations dropped 82 percent from 80,263 in 1982 to 13,459 in 1990. The second measure of enforcement activity is the average number of daily patrol units. This measure remained relatively constant in the 1985–1991 period.

Forestry and Horticulture Indicators

Several indicators pertain to DPR's forestry and horticulture responsibilities, which are planting, pruning, inspecting, and removing trees. In 1990, more than 210,000 trees were inspected, up 48 percent over 1983 but down 11 percent from the peak in 1988. In 1991, however, inspections dropped precipitously due to budget cutbacks, falling 54 percent to fewer than 97,000. Tree removals increased 152 percent between 1979 and 1990, while trees pruned rose 265 percent. Both activities also were curtailed because of budget reductions—removals dropped 59 percent, and prunings 62 percent.

Recreation Indicators

The indicators available for DPR's recreation programs are limited, but they point to dramatic service reductions in recent years. Since 1986, the city has recorded the number of service hours at recreation and senior citizen centers. The number of hours increased 16 percent between 1986 and 1988 but fell 52 percent in the three most recent years. The number of "monthly average sites with structured recreation programs" was halved between 1985 and 1989. The city then stopped reporting this measure in 1990. Recent declines also are evident in the number of theater performances offered, the number of mobile unit visits, and the number of visits to recreational facilities. Finally, the number of participants in structured programs fell 35 percent from fiscal year 1988 to 1989, before being dropped as a performance measure in 1990.

Other Indicators

For its "technical services," DPR uses indicators relating to repair of facilities and maintenance of vehicles. Nearly one-fourth of DPR's vehicles were out of service at any given time in 1977. This fell to 10 percent by 1987, but by 1990 it had risen to 18 percent.

Raising Revenues

Another task of DPR is collecting revenues from rentals, privileges, and permits. Rental fees are paid to the city by organizations using public facilities, primarily Yankee Stadium and Shea Stadium. Some rental revenue also is received for advertisements in the city's stadia, as well as for use of docks and wharfs.

The majority of revenues is from the granting of privileges on concessions for the commercial use of parks. Concessions have become more prevalent since the early 1980s. Currently, five of the city's six skating rinks are concessioned, as are all of its golf courses. Aside from the fees they earn, concessions reduce the department's maintenance responsibilities. This permits the department to focus its thin maintenance resources on other properties. In addition, revenues from the concessions are greater than the excess (or deficit) of revenues over expenses when DPR operated the facilities.[14]

Permits are required to use many of the city's athletic facilities, including ballfields, tennis courts, and skating rinks, and to hold special events on city-

Table 14.7   City of New York Department of Parks and Recreation Operating Revenues in Constant Dollars, Selected Fiscal Years 1945–1990 (dollars in thousands)

Fiscal Year	Permits	Privileges and Rentals	Studies and Surveys	Grants and Trusts	Federal Aid	State Aid	Miscellaneous	Net Change in Estimate of Prior Payables	Total
1945	$2,505.8	$4,896.8	—	—	—	—	$36.2	—	$7,438.8
1950	3,530.0	5,830.4	—	—	—	—	20.4	—	9,380.8
1955	6,522.6	8,136.7	—	—	—	—	61.8	—	14,721.1
1960	6,262.2	8,828.4	—	—	—	—	131.8	—	15,222.3
1965	8,312.3	8,435.8	—	—	—	—	135.4	—	16,883.4
1970	9,061.2	15,310.3	—	—	—	—	235.0	—	24,606.5
1975	9,398.8	8,958.7	—	—	—	—	286.5	—	18,643.8
1978	6,070.7	6,825.3	—	—	—	$809.5	2,160.9[a]	—	15,866.3
1979	6,180.2	7,413.5	—	—	—	1,493.8	2,118.2[a]	($80.9)	17,125.1
1980	5,645.9	8,121.2	—	—	—	1,420.9	1,647.9[a]	(91.2)	16,744.7
1981	4,573.8	8,790.3	—	—	$90.4	1,275.0	454.3	(5.8)	15,178.0
1982	4,618.1	7,846.7	—	—	63.2	1,487.8	628.5	(0.1)	14,644.3
1983	4,863.3	7,512.0	—	—	357.7	474.4	359.3	(0.9)	13,565.8

1984	2,877.3	9,314.5	—	—	314.5	417.0	834.5	34.0	13,791.8
1985	2,587.9	8,687.7	$176.6	$13.6	—	280.9	236.7	(12.4)	11,971.0
1986	2,290.9	10,555.6	224.9	77.0	—	378.2	177.2	(23.7)	13,680.0
1987	1,919.6	13,057.8	88.9	148.9	—	351.3	347.9	0.9	15,915.2
1988	1,433.4	13,546.5	175.4	114.9	—	368.8	265.9	(2.9)	15,901.7
1989	1,319.7	15,036.0	491.3	124.0	—	353.3	216.4	15.6	17,556.4
1990	1,357.0	15,911.5	53.5	50.0	—	248.3	445.2	(226.4)	17,839.2
Percentage change									
FY 1945–90	(45.8%)	224.9%	—	—	—	—	1129.8%	—	139.8%
FY 1945–75	275.1	83.0	—	—	—	—	691.4	—	150.6
FY 1975–90	(85.6)	77.6	—	—	—	—	55.4	—	(4.3)
FY 1978–90	(77.6)	133.1	—	—	—	(69.3%)	(79.4)	—	12.4

Sources: City of New York, *Comprehensive Annual Financial Report of the Comptroller,* fiscal years 1945–1990 editions. Conversions to constant dollars based on U.S. Department of Labor, Bureau of Labor Statistics, Middle Atlantic Regional Office, "Consumer Price Index for All Urban Consumers (CPI-U) in the New York–Northeastern New Jersey Area" (fiscal-year average).

Note: Totals may not add due to rounding. Constant dollars are fiscal year 1989 dollars.

*a*Includes "Administrative Services to Public."

owned property. Revenues are raised from the sale of these permits, as well as from locker and storage use at park facilities. The other revenues received by DPR can be grouped in four categories: intergovernmental aid, grants and trusts, studies and surveys, and miscellaneous.

Table 14.7 shows DPR's revenues in selected fiscal years since 1945 in constant dollars. Revenues rose more than 230 percent from 1945 to 1970, but in the first half of the 1970s they declined 24 percent due to a sharp drop in concession and rental revenues. In the following years permit revenues also dropped, causing 1978 revenues to fall below 1965 levels.

The most steady revenue trend has been the decline in permit revenues. From a 1975 high of nearly $9.4 million, they fell to just $1.3 million in 1989. Other revenue growth has helped offset the loss, but the trend in permit revenue suggests that the DPR should pay more attention to this revenue source.

New Yorkers and Their Parks

An important determinant of the quality of municipal services is citizen behavior. Service delivery is an interaction between providers and consumers; both park workers and park users play critical roles in determining the quality of New York City's parks. This section focuses on how New Yorkers use—and misuse—their parks.

Citizen Use of the Parks

The previous section described the limited data available regarding participation in recreation and other DPR programs. Unfortunately, few other data are regularly collected, and their integrity is questionable. The method of compiling indicators such as "visits to recreation facilities" in some cases consists of a DPR employee counting the number of people who enter on a given day and then extrapolating to create an annual figure. Moreover, such volume counts reveal little about the *nature* of use. For these reasons, citizen use of most DPR facilities remains largely an uncharted phenomenon. The notable exceptions are periodic in-depth studies conducted at selected prominent facilities.

The Central Park Conservancy is a leader in fostering studies of park usage. A 1982 study of Central Park estimated that approximately 3 million different persons visit Central Park a total of 14.2 million times in a given year.[15] A similar investigation in 1973 estimated the total number of visits to be 13 million. The authors suggested several explanations for the growth, including warmer weather, more frequent and larger political and cultural events held in parks (attracting hundreds of thousands of people), and renewed interest in physical fitness.

The study also indicated how Central Park was being used. While its use for athletics rose, the study found that fully 80 percent of the visitors used the park for "passive" activities, like people watching, picnicking, reading, and sunbathing.

With respect to visitor characteristics, the study found users to be increasingly representative of the population as a whole (with the exception of women, who are less likely to use Central Park). The study also revealed that 57 percent of the park visitors were white, 20 percent black, and 20 percent Hispanic. The 1973 study indicated that 77 percent of the visitors were white, and 12 percent black, and 8 percent Hispanic.

The Parks Department has contracted user studies of Van Cortlandt and Pelham Bay parks and Prospect Park. The Bronx parks study, conducted in 1986 and 1987, showed that visitors were almost evenly divided between male and female and tended to be middle-aged or older.[16] Racial minorities accounted for more than half of the visitors. The study estimated that more than 763,000 persons visit Van Cortlandt Park and 1,000,000 visit Pelham Bay Park annually. As with Central Park, the majority of visitors come for passive activities.

The Prospect Park study was published in 1988.[17] It estimated that the park received 4,370,000 visitors in 1987, approximately 14 percent higher than the number reported in the last study of Prospect Park in 1982. The ratio of male to female visitors was approximately three to two. During the summer months, between 51 and 68 percent of the visitors were black or Hispanic, although the proportion of white visitors increased during the spring and fall. Prospect Park too was most often used for passive activity.

One examination of general park use in New York City was a telephone survey performed by DPR's Office of Management Planning and Analysis in 1988.[18] Among other things, it found that more than 34 percent of the respondents do not use neighborhood parks, 79 percent had never used a DPR recreational facility, and 85 percent had never asked a parks employee for assistance. The leading need for improvement identified by the respondents was litter and cleanliness; in fact, litter was the thing most disliked by the respondents. When asked to judge the condition of facilities in the parks, 35 percent believed comfort stations were in poor condition, 42 percent believed the drinking fountains were in poor condition, and almost one-fourth believed the benches were in poor condition.

Citizens' Misuse of the Parks

Unfortunately, some visitors to the city's parks exhibit inappropriate, or even criminal, behavior. This behavior ranges from the relatively innocent act of littering to murder.

The public's perception of the safety of the parks is a key factor affecting park use. Recent data on this subject show that people believe that the parks—if not safe—are safer than they used to be. The 1982 Central Park study found that 56 percent of those questioned believed that Central Park was as safe or safer than two years before. A 1989 follow-up placed the share at 72 percent.[19] Respondents also identified the following problems with Central Park (from most to least frequently mentioned): homeless persons, rats, noise, gangs/muggers, drugs/dealers, trash/litter, bikers/joggers, traffic/cars, and pets/pet dirt.

Other responses from the 1989 study contradict the idea that people believe the park is safe. The majority of respondents take special precautions before coming to Central Park, including not coming after dark and not carrying money.

The Parks Department telephone survey also provides some pertinent data on perceptions of park safety. Sixty-two percent of the respondents believed their neighborhood parks were as safe or safer than three years earlier. Some 29 percent felt their park was unsafe during the day, compared to 78 percent after the sun sets. When asked what improvement they would most like to see in their parks, "more crime prevention measures" and "less litter" were most frequently mentioned.

Vandalism

Data on the amount and cost of vandalism in the city's parks are published in *The Mayor's Management Report*. The cost of reported vandalism in city parks rose 40 percent between 1977 and 1990 after adjusting for inflation.[20] The number of vandalism incidents also has risen considerably, 103 percent since 1984. DPR attributes much of this growth to the decline in fixed-post staffing of the parks.[21] The presence of a parks worker in a park apparently acts as a deterrent to vandalism.

Crime

According to the findings described previously, most people believe the parks are getting safer, but are fewer crimes actually being committed in the parks? Unfortunately, practically no information is available on crime in the parks. The notable exception is crime in Central Park, which is available because Central Park comprises a separate police precinct.

Central Park crime data show a 59 percent downturn during the 1982–1989 period.[22] Robbery, which accounted for more than half of the nearly 5,600 crimes reported over the period, plummeted 73 percent. Murder and manslaughter disappeared completely. At the same time, enforcement efforts improved. The number of arrests decreased at less than one-third the rate of reported crimes.

Homelessness

As the plight of the homeless is receiving increasing attention, so too is the presence of the homeless in the city's parks. There are no accurate data on the number of people living in parks, but some advocates for the homeless put the figure at several thousand.[23] During the 1982 Central Park study, a sweep of Central Park found fewer than 25 people sleeping in the park, some of whom were likely to have been simply sleeping off a drunk from the night before. In 1989, they found 105 persons, excluding those who were obviously not homeless.

Clearly, there are more people living in the city's parks than ever before. The reasons are not difficult to fathom. Parks provide a comparatively safe and comfortable place for the homeless to sleep, a place where they are seldom harassed. Furthermore, DPR has historically been lax in enforcing its regulations regarding the homeless, perhaps in recognition of the fact that the task of preventing them from sleeping in the parks would be monumental. However, in 1991 the city closed Tompkins Square Park (a well-known roost for squatters), perhaps signaling an end to DPR's lax enforcement.

Homeless persons present a number of problems and challenges to the Parks Department. Cleanliness is a problem—many of the homeless persons living in the parks exacerbate the difficulty of keeping facilities clean. Safety is another problem—a substantial share of the homeless are addicted to drugs and alcohol; many are formerly institutionalized mental patients or have become severely disoriented as a result of years of living on the street. Both of these factors act as disincentives to park usage. Potential park visitors, especially those with small children, are wary of homeless persons and consider them dangerous.

Policy Directions

When the facts about DPR assembled in this chapter are combined with the city's fiscal outlook, the conclusions are grim. The vast inventory of parkland and other properties assembled by the city since colonial days is not adequately maintained. For more than 20 years, through fiscal crises and better days, parks commissioners have struggled unsuccessfully to acquire the resources necessary to maintain and operate their facilities. As a consequence, three of ten parks and playgrounds are in fair or poor condition, park facilities such as drinking fountains and comfort stations work only three-quarters of the time, and recreational services are skeletal at best.

The gap between current resources and those needed to run the existing system adequately is beyond the city's ability to close. A departmental study in 1981 defined full-time staffing levels to perform adequately its several tasks.[24] Although the study relied primarily on the judgments of then-current managers rather than outsiders and contemplated no productivity improvements, it nonetheless is a reasonable baseline for considering staff requirements. The results, summarized in Table 14.8, show that staff would have to increase between 3,042 and 5,028, or from 80 to 130 percent. If DPR staffing falls by 1,200 positions from 1990, as is projected for fiscal year 1992, the needed growth would range from 160 to 240 percent.

Similar gaps exist with respect to capital investments. While the city's

Table 14.8 Results of Staffing Level Survey

Function	Benchmark Study Level	1990 Level
Maintenance and operations	4,672–5,939	2,731
Technical services	716–795	548
Recreation	1,027–1,337	285
Forestry and horticulture	455–781	260
Total	6,870–8,852	3,824

1988 ten-year plan provided a large sum for parks improvements, it still left much accumulated neglect unaddressed, especially in the larger parks and at recreational facilities. The current ten-year strategy for 1992–2001 is substantially smaller in scope, leaving most of DPR's capital needs unaddressed.

The fiscal and political reality is that these gaps are unlikely to be closed. An economic recession is causing local revenues to shrink, and competitive pressures limit the extent to which this can be countered with higher tax rates. The Parks Department budget was drastically reduced as the city struggled to close a nearly $4 billion budget gap for fiscal year 1992, and there is little prospect for additional aid from the federal and state governments.

The record suggests that in the political battles that shape retrenchment policies within city government, DPR will be a big loser. Experience after the 1975 and 1991 crises suggests that DPR will continue to suffer reductions substantially in excess of citywide averages. With the added pressure to find resources with which to combat the rising tide of crime, homelessness, and AIDS, DPR will find its struggle to retain its current meager funding even more difficult.

Yet grim prospects ought not be an excuse for inaction or despair. Following two policy directions—securing new designated revenues and achieving greater productivity in maintenance functions—could relieve some of the pressure on DPR.

Expanding Designated Revenues

Although DPR is likely to suffer in the political battles over scarcer local tax levy funds, it has opportunities to tap other resources. The current commissioner already has identified one such opportunity and is seeking to expand private efforts to support park maintenance and improvements. The Central Park Conservancy alone contributed $10.5 million to the maintenance and operation of Central Park in 1989.[25] Expansion of the Adopt-a-Park program and similar efforts should be encouraged, but with two important corollaries.

First, new private funds should not substitute for local tax funds. As private support grows, this should not be a reason to pare public support. A clear understanding between DPR and citywide budget officials should specify that these efforts will not result in offsetting cuts in local appropriations. Second, it is likely that these private efforts will be more successful for facilities in wealthier neighborhoods than in poorer ones, leading to greater disparities in park conditions among neighborhoods. Therefore, DPR should be certain to maintain or even increase resources devoted to otherwise underserved areas as private support for other facilities increases.

It is important to stress that private efforts need not be limited to monetary contributions. Neighborhoods, as well as businesses, can "adopt" smaller parks and playgrounds by providing volunteer labor to clean up and do simple maintenance. A large in-kind contribution in the form of volunteer workers could enable neighborhood groups to supplement the resources available to DPR, including its existing volunteer efforts. For instance, one conservancy program provided nearly 11,600 volunteer hours for maintaining Central Park in 1989, and a single-day event brought 3,200 volunteers into the park to clean up and solicit donations from visitors.[26]

In addition to philanthropy and volunteers another resource which DPR could tap more fully is user fees. The analysis of departmental revenues indicated that constant-dollar permit revenues, the principal form of user fees, have declined significantly in recent years. This is partly related to the shifting of golf courses (and hence golf permit revenues) to private concessions, but it also suggests such revenues might be used more effectively as a new resource. DPR has initiated a comprehensive review of the possibilities for new charges for services, as well as of the level of current charges. The preliminary budget for fiscal year 1992 included a proposed doubling of the fee for reserving a ball field from $4 to $8. If the recently initiated review of user fees is truly comprehensive and imaginative, then user fees might prove a significant source of new revenues. As with contributions, any such new revenues should be collected with a clear understanding between DPR and citywide budget officials about the extent to which they might be offset by reductions in local tax levy support.

Greater Productivity in Maintenance and Operations

The bulk of DPR's fiscal and human resources are allocated to routine maintenance and operations. These activities are managed through a borough command structure and personnel system that is hierarchical and closed. People have well-defined tasks, well-established work patterns, and achieve occupational mobility by slowly moving up the chain of command. Most of those at the higher levels are "insiders" schooled in the ways of the system.

Such organizations, be they police departments or parks departments, tend to be resistant to change and sometimes perpetuate modes of operation that are unresponsive to new conditions. Specific and detailed data about the productivity of DPR's units are not available (perhaps in part because of the agency's traditions), but it is reasonable to believe its productivity could be improved through managerial improvements. An organization that performs its work with small teams in numerous decentralized locations inevitably faces supervisory problems and difficulties in enforcing and improving workload norms.

For managers to provide more efficient services, they will require improved performance indicators. The Parks Department, together with the Mayor's Office of Operations, should continue to refine the scorecard rating system. In addition, improved measures are required for recreational services, forestry and horticulture functions, and other aspects of the department's activities.

Managerial innovations are likely to become more frequent if a wider range of talented individuals is made eligible for managerial positions within DPR. Many central office positions are widely recruited, and the opening of senior-level positions within the borough offices to skilled managers from a wide range of organizations might stimulate innovation at DPR.

Even greater gains might be achieved by a fundamental reorganization of the way maintenance and operation activities are performed. Two complementary approaches can be identified. First, specific groups of workers could be organized as small firms that are contracted to maintain designated facilities. Through the use of an improved scorecard rating system to enforce standards of maintenance, the workers could be paid fixed sums for achieving the standards. The pay could vary with the extent to which standards are achieved and with the number or scope of properties maintained. Simply put, more productive groups of workers could take on more assignments and earn more money. Parks are one municipal service in which it is possible to relate workers' pay to their performance, and this would be an effective policy to follow.

This approach could be expanded to include performance contracts with private firms. Groups of municipal workers could compete with private firms for the task of maintaining specific properties. Municipal workers would have the opportunity to demonstrate their efficiency and earn the rewards it brings, but they also would be held to competitive standards.

Finally, efforts to make municipal parks better for recreation will require greater interagency efforts to deal with the problems posed by homelessness, crime, and other social problems that plague the parks as well as other portions of the city. Joint efforts with the Human Resources Administration, the Police Department, and voluntary neighborhood groups should be encouraged to apply the resources and expertise of these organizations to the challenges facing parks managers.

The Remaining Gap

How far could greater productivity and more nontax resources go toward filling the previously identified resource gap that is equivalent to between 80 and 130 percent of 1990 staff levels? The answer is necessarily highly speculative, but some plausible estimates can be put forth.

In recent municipal history the most significant productivity initiative was the shift from three-person to two-person trucks for refuse collection in the Sanitation Department. This represents a productivity gain of one-third. If management initiatives and competitive approaches for DPR staffing yielded equivalent results, then a staffing gap of between 80 and 130 percent could be reduced to a gap of between 50 and 100 percent. This would be substantial progress, but it would still leave parks inadequately maintained.

Additional private resources and user fees could narrow the gap further. In the latest year for which data are available (1990), DPR raised about $18 million, or about 10 percent of its operating budget, from user-fee-type revenues. Assuming a thorough review of revenue opportunities led to a doubling of that figure, it would represent another 10 percent increase in DPR resources. This, combined with the productivity gains, could narrow the gap to between approximately 40 percent and 90 percent of 1990 resources; this is the equivalent of about between 1,530 and 3,440 staff.

Could private philanthropy and volunteer efforts yield the equivalent of this many additional staff? The answer is unknown, but it surely is worth exploring. The alternative is continued deterioration of the park system as a whole or in part, through a de facto triage policy of selective neglect.

_____15

THE HEALTH AND HOSPITALS CORPORATION

The medical care system in New York City is unique. Its distinguishing features include its enormous size, with an abundant supply of both physicians and hospital beds. But the special character of New York medicine also is rooted in two other characteristics, the large role of teaching hospitals and the large role of the municipal system.[1] Whereas New York City accounts for only about 3 percent of the nation's population, it is home to nearly 11 percent of all medical residents, and nearly seven of every ten hospitals in town are involved in graduate medical education. (Nationally, less than one hospital in ten is a teaching hospital.) The large scale of the municipal system is evident in the fact that the Health and Hospital Corporation's multiple facilities account for about one-fifth of all inpatient care in the city and over 40 percent of the hospital-based ambulatory care. In contrast, most large cities have no local public hospital, and in those that do, it typically plays a much smaller role.

This chapter focuses on the agency currently responsible for operating the city's health care facilities, the Health and Hospitals Corporation (HHC). The first section relates the history of HHC's creation and its first 20 years of operation; the second section focuses on the efficiency of its operations in the late 1980s; the third considers the contribution of HHC to providing access to care for the indigent; the final section presents recommendations to enable HHC to realize better its objectives of both operating efficiently and providing care to the poor.

329

Evolution of Current Policies

Historically, New York City's provision of medical care to needy individuals through municipally operated institutions has been a source of pride as well as a target of reform. In the nineteenth century the city provided medical care for poor individuals at infirmaries attached to its poorhouses, and these facilities evolved into separate hospitals. In 1929 responsibility for operating these facilities was shifted from the Welfare Department to a newly created Department of Hospitals.

During the Depression the scale of operation expanded to meet a growing need as an estimated 60 percent of the city's population was eligible for care at public expense under then-prevailing rules.[2] Municipal hospitals became overcrowded, and the city launched a major program of purchase of hospital care for indigents from underutilized voluntary hospitals. At prices less than the full cost of care, the city eventually purchased care for about one-third of its total indigent patient load from voluntary hospitals as well as operating a large municipal hospital system at nearly 100 percent occupancy.

During the Depression, the reform administration of Mayor Fiorello La Guardia instituted a number of administrative changes designed primarily to remove political patronage and corrupt practices from the Department of Hospitals. Employees were placed under the civil service system, purchases of supplies and letting of contracts were subject to careful review and centralized standards, and the Bureau of the Budget, created in 1933, was given authority to monitor expenditures.

The 15 years following World War II witnessed a decline in the standing of the municipal hospital system. Four major factors underlay this decline. First, the physical plant deteriorated seriously. Inadequate and overutilized even before the war, municipal facilities received little new investment during the Depression and war years.

Second, economic and technological forces were working to reduce demand for municipal hospital services while making hospital care a more expensive product. Group hospital insurance for the working population became widespread during this period, reducing demand for municipal hospital services and increasing occupancy at the newer voluntary facilities. Improvements in the nature of medical care made it a more expensive service as its technological component grew.

Municipal appropriations for the Department of Hospitals did not keep pace with these cost pressures, leading to a perception that the municipal hospitals were underfunded. Equipment was not always modern. Staffing often was inadequate, particularly for nursing and other technical positions that could not be filled at permitted salaries, with the result that municipal hospitals came to rely on less-skilled employees.

Third, changes in physician education and supply made it increasingly difficult for the municipal facilities to recruit and maintain adequate physician staff. Due to the American Medical Association's control over medical school capacity, the nation's physician supply did not keep pace with population growth. Given a wider range of choices than they had during the Depression, doctors in the postwar era generally chose to serve middle-class patients with health insurance. Younger and better-trained doctors followed their more affluent patients to the suburbs. By the end of the 1950s most of the municipal hospitals were relying heavily on foreign-trained doctors for staff and several institutions were threatened with loss of accreditation because of inadequate staff.

Finally, the administrative reforms of the La Guardia era came to be perceived as bureaucratic obstacles to efficient management in the new period of more technologically sophisticated medical care. Centralized control over the budget, civil service procedures, and purchasing regulations led to rigidities in the operation of the municipal hospitals. The combination of old and poorly maintained facilities, underfunding for operations, a shortage of medical staff, and inappropriate administrative controls led to a serious deterioration in the quality of services available at municipal hospitals in the postwar era.

Establishment of the Affiliation System

The deterioration in the level of service at municipal hospitals eventually led to strong political pressures to take remedial action.[3] In February 1959, Mayor Robert F. Wagner appointed a blue-ribbon Commission on Health Services chaired by David Heyman, an investment banker active in creating the Health Insurance Plan of Greater New York. The Heyman Commission report in July 1960 was followed six months later by a similar effort sponsored by the Hospital Council of Greater New York. While the two commission reports differed in their emphases, both highlighted the staff problems of the municipal hospitals and identified closer relations with medical schools and voluntary teaching hospitals as a partial solution.

To cope with the situation, Mayor Wagner appointed a new hospitals commissioner, Dr. Ray Trussel from Columbia University's medical center, and mandated him to develop teaching affiliations for each of the municipal hospitals. During his tenure (1961–1965), Commissioner Trussel succeeded in developing contractual relations for professional medical staff for all of the municipal hospitals except Sydenham, a small facility in Harlem to which community physicians admitted private patients, and Seaview, a chronic care hospital on Staten Island. The common element in the affiliation arrangements was payment of city funds on a cost-plus basis in exchange for provision of services by salaried physicians who would oversee the activities of municipal hospital interns and residents. In effect, all of the municipal hospitals (with the previously noted exceptions) became teaching hospitals.

The affiliation contracts generally were successful in achieving their initial goal of improving the quality of physician services. Recruitment of staff at the municipal hospitals was greatly eased by the links with teaching institutions, although some of the hospitals that were affiliated with less well-known voluntary teaching hospitals still were obliged to depend heavily on foreign medical graduates.

The Creation of the Health and Hospitals Corporation

The enactment of federal Medicaid and Medicare legislation in 1965 coincided with the election of a reform mayor in New York City. The new mayor, John V. Lindsay, had promised improved municipal hospitals as part of his campaign. The new federal programs made this goal appear realistic. Lindsay appointed a blue-ribbon commission under the chairmanship of Gerard Piel in 1966 which reported in 1967 with a call for fundamental changes in the local health care system.

The Piel Commission's goal was elimination of the dual system of health care with lower standards for the poor. The members believed that Medicare and Medicaid not only would provide the resources to accomplish this goal but also justified a stronger public role in managing the entire city's health care system. Under Medicare and Medicaid the voluntary hospitals were likely to be deriving more than one-half of their revenues from public sources, which in the mind of commission members justified public control over all health care institutions in the city. The commission also was concerned about the operation of the municipal hospitals and sought to improve their management by reducing oversight by the citywide budget and personnel agencies.

The commission recommended creation of a new public benefit corporation, the Health Services Corporation, that would be responsible for coordinating all public funds for health care in the city and would be able to use this leverage to establish regional networks of facilities consisting of both municipal and voluntary institutions. It would collect third-party revenues but also receive a lump sum payment from the city. The new corporation also would be responsible for operating the municipal hospitals without the constraints of a civil service system or reliance on centralized municipal purchasing agencies. The corporation would be governed by a board of nine prominent citizens appointed by the mayor, none of whom would be employees of the city.

In 1969, a political agreement was forged among the mayor, the city council, and the municipal hospitals employees' union leaders that resulted in state legislation creating the New York City Health and Hospitals Corporation. The HHC was given responsibility for operating the municipal hospitals and other health care facilities that the city might assign it. Ownership of the facilities as well as responsibility for capital improvements remained with the city. However, HHC was responsible for collecting all third-party revenues and would be given a lump sum appropriation from the city. The amount of the city subsidy was set at $175 million in the first year with subsequent adjustments for inflation and changes in the responsibilities the city asked HHC to undertake. The HHC was freed from direct control by the city's budget agency and was able to make its own purchasing arrangements. In addition, HHC was empowered to create subsidiary corporations to operate individual facilities, a provision included to permit greater decentralization of municipal hospital operations.

While HHC incorporated some of the structural features recommended by the Piel Commission, the compromises necessary to obtain the authorizing legislation led to several important deviations from the original model. The

HHC's board was expanded to 16 people with more responsiveness to the local political establishment than the commission recommended. To gain support of the union leaders, the legislation provided civil service protection for all nonmanagerial municipal hospital employees and retained the municipal employees' union as collective bargaining agent; also, informal commitments were made to the union to limit and eventually reduce the hiring of nonphysician personnel through the affiliation contracts.

The HHC began operations on July 1, 1970, with little lead time for planning. In its early years it continued to rely heavily on the city overhead agencies for personnel, purchasing, and financial management. Since it inherited a weak billing and collections system from the Department of Hospitals, HHC found it could not achieve initial targets for third-party revenue collections and thus was obliged to rely on the city for working capital. Financial autonomy and greater management flexibility proved difficult to achieve. Because of its numerous early difficulties HHC was viewed by many as a disappointment. In 1973, a State Study Commission issued a well-publicized report concluding that "the people of New York City are not being materially better served by the Health and Hospitals Corporation than by its predecessor agencies."[4]

Impacts of the 1975 Fiscal Crisis

The immediate impact of the fiscal crisis was sharp staff reductions and expenditure limits for HHC. The HHC payroll (excluding affiliate employees) had grown from 40,036 in 1970 to 49,080 in 1975; in the next three years it was cut 17 percent to 40,750 and then reached a low of 40,431 in 1980. Total HHC expenditures, which had risen 56 percent from $663 million to $1,034 million between 1970 and 1975, were tightly controlled for the next five years and reached only $1,238 million in 1980.[5]

The volume of services provided by HHC was affected only modestly by these resource reductions. However, a trend toward reduced lengths of stay meant that HHC's continued provision of care to the same number of people admitted required fewer days of care and hence fewer hospital beds. The HHC had almost an identical number of general care admissions in 1972 and 1982, but average length of stay fell from 11 days to 8.3 days. Accordingly, the number of days of care fell almost 23 percent during this period.

The reductions in lengths of stay and total days of care were accompanied by reductions in the bed capacity of the HHC system. (See Table 15.1.) Between 1975 and 1980, inpatient general care services were closed at Morrisania, Gouverneur, Francis Delafield, Fordham, and Sydenham hospitals, and the bed capacity of most other HHC facilities was reduced. For example, Metropolitan Hospital, which was at one time targeted for closure but remained open, saw its general care bed capacity cut from 626 in 1975 to 522 in 1980 to 407 in 1985. For all HHC hospitals, the decline in general care bed capacity was 18 percent between 1975 and 1980.

The fiscal crisis also helped bring about changes in the relationships be-

Table 15.1 New York City Health and Hospitals Corporation General Care Beds by Facility, 1975, 1980, 1984, and 1990

General Care Hospital	1975	1980	1984	1990
Bronx Municipal	724	656	640	537
Fordham	406	Closed	Closed	Closed
Lincoln	292	509	517	513
Morrisania	311	Closed	Closed	Closed
Coney Island	408	378	374	399
Cumberland	334	310	Closed	Closed
Greenpoint	174	174	Closed	Closed
Kings County Hospital Center	1,138	1,008	877	784
Bellevue	828	789	786	806
Francis Delafield	195	Closed	Closed	Closed
Harlem	793	688	639	540
Metropolitan	626	522	407	354
Sydenham	193	120	Closed	Closed
City Hospital at Elmhurst	654	583	493	397
Queens Hospital Center	673	540	454	377
Gouverneur	119	Closed	Closed	Closed
North Central Bronx	—	352	347	295
Woodhull	—	—	322	353
Total	7,868	6,629	5,856	5,355

Sources: Health and Hospital Planning Council of Southern New York, *Hospital and Related Facilities in Southern New York*, 1975 edition; United Hospital Fund, *Hospitals and Related Facilities in Southern New York*, 1980 edition; data for 1984 provided by the United Hospital Fund; data for 1990 from United Hospital Fund, *Health Care Annual*, 1991.

tween HHC and the city general government. The fiscal monitors established by the State exercised supervision over HHC as well as the city. The procedures developed for financial planning delegated to the city responsibility for submitting a plan for HHC which was consistent with the city's own budget. That is, HHC had to develop a budget that required no more city funds than the city was including in its financial plan for HHC, and this figure had to be viewed as reasonable by the fiscal monitors. The effect of this coordinated financial oversight was to give the city more direct control over HHC budget planning and to make the processes of both agencies subject to greater public scrutiny. After some initial battles between the HHC leadership and the Financial Control Board, which eventually led to the dismissal of an HHC president in 1976, the city's Office of Management and Budget and HHC developed smoother working relationships for arriving at compatible financial plans.

The need to contain spending and the desire to reduce HHC bed capacity also led Mayor Edward I. Koch, who took office in 1978, to seek greater political control over the HHC board and to involve his appointees more closely in the management of HHC. During Mayor Koch's first term this goal led to conflict with three successive HHC presidents, each of whom served only a relatively short period before leaving over disagreements with the mayor. In 1981, Mayor Koch selected, and the board approved, Stanley Brezenoff as president. Brezenoff had served as a commissioner since 1978 and brought both organizational stability and personal loyalty to the mayor to the office of HHC president. Brezenoff was elevated to deputy mayor in 1984, but his successors were recruited to HHC by him and also served under him. The combination of new board appointees by Mayor Koch and selection of presidents sensitive to the mayor's desire to exercise close control over HHC changed HHC's character. Instead of being a semiautonomous body, it operated much like other mayoral agencies.

Fiscal Recovery and Progress at HHC

In fiscal year 1981 the city achieved a balanced budget, and the local economic and fiscal climate improved in the following years. In 1981 Mayor Koch successfully ran for reelection with promises to expand and improve services, and subsequently new resources were devoted to most municipal agencies as well as to HHC. In addition, a new state program for reimbursement of hospitals by Medicaid, Medicare, and Blue Cross was adopted in 1982, and this provided additional resources through both increased reimbursement rates and special earmarked funds for care for the medically indigent. Moreover, the more stable management of HHC in the early 1980s facilitated realization of many of the collections improvements planned in earlier years.

As a result of this combination of circumstances, HHC's total expenditures increased 95 percent, from $1,238 million in 1980 to $2,417 million in 1988. In the same period the share of expenditures financed by a city subsidy fell from 35 to 23 percent. (See Table 15.2.) Thus, HHC financed its budgetary expension primarily through greater third-party revenues.

The new revenues together with a more harmonious relationship with city officials and greater stability in corporate leadership enabled HHC to undertake several programmatic initiatives. Four of these efforts are described briefly next.[6]

Reduced the Nursing Shortage

The HHC acute care hospitals suffered from a chronic shortage of registered nurses. After 1980, increased funding was made available to support nursing positions and the number of registered nurses was expanded 29 percent, from 5,098 in 1981 to 6,565 in 1985. However, HHC was not always able to recruit successfully for budgeted positions and had to rely on per diem nurses to meet a substantial portion of its needs.

Programs were launched to enhance recruiting and to reduce expenses for per diem nurses. To make HHC a more attractive workplace for nurses, HHC developed a flexible work schedule program, made forgivable loans available to senior nursing students, and created a career ladder program to permit promotion of practical nurses to registered nurses. In 1983 HHC created a subsidiary corporation, Nurse Registry, Inc., to serve as a source of per diem nurses and reduce reliance on overtime.

Table 15.2 New York City Health and Hospitals Corporation Expenditures and Revenues, Selected Fiscal Years 1975–1990 (dollars in millions)

Financial Category	1975	1980	1985	1986	1987	1988	1989	1990
Revenues, total	$1,041	$1,261	$1,946	$2,016	$2,259	$2,327	$2,581	$2,782
Third party, subtotal	592	773	1,447	1,528	1,655	1,824	1,907	2,143
Medicaid	368	431	931	977	1,126	1,143	1,109	1,335
Medicare	142	216	238	270	246	336	389	406
Blue Cross	39	56	91	86	88	118	119	114
Others[a]	42	69	187	195	195	227	270	388
New York City subsidy	414	447	465	458	568	455	626	481
Other revenue	35	41	34	30	36	48	48	58
Expenditures	$1,034	$1,238	$2,018	$2,086	$2,230	$2,417	$2,646	$2,890
Surplus (deficit)	7	23	(72)	(70)	29	(90)	(65)	(108)
Subsidy as percentage of total revenue	40%	35%	27%	25%	24%	23%	26%	17%

Source: Audited Annual Financial Statements of the Corporation.
[a]Includes bad debt and charity care pool.

Improved Medical Records System

Another chronic problem for HHC hospitals has been poorly equipped and staffed medical records units. In recognition of the need for better medical records management for a variety of purposes, including higher-quality care, reduced duplicative testing, and better utilization review, HHC launched a "medical records initiative" in May 1982. The program provided additional funds as well as central office management attention to deal with the problem. The passage of a new diagnosis-related system for payment under Medicare provided additional incentives for improved medical records.

The initiative resulted in substantial reductions in the number of incomplete records at most facilities. By 1985 all hospitals except Kings County met the state standard of having at least 50 percent of all records up to date within fifteen days of discharge. Automated chart tracking systems were installed in five acute care hospitals.

Revised Ambulatory Care Programs

A major effort of the HHC board and staff was to serve better its role as "family doctor" to most of the city's poorer residents. In November 1982 the board adopted a formal Ambulatory Care Initiative that called for the reorganization of most high-volume clinics into family-oriented services staffed by primary care specialists and others organized into primary care teams.

By mid-1986 this program had been implemented in the general medicine clinics of all acute care hospitals, in the pediatric clinics of ten hospitals, and in the obstetric and gynecological services of nine hospitals. The model was also implemented in all three services at all Neighborhood Family Care Centers. In addition, these initiatives include the development of special arrangements for staffing a demonstration program (Citycaid) at Metropolitan Hospital and implementation of a private practice group plan for Coney Island Hospital. Finally, more accessible primary care was promoted by the creation of smaller clinics at decentralized sites. By mid-1985, forty such satellite clinics were in operation.

Expanded Psychiatric Services

A long-term state policy to reduce the number of mentally ill persons cared for at state mental hospitals created chronic overcrowding at municipal hospital acute psychiatric care units. The HHC sought to address this problem by developing better coordination for admission of patients to state facilities, by expanding the bed capacity of psychiatric units at HHC facilities, and by expanding HHC outpatient mental health services. Specifically, the psychiatric bed capacity at HHC hospitals was increased from 1,137 in 1982 to a planned 1,329 in the 1986 fiscal year through changes at several facilities as well as the opening of a psychiatric unit at the new Woodhull facility. In addition, new psychiatric ambulatory care programs were launched, including one aimed at homeless individuals.

The Current Climate—Coping with New Demands

By the late 1980s, the fiscal and public health climate had changed dramatically, causing HHC to cope with new demands while resources were curtailed. Like other municipal services—and like many voluntary hospitals—HHC entered the 1990s beset with problems.

The origins of the fiscal difficulties can be traced to the stock market crash of October 1987. After that traumatic event, growth in the New York City economy slowed as financial sector firms cut employment and suffered reduced profits. The slowed economy lowered expected city revenues and led to reductions in available funds for HHC from the city. In addition, the same slower economic growth hurt the state government's revenues, and the state has not funded its health care programs generously.

At the same time that resources were evaporating, new demands emerged for the local health care system. After a long period of decline, demand for inpatient care increased citywide. (See Table 15.3.) After falling 11 percent during the 1980–1986 period, general care days rose 2.2 percent between 1986 and 1988. The post-1986 increase in demand was felt more sharply by the municipal hospitals. The number of general care days provided by that system increased nearly 6 percent; the increase in psychiatric care was nearly 10 percent. However, in 1989 this upward trend ended as demand fell slightly.

The reasons for the unanticipated changes in demand trends are not yet fully understood, but several factors are clear. First, AIDS emerged as a major epidemic and required more hospital care than was expected. Between 1987 and 1989, AIDS patients in New York City hospitals increased from 1,071, or 3.5 percent of the average daily total, to 1,852, or 6.3 percent. Municipal hospitals care for a disproportionately large share of AIDS patients.

Second, there is an unforeseen rise in demand for psychiatric care. This appears to be related to increased substance abuse, notably the cocaine derivative known as crack. As seen in Table 15.3, psychiatric days increased 22 percent between 1983 and 1988, including a 29 percent increase in the municipal system.

Third, births have not fallen as was anticipated by health planners. Obstetric care days rose 4 percent in the 1986–1988 period and another 2 percent in 1989. There was also an increased need for intensive newborn care as the number of low birth weight and other problematic infants increased. This too is related to greater substance abuse.

Finally, length of stay has not declined in accord with previous trends and national patterns. The average among general care patients in New York City was 8.8 days in 1988, the same as in 1985. In contrast, the national average in 1988 was 7.2 days. The reasons for the difference include a shortage of nursing home beds, which causes some patients to remain in hospitals while awaiting nursing home placement, but social factors also play a role. For

Table 15.3 General Care Hospital Days in New York City, 1980–1989

| | Total | | | | | Municipal Hospitals | | | | |
| | | General Care | | | | | General Care | | | |
Year	Total[a]	Medical/ Surgical	Pediatrics	Obstetrics	Psychiatric Care	Total[a]	Medical/ Surgical	Pediatrics	Obstetrics	Psychiatric Care
1980	10,466,894	9,121,979	NA	NA	955,271	1,833,364	1,483,265	NA	NA	NA
1981	10,353,004	9,014,578	796,128	542,298	1,019,572	1,797,650	1,450,705	208,951	137,994	449,396
1982	10,359,266	9,038,837	781,067	549,362	1,031,053	1,822,317	1,453,386	222,265	146,666	446,267
1983	10,319,272	8,933,049	777,695	548,528	1,029,586	1,795,555	1,418,930	222,126	154,899	449,079
1984	NA	NA	NA	NA	NA	NA	NA	NA	NA	NA
1985	NA	NA	NA	NA	NA	NA	NA	NA	NA	NA
1986	9,155,085	7,794,676	772,005	548,404	1,176,093	1,665,878	1,275,900	229,690	160,288	526,977
1987	9,298,755	7,958,444	770,390	569,921	1,248,060	1,754,942	1,360,632	230,149	164,161	556,836
1988	9,358,589	8,019,080	767,835	571,674	1,259,295	1,760,836	1,364,057	233,711	163,068	579,314
1989	9,212,523	7,847,931	781,083	583,509	1,109,334	1,712,012	1,310,152	240,454	161,406	503,408
Percentage change										
1980–86	(11.0%)	(2.6%)	NA	NA	23.1%	(4.0%)	(14.0%)	NA	NA	NA
1986–88	2.2	2.9	(0.5%)	4.2%	7.1	5.7	6.9	1.8%	1.7%	9.9%
1988–89	(1.6)	(2.1)	1.7	2.1	(11.9)	(2.8)	(4.0)	2.9	(1.0)	(13.1)

Source: Data from United Hospital Fund of New York presented in Kenneth Thorpe, "Health Care," in Charles Brecher and Raymond D. Horton, eds., *Setting Municipal Priorities 1990* (New York: New York University Press, 1989), p. 344, and in United Hospital Fund of New York, *Health Care Annual*, 1990 and 1991 editions.

Note: NA, not available.

[a]General care total excludes psychiatric days.

example, concentrated in municipal hospitals are many homeless patients who are not easily discharged and many abused or abandoned children who also take a long time to place outside the hospital.

The 1986–1988 reversal in demand trend was especially problematic because the supply of hospital beds had been shrinking as part of longer-run plans. The New York State Department of Health (DOH) has authority to regulate capital investments; hospitals cannot build or renovate facilities without its approval. To guide its investment decisions, DOH developed and periodically revises a plan that is based upon demand estimates for inpatient care. It seeks to balance the number of hospital beds with its estimates of demand.

When these planning efforts started in the 1960s, the consensus was that the city was "overbedded" and that reducing supply would both increase hospital efficiency and permit services to be concentrated in higher-quality facilities. For the 1980s, DOH expected continued reductions in average length of stay and fewer surgical admissions due to expanded ambulatory surgery. It also underestimated the impact of AIDS. As a result DOH plans called for reduced hospital bed capacity in New York City.

These plans were largely achieved. (See Table 15.4.) Between 1980 and 1988, the number of general care hospital beds citywide dropped 12 percent. At the municipal hospitals, one of five beds was closed; municipal hospital general care bed capacity fell from 6,629 to 5,241.

The obvious consequence of increased demand and reduced supply is very high occupancy rates. (See Table 15.5.) Although New York City traditionally had occupancy rates above the national average, the discrepancy has grown in recent years. Until 1982, occupancy rates in New York City were approximately 10 percentage points higher than the comparable national figure. Subsequently, national rates decreased sharply, falling from 75 to 64 percent between 1982 and 1988. Locally, occupancy rates fell slightly in the 1982–1986 period but rose again to nearly 87 percent—nearly 23 percentage points above the national average—in 1988. The city's municipal hospitals experienced the most rapid rise, from 81 to 92 percent in the 1985–1988 period. In 1989 the modest decline in demand eased the situation somewhat, occupancy rates fell to 86 percent—still 20 percent above the national average.

The consequences of these extraordinarily high occupancy rates is an overcrowded system. Admissions cannot be made from the emergency room because beds are not available. This leads to backups of patients in the emergency room. These overcrowded facilities have attracted considerable media attention, and the New York City hospital industry—and especially its municipal component—was seen as entering the 1990s in a particularly stressed condition.

Trends in Performance

How well do the arrangements that have evolved for operating HHC serve the public? The performance of HHC can be assessed in terms of its efficiency in

Table 15.4 General Care Hospital Beds in New York City, 1980–1990

| | Total | | | | | Municipal Hospitals | | | | |
| | General Care | | | | | General Care | | | | |
Year	Total[a]	Medical/ Surgical	Obstetrics	Pediatrics	Psychiatric Care	Total[a]	Medical/ Surgical	Obstetrics	Pediatrics	Psychiatric Care
1980	33,596	28,723	2,018	2,855	2,812	6,629	5,279	512	838	1,367
1981	32,778	27,945	1,986	2,847	3,006	6,072	4,753	499	820	1,353
1982	32,656	27,863	1,914	2,879	3,074	6,078	4,753	499	826	1,368
1983	32,708	28,086	1,882	2,740	3,110	5,964	4,667	487	800	1,368
1984	32,051	27,522	1,882	2,707	3,179	5,770	4,515	494	761	1,401
1985	32,016	27,446	1,804	2,776	3,243	5,856	4,569	500	787	1,436
1986	31,251	26,776	1,805	2,670	3,305	5,871	4,578	500	793	1,565
1987	30,263	25,807	1,797	2,659	3,563	5,632	4,339	500	793	1,580
1988	29,427	24,980	1,797	2,650	3,691	5,241	3,948	500	793	1,635
1989	29,610	25,070	1,886	2,654	3,411	5,243	3,916	500	827	1,672
1990	29,506	24,988	1,885	2,663	3,238	5,355	4,027	500	828	1,447

Sources: See Table 15.3. Figures for 1980 and 1981 are as of January 1; figures for 1982 to 1990 are as of December 31 of the preceding year.
[a]General care total excludes psychiatric beds.

Table 15.5 General Care Hospital Occupancy Rates, New York City and United States, 1980–1989

Year	United States, All Community Hospitals	New York City		
		Total[a]	Municipal	Voluntary
1980	75.6%	86.6%	78.9%	88.3%
1981	76.0	86.5	81.0	87.5
1982	75.3	86.9	82.0	88.0
1983	73.5	87.6	83.0	88.7
1984	69.0	86.9	84.0	87.9
1985	64.8	83.6	80.8	84.4
1986	64.3	82.4	81.0	83.4
1987	64.9	86.6	91.7	86.4
1988	64.5	86.9	91.8	86.2
1989	66.2	85.9	87.6	85.5

Sources: National data from American Hospital Association, *Hospital Statistics,* 1986 and 1989 editions; New York City data from sources noted in Table 15.3.

[a]Includes proprietary and state general care hospitals not shown separately.

providing services and the quality of its output. In recent years the agency's top managers have emphasized a systemwide approach seeking to coordinate services at multiple facilities. This suggests that a focus on services provided by HHC as a whole, rather than the performance of individual facilities such as Bellevue and Harlem hospitals, is the best approach for assessment. Accordingly, the agency is analyzed in terms of five service activities: acute medical inpatient care, psychiatric inpatient care, long-term care, ambulatory care, and the Emergency Medical Service (EMS). The period examined is fiscal years 1983–1988, one for which relatively detailed data were available.

Acute Medical Inpatient Care

Expenditures for acute medical inpatient care remained virtually stable in real, or inflation-adjusted, terms during the period examined. However, there were significant changes in the volume of such services provided, and these changes point to a reduction or improvement in the unit cost of services. (See Table 15.6.) The trends supporting a reduced unit cost are an increased number of patients treated (measured as the number of discharges) accompanied by a reduced length of stay for these patients. In addition, there is evidence that these patients suffered from more complex conditions that otherwise would have required more, not less, resources. For the period since fiscal year 1984, a measure of the relative intensity of services required by patients—the Medicare program's Casemix Index—is available. This figure rose from 0.755 to 0.802 over the 1984–1987 period, meaning that the resources required to care for the "average" patient rose from about 75 percent to over 80 percent of the norm established by the federal Health Care Financing Administration. (In general, HHC's patients are below the norm because a

Table 15.6 Cost and Volume of HHC Acute Medical Inpatient Services, Fiscal Years 1983–1988

Indicator	1983	1984	1985	1986	1987	1988	Percentage Change 1983–87
Current-dollar operating expenses (millions)	$882.4	$981.5	$1,003.0	$995.5	$1,030.5	NA	16.8%
Constant-dollar operating expenses (millions)^a	$1,085.0	$1,156.1	$1,131.7	$1,085.6	$1,030.5	NA	(0.5)
Patients treated (discharges)	218,131	214,923	218,486	220,570	223,062	216,283	2.3
Average length of stay (days)	9.1	9.1	8.9	8.4	8.4	9.1	(7.9)
Casemix index^b	0.749	0.755	0.761	0.797	0.802	NA	7.1
Adjusted number of discharges^c	163,380	162,267	166,268	175,794	178,896	NA	9.5
Patients admitted from emergency rooms							
Number	153,902	152,522	159,643	156,903	161,598	158,597	5.0
As a percentage of all patients	70.6%	71.0%	73.1%	71.1%	72.4%	73.3%	2.7
Constant-dollar cost per adjusted dis-charge	$6,641	$7,125	$6,806	$6,175	$5,760	NA	(13.2)
Beds	6,672	6,555	6,628	6,370	5,997	6,024	(10.1)
Average percentage of beds occupied	81.7%	82.0%	80.4%	79.6%	85.7%	89.0%	4.9

Sources: Authors' calculations based on data provided by the Office of the Vice President for Finance, New York City Health and Hospitals Corporation. Conversion to constant dollars based on U.S. Department of Labor, Bureau of Labor Statistics, Middle Atlantic Regional Office, "Consumer Price Index for All Urban Consumers (CPI-U) for the New York–Northeastern New Jersey Area" (fiscal-year average).

Note: NA, not available.

^{a}Constant dollars are fiscal year 1987 dollars.

^{b}Figure for 1983 estimated by the authors based on 1984–1985 change.

^{c}Actual discharges multiplied by casemix index.

large proportion of them receive normal deliveries, abortions, and other treatments that are not as resource-intensive as most other types of inpatient care.)

Additional evidence pointing to more complex cases is the general increase in the number and proportion of patients admitted from the emergency room. Such patients arguably must be treated at a later stage of a disease and/or suffer from more traumatic illnesses than those admitted on a scheduled basis. Also, the number of simpler surgical procedures performed on an outpatient basis rather than with an overnight admission has increased (data presented later), further indicating that procedures done on an inpatient basis are, on average, becoming more complex.

If all other things remained constant, the reduction in unit costs for acute medical inpatient care should be taken as a significant improvement in efficiency at HHC. And there is some further evidence to support this praise. The agency reduced its bed capacity to reflect the shift toward shorter stays; between 1983 and 1988 one of every ten acute medical beds was removed from service. This increased the proportion of beds occupied on the average day from under 82 percent to 89 percent during the period.

However, one important cautionary note must be sounded before concluding that all the reduction in cost per discharge derives from more efficient management. It is possible that the lower unit costs resulted in lower quality of care. But quality of medical inpatient care is difficult to gauge, and HHC has done a poor job of assembling management information systems that address this complex issue. A distinction can be made between the monitoring of quality of care through management information systems using quantitative indicators and the monitoring of quality of care through procedures including reviews of individual patient records or supervising reviews of the performance of personnel. The HHC maintains that it has a strong "quality assurance" program that requires review of records at each level of the organization. However, findings or results for those procedures are kept confidential. The limited publicly available evidence relating to quality is mixed.

In *The Mayor's Management Report* the only indicator used to assess quality of medical inpatient care is the percentage of medical records completed within 15 days of the patient's discharge. This indicator is used because HHC historically had a bad record in maintaining its files and fell behind the requirements of the Joint Commission on the Accreditation of Health Care Organizations that at least 50 percent of these records be complete within a month of discharge. Consequently, HHC identified meeting medical records requirements as an important management goal. Although completing a record bears little direct relationship to quality of care during a hospital stay, the ability to achieve management's goals in this area and the logical relationship among good record keeping, availability of clinical information for doctors and nurses, and high-quality care suggest the indicator is worth considering.

Unfortunately, the indicator points to lower quality. The percentage of records completed within 15 days fell from 61 percent in fiscal year 1983 to 58 percent in 1984, 60 percent in 1985, 49 percent in 1986, and 56 percent in 1987. While there was some fluctuation, the performance dropped from 1983

Occupational Group	1983	1984	1985	1986	1987	Percentage Change 1983–87
Physicians	5,197	5,225	5,340	4,917	5,432	4.5%
Attending and supervisory	2,387	2,378	2,421	2,016	2,450	2.6
Residents	2,810	2,847	2,919	2,901	2,982	6.1
Nurses	9,006	8,706	8,940	9,272	8,625	(4.2)
Registered nurses	7,077	6,817	7,078	7,562	6,923	(2.2)
Practical nurses	1,929	1,889	1,862	1,710	1,702	(11.8)
Technicians	9,407	9,808	9,777	9,944	10,630	13.0
Aides	5,431	5,213	5,141	4,997	5,263	(3.1)
Housekeeping	8,937	8,830	8,997	9,128	9,327	4.4
Clerks	8,785	8,821	8,666	8,415	8,425	(4.1)
Management and supervisors[a]	2,022	2,262	2,510	2,705	2,951	45.9
All other	26	221	31	20	0	(100.0)
Total	48,810	49,085	49,401	49,396	50,653	3.8%

Source: Unpublished data provided by the Office for Budget Reporting and Supporting Services, New York City Health and Hospitals Corporation.

Note: Figures are for December of years shown. Figures differ from totals shown in Table 15.1 because figures in Table 15.1 are for June of year indicated. All figures include both direct and affiliate employees.

[a]Includes all employees not covered by collective bargaining agreements.

to 1987. Moreover, the data exclude Kings County Hospital because its record-keeping system is so far behind that the goals are considered inappropriate.

Additional inferences about quality of care can be drawn from the staffing pattern of the organization, particularly the number of direct care workers such as physicians and nurses. However, HHC does not maintain information on the allocation of staff among its service lines; the only available relevant data are end-of-calendar-year employment by occupational group. (See Table 15.7.) From December 1983 to December 1987, the number of workers grew by 4 percent, or 1,843 full-time positions; but most of this growth (1,257 positions) was concentrated in the most recent year. The overall growth was linked to an increase in physician staff somewhat greater than for other groups, but the trend for nurses is more troubling. The number of practical nurses declined steadily and was about 12 percent lower at the end of 1987 than 1983. The HHC was able to increase its registered nurse staff in 1985 and 1986, but in 1987 this trend reversed sharply and fewer regularly employed nurses were available for patient care at the end of 1987 than 1983.

The HHC responded to its difficulty in attracting nurses in several ways. First, in 1983 HHC created a subsidiary unit, Nurse Referrals, Inc. (NRI), to employ nurses on a per diem basis. This permitted a reduction in overtime demands on nurses in exchange for more favorable compensation for nurses working extra shifts as well as facilitating additional nurses working in municipal hospitals on a per diem basis. Figures are not available for fiscal years 1983 and 1984, but the following figures show the full-time equivalent number of nurses employed by NRI in subsequent fiscal years:

	1985	1986	1987
Registered nurses	597	515	983
Practical nurses	57	104	133

As these figures suggest, NRI helped overcome the losses in nurse staffing. However, this pattern of per diem employment is generally considered less desirable than employment of full-time staff because the personnel working per diem shifts are either working extended hours or are newcomers to the particular hospital setting and do not provide continuity of care.

In addition, HHC in 1988 granted salary increases for nurses much greater than those of other HHC and other municipal workers. Other measures (offering scholarships and improved benefits, for example) have been taken to attract nurses to HHC. However, the combination of reduced regular nurse staffing and greater reliance on per diem staff in the period examined suggests that in this aspect of quality there were not clear improvements.

No other data relating to the quality of medical inpatient care are maintained and publicly reported by HHC, despite earlier, repeated recommendations by outside organizations to do so. The only other available evidence relating to quality is provided by outside monitors and is typically "one shot" in character rather than consistent trend data. These limited data, such as the federal Health Care Financing Administration's review of mortality at individual hospitals, suggest HHC's facilities performed below national standards in 1987, but the interpretation of these data is problematic.[7] It is not possible to determine whether the situation became better or worse over time.

In sum, HHC's performance in delivering medical inpatient care is mixed or, perhaps more aptly, cloudy. Between 1983 and 1987 the services were delivered more efficiently in the sense that real unit costs fell significantly. This gain is attributable largely to the reduced average length of stay for patients admitted with conditions that on average have become more serious. Whether these patients received better-quality care, however, remains uncertain, although the limited available evidence suggests some of the cost savings reflect reduced standards as well as improved management.

Psychiatric Inpatient Care

Psychiatric inpatient care is provided at each of HHC's 11 acute care hospitals, with particularly large services at Bellevue and Kings County. In fiscal year 1988 these two facilities had 349 and 272 psychiatric beds, respectively, accounting for fully 44 percent of the corporation's total psychiatric inpatient capacity.

Resources allocated for inpatient psychiatric care increased 63 percent between 1983 and 1987. Adjusted for inflation, the increase was 38 percent.

The additional resources were not used to serve more patients. The number of patients treated on an inpatient basis for psychiatric conditions

Table 15.8 Cost and Volume of HHC Psychiatric Inpatient Services, Fiscal Years 1983–1988

Indicator	1983	1984	1985	1986	1987	1988	Percentage Change 1983–87
Current-dollar operating expenses (millions)	$105.5	$112.1	$152.0	$151.5	$171.5	NA	62.6%
Constant-dollar operating expenses (millions)[a]	$123.9	$126.1	$163.8	$157.2	$171.5	NA	38.4
Patients treated (discharges)	18,941	19,002	19,269	18,881	18,603	18,658	(1.8)
Days of care	392,912	405,690	421,675	439,991	476,832	505,393	21.4
Average length of stay (days)	20.7	21.3	21.9	23.3	25.6	27.1	23.6
Patients admitted from emergency room (percent of total)	88.6%	88.5%	88.3%	88.9%	88.5%	91.2	(0.1)
Constant-dollar cost							
Per discharge	$6,542	$6,638	$8,501	$8,358	$9,219	NA	40.9
Per day	$315	$311	$388	$359	$360	NA	14.0
Beds	1,166	1,206	1,306	1,361	1,361	1,423	16.7
Average percentage of beds occupied	92.3%	92.2%	88.5%	88.6%	96.0%	97.3%	—
Full-time equivalent professional staff	NA	268	410	374	300	288	11.9[b]
Psychiatrists	NA	181	233	247	198	202	9.5[b]
Psychologists	NA	59	75	70	67	63	13.5[b]
Social workers	NA	28	102	57	35	23	23.9[b]
Ratio: FTE professional/patient[c]	NA	0.242	0.355	0.310	0.229	0.208	(5.1)[b]
Patients transferred to state mental hospitals (percent of total discharges)	11.7%	9.7%	8.6%	5.5%	6.5%	6.8%	—

Sources: Authors' calculations based on data provided by the Office of the Vice President for Finance, New York City Health and Hospitals Corporation. Conversion to constant dollars based on U.S. Department of Labor, Bureau of Labor Statistics, Middle Atlantic Regional Office, "Consumer Price Index for All Urban Consumers (CPI-U) for the New York–Northeastern New Jersey Area" (fiscal-year average).

Note: NA, not available.

[a]Constant dollars are fiscal year 1987 dollars.

[b]Figure is for 1984–1987.

[c]FTE professional staff divided by average daily census.

was relatively stable throughout this period with a modest net decline of under 2 percent between 1983 and 1987. Thus, the average constant-dollar cost per psychiatric discharge rose 41 percent from about $6,500 in 1983 to $9,200 in 1987. (See Table 15.8.)

The substantial rise in costs can be divided among two components, longer lengths of stay and higher costs per day. Both cost pressures result from apparent inefficiencies, but the source of the problem is different in each case.

The average length of stay for psychiatric patients increased steadily from 20.7 days in 1983 to 25.6 in 1987 and 27.1 in 1988. The cause of this increased length of stay is not readily apparent. There has not been any dramatic shift in the nature of psychiatric treatment that would require the longer stays. However, there is limited evidence that HHC's psychiatric inpatients are suffering more severe problems. For example, the share of patients admitted from the emergency room was virtually stable from 1983 through 1987 but rose slightly in 1988. In addition, the share of psychiatric patients with drug addictions as well as a basic psychiatric problem rose from 39 to 47 percent from 1985 to 1987.

Probably more significant than the modest changes in patient characteristics is the increasing shortage of alternative forms of treatment and alternative housing arrangements for those admitted. Patients remain in the hospital longer primarily because there is no place else for them to go. One sign of this is the decline in the share of HHC patients transferred to state mental facilities from about 12 percent in 1983 to under 7 percent in 1987 and 1988.

At an average cost of about $360 per day, municipal hospitals are an inefficient place to maintain the mentally ill, but neither HHC nor other state and local agencies are developing viable options. Since outpatient treatment assumes alternative living arrangements, this is obviously a vital component outside HHC's control. Thus one important source of inefficiency in HHC's psychiatric inpatient services is largely outside its control and related to failure by other agencies to develop alternative forms of care.

However, the 14 percent rise in the constant-dollar cost per day for psychiatric inpatient care is more directly related to HHC management policies. Arguably, with patients remaining in the hospital longer, the average daily cost should fall because the earliest days in which most diagnostic work is completed are the most costly. The rise in daily costs does not seem related to any substantial improvement in the quality of care provided. As with medical inpatient care, the psychiatric inpatient care lacks any meaningful monitoring of service quality. However, available data on professional staff relative to workload suggest declines in quality. The amount of treatment or therapeutic time per patient is typically related to the availability of staff who provide such services, specifically psychiatrists, psychologists, and social workers. However, the number of such personnel relative to the average daily number of patients actually fell from 1984 to 1988 with declines since 1985. (No data are available for 1983.) On an average day in 1985 there were nearly 3.6 such staff for every 10 patients compared to just 2.1 in 1988.

Long-Term Care

The HHC operates five independent long-term-care facilities and a nursing home unit within its Elmhurst Medical Center. All the facilities except one are classified as skilled nursing facilities, meaning they have nursing services available on-site at all times; the Neponsit Home is classified as a health-related facility, meaning its patients do not have such intensive nursing services available.

The 22 percent expansion in constant-dollar expenditures for long-term care is partly explained by an expansion of services and partly related to apparent inefficiencies. The expansion in service is due primarily to the acquisition by HHC of the Neponsit Home from the Human Resources Administration (HRA) in fiscal year 1986. The HHC's number of long-term-care beds rose notably that year and increased about 10 percent over the 1983–1987 period. (See Table 15.9.) With high and steady occupancy rates in the 95 percent range, the greater bed capacity has meant more services. The days of care provided rose about 8 percent over the 1983–1987 period.

But the 8 percent increase in service volume does not fully explain the 22 percent increase in real spending. The difference is a 13 percent increase in the average daily cost of long-term care; by 1987 the daily cost at municipal facilities was $196. The substantial increase in daily costs does not appear to be related to a shift toward patients requiring more intensive services. A sophisticated measure of patients' needs was initiated only recently; the available evidence over the longer period points to a decrease in average needs. Specifically, the acquisition of a health-related facility as the principal means of expanding services has lowered the average intensity of services because previously all care was in skilled nursing facilities.

It is conceivable that the higher unit costs for patients with somewhat less intensive needs has resulted in higher-quality care. Limited evidence points to some improvements. Since 1986 periodic inspections of HHC's long-term-care facilities by the State Health Department have uncovered a decreasing number of deficiencies. For four facilities (Goldwater, Coler, Gouverneur, and Seaview) the total number of deficiencies fell from 65 in 1986 to no deficiencies in 1988. In the other two facilities (Elmhurst and Neponsit) the number of deficiencies increased from 1986 to 1987 and data were not made available for 1988. Other than these minimal standards monitored by the state, HHC has no data to reflect quality of long-term care. The interpretation that the rising unit costs are related to reduced efficiency is supported by comparable data for other long-term-care facilities in New York City. The New York State Health Department reports that other nursing homes in New York City had average costs of approximately $116 per day, well below HHC's figure.

In sum, HHC has expanded its long-term-care services, a desirable outcome in a city with serious shortages of nursing home beds. But the resources used to achieve the modest service expansion are far greater than the added volume justifies. Much of the added money appears to be underwriting increasingly inefficient services rather than more or higher-quality services.

Table 15.9 Cost and Volume of HHC Long-Term-Care Services, Fiscal Years 1983–1988

Indicator	1983	1984	1985	1986	1987	1988	Percentage Change 1983–87
Current-dollar operating expenses (millions)	$129.4	$154.0	$159.0	$174.0	$185.0	NA	43.0%
Constant-dollar operating expenses (millions)[a]	$152.0	$173.3	$171.4	$181.2	$185.0	NA	21.7
Annual days of care	876,227	884,895	876,883	946,345	944,833	940,826	7.8
Percentage of days in health-related facilities	0.0	0.0	0.0	7.7	8.8	8.9	—
Constant-dollar cost per day	$173	$196	$195	$192	$196	NA	12.9
Beds	2,493	2,529	2,529	2,760	2,754	2,702	10.5
Average percentage of beds occupied	96.3%	95.9%	95.0%	93.9%	94.0%	95.4%	—

Sources: See Tables 15.5 and 15.8.

Note: NA, not available.

[a]Constant dollars are fiscal year 1987 dollars.

Ambulatory Care

The HHC's ambulatory care services are provided through outpatient departments and emergency rooms at each of the 11 acute care hospitals, at one nursing home (Gouverneur), and at a network of freestanding clinics with referral arrangements with the hospitals. The bulk of the services are classified as either outpatient department or emergency room visits; the remainder are a composite of specialized services including ambulatory surgery, renal dialysis, and methadone maintenance treatment. (See Table 15.10.)

The HHC's large volume of ambulatory care earns it the reputation of "family doctor" to the poor. Those using the emergency rooms and outpatient departments are primarily low-income families seeking care for relatively routine medical problems. There is a historic pattern of inappropriate use of emergency rooms, with patients using these facilities for "walk-in" care for nontraumatic conditions rather than setting up appointments in advance at the outpatient departments. The outpatient departments, however, are viewed by many patients as unsuitable because of long delays and waits for appointments, a specialty orientation that requires visits to separate doctors at separate departments for different conditions, and frequent rotation of staff (primarily residents), which leads to a different physician providing care for the same condition at each visit.

In order to improve its performance as family doctor HHC launched an Ambulatory Care Initiative early in fiscal year 1983. The policy called for reorganization of outpatient departments so that patients would be assigned to a primary care practitioner (pediatrician, gynecologist, or internist) who would be responsible for coordinating their care. In addition, appointment systems were to be improved to reduce the delay in setting up appointments and the waiting time for appointments. The expected results included a shift of nontraumatic care from emergency room visits to outpatient department visits, a greater proportion of care provided by the primary care physicians rather than in specialty clinics, and greater continuity of care for the patients.

The HHC phased in the policy at all its high-volume clinics. No systematic evaluation of the program has been conducted, but new data collection efforts were established for the reorganized clinics with new performance measures. These measures include the percentage of visits to the same physician for patients with multiple visits, the percentage of two-year-old children enrolled in clinics who receive all their immunizations on schedule, waiting time for first appointment, and appointment waiting time on the day of the visit.

The available data suggest three generalizations about the ambulatory care initiative. First, the resource allocation decisions do not seem well coordinated with the policy. The policy suggests that ambulatory care would receive a high priority. This has been the case, with real resources increased about 40 percent. But within ambulatory care the outpatient departments should have been favored over the emergency room and specialized services. This is not the case. The emergency room allocation grew slightly more rapidly than the outpatient department allocation; since emergency room visits fell more

Table 15.10 Cost and Volume of HHC Ambulatory Care Services, Fiscal Years 1983–1988

Indicator	1983	1984	1985	1986	1987	1988	Percentage Change 1983–87
Current-dollar expenditures (millions)	$365.5	$428.0	$462.0	$528.0	$602.0	NA	64.7%
Constant-dollar expenditures (millions)[a]	$429.3	$481.6	$497.9	$550.0	$602.0	NA	40.2
Emergency room	102.7	114.8	114.2	121.9	139.0	NA	35.4
Outpatient clinics	307.4	342.0	353.5	383.3	414.0	NA	34.7
Selected specialties[b]	19.3	24.8	30.2	44.8	49.0	NA	154.4
Emergency room visits	1,307,386	1,266,444	1,287,821	1,253,506	1,204,029	1,226,628	(7.9)
Outpatient clinic visits[c]	3,636,643	3,598,748	3,601,163	3,631,942	3,598,607	3,511,495	(1.0)
Constant-dollar cost per emergency room visit	$79	$91	$89	$97	$115	NA	47.0
Constant-dollar cost per outpatient clinic visit	$85	$98	$98	$106	$115	NA	36.1
Indicators for selected outpatient clinics[d]							
Delay for nonurgent appointments (days)	NA	NA	NA	13.3	13.2	13.6	NA
Appointment waiting time (minutes)	NA	NA	NA	55.0	47.5	47.3	NA
Outpatient waiting time (minutes)	NA	NA	NA	78.0	70.3	71.1	NA
Percentage of patients with visits to the same provider	NA	NA	NA	84.0%	91.7%	92.6%	NA
Percentage of children immunized on schedule	NA	NA	NA	86.0%	91.7%	92.3%	NA

Sources: Indicators for selected outpatient clinics are from City of New York, Mayor's Management Report, September 1987 and 1988 editions; all other figures, see Table 15.8.

Note: NA, not available.

[a] Constant dollars are fiscal year 1987 dollars.
[b] Includes ambulatory surgery, renal treatment, methadone maintenance, psychiatric day care, home care, and WIC.
[c] Excludes services listed above in note b.
[d] Figures refer only to reorganized clinics reporting information; the number of clinics and visits covered by these indicators is not specified by HHC or the Mayor's Office of Operations.

rapidly than other visits, the real resources per visit in the emergency room were enhanced more than those in the outpatient departments. Whereas in 1983 expenses per outpatient department visit exceeded those for emergency room visits by about 10 percent, by 1987 the two were nearly identical. This seems inconsistent with a policy designed to shift utilization to the outpatient departments.

Second, although there has been some relative shift in utilization to outpatient departments, this seems unrelated to changes or actions established by HHC policies. There was a steady decline in emergency room visits during the 1983–1987 period, but it is not clear this was due to a shift to outpatient department utilization. The outpatient department visits fluctuated during this period with a net decline of 1 percent. In 1988 outpatient visits fell another 2.6 percent while emergency room visits rose slightly. Overall, the broad trends in use of municipal ambulatory care facilities seem unrelated to the specific changes associated with the Ambulatory Care Initiative, and more analysis is required to determine the impact of the program.

The lack of patient incentives to make and keep appointments even under the new system is suggested by the data on waiting time. A patient who walks into a clinic to seek care was required to wait an average of 71 minutes in fiscal year 1988. A patient calling to make an appointment would have to wait an average of nearly two weeks (13.6 days) for the appointment and on the day of the appointment would wait 47 minutes after the time of the appointment. While part of the delay (in days) in obtaining an appointment is related to the effort to enhance continuity in the doctor–patient relationship, the difference in waiting time (47 versus 71 minutes) may not be a sufficient incentive to shift visits to the new appointment system.

Third, HHC has no data to indicate if the reorganized (and more expensive) clinics are serving patients better. The limited quality of care indicators are available only for the reorganized clinics after they are reorganized, so no before-and-after comparisons are possible. The data suggest that in recent years these reorganized clinics are doing better. There is more continuity of care in the sense that a greater portion of patients with multiple visits see the same practitioner, and more children are reported to be immunized on schedule. However, it should be stressed that the indicators relate only to patients served in the reorganized clinics, and no data are made available to indicate whether a greater or lesser number and proportion of HHC patients are served in those clinics versus the remaining specialty clinics. That is, there is no reported denominator for these percentage measures, so it is impossible to know the extent to which the reorganized clinics are serving the population dependent on HHC facilities.

In sum, HHC took steps to do a better job of delivering ambulatory care and devoted considerable new resources to the task. But the resources were not well targeted, and there is no systematic evidence to determine if better care resulted. The average real cost of both emergency room and outpatient department visits increased more than one-third, but little is known about what these added funds bought.

Ambulance Services

The EMS operates ambulances that primarily respond to telephone requests. The ambulances are stationed at municipal and voluntary hospitals as well as off-site; they bring patients to the nearest hospital that has space for the patient. Calls are screened over the telephone so that ambulances are dispatched in response only to calls that appear to require emergency medical assistance.

The constant-dollar resources allocated to EMS increased 17 percent during the 1983–1987 period. (See Table 15.11.) Available data on personnel indicate a significant expansion in 1985 and again in 1988. However, the number of ambulances owned by the EMS actually fell in 1984 and 1985, was increased in 1986, but then decreased again in 1987. In 1988 a substantial number of new ambulances were added, bringing the fleet size from 176 in 1983 to 209 in 1988.

Although the number of ambulances did not rise steadily, the growing number of personnel and other resources yielded a greater service capacity because the available ambulances were operated more intensely. The average number of tours increased 15 percent from 1983 to 1987 and increased another 35 percent in 1988. Whereas in 1983, on average, about 107 ambulances were being operated at any given time, the figure was about 120 in 1987 and jumped to about 163 in 1988. (The total number of tours shown in Table 15.11 is divided by 3 to yield the average number of ambulances available at a given time during the day.)

The demand for ambulance services grew more steadily and rapidly than EMS capacity during the 1983–1987 period. While the number of completed tours rose 16 percent, the number of calls to EMS rose nearly 22 percent and the number of ambulance responses rose 21 percent. As a result the average EMS crew responded to 5.6 emergencies per tour in 1987 compared to 5.4 in 1983. However, in fiscal year 1988 this disparity was reversed and the number of tours rose 35 percent while the number of runs increased only 5 percent. Thus, the number of responses per tour fell to a low of 4.4 in 1988.

The quality of EMS services is best gauged by the speed with which ambulances respond to emergencies. During the 1983–1986 period, this measure greatly improved as average response time dropped by nearly 3 minutes and response time for the most important calls dropped by 2 minutes to about 9 minutes. These gains in quality were accompanied by gains in efficiency as the runs per tour increased and the constant-dollar cost per run fell.

However, in 1987, the quality and efficiency of service fell. For 1988 EMS changed the way in which it monitors response time as well as the way in which it classifies ambulance runs. Consequently, it is not possible to know from available statistics whether quality improved in the most recent year. However, highly publicized delays in responses during the summer of 1988 indicate the management of this service deteriorated during fiscal year 1988. With significantly expanded capacity the agency provided seemingly worse service.

Improved management of EMS should have multiple goals. Not only

Table 15.11 Cost and Volume of Emergency Medical Services, Fiscal Years 1983–1988

Indicator	1983	1984	1985	1986	1987	1988	Percentage Change 1983–87
Current-dollar operating expenses (millions)	$57.6	$67.0	$68.0	$72.0	$79.0	NA	37.2%
Constant-dollar operating expenses (millions)[a]	$67.7	$75.4	$73.3	$75.0	$79.0	NA	16.8
Employees	NA	1,884	1,924	1,920	1,929	2,447	2.4[b]
Ambulances	176	163	154	181	163	209[c]	(7.2)
Average daily tours completed	313	352	366	361	362	490[c]	15.5
Number of calls	710,509	735,479	799,264	837,363	864,000	455,885[c]	21.6
Number of runs	612,508	634,034	689,021	720,672	742,085	782,033	21.2
Runs per tour	5.4	4.9	5.2	5.5	5.6	4.4	3.7
Average response time (minutes)							
All runs	13.3	11.7	9.7	10.6	13.9	NA	4.7
Priority 1 runs	11.7	10.4	9.4	9.1	11.2	NA	(4.4)
Constant-dollar cost per run	$109	$117	$105	$104	$109	NA	(0.1)

Sources: Operating expenditures provided by the Office of the Vice President for Finance, New York City Health and Hospitals Corporation; employees data provided by the Office of Budget Reports and Supporting Services; all other figures are from City of New York, *Mayor's Management Report*, September 1983–1988 editions. See Table 15.8.

Note: NA, not available.

[a]Constant dollars are fiscal year 1987 dollars.

[b]Figure is for 1984–1987.

[c]Figures are for period January–July 1988.

should capacity be better used in the sense that more vehicles should be available for service, but greater effort should be made to educate citizens in order to better control demand and inappropriate use of services. For example, in fiscal year 1987, only about half the calls required a "priority 1" response, indicating there was a life-threatening situation. Fully 120,000 calls—or about one of every seven—did not require an ambulance response and the remaining calls were less threatening situations in which alternative responses or actions by citizens might have been more efficient or effective. The recent declines in service suggest that the way in which EMS is being used by citizens as well as the way in which it is being managed by HHC requires examination and monitoring.

Access to Care

An assessment of the role of HHC in the city's health care system should consider the institution's mission to provide care for all regardless of income. How well does HHC serve this function?

Within New York City there is generally equal access to some form of care for both poor and nonpoor residents. Survey data suggest that about an equal share of poor and nonpoor adults see a physician at least once during the year (78 percent versus 79 percent).[8] Some 13 percent of poor adults and 6 percent of poor children are hospitalized compared to only 9 percent of nonpoor adults and 4 percent of nonpoor children. This differential in hospitalization rate does not take into account differences in health status, but it suggests relatively good access for the poor. Troubling, though, is the fact that substantially fewer poor children see a doctor each year than is true for nonpoor children (81 percent versus 91 percent), but in both cases the proportion is relatively high.

The HHC plays a major role in ensuring a high degree of access to medical care for poor residents. It devotes the overwhelming share of its resources to those with Medicaid coverage and those medically indigent with no insurance coverage (frequently dubbed "self-pay" or, more accurately, "no pay" patients). These patients comprise over 68 percent of all HHC inpatient discharges, nearly 80 percent of the corporation's outpatient department visits, and 82 percent of its emergency room visits.[9]

The strong role of public hospitals in guaranteeing access to care for the indigent, particularly the uninsured lacking Medicaid coverage, was evident in an analysis of public hospitals nationwide.[10] Among 99 of the 100 largest cities in the United States, fully 48 had at least one local public hospital. Another 22 cities had a state, rather than local, public hospital, typically a hospital operated by a state university system in conjunction with its medical school. Finally, another 29 cities had no public general care hospital.

The volume of care delivered to the uninsured poor population differed among the types of communities. Cities with state and local public hospitals provided a higher average volume of uncompensated care per uninsured poor person than cities without any public hospital. Specifically, the three types of city with some form of public hospital provided between 31 and 34 uncompensated adjusted admissions per 100 uninsured poor people; in contrast, the figure for cities with no public hospital was only 24. Another way to express these differences is to estimate for an average-sized city among the 100 largest how many additional adjusted admissions are provided in cities with a public hospital. These calculations indicate that the presence of a public hospital increases the number of uncompensated adjusted admissions by over 4,000 annually.

The presence of a public hospital not only increases the volume of care provided to the uninsured poor; it also reduces the uncompensated care burden for private hospitals. Uncompensated care averages 5.9 percent of all hospital charges in cities with no public hospital and 6.5 percent in cities with some type of public hospital. However, in cities with no public hospital, all this financial burden was borne by private hospitals. In contrast, cities with a public hospital provided more uncompensated care in total with less financial burden on private hospitals. In these cities private hospitals had uncompensated care equal to just 4.4 percent of charges while the public hospitals' much higher proportion raised the citywide average to 6.5 percent.

Yet substantial variation across cities in underlying demand and supply characteristics could make the results implied by this bivariate analysis statistically insignificant and misleading. To account for these differences across cities and to isolate the impact of a public hospital on access requires a more sophisticated approach. Accordingly, a multiple regression model was developed using variables relating to the characteristics of the city's population (age and minority status) and its health care system (bed supply and teaching activity). Controlling for the relevant factors did not eliminate the significance of the presence of a public hospital in a city.

These findings have clear implications for public hospitals. Those cities currently operating public hospitals cannot safely assume that closing these facilities will not have adverse impacts on the area's poor, uninsured residents. Care for this group will not automatically be provided by local private hospitals when the public facility is closed. The local tax funds allocated to support a public hospital are likely to buy some additional care for the poor and not merely offset philanthropic or other revenue sources available to private institutions.

However, readers should recognize that access to care is not the only, or even the highest priority pursued by public officials. The findings summarized here do not speak adequately to the quality of care in HHC hospitals and suggest HHC hospitals have in some respects become less efficient. The unambiguous findings regarding the favorable impact of HHC on access to care among the uninsured poor should be weighed against the less favorable evidence relating to efficiency and quality. HHC hospitals, like all health care providers, should not only serve a social mission, but they should do so efficiently and with qualitative distinction.

Next Steps for Reform

The HHC serves an important mission, but it does so at a high price. Reforms should be designed to maintain the organization's capacity to serve the poor while permitting greater efficiencies. The greatest opportunity for such change is to modify the current affiliation policy.

The general policy of securing medical staff through contracts with affiliated teaching institutions adds to HHC costs, through both direct supervision charges and indirect costs resulting from additional tests, more extensive diagnostic procedures, and more intensive treatment for the sickest patients. While expensive, the affiliation arrangements are generally recognized as having contributed significantly to improved quality of care at municipal facilities. At the time the affiliation contracts were initiated, physicians were in short supply; the contracts have helped ensure adequate physician supply at municipal facilities, as the figures on physician staff levels cited earlier indicate.

However, the contribution of the affiliation arrangements to quality care varies widely among municipal facilities. Not all affiliates are attractive to physicians, particularly graduates of U.S. medical schools. The variation in the share of U.S. medical graduates filling available positions is related to the performance of the voluntary affiliate. Most of the institutions with "close" affiliation relationships are relatively successful in attracting U.S. medical graduates to their municipal affiliates: New York University's performance at Bellevue, Montefiore's at North Central Bronx, and Einstein's at Bronx Municipal are examples. In contrast, those institutions with weaker ties to their municipal affiliates are less able to secure U.S. medical graduates for the municipal facility: Columbia's performance at Harlem and Mt. Sinai's performance at Elmhurst are illustrative. There are exceptions to the rule (notably Downstate and Kings County), but in general affiliation relationships that produce the best quality care for the municipal facilities are those where the two institutions are well integrated.

Affiliation contracts benefit physician care in the municipal hospitals, but they divide operational authority within the municipal system and thus weaken hospital management. Until recently affiliation contracts were negotiated and monitored almost exclusively by HHC's central office. Recently, greater responsibility was shifted to the hospital directors. However, the affiliates often do not feel directly accountable to the institution they are hired to serve; instead, they look to central office leadership to resolve problems at the hospitals. A further complication is that some affiliation contracts cover nonphysicians, who are represented by a different union than the one representing municipal hospital employees. Thus, voluntary hospital employees may work in municipal facilities for supervisors located elsewhere and side by side with municipal hospital employees who are represented by a different union and working under different collective bargaining contracts. This situation limits municipal hospitals managers' authority and complicates labor–management relations.

Another set of problems with the affiliation relationships involves the fit between the programmatic needs of the teaching institutions and those of the municipal hospitals. The principal mission of the municipal hospitals is to provide services to the city's indigent population. Although the poor—like everyone else—are occasionally afflicted by unusual or very critical diseases, the bulk of their medical needs—like everyone else—are for primary medical care, often best provided on an outpatient basis, and relatively routine inpatient procedures. The research and teaching mission of the affiliates, however, causes them to place high priority on specialized care utilizing complex procedures. The adverse consequences include use of scarce resources for expensive specialized equipment, maintenance of a relatively large number of residencies at municipal hospitals in medical specialties other than primary care, and organization of outpatient services into highly specialized clinics rather than more comprehensive arrangements that would simplify care of patients with multiple illnesses. Teaching and research concerns dominate because HHC has no alternative source of physician supply and, therefore, limited bargaining power over the affiliates.

A number of developments suggest that alternatives to the affiliation arrangements may be both feasible and desirable. First, the growing numbers of physicians nationally and locally have made it easier for all types of institutions to recruit medical staff. In most specialties it no longer is difficult to recruit well-qualified young physicians at reasonable levels of compensation. Second, the possibility of future state regulation of graduate medical education would mean reduced numbers of residencies and greater proportions of residencies in primary care specialties.[11] The reduced numbers of residencies and accompanying restrictions on recruitment of foreign medical graduates may make some residency programs in some of the municipal hospitals no longer viable. This could effectively eliminate the possibility of teaching affiliations for those hospitals without current high-quality residency programs. On the other hand, the greater emphasis on primary care specialties within the network of graduate medical education programs will make the municipal hospitals desirable sites for such residencies. Because the HHC's service mission is strongly weighted toward provision of primary care to the indigent, municipal facilities have a large population suited to primary care residencies. Thus the proposed types of regulation may make at least some parts of the municipal system even more attractive as locations for residencies.

The overall outlook with respect to medical staffing policy is a potential for both reduced costs and increased quality by reconsidering current arrangements. The HHC leadership should be in a better position to secure lower-cost medical care services without maintaining large, expensive, highly specialized teaching programs that are not well suited to the primary care mission of the municipal hospitals.

Notes

Chapter 1

1. Wallace S. Sayre and Herbert Kaufman, *Governing New York City: Politics in the Metropolis* (New York: Russell Sage Foundation, 1960). (A paperback edition with a new introduction was published by W. W. Norton and Company in 1965. All citations refer to the 1965 edition.)

2. Ibid., pp. 709–710.

3. Ibid., pp. 720–721.

4. Ibid., p. 738.

5. Ibid., p. 20.

6. For an examination of these and other demographic trends in New York City and New York State see Katherine Trent and Richard Alba, "Population," in Gerald Benjamin and Charles Brecher, eds., *The Two New Yorks: State and City in a Changing Federal System* (New York: Russell Sage Foundation, 1988), pp. 81–106.

7. The figures are unpublished data from the Immigration and Naturalization Service presented in Emanuel Tobier, "The New Immigration in the New York Metropolitan Region: Characteristics and Consequences," Report to the Port Authority of New York and New Jersey, 1987.

8. David Rogers, *110 Livingston Street* (New York: Random House, 1969), and Marilyn Gittell, *Participants and Participation* (New York: Praeger, 1967).

9. Edward Rogowsky, Louis Gold, and David Abbott, "Police: The Civilian Review Board Controversy," in Jewell Bellush and Stephen David, eds., *Race and Politics in New York City* (New York: Praeger, 1971), pp. 59–97.

10. For examples, see John H. Mollenkopf, *The Contested City* (Princeton, NJ: Princeton University Press, 1983); Paul Peterson, *City Limits* (Chicago: University of Chicago Press, 1981); and Clarence Stone and Heywood Sanders, eds., *The Politics of Urban Development* (Lawrence: University Press of Kansas, 1987).

11. Jack Newfield and Paul DuBrul, *The Abuse of Power* (New York: Viking Press, 1977); Norman Fainstein and Susan Fainstein, "Governing Regimes and the Political Economy of Development in New York 1946–1984," in John Mollenkopf, ed., *Power, Culture, and Place* (New York: Russell Sage Foundation, 1988), pp. 177–182.

12. Martin Shefter, *Political Crisis/Fiscal Crisis* (New York: Basic Books, 1985).

13. An earlier version of this chapter was presented at the 1990 Annual Meeting of the American Political Science Association: Charles Brecher and Raymond D. Horton, "Political Change in New York City, 1961–89."

14. This chapter is a modified version of Robert A. Cropf, "What Were the Benefits of Public Financing of Municipal Campaigns?" *CBC Quarterly,* Volume 10, Number 2 (Spring 1990), pp. 1–14.

15. This chapter is based on material prepared by Patricia Fry as a consultant to the Citizens Budget Commission. Earlier versions appeared as Patricia Fry, *Improving the Operating Budget Process of the City of New York* (New York: Citizens Budget Commission, May 1987), and Patricia Fry, "The City's Budget Process: Good, But Not Good Enough," *CBC Quarterly,* Volume 7, Number 2 (Spring 1987), pp. 1–9.

16. This chapter is adapted from Raymond D. Horton, "Collective Bargaining and Budgeting in New York City," *CBC Quarterly,* Volume 5, Number 2 (Spring 1985), pp. 1–6.

17. This chapter is based on material presented in Charles Brecher and Robert Cropf, *Implementing Capital Projects* (New York: Citizens Budget Commission, May 1988), and Charles Brecher and Robert Cropf, *Toward Greater Accountability for the Implementation of Capital Projects* (New York: Citizens Budget Commission, November 1989).

18. This chapter draws on Raymond D. Horton, *Municipal Tax Policy in New York City: Opportunities for Reform* (New York: Citizens Budget Commission, June 1986).

19. This chapter is based on Dean Michael Mead, "Property Taxes in New York City: The Promotion of Inequality," *CBC Quarterly,* Volume 9, Numbers 3 and 4 (1989), pp. 1–6.

20. This chapter appeared previously as Raymond D. Horton, "Expenditures and Services," in Charles Brecher and Raymond D. Horton, eds., *Setting Municipal Priorities, 1988* (New York: New York University Press, 1988), pp. 105–130.

21. This chapter is a modified version of Charles Brecher and Dean Michael Mead, *Toward a Responsible Municipal Wage Policy: Guidelines for the 1990 Round of Bargaining* (New York: Citizens Budget Commission, July 1990).

22. This chapter is a modified version of Raymond D. Horton and Elisabeth Hultcrantz, *The State of the Uniformed Services: Recommendations for Improved Performance* (New York: Citizens Budget Commission, January 1990).

23. This chapter is a modified version of Charles Brecher and Dean Michael Mead, *Managing the Department of Parks and Recreation in a Period of Fiscal Stress* (New York: Citizens Budget Commission, March 1991).

24. This chapter draws on Charles Brecher, Kenneth E. Thorpe, and Cynthia Green, "New York City Health and Hospitals Corporation," and Kenneth E. Thorpe and Charles Brecher, "Comparative Analysis of Efficiency and Access," in Stuart H. Altman, Charles Brecher, Mary Henderson, and Kenneth Thorpe, eds., *Competition and Compassion: Conflicting Roles for Public Hospitals* (Ann Arbor, MI: Health Administration Press, 1989), pp. 45–92, 175–200; Charles Brecher and Stuart Altman, "City Hospitals: What—Not Who—Needs to Be Changed?" *CBC Quarterly,* Volume 6, Number 4 (Fall 1986), pp. 1–11; Charles Brecher, "Health," in Brecher and Horton, *Setting Municipal Priorities, 1988,* pp. 220–248; Kenneth Thorpe, "Health

Care," in Charles Brecher and Raymond D. Horton, eds., *Setting Municipal Priorities, 1990* (New York: New York University Press, 1989), pp. 339–361; and Charles Brecher and Elisabeth Hultcrantz, *The State of Municipal Services: Hospital and Social Services Between 1983 and 1988* (New York: Citizens Budget Commission, February 1989).

Chapter 2

1. The "stakes and prizes" approach is used in Wallace S. Sayre and Herbert Kaufman, *Governing New York City: Politics in the Metropolis* (New York: Russell Sage Foundation, 1960), pp. 39–66.

2. For a more complete discussion of these categories see Paul Peterson, *City Limits* (Chicago: University of Chicago Press, 1981), especially Chapter 3.

3. For an elaboration of these points see Robert Berne and Emanuel Tobier, "The Setting for School Policy," in Charles Brecher and Raymond D. Horton, eds., *Setting Municipal Priorities, 1988* (New York: New York University Press, 1987), pp. 131–162.

4. The data in Table 2.2 reflect total spending net of debt service. This is appropriate because the figures include capital spending financed through borrowing. Counting both debt service and capital spending could be interpreted as "double counting" for this analysis.

5. See Richard Musgrave and Peggy Musgrave, *Public Finance in Theory and Practice* (New York: McGraw-Hill, 1980), pp. 532–538.

6. An important development emerging in the 1960s was the Supreme Court's more rigorous application to state governments of the 14th Amendment, which prohibits state actions that deny individuals due process and equal protection of the law. Since cities are viewed legally as instruments of state government, the prohibition and related mandates were applied to local governments as well.

7. Charles H. Levine, Irene S. Rubin, and George C. Wolohojian, *The Politics of Retrenchment* (Beverly Hills, CA: Sage Publications, 1981).

8. Terry Nichols Clark and Lorna Crowley Ferguson, *City Money* (New York: Columbia University Press, 1983), especially Chapter 4.

9. Sayre and Kaufman, *Governing New York City*, p. 505.

10. For discussion, see Matthew Drennan, "Local Economy and Local Revenues," in Brecher and Horton, *Setting Municipal Priorities, 1988*, pp. 15–44.

11. The debt service item shown in Table 2.6 is less informative as a measure of the influence of municipal financiers than the borrowing item in Table 2.5. This is because debt service includes payment of principal and interest on debt sales in prior years, whereas borrowing reflects new activity during the period.

12. This figure is the combination of the labor cost item in Table 2.6 and the borrowing item in Table 2.5. The figures are not mutually exclusive, so the figure is a maximum. If the debt service item from Table 2.6 is used, the figure falls to 71 percent. For reasons indicated in Note 11, the debt service item is less meaningful.

13. Sayre and Kaufman, *Governing New York City*, p. 514.

Chapter 3

1. These charter reform procedures are required only for changes affecting the powers of elected officials. Amendments not altering these powers can be made by act of the city council. However, a referendum in November 1988 approved some changes that did not significantly alter the powers of elected officials. They incorporated in the

charter the local legislation establishing a public financing program for municipal elections, created a Conflicts of Interest Board, required many city agencies to maintain an inventory of assets, required special elections to fill certain vacancies, and made other changes.

2. Council members generally serve four-year terms. The 25 district members elected in 1961 thus served until 1965. The at-large members first elected in 1963 served two years until 1965, when they joined the district members in serving four-year terms.

3. Gerald Benjamin, "Full-Time Service and Earned Income Limitations for Council Members," Paper prepared for the New York City Charter Revision Commission (no date), pp. 11–12.

4. Urban Analysis Center, Graduate School and University Center, City University of New York, *The City Council of New York and the President of the City Council,* Report prepared for the State Charter Revision Commission for New York City (December 1973), p. 26.

5. Charles Brecher and James M. Hartman, "Financial Planning," in Charles Brecher and Raymond D. Horton, eds., *Setting Municipal Priorities: American Cities and the New York Experience* (New York: New York University Press, 1984), pp. 223–228.

6. See Frank J. Mauro and Gerald Benjamin, eds., *Restructuring the New York City Government: The Reemergence of Municipal Reform* (New York: Academy of Political Science, 1989), pp. 53–82.

7. City of New York, Department of General Services, *The Green Book 1990– 1991; The Official Directory of the City of New York,* pp. 243–248.

8. City of New York, *Adopted Budget Fiscal Year 1990,* pp. 310E–318E.

9. See Wallace S. Sayre and Herbert Kaufman, *Governing New York City: Politics in the Metropolis* (New York: W. W. Norton and Company, 1965), p. 619.

10. For a history of New York State primary election law changes see Howard A. Scarrow, *Parties, Elections and Representation in the State of New York* (New York: New York University Press, 1983), especially Chapter 2.

11. Gerald Benjamin, "Filling Vacancies in the Council and Borough Presidencies," Paper prepared for the New York City Charter Revision Commission (undated), p. 3.

12. Royce Crocker, *Voter Registration and Turnout: 1948–1988* (Washington, DC: Congressional Research Service, March 15, 1989), p. 11.

Chapter 4

1. Wallace S. Sayre and Herbert Kaufman, *Governing New York City: Politics in the Metropolis* (New York: W. W. Norton and Company, 1965), pp. 513–514.

2. Martin Shefter, *Political Crisis/Fiscal Crisis: The Collapse and Revival of New York City* (New York: Basic Books, 1985).

3. Sayre and Kaufman, *Governing New York City,* p. 514.

4. For a classic presentation see Edward C. Banfield and James Q. Wilson, *City Politics* (Cambridge, MA: Harvard University Press, 1963).

5. Robert L. Lineberry and Edward P. Fowler, "Reformism and Public Policy in American Cities," *American Political Science Review,* Volume 61 (September 1967), pp. 701–716.

6. Banfield and Wilson, *City Politics.*

7. See Nathan Glazer and Daniel Patrick Moynihan, *Beyond the Melting Pot* (Cambridge, MA: MIT Press, 1963).

8. See Michael Preston, Lenneal J. Henderson, Jr., and Paul L. Puryear, eds., *The New Black Politics: The Search for Political Power* (New York: Longman, 1987), and

Rufus P. Browning, Dale Rogers Marshall, and David H. Tabb, *Racial Politics in American Cities* (New York: Longman, 1990).

9. See Rufus P. Browning, Dale Rogers Marshall, and David H. Tabb, *Protest Is Not Enough* (Berkeley: University of California Press, 1984), and Paul Kleppner, *Chicago Divided: The Making of a Black Mayor* (DeKalb: Northern Illinois University Press, 1985).

10. Quoted in *The New York Times,* September 8, 1961.

11. John C. Walter, *The Harlem Fox: J. Raymond Jones and Tammany, 1920–1970* (Albany: State University of New York Press, 1989), p. 155.

12. Ibid., pp. 150–161.

13. Quoted in *The New York Times,* April 26, 1965.

14. See the statement by Buckley reported in *The New York Times,* June 25, 1965.

15. John V. Lindsay, *The City* (New York: New American Library, 1970), p. 20.

16. *The New York Times,* February 20, 1969.

17. Nathan Glazer and Daniel Patrick Moynihan, *Beyond the Melting Pot,* 2nd ed. (Cambridge, MA: MIT Press, 1970), p. xxvii.

18. After the disappointing performance of Procaccino in 1969, the Democratic party leadership secured state legislation requiring a runoff election if no candidate received at least 40 percent of the vote in the primary.

19. Data from Board of Election disclosure statements presented in Robert Franks, "The Need for Reform of New York State's Election Laws," masters thesis, New School for Social Research, October 1980.

20. Quoted in *The New York Times,* September 11, 1977. Additional information on Koch's strategy is presented in Edward I. Koch, *Mayor: An Autobiography* (New York: Simon and Schuster, 1984), pp. 29–44.

21. Quoted in *The New York Times,* September 12, 1977.

22. Koch's publicly stated reason for seeking both nominations was to strengthen his bargaining position on behalf of the city with Republicans controlling the state Senate and in the White House. See Koch, *Mayor,* pp. 303–304.

23. For each candidate's version of the campaign see Koch, *Mayor,* pp. 325–342 and Mario M. Cuomo, *Diaries of Mario M. Cuomo: The Campaign for Governor* (New York: Random House, 1984).

24. Figures were compiled from newspaper accounts and presented in "Reform of Campaign Finance: How Wide Is the Support?" *CBC Quarterly,* Volume 6, Number 1 (Winter 1986), p. 1.

25. Much of the following account of scandals draws upon Jack Newfield and Wayne Barrett, *City for Sale: Ed Koch and the Betrayal of New York* (New York: Harper and Row, 1988).

26. For a more complete and somewhat different treatment of this issue see Asher Arian, Arthur S. Goldberg, John H. Mollenkopf, and Edward T. Rogowski, *Changing New York City Politics* (New York: Routledge, 1991).

Chapter 5

1. *Buckley v. Valeo,* 424 U.S. 1 (1976).

2. Herbert E. Alexander, *Financing Politics: Money, Elections, and Political Reform* (Washington, DC: Congressional Quarterly Press, 1989), p. 60.

3. Elizabeth Drew, *Politics and Money* (New York: Macmillan, 1983), p. 9.

4. Figures for 1976, 1980, and 1984 elections are from Herbert E. Alexander, *Financing the 1976 Election* (Washington, DC: Congressional Quarterly Press, 1979); Herbert E. Alexander, *Financing the 1980 Election* (Lexington, MA: Lexington

Books, 1983); and Herbert E. Alexander and Brian A. Haggerty, *Financing the 1984 Election* (Lexington, MA: Lexington Books, 1987). The figure for 1988 is from a Federal Election Commission press release, August 25, 1989.

5. For example, see Philip M. Stern, *The Best Congress Money Can Buy* (New York: Pantheon Books, 1988). He describes a number of incidents involving so-called independent expenditures.

6. Figure for 1980 election is from Alexander, *Financing the 1980 Election*. The 1988 figure is from Alexander, "Financing the Presidential Elections, 1988," Paper presented at the International Political Science Association Roundtable, September 8–10, 1989.

7. From Alexander, "Financing the Presidential Elections, 1988."

8. Alexander and Haggerty, *Financing the 1984 Election*, p. 119.

9. Stern, *The Best Congress Money Can Buy*, p. 25.

10. Ibid., p. 24.

11. For a discussion of recent congressional scandals see Stern, *The Best Congress Money Can Buy*, and Brooks Jackson, *Honest Graft: Big Money and the American Political Process* (New York: Alfred A. Knopf, 1988).

12. Frank J. Sorauf, *Money in American Elections* (Glenview, IL: Scott, Foresman and Co., 1988), p. 262.

13. Ibid.

14. Data are from Table 13 in the Council of State Governments, *Campaign Finance, Ethics and Lobby Law Special Edition Blue Book, 1988–89* (Lexington, KY: Council of State Governments, 1988).

15. Ibid., Table 15.

16. Data for New Jersey are from New Jersey Election Law Enforcement Commission; data for Michigan are from Michigan Department of State.

17. City of Seattle, Office of Election Administration, "Office of Election Administration Report 1979–1987," June 1988, p. 13.

18. City of Tucson, Mayor and Council Memorandum, "Campaign Finance Administration Report, Public Matching Funds—Water Bill Check-Off," Attachment 6.

19. State of New York, Commission on Government Integrity, "Campaign Financing: Preliminary Report," December 21, 1987.

20. State of New York, Commission on Government Integrity, "Restoring the Public Trust: A Blueprint for Government Integrity," December 1988.

21. Steven Sanders, "Lets Purify New York's Campaign Financing," *The New York Times*, March 9, 1988, p. 27.

22. "Panel Urges Changes in Campaign Financing," *The New York Times*, February 13, 1990.

23. Figures in this paragraph are from State of New York, Commission on Government Integrity, "Unfinished Business: Campaign Finance Reform in New York City," September 28, 1988. These figures exclude refunded contributions which were included in earlier data reported by the press.

24. "Leichter Says Builders Gave Most to Members of Board of Estimate," *The New York Times*, November 27, 1985, II, p. 4.

25. Ibid.

26. Press release from State Senator Franz S. Leichter, February 25, 1988.

27. City of New York, *Comprehensive Annual Financial Report of the Comptroller for the Fiscal Year Ending June 30, 1990*, October 31, 1990.

28. State of New York, Commission on Government Integrity, "Unfinished Business," September 28, 1988.

29. Unpublished data from New York City Campaign Finance Board.

30. The total vote in the Democratic primary was 681,954 in 1985 and 1,060,909 in 1989. The total vote in the general election was 1,170,904 in 1985 and 1,782,709 in 1989. Data are as reported in the *The New York Times*. See Table 5.9 for sources.

31. New York City Campaign Finance Board, press release, March 27, 1990.

32. New York City Campaign Finance Board, "1991 City Council Primary Elections Summary," September 5, 1991.

Chapter 6

1. For an enumeration of the standards of the New York State Financial Emergency Act for the City of New York, see generally Sections 8.1 and 8.2 thereof.

2. See the *CBC Quarterly,* Volume 7, Number 1(Winter 1987), p. 15.

Chapter 7

1. For a review of the literature on the relative chilling effects of various impasse procedures on negotiated settlements, see Marion M. Extegt and James R. Cheluis, "The Behavioral Impact of Impasse Resolution Procedures," *Review of Public Personnel Administration,* Volume 5, Number 2 (Spring 1985), pp. 37–48.

2. The information in this paragraph is drawn from two primary sources, Government Employee Relations Report (GERR) and Commerce Clearing House reports. The states with long-established public sector bargaining laws that now employ final-offer arbitration include Connecticut, Michigan, Minnesota, and Ohio. Conventional arbitration remains in effect in states other than New York with long backgrounds in public sector bargaining, including Oregon, Pennsylvania, and Wisconsin. Some states utilize one system or the other depending on the kind of issues involved in impasse procedures. For example, Michigan employs final-offer arbitration for wage disputes but conventional arbitration on noneconomic disputes.

3. This timetable may be modified, if necessary.

4. DC 37's contract was 39 months in duration, and expired on September 30, 1990.

Chapter 8

1. David A. Grossman, "Debt and Capital Management," in Charles Brecher and Raymond D. Horton, eds., *Setting Municipal Priorities: American Cities and the New York Experience* (New York: New York University Press, 1984), p. 274.

2. The state law which established the SCA required the city to provide a $4.3 billion appropriation for the SCA in fiscal year 1990. However, as part of the conditions of the appropriation, expenditures cannot exceed $889,805,000 in fiscal year 1990, $1,570,080,000 in fiscal year 1991, $2,480,215,000 in fiscal year 1992, $3,390,410,000 in fiscal year 1993, and $4,300,575,000 in fiscal year 1994.

3. Edward I. Koch, "New Capital Project Tracking System," memorandum to agency heads dated July 19, 1989.

4. This section of the report deals only with line item projects. Information is not available to complete a similar analysis for continuing projects. With the demise of the Board of Estimate, the council is now the sole legislative body empowered to authorize capital projects.

5. Mayor's Private Sector Survey, *The New York City Service Crisis: A Management Response,* September 1989, pp. 35–46.

Chapter 9

1. A classic work on this subject is Temporary Commission on City Finances, *Better Financing for New York City* (New York: The Commission, 1966). The work of the commission led to a series of revenue measures enacted in 1966 that were designed to make local taxes more sensitive to changes in local economic activity. Increases in "income elasticity" sought by the commission resulted from changing the base of business taxation from gross receipts to net income, imposing a progressive income tax, and increasing stock transfer tax rates. For a discussion of these changes and a general review of municipal tax policy in the late 1960s, see Dick Netzer, "The Budget: Trends and Prospects," in Lyle C. Fitch and Annmarie Hauck Walsh, eds., *Agenda for a City: Issues Confronting New York* (Beverly Hills, CA: Sage Publications, 1970), pp. 651–714. A more recent effort to examine the system is City of New York, Tax Study Commission, *Final Report of the Tax Study Commission,* December 1989.

2. The taxpayer-consumer under this conception is viewed as a footloose "shopper" constantly looking for the governmental jurisdiction that offers the optimal location, i.e., the one that offers the best mix of local taxes (as low as possible) and local services (as rich as possible). For the classic exposition of this outlook, see Charles M. Tiebout, "A Pure Theory of Local Expenditures," *Journal of Political Economy,* Volume 64 (October 1956), pp. 416–424.

3. There is a substantial literature on this topic, though relatively few studies concern New York. For such a study that also contains references to the general literature, see Christopher Jones, "The Effect of the Corporate Sales and Property Taxes on Business Locational Decisions," prepared for the New York State Legislative Commission on the Modernization and Simplification of Tax Administration and the Tax Law, June 29, 1984. For a contrary conclusion emerging from a review of the same literature, see Michael Wasylenko, "Business Climate, Industry and Employment Growth: A Review of the Evidence," Syracuse University Metropolitan Studies Program, Occasional Paper No. 98 (October 1985).

4. Computed from data in U.S. Department of Commerce, Bureau of the Census, *Local Government Finances in Selected Metropolitan Areas, 1982–83* (Washington, DC: U.S. Government Printing Office, 1984).

5. For discussion, see Temporary Commission on City Finances, *The City in Transition: Prospects and Policies for New York* (New York: Arno Press, 1977), pp. 43–58.

6. Raymond D. Horton, "Human Resources," in Charles Brecher and Raymond D. Horton, eds., *Setting Municipal Priorities, 1986* (New York: New York University Press, 1985), pp. 173–175.

7. For analysis of the reasons for the local economy's recovery after 1977, see Matthew Drennan, "The Local Economy and Local Revenues," in Charles Brecher and Raymond D. Horton, eds., *Setting Municipal Priorities, 1983* (New York: New York University Press, 1982), pp. 15–45.

8. Charles Brecher and Raymond D. Horton, "Introduction," in *Setting Municipal Priorities, 1981* (Montclair, NJ: Allenheld Osmun, 1980), p. 2.

9. This characterization of general service improvements beginning in the early 1980s is supported by reports of the Citizens Budget Commission entitled *The State of Municipal Services,* published since 1981.

10. For a discussion of the criteria that is representative of the public finance literature, see Richard A. Musgrave and Peggy B. Musgrave, *Public Finance in Theory and Practice,* 4th ed. (New York: McGraw-Hill, 1984), pp. 219–266.

11. See Dick Netzer, "The Budget," p. 673; also see Advisory Commission on

Intergovernmental Relations, "Tax Burdens of Families Residing in the Largest City in Each State," Staff Working Paper 3R, August 1984.

12. Advisory Commission on Intergovernmental Relations.

13. Howard Chernick, "Taxes," in Charles Brecher and Raymond D. Horton, eds., *Setting Municipal Priorities, 1988* (New York: New York University Press, 1988), pp. 45–79.

14. For measures of the elasticity of various municipal taxes in New York City, see Matthew Drennan, "Local Economy and Local Revenues," in Charles Brecher and Raymond D. Horton, eds., *Setting Municipal Priorities, 1986* (New York: New York University Press, 1985), p. 39.

15. The data on assessment ratios and effective tax rates are from Charles Brecher and Herbert Ranschburg, "Time to Clean Up the New York City Property Tax Mess," *CBC Quarterly,* Volume 1, Number 2 (October 1981), pp. 1–5. They, in turn, relied on Graduate School of Public Administration, New York University, *Real Property Tax Policy for New York City,* December 31, 1980.

16. The subject of nonuniform assessment practices leading to intraclass inequity has been documented most completely by the New York Public Interest Research Group. See, most recently, Frank Domurad, Dan Kaplan, and Gene Russianoff, *City of Unequal Neighbors III: A Study of Three-Family Home Property Tax Assessments in New York City* (New York: New York Public Interest Research Center, 1983). Also see Frank Domurad, Dan Kaplan, and Gene Russianoff, *City of Unequal Neighbors: A Study of Residential Property Tax Assessments in New York City* (New York: New York Public Interest Research Group, 1981); and Frank Domurad and Gene Russianoff, *City of Unequal Neighbors—One Year Later* (New York: New York Public Interest Research Group, 1982).

17. See Real Estate Board of New York, *Sudden Peril—The Negative Impact of New York City's Real Property Assessment Policy* (April 1983).

18. Data in this paragraph from City of New York, Department of Finance, *Annual Report on Tax Expenditures of the City of New York, Fiscal Year 1991* (April 1991).

19. See Drennan, "Local Economy and Local Revenues."

20. Ibid.

21. For discussion on this point, see Dick Netzer, "Taxes," in *Setting Municipal Priorities, 1982,* pp. 129–130.

22. For elaboration of this proposal and others to make the municipal system more progressive, see Chernick, "Taxes."

Chapter 10

1. City of New York, *Comprehensive Annual Financial Report of the Comptroller,* fiscal years 1980 and 1990 editions.

2. New York City Tax Study Commission, "The New York City Real Property Tax System under S-7000A," p. 5.

3. *In the matter of Pauline Hellerstein, Appellant, v. Assessor of the Town of Islip, Respondent* (37 NY2d 1). See also *Hellerstein v. Assessors of Town of Islip* (44 AD2d 689, modified).

4. New York University, Graduate School of Public Administration, *Real Property Tax Policy for New York City: A Study Conducted under Contract with the Department of Finance, City of New York,* December 31, 1980, p. II-47.

5. Since the enactment of S-7000A, the definition of Class I property has been expanded to include some vacant land zoned as residential and buildings of three or

fewer stories all of whose units have always appeared on the assessment roll as condominiums.

6. Although this chapter focuses on the continuing problem of "interclass" inequality, it is worth noting that a similar lack of progress has been made toward resolving "intraclass" inequality, or the variation of rates of assessment among properties of the same classification. In fact, S-7000A's assessment limitations have exacerbated the intraclass inequality by keeping assessment increases uniform during the 1980s while market values increased at varying paces. Properties that realized larger increases in market value saw their assessments reduced to a smaller percentage of their market value than properties that realized smaller or no increases in market value. For a further discussion see State of New York, Office of the State Deputy Comptroller for the City of New York, "Inequities in New York City Real Property Assessments," Report 20-90, January 11, 1990. See also Note 17, Chapter 9.

7. The modest growth in Class III assessments is the result of agreements between the city and the utilities pursuant to legal suits, and a 1987 amendment to the RPTL removing telecommunications equipment from the property tax base (to be phased in by 1993).

8. State of New York, Executive Department, Board of Equalization and Assessment, memorandum to State Board members, October 18, 1988, p. 3.

9. New York City Tax Study Commission, p. 27.

10. "Statement by Mayor Edward I. Koch and City Council Majority Leader Peter Vallone," 56-89, February 14, 1989; and remarks made by Mayor Koch and Majority Leader Vallone at a public hearing co-chaired by New York State Assemblymen Eric N. Vitaliano, George Friedman, and James F. Brennan, CUNY Graduate Center, February 15, 1989.

11. Ibid.

12. New York City Partnership, Property Tax Task Force, "Policy Recommendations," May 11, 1989.

Chapter 11

1. The terms "exit" and "voice" are from a provocative book by Albert O. Hirschman, *Exit, Voice, and Loyalty* (Cambridge, MA: Harvard University Press, 1970). Exit, in his framework, is one option confronting the members of failing organizations; voice is the other. Instead of jumping the sinking ship, members can try changing the organization from within. Loyalty, Hirschman's third key concept, affects the exit–voice choice.

2. Wilbur R. Thompson, *A Preface to Urban Economics* (Baltimore, MD: Johns Hopkins Press, 1965), pp. 24–27.

3. Edward Hamilton, "On Nonconstitutional Management of a Constitutional Problem," *Deadalus,* Volume 107 (Winter 1978), pp. 111–128.

4. Perhaps the best known of the studies questioning the spending-service hypothesis is James S. Coleman, Ernest Q. Campbell, Carol J. Hobson, James McPartland, Alexander M. Mood, Frederic D. Weinfeld, and Robert L. York, *Equality of Educational Opportunity* (Washington, DC: U.S. Government Printing Office, 1966). That study, known as the Coleman Report, concluded that educational achievement was not affected significantly by changes in educational expenditure. As might be expected, the Coleman Report prompted an avalanche of studies scrutinizing its conclusion. The results of these studies have been reviewed by Eric A. Hanushek, whose conclusion is that the post-Coleman Report research fails to show a systematic relationship between school spending and student achievement. See his "Throwing Money at Schools," *Journal of Policy Analysis and Management,* Volume 1 (Fall 1981), pp. 19–41, and

"The Economics of Schooling: Production and Efficiency in Public Schools," *Journal of Economic Literature*, Volume 24 (September 1986), pp. 1141–1177. In addition, see Ira Sharkansky, "Government Expenditures and Public Services in the American States," *American Political Science Review*, Volume 16 (December 1967), pp. 1066–1077, and for a partial replication and partial rebuttal of the Sharkansky study, see Gillian Dean and Kathleen Peroff, "The Spending–Service Cliche: An Empirical Reevaluation," *American Politics Quarterly*, Volume 5 (October 1977), pp. 501–517.

5. See Charles Brecher, *Where Have All the Dollars Gone?* (New York: Praeger, 1974).

6. Raymond D. Horton and Mary McCormick, "Services," in Charles Brecher and Raymond D. Horton, eds., *Setting Municipal Priorities, 1981* (Montclair, NJ: Allanheld, Osmun, 1980), pp. 85–112.

7. Dennis C. Smith, "Police," in Charles Brecher and Raymond D. Horton, eds., *Setting Municipal Priorities, 1982* (New York: Russell Sage Foundation, 1981), pp. 220–263.

8. Raymond D. Horton and John Palmer Smith, "Expenditures and Services," in Charles Brecher and Raymond D. Horton, eds., *Setting Municipal Priorities, 1983* (New York: New York University Press, 1982), pp. 77–119.

9. Each of the annual reports published by the Citizens Budget Commission is titled *The State of Municipal Services,* and John Palmer Smith was author or co-author of each. Their volume numbers and dates of publication, respectively, are 49, February 1982; 50, January 1983; 51, April 1984; 52, June 1985; and 53, December 1986.

10. Josh Barbanel, "City Services Found Improved," *The New York Times,* June 24, 1985, p. 1.

11. See Citizens Budget Commission, *The State of Municipal Services,* December 1986, p. 2.

12. Ibid., pp. i–ix.

13. City of New York, Mayor's Press Office, Statement of Mayor Edward I. Koch, December 26, 1986.

14. Letter from Barbara Gunn, director, Office of Operations, to Raymond D. Horton, dated December 17, 1986.

15. This is a summary interpretation of comments made by Mary Keegan, deputy director, Office of Management and Budget, at a December 1986 meeting requested by city officials to discuss a draft of the 1986 Citizens Budget Commission report.

16. For a very thoughtful treatment of the weaknesses and potential applications of input–output analysis to what are called "idiosyncratic" services, see Richard J. Murnane and Richard R. Nelson, "Production and Innovation when Techniques Are Tacit," *Journal of Economic Behavior and Organization,* Volume 5 (1984), pp. 353–373.

17. A good review is Harry P. Hatry, "The Status of Productivity Measurement in the Public Sector," in Frederick S. Lane, ed., *Current Issues in Public Administration,* 2nd ed. (New York: St. Martin's Press), pp. 427–445. For an earlier, but still valuable work, see John P. Ross and Jesse Burkhead, *Productivity in the Local Government Sector* (Lexington, MA: D. C. Heath & Co., 1974).

18. The most extended analysis can be found in John Palmer Smith, *The Relationship of Resources and Municipal Service Provision in New York City, Fiscal Years 1978–1982* (Columbia University, unpublished doctoral dissertation, 1983); also see Horton and McCormick, "Services," and Horton and Smith, "Expenditures and Services."

19. For a prototypical expression of this view, written in response to the first Hanushek review cited in Note 4, see Bruce D. Spencer and David E. Wiley, "The Sense

and Nonsense of School Effectiveness," *Journal of Policy Analysis and Management,* Volume 1 (Fall 1981), pp. 43–52.

20. The specter of the city's inability to dispose of its refuse is no abstraction. See John Kaiser, "Sanitation," in Charles Brecher and Raymond D. Horton, eds., *Setting Municipal Priorities, 1986* (New York: New York University Press, 1985), pp. 412–442. Noting the city's need to build incinerators to replace rapidly filling landfills, Kaiser referred to the waste disposal problem as a "time bomb ticking away" (p. 434).

21. Kaiser, "Sanitation." Also see James Hartman, "Sanitation," in Charles Brecher and Raymond D. Horton, *Setting Municipal Priorities, 1982* (New York: Russell Sage Foundation, 1981), pp. 291–321.

22. In 1981, the last year for which comparative data have been collected, the hourly compensation of sanitation workers in New York City was 47 percent higher than the average in the 12 largest American cities. In contrast, the hourly compensation of the city's police officers and firefighters exceeded the big-city averages by 12 percent and 37 percent, respectively. For greater detail on comparative compensation of sanitation workers and selected other titles, see Elizabeth Dickson and George E. Peterson, *Public Employee Compensation: A Twelve City Comparison,* 2nd ed. (Washington, DC: Urban Institute Press, 1981). For more detail on the relationships described above, see Raymond D. Horton, *Toward a Responsible Municipal Wage Policy* (New York: Citizens Budget Commission, July 1984), pp. 25, 27.

23. For discussion, see Wallace S. Sayre and Herbert Kaufman, *Governing New York City,* 2nd ed. (New York: W. W. Norton & Co., 1965), pp. 249–264. Sayre and Kaufman wrote that commissioners of the Department of Sanitation direct the agency "within the limited range of discretion [their] bargaining resources and skills can win from the leaders of the sanitation bureaucracy" (p. 301).

24. Hartman, "Sanitation," p. 295. Unless otherwise indicated, the statistical information in this discussion of the Department of Sanitation's performance in the 1970s is from that chapter.

25. For the complete data series, see City of New York, *The Mayor's Management Report,* September 17, 1986, pp. 105–110.

26. A detailed description of the expenditure allocation methodology, which was developed with the assistance of officials of the Office of Management and Budget and the Department of Sanitation, plus the supporting data, are available upon request. In brief, the methodology relies on expenditure data found in the city's expense budgets, in particular detail from the current modified budget plus amounts appropriated for fringe benefits, pension benefits, and debt service for the next year. By combining these data it is possible to estimate total departmental spending for a given fiscal year, as well as to identify spending for the components of capital, other, and labor (including personal services, fringe benefits, and pension benefits). Then, two allocation assumptions were utilized to disaggregate the data for refuse collection: first, that spending for fringe benefits, pension benefits, and other reflect the share of department personnel assigned to refuse collection; second, that 70 percent of department capital spending was for refuse collection. Finally, the disaggregated amounts were adjusted for fiscal-year average price changes during the 1980–1986 period to yield the constant-dollar expenditures shown in Table 11.2.

27. Accounting for capital spending raises some difficult conceptual and empirical questions. The cost-accounting method described in Note 26 uses authorized appropriations for debt service in a given year, which includes sums to repay principal and interest on debt incurred prior to the year for which the appropriation is made (as well perhaps as small shares reflecting interest payments for bond sales scheduled in the current year). However, the equipment purchased with the proceeds of prior bond sales

should still be in current operation, provided the actual life of the equipment corresponds to the "period of probable usefulness" governing the repayment of debt and interest. An alternative approach is to amortize the cost of current bond sales. However, this approach would understate current capital costs by excluding the cost of equipment currently in use but previously purchased.

28. This figure is derived from data in Raymond D. Horton, *Toward a Responsible Municipal Wage Policy: The 1988 Round of Collective Bargaining* (New York: Citizens Budget Commission, August 1987), p. 16, Table 2. The fact that the 16.7 percent increase in real base pay exceeded the 14.8 percent rise in average compensation reflects a number of factors, the most important of which is that some nonsalary benefits do not rise proportionately with base pay.

29. Harold D. Lasswell, *Politics: Who Gets What, When, How* (New York: Whittlesey House, 1936).

30. The city received the award for Distinguished Budget Presentation by the Government Finance Officers Association for fiscal year 1986.

Chapter 12

1. For a fuller description of OLR's (until 1991 the Office of Municipal Labor Relations) responsibilities, see City of New York, Office of the Mayor, Office of Municipal Labor Relations, *1988 Annual Report*.

2. Data on union membership in this and the following paragraphs was supplied by OLR.

3. Pattern bargaining, as defined for the purposes of this chapter, differs slightly from OLR's definition. The OLR defines pattern bargaining as the custom of awarding contracts of equal net worth to all employees. Further negotiations for salary floors and equity funds led to variations in annual base salary increases in order to maintain a total net worth equal to that of other agreements.

4. Elizabeth Dickson and George E. Peterson, *Public Employee Compensation: A Twelve City Comparison*, 2nd ed. (Washington, DC: Urban Institute Press, 1981).

5. An earlier review of the settlements between 1976 and 1984 can be found in Raymond D. Horton, *Toward a Responsible Municipal Wage Policy* (New York: Citizens Budget Commission, July 1984).

6. Fiscal year CPI-U computed from U.S. Department of Labor, Bureau of Labor Statistics, Middle Atlantic Regional Office, "Consumer Price Index for All Urban Consumers, New York–Northeastern New Jersey Area."

7. Data supplied by Office of Labor Relations.

8. Potential hiring figures computed from data supplied by OLR for total cost of first-year police officers and teachers.

9. The Mayor's Private Sector Survey, *The New York City Service Crisis: A Management Response*, September 1989.

10. Raymond D. Horton and Elisabeth Hultcrantz, *The State of the Uniformed Services: Recommendations for Improved Performance* (New York: Citizens Budget Commission, January 1990).

11. Attrition data supplied by OLR. Figures are for fiscal year 1989. Although attrition for civilian employees ranges from 19 to 17 percent, a substantial portion of that represents movement from agency to agency within the city system rather than movement from city to other employment. Net citywide attrition for fiscal year 1989 was 8 percent.

12. Precise data on employee length of service are not available, but an analysis from OLR indicates that 68 percent of both uniformed and civilian employees in major collective bargaining units as of June 30, 1990, were hired after June 30, 1980.

Chapter 13

1. An analysis of the 1983–1987 period is presented in Raymond D. Horton, *The State of Municipal Services: The Uniformed Services Between 1983 and 1987* (New York: Citizens Budget Commission, April 1988).

2. See Maarten de Kadt, "Solid Waste Disposal," in Charles Brecher and Raymond D. Horton, eds., *Setting Municipal Priorities, 1990* (New York: New York University Press, 1989), p. 199.

3. The plant was approved by the Board of Estimate in 1987 but the state of New York has yet to issue a construction permit. Indications are that one will be issued when the city prepares an acceptable plan for disposal of the ash remaining after incineration.

4. Local Law No. 19, *New York City Administrative Code* SS16-301 et seq. Local Law No. 19 requires the commissioner of the Department of Sanitation to adopt and implement regulations requiring separation of recyclables for residential, commercial, and institutional buildings. The goal is to recycle 25 percent of the city's solid waste by 1994—in 5 percent increments over the next five years—and 40 percent by 1997. In addition, the goals include 10 percent source reduction by 1997.

5. According to the Department of Sanitation, municipal recycling in 1989 totaled 67,000 tons; bottles and cans recycled under the bottle law amounted to 135,900 tons.

6. The Productivity Analysis Report (PAR) index measures collection productivity by comparing hours worked and tons collected against predetermined standards.

7. According to department officials this decline is due to the recycling effort, which they argue reduces productivity.

8. Estimate provided by New York State Department of Environmental Conservation.

9. De Kadt, "Solid Waste Disposal," pp. 199–219.

10. Ibid., p. 211.

11. Information provided by the Fire Department.

12. The city maintains data on the share of reported felonies the police believe they have solved by making felony arrests (the felony clearance rate). In 1989, the rate was 20.2 percent. However, if the actual numbers of felonies approximate the numbers estimated in the text, almost 1.5 million, then the felony clearance rate was less than 8 percent.

13. John Palmer Smith and Ester Fuchs, "Criminal Justice," in Charles Brecher and Raymond D. Horton, eds., *Setting Municipal Priorities, 1986* (New York: New York University Press, 1985), p. 360.

14. The compensation data were provided by the New York City Office of Labor Relations.

15. This is a simple average based on average daily population and admissions ($17,439 \times 365 \div 119,600$).

16. Unpublished data provided by the Department of Correction.

17. Various official documents identify reduction of overtime costs as an important goal. See, for example, *The Mayor's Management Report,* and the Mayor's Private Sector Survey, *The New York City Service Crisis: A Management Response,* September 1989, p. 73.

18. See Diana Gale and Timothy Croll, "Coping with Seattle's Solid Waste Crisis," *Waste Alternatives* (June 1989), pp. 10–16.

19. The relationship between the number of officers transferred from administrative positions to enforcement strength is not one to one because police officers average only 207 tours a year, or 57 percent of the 365-tour total.

20. Impasse Panel Report and Recommendations, I-130-77 (June 10, 1977). In rejecting the argument of the Patrolman's Benevolent Association that one-officer cars should not be permitted for safety reasons, the impasse panel concluded: "The Panel recognizes that police work may be dangerous and is inherently associated with a risk factor. The Panel is also aware that there presently exist other forms of one-man duty such as foot patrol, scooters and motorcycles. It does not appear to the Panel that the risk feature involved in this one-man car plan would be greater than other forms of one-person duty. Indeed, it might be safer under certain circumstances than other forms of one-person duty since the police officer would have the benefit of a vehicle shielding him from the elements and certainly would be less prone to vehicular accidents associated with scooters and motorcycles. The use of one-man cars is not a unique practice and many other cities are engaged in this manning procedure. Therefore, the Panel finds no safety impact in the implementation of the City's Plan."

21. The ENFORTH Corporation, *A Systematic Analysis of the Arrest to Arraignment Process—Final Phase Report: Detailed Description of the Arrest to Arraignment Process* (1989).

22. A supervised detention program was begun in 1989 but discontinued because strict requirements for participation set by the state legislature made the program inoperable. During the first three months of the program almost 15,000 inmates were screened for participation, but only 661 were declared eligible. Of the 661, only 25 passed final screening. According to Correction officials, eligibility requirements set by the state need to be loosened. One is the "trigger" requirement, which permits supervised detention only when the inmate population exceeds 101 percent of capacity. Another is the prohibition against supervised detention for inmates with a prior felony conviction for drug possession.

Chapter 14

1. This section draws heavily from City of New York, Department of Parks and Recreation, *Three Hundred Years of Parks: A Timeline of New York City Park History,* January 1988.

2. August Heckscher, *Open Spaces: The Life of American Cities* (New York: Harper and Row, 1977).

3. Ann L. Buttenwieser, *Manhattan Water-Bound* (New York: New York University Press, 1987).

4. This section draws heavily from Robert A. Caro, *The Power Broker: Robert Moses and the Fall of New York* (New York: Vintage Books, 1975).

5. The data presented in this section in some cases vary greatly from inventory figures currently being published by the Office of Management and Budget. Most notable is the difference in acreage, 26,304 acres shown in Table 14.1 versus the 25,058 acres cited in the 1982 inventory. However, the 1982 inventory is the only comprehensive listing of DPR properties currently available, and thus it is utilized despite some substantial changes since its compilation.

6. Figures in this section are from City of New York, Office of Management and Budget, *Ten-Year Capital Strategy Fiscal Years 1992–2001,* May 10, 1991.

7. Central Park Conservancy, *Annual Report,* 1981–1989 editions.

8. City of New York, Office of Management and Budget, *Message of the Mayor,* May 10, 1991; and City of New York, Office of Management and Budget, *Adopted Budget Fiscal Year 1992.*

9. Ibid.

10. The Parks Department also hires some employees on a part-time basis; how-

ever, this is a very small part of total personal services spending and thus is not included in this discussion.

11. City of New York, Office of Management and Budget, *Planned Headcounts 7/1/91 QAS Plan.*

12. City of New York, Office of Operations, *The Mayor's Management Report,* fiscal years 1978–1991 editions.

13. Ibid.

14. DPR's revenue division has stated that, prior to concessioning its golf courses, DPR annually spent approximately $2 million more on maintenance than it took in through greens fees. DPR currently collects over $1 million from its golf course concessionaires. Thus, there is a net gain of at least $3 million, before accounting for the freeing of DPR personnel to perform other tasks.

15. William Kornblum and Terry Williams, *New Yorkers and Central Park: A Report to the Central Park Conservancy* (New York: Evaluation and Policy, Inc., April 1983).

16. Rolf Meyersohn, *Van Cortlandt Park and Pelham Bay Park and Their Visitors, 1986–87: A Report Prepared for the City of New York Department of Parks and Recreation* (New York: Center for Social Research, Graduate School and University Center of the City University of New York, 1987).

17. Jacob B. Ukeles Consulting Services, "Prospect Park User Study and Maintenance Management Plan: Submitted to the New York City Department of Parks and Recreation" (1988).

18. Data on the telephone survey is from a Memorandum to Henry J. Stern, entitled, "Telephone User Survey—Report I," dated November 1, 1988.

19. William Kornblum and Terry Williams, *New Yorkers and Central Park: 1989,* Report to the Central Park Conservancy and the Central Park Task Force (New York: Center for Social Research, CUNY Graduate School, December 1989).

20. City of New York, Office of Operations, *The Mayor's Management Report,* fiscal years 1978–1991 editions.

21. Ibid., September 17, 1990, p. 154.

22. City of New York, Police Department, Central Park Precinct.

23. Telephone interviews were conducted in late August 1990 with Keith Summa of the Coalition for the Homeless and Diana Sonde of Project Reachout.

24. City of New York, Department of Parks and Recreation, Office of Operations Analysis, "Citywide Staffing Benchmark Project" (March 1981).

25. Central Park Conservancy, *1989 Annual Report.*

26. Ibid.

Chapter 15

1. This paragraph draws on information in Kenneth Thorpe, "Health Care," in Gerald Benjamin and Charles Brecher, eds., *The Two New Yorks* (New York: Russell Sage Foundation, 1988), pp. 355–382.

2. Much of the historical material in this section is adapted from Miriam Ostow, "Affiliations," in Eli Ginzberg and the Conservation of Human Resources Staff, *Urban Health Services: The Case of New York* (New York: Columbia University Press, 1971).

3. The following paragraphs draw upon material in Robert Alford, *Health Care Politics* (Chicago: University of Chicago Press, 1975), Chapter 2.

4. State Study Commission for New York City, *Health Care Needs and the New York City Health and Hospitals Corporation,* April 1973, p. 175.

5. Data in this and the next paragraph from Charles Brecher, Kenneth Thorpe, and Cynthia Green, "New York City Health and Hospitals Corporation," in Stuart Altman, Charles Brecher, Mary Henderson, and Kenneth Thorpe, eds., *Competition and Compassion: Conflicting Roles of Public Hospitals* (Ann Arbor, MI: Health Administration Press, 1989), pp. 45–92.

6. This discussion draws from sections on HHC in City of New York, Office of Operations, *The Mayor's Management Report,* annual editions.

7. For a discussion of some of the issues in interpreting the HCFA mortality data as an indicator of quality in public hospitals see New York State Department of Health, Office of Health Systems Management, "A Critique of the 1987 HCFA Mortality Study Based on New York State Data," undated paper; and "Comments on HCFA Release of Medicare Mortality Rate Information," Memorandum from Larry S. Gage, president, National Association of Public Hospitals, to William Roper, administrator, Health Care Financing Administration, December 6, 1988.

8. See Louis Harris and Associates, "Health Care in New York City," Study No. 814009, October 1982, and Howard E. Freeman and Hye Kgung Lee, "New Yorkers' Perceptions of Their Health Care," *New York Affairs,* Volume 9, November 2, pp. 74–81.

9. See data presented in Charles Brecher, "Health," in Charles Brecher and Raymond D. Horton, eds., *Setting Municipal Priorities, 1988* (New York: New York University Press, 1987), Tables 8.6 and 8.7.

10. See Kenneth E. Thorpe and Charles Brecher, "Comparative Analysis of Efficiency and Access," in Stuart Altman et al., *Competition and Compassion.*

11. See *Report of the New York State Commission on Graduate Medical Education* (Albany: The Commission, 1986).

Index

Running paths, 307
Runoff elections, 71, 92, 97, 99, 128
Ryan, William Fitts, 83

S-7000A, 212, 212–214, 216
Salaries
  municipal officials, 50
  police, 283
Sales tax, 22, 197–198, 199, 200,
  203–204
Samuels, Howard, 88
Sanders, Steven, 125
Sanitation, Department of. See
  Department of Sanitation
Sayre, Wallace, 4, 5, 6, 8, 9, 15, 30,
  43, 77
Scheuer, James, 88
School boards, 57, 58–59
School Construction Authority (SCA),
  169, 170
School decentralization law of 1969,
  59
Schools, public. See Public schools
Screvane, Paul, 80, 82, 83, 84
Seaview Hospital, 349
Service-demanding interest groups, 77,
  78, 80, 83, 85, 89, 94, 99, 108
Services, municipal. See Municipal
  services; Spending-service
  relationship
Setting Municipal Priorities studies,
  222, 224
Seward Park, 303
Shea Stadium, 305, 317
Shefter, Martin, 9, 77, 78
Skating rinks, 307, 317
Small Parks Act, 302
Smith, Dennis C., 223
Soft money, 119
Spending. See Expenditures
Spending-service relationship, 221–239
  assumptions and tools for study of,
    224–225
  collective bargaining in, 239
  competition in, 224–225
  consumer behavior in, 223, 237
  firefighting, 223, 226
  input measurement, 227
  input-output model of, 13, 225–239
  input-output model of, revised, 234–
    236

jails, 226
management behavior in, 223, 237,
  238
output measurement, 226–227
performance evaluation, 237–238
police, 223
policy implications of input-output
  model, 238–239
public schools, 226
recommendation, 239
refuse collection, 223, 226, 228–236
research problems, 225–228
studies of, 222–224
Stark, Abraham, 80
State aid, 22
State Board of Equalization and
  Assessment (SBEA), 211–212,
  215, 216
Staten Island, elections in, 64
Stein, Andrew, 66–68, 103, 126, 130,
  131–132, 133, 135
Stevenson, Adlai, 80
Stock market crash of October 1987,
  146, 338
Street Cleaning, 268, 270
Supplemental Security Income (SSI)
  program, 38
Supreme court judges, 57, 58
Sutton, Percy, 94, 95, 97–99, 99, 132
Sydenham Hospital, 333

Tammany Hall Democratic Club, 302,
  303
Tax Commission, 51
Tax Equity and Fiscal Responsibility
  Act of 1982, 252
Taxi and Limousine Commission, 51
Tax policy, 185–208
  aggregate tax trends, 187–189
  auto taxes, 200
  business community and, 31
  business income tax, 198, 206
  changing composition of local taxes,
    192–193
  commercial occupancy tax, 207–208
  cost of doing business in NYC, 195,
    206
  costs of administration, 200
  efficiency of, 197, 201–204, 206,
    207
  efficiency of business income tax, 206